D1602794

Pitt Series in
POLICY AND INSTITUTIONAL STUDIES

History and Context in Comparative Public Policy

Douglas E. Ashford
EDITOR

UNIVERSITY OF PITTSBURGH PRESS
Pittsburgh and London

Published by the University of Pittsburgh Press, Pittsburgh, Pa., 15260

Eurospan, London

Manufactured in the United States of America

Library of Congress Cataloging-in-Publication Data

History and context in comparative public policy / Douglas E.
Ashford, editor.
p. cm.—(Pitt series in policy and institutional studies)
ISBN 0-8229-3694-1
1. Policy sciences. 2. Welfare state. 3. Comparative government.
I. Ashford, Douglas Elliott. II. Series.
H97.H57 1992
320′.6—dc20 91-18192
CIP

A CIP catalog record for this book is available from the British Library.

Contents

PART III
In Search of Agency

Preface

THIS BOOK is the product of a conference on comparative public policy held at the University of Pittsburgh in May 1988. If the elapsed time seems long, it is in no small part due to the challenging issues raised by the participants and the provocative papers they prepared. It will come as no surprise to those who have organized conferences that the contributors insisted on talking about their own perspectives as well as the theme of the conference, so time was needed to sift through the various messages. I hope that the richness and diversity of their contributions permeates this book, for in my view, comparative policy studies have only begun to reveal the insight and knowledge that they could provide social science. In a nutshell, that is the theme of this book.

This tribute made, our meeting was about a project initiated nearly twenty years ago. In the early 1970s, I began to think about the inability of political science to deal with an action frame of reference and, after some years examining center-local relations in Europe, I realized that most macrotheories were incapable of dealing with microlevel complexities. Out of this grew the policy and politics seminar at Cornell, made possible with the support of the U.S. Office of Education and the Cornell Center for International Studies. In the late 1970s, the Ford Foundation provided a grant to enable me and my collaborators, T. J. Pempel and Peter Katzenstein, to launch a series of books on policy making and politics in the advanced industrial societies. The series was still growing in 1990 and, with the addition of Canada, now covers seven countries. Our effort to construct a comparable framework for these books has much to do with this book.

The book series was founded on the conviction, much more controversial in the 1970s than today, that macrolevel theories need to be tested against microlevel realities. *Realities* is of course a waffle word, but we were all aware then, as now, that policy-making studies often contradict macrolevel theories about particular sectors, public-private boundaries, and center-local relations. In a word, policy was not only the product of easily compared inputs and easily measured outputs but also the product of historical experience, institutional traditions, and political opportunity. All these suspicions put us in opposition to the behavioral dominance of political science, but they also sensitized us to an action frame of reference.

As I think this book indicates, compared to progress in most areas of political studies, the advance of policy studies over the past decade or so is truly phenomenal. There are a multitude of new theoretical perspectives, an ever expanding realm of empirical interests, and, with some dispute, some fundamental qualifications to the deductive-hypothetical model that has prevailed in American and much of European political science since the war. In the history of political science from 1950 to 1990—and quite possibly the other social sciences—the growth of policy studies will have a major place.

After nearly two decades, it is difficult to write a concise account of all the persons and agencies to whom this book is indebted. The Cornell Western Societies Program provided substantial encouragement at the early stages. The Council of European Studies supported a research group that contributed to a conference on comparative policy studies early in our work, the results of which were published in 1978. The U.S. Office of Education provided funds that enabled me and my collaborators to teach together for several years and to thrash out the format for our policy book series. There followed a grant from the Ford Foundation to recruit authors for additional books. The conference in Pittsburgh to assess the series was supported by the Council for European Studies as well as by funds from the Western European Program at the University of Pittsburgh, the Graduate School of International and Public Affairs, the University Research Center of the University of Pittsburgh, and the Program on Comparative Public Policy. No specific accounting can be made of the many scholars who attended the conference and contributed papers, but the result is indisputably the product of cooperation and common concern over many years.

For one who has always been somewhat skeptical about professional isolation from the real world, this book provides much pleasure. If the net seems too widely cast or the conceptual focus too broad, it is because of my own conviction that political science has in a sense come full circle. Having spent a generation since the war showing that it can emulate if not reproduce the objective standards of natural science, political science is now engaged in a more vital process of showing once again (there was much less doubt a century ago) that it can contribute to the common understanding.

History and Context
in Comparative Public Policy

1

Introduction: Of Cases and Contexts

Douglas E. Ashford

AN INTERESTING argument can be made that comparative policy studies have made fundamental contributions to theory formation in political and other social sciences. To fully appreciate the force of such an argument, it is necessary to momentarily, possibly even definitively, suspend the conventional foundations of behavioral science and reconstruct how social scientists generally, and political scientists in particular, seek to understand behavior. An important starting point is to recall that no more than a decade ago policy analysis was understood as a relatively primitive form of investigation; that is, it had little formal theory, virtually no consensus about preferred methodologies, and, despite an enormous amount of detailed cases (possible *because* of the enormous amount of case studies), little idea of how to generalize about its contribution to human understanding. Put simply, in the 1960s and probably well into the 1970s policy analysis had no informing generalization to guide research. For the most part, case studies were randomly selected and randomly used, often for such perfectly good reasons as instruction about the real world. More ambitious use of cases was still derived from mainstream issues and topical concerns. In a decade or less, policy studies—and more narrowly, comparative policy studies—have come a long way. A basic aim of this book is to point out that policy studies are no longer the handmaiden of established areas of political or social inquiry, nor do they remain methodological parasites on the back of political science, sociology, or history.

Because this volume highlights the diversity of approaches to comparative policy studies and, implicitly if not explicitly, the limitations of conventional social science approaches to comparative studies, it is worth reflecting on the common question about any case study: What is it a case of? Until fairly recently, the implied question really was, How can one relate this case to some lawlike statement about social behavior? Not surprisingly, *case studies* became a term of reproach among professional social scientists, since they could be related to nearly any lawlike statement. The philosophical and epistemological limitations of cases should be made explicit early in the presentation of this book. It juxtaposes contrasting frameworks of social explanation and social understanding beyond the view of standard social science, which is that social science should emulate, if not reproduce, natural science by the prudent application of lawlike generalizations (Hempel 1965; Popper 1959). Indeed, the aim of the book is to redefine the meaning of cases and to differentiate their use in different frameworks of explanation—historical, ethical, and philosophical—as well as their application to normal hypothetical-deductive forms of political reasoning. Broadly speaking, until the 1970s queries about the use of cases for comparative studies were of only one kind: How can we fit cases into the established paradigm of explanation prevailing in political science as well as the other social sciences (Eckstein 1975; Lijphart, 1971, 1975)?

While it may seem trivial to note that the use of cases in comparative or other research design depends on the intention of the analyst, it is remarkable that other ways of using case studies have been effectively ignored. The reasons for this are not simply the tyranny of the mind imposed by a dominant form of explanation but are deeply imbedded in the various ways that nations historically related the social sciences to major national issues (Hennock 1976; Collini et al. 1983; Burrow 1981). Though not a major theme of this book, it is noteworthy that the renewed debate about the nature of social and political explanation was often ignited by studies that were essentially policy evaluations and critiques of the dominant theories of the moment (Crozier 1964; Lowi 1969; Beer 1973). Many of the works that raised new problems of social research were, among other things, complex policy studies that questioned important generalizations of conventional social science. They did so by constructing new contextual statements in order to link cases rather than relying on prevailing modes of knowledge accumulation. The authors did not necessarily dismiss familiar hypothetical-deductive models but were also sensitive to how their cases did not fit into larger lawlike assertions.

The essays in this book are intended to elaborate on how contextual meanings can be attached to comparative policy studies. The introductions to each section try to make such broad distinctions clear, but for the sake of clarity, if not analytical rigor, it may help to pose the most ambitious notion of *case*. A particular policy study is not simply a building block for one or more lawlike generalizations as conceived in normal social science but is simultaneously a historical narrative, a portrayal of particular motives and intentions at work in a particular setting, an account of prevailing ethical and moral standards at work in political and social life at some moment in history, and an exercise in defining political and social reality for policy makers and the public. As these suggestions imply, a case study is amenable to many different interpretations—historical, ethical, and philosophical. But its intellectual fascination and, to some extent, its intellectual intransigence within conventional social science, arise from the ease with which a microscopic slice of reality can be manipulated. Put in more experimental terms, a case study invites the analyst to construct a context or, more simply, to disregard received wisdom when interpreting how the case might be linked to other cases. Doing so entails some form of generalization but not necessarily the conventional explanatory form of more rigorous social science. It is not entirely coincidental that one of the most respected practitioners of case study analysis and generalization, Wildavsky (1979), uses the metaphor of Diogenes in search of light to explain how his work relates to the business of government and politics.

The aim of this book is not to reduce comparative policy studies to incoherence but only to suggest that the language of normal social science does not address important issues about contextual knowledge. While it is true that many enthusiastic exponents of empirical social science expressed real doubts about the overall validity of scientific methods—Popper (1959) and Lakatos (1970) being conspicuous examples—on the whole, mainline social science was content to confine social science to the Kuhnian plateaus of learning and investigation. Cases thus became an important launchpad in the search for contextual knowledge. In this respect, it is perhaps fair to state that policy studies, in particular comparative policy studies, have had an important place in the paradigmatic explosion of social science over the past decade or more. For example, one distinguishing feature of critical theory is that the investigator is not only at liberty to explore the various meanings that might be attached to a study but is morally obligated to do so (Habermas 1973). Forester (1985) argues, for example, that a critique of the possible uses of a case study is an integral part of social research. Thus, some approaches to contextual questions not only reject the established aim of conventional social science but self-consciously demand that the investigator evaluate alternative interpretations. Less radical, but nonetheless closely associated in its intellectual demands, is interest in how policy makers themselves construct frameworks of reality or designs in making decisions (Linder and Peters 1988; Alexander 1982).

Perhaps the most elaborate attempt to rescue case studies for normal social science is Eckstein's essay (1975) for the *Handbook of Political Science*. His elaboration of the appropriate use of crucial cases is an effort to relate case studies to conventional approaches to comparative politics and to integrate case studies within normal social science. Eckstein is not entirely happy with Verba's (1967) suggestions that cases be relegated to heuristic significance in the elaboration of serious social science, but he still sees no difficulties in limiting their use to the customary rules of behavioral inquiry. Eckstein (1975, 104) notes that "discipline configured" case studies may underestimate the problems of interpreting cases, and he expands on Verba's cautious suggestion to note the possibility of using case studies to find neglected variables to generate weak theories. His appreciation of the history of social science leads him to suggest that the elaborate cases expounded by Tocqueville and Bagehot helped generate theory. He is clearly uncomfortable with too radical an expansion of the meaning of case studies and is quick to qualify his argument about the detailed country studies that concentrated on the policy processes. Although the analytical process by which such elaborate studies of decision making are translated into comparative generalizations is not explored, he sees his own study of Norway (Eckstein 1966) as a useful example of such a plausibility probe (1975, 108–13).

Keeping in mind that in the 1960s Eckstein's interest in comparative case studies was adventurous, it is worthwhile examining his description of cases in order to see more clearly how these diverse and detailed slices of reality became, as it were, a minefield in the path of normal social science. Lest his exploration of case studies be underestimated, it is also important to recall that in the late 1960s standard behavioral research had become a virtual dogma of political science. Easton (1953) had dismissed the state as a meaningful unit of political analysis, and Almond and Coleman (1960) had launched their ambitious study that would presumably bring all political cultures within the orbit of behavioral research. As an academic product, case studies were firmly relegated to teaching devices for public administration and law schools, whose practical concerns were best distanced, if not ignored, by professional political scientists. Eckstein does not fundamentally differ from the dominant view of what constitutes social explanation, but he is sufficiently curious to give a revealing, and perhaps inadvertently a damning, account of the difference between what he calls "experimental" and "clinical" inquiries. Even a brief account will show that each of his contrasts between scientific research and detailed particularistic case studies leave some fundamental questions unanswered (1975, 81–83).

He first points out that in the social as in the natural sciences, experimental studies are designed with a limited number of variables and in situations where the presence or absence of the variables can be empirically established. He contrasts this with the clinical situation that tries to capture the "entire individual" (1975, 81). The choice of words is significant. Consciously or not, he accepts the best advice of the leading behaviorists of the day that the most worthwhile unit of observation is the individual (Eulau 1958) and that the behavioral analysis of collective decisions is not promising. The perfection of individual behavioral studies will presumably provide more advanced methodology, allowing us to aggregate, translate, or possibly, as Kiser and Ostrom suggest (1982, 179–232), logically infer large-scale behavior from laws of individual behavior. Acquiescence to the rules of normal social science ignores the possibility that theories with less demanding rules of inquiry and radically different definitions of man might not find discourse about societies, cultures, traditions, and institutions as confusing. Though not explored in his account, in the Kuhnian sense Eckstein apparently condemns us to work on the plateaus of human knowledge. There is no mention that even a decade ago there were important arguments (largely outside political science) about the nature of explanation and discovery (Hansen 1958) that questioned whether science itself progressed by relying entirely on experimental methods.

Second, Eckstein correctly contrasts the routinized procedure of experiments with the intuitive and searching procedures of most case studies. Perhaps inadvertently, he uses the term *Verstehen* to characterize the kind of internal validity that other forms of explanation seek. There are major philosophical arguments about the difference between explanation and understanding in political science (Ball 1987; Bernstein 1976; Gunnell 1969), as well as fundamental ethical and philosophical controversies about the assumptions needed to understand human behavior (Moon 1975; Toulmin 1963; Hardin 1982). Though now largely forgotten, many of their questions were contained in the community power debate of the 1960s, but in the age of pluralist theory, the entire controversy over the substitution of method for theory (and implicitly, the limited understanding of complete reliance on routine experimental methods) was little noticed. It was of course essential to the defense of the pluralist school and to their approach to community power studies that the explanatory underpinnings of *Who Governs?* (Dahl 1961) be defended from charges that other political forces might not be as easily explained. Both Polsby (1960) and Wolfinger (1960) battled nobly on behalf of Dahl, though other Yale products raised questions. Lowi (1964), for example, suggested that organizations and leadership may independently affect city politics. Without reviewing the entire community power literature (Hawley and Svara 1972), it is perhaps fair to say the impassioned methodological debate was at least prima facie evidence that the individualist assumptions of what was perhaps the most illustrious product of political science in the 1960s raised a multitude of questions about the completeness, even the impartiality, of routinized inquiry.

Third, experiments and clinical studies are contrasted in relation to their results. The former provide findings that confirm or deny hypothetical models, and therefore are presumably of no further interest in other settings and have no specific relevance to other theories, while the latter present difficult problems of interpretation. Again, without plunging into controversies over the nature of explanation, it is by no means obvious that natural science is limited to the particular explanation at hand, nor do natural scientists actually behave in this way. Precise methods permit all scientists to explore defined problems, but even in natural science there are often, as in the case of the discovery of the atom bomb, major controversies of emphasis, justification, and consequences. To be sure, rigorous methods clearly separate these issues from scientific inquiry, but even antiseptic inquiry may return to haunt science and to affect future research. Thus, interpretation may be no more than an explicit, if not rigorous, burden laid on the investigator to assess findings in more than one way, that is, in more than one setting or context. Its explicit recommendation is to assess the results in terms of their meaning to the human objects of the experiment and in terms of their probable consequences on human objects is not entirely unreasonable (Fischer 1985, 231–57). A more philosphical version of this critique is Goodin's telling comment (1982, 20) that incrementalism recommends thinking small so as not have to think at all.

Eckstein's last contrast also follows the convention that only experimental methods make persuasive claims on theoretical knowledge. Experiments accumulate in the form of generalized knowledge to reinforce theory, while the clinician's preoccupation with the unique and particular can only pursue action objectives. Even at that time, this formulation itself of routine social science was criticized by Bachrach and Baratz (1963). Similar objections are now echoed in certain versions of critical theory, in the renewed interest in deep structures (Geertz 1973), and in renewed controversies about historical explanation. The notion that social investigation inescapably has action objectives as well as pure theoretical objectives is not new to the 1980s but was advocated by many critics of behavioral studies more than twenty years ago (Mills 1956; Gouldner 1957; Berger and Luckmann 1966). Numerous studies show how hypothetical social research has real consequences. One of the most fascinating examples is Burns's study (1941) of British unemployment policies, which indicates how the presumably value-free and hypothetical constructs used to assess British unemployment led policy makers to misperceive the problem and quite possibly to exaggerate its importance. The sociology of knowledge, where much of this discussion occurs, is not simply an unfortunate consequence of misconceived empirical inquiry but an elaboration of the link between research and its application. Behavior is affected by theories as well as findings. A central issue in more recent policy studies has been to understand how these linkages work and to explain the limitations of our own explanations.

For those interested in policy studies, there is then a sense of déjà vu in many of the more passionate contemporary controversies about the uses of case studies and their relation to human understanding. Whether imagined in historical, ethical, or action-based terms, the relevance of contextual knowledge to the evaluation of scientific knowledge has probably been clear for a decade or more. The theoretical debates that now encompass political science are in no small part due to the renewed search for contextual foundations to interpret scientific knowledge and to more systematically advance our understanding of unique and particular situations. In the diverse ways apparent in Eckstein's careful analysis twenty years ago, the contextual questions were never absent; they were simply not discussed. Not the least surprising effect of revived interest in contextual issues is the renewed effort to uncover how the exponents of experimental science actually thought about the matters that seem to have been so easily dismissed. Thus, it is symptomatic of the new vitality of contemporary social research that one can find, for example, essays linking Parsons's social action theory, often dismissed as a futile and reactionary effort to impose scientific rigor on all the social sciences, with Habermas's demands for moral sensitivity in social science (Clegg 1989, 129–48).

The revived interest in public policy, and in comparative policy studies, originates in two questions that the predominant pluralist theory of the 1960s, and the closely associated interest in rational decision making, could not resolve. Quite apart from the theoretical import of pluralism in the development of political theory more generally, behavioralism (as transplanted into political science after the war and over the 1950s) rejected the ideas of the state, legal order, and public administration as significant concerns of political inquiry. The new science of politics even rejected Laswell's efforts to build on the prewar work of Meriam, Gosnell, and others to produce a branch of political science focusing on problem solving. Eulau (1958, 49) perhaps the most exacting of the behaviorists, considered the policy sciences "old public administration in a refurbished wardrobe." This sentiment was largely shared at Yale, where Dahl, Lindblom, and their disciples found pluralist behavior grounded in American ideals; indeed, in the behavioral comparative politics of Almond, it was extended to comprise all political ideals, all political cultures, and, apparently, all moments in history. There has perhaps never been such an energetic, and for a moment such a successful, effort to monopolize political thinking since the early nineteenth-century French positivist August Comte anticipated the arrival of high priests of humanity to provide universal knowledge for all societies (Bryant 1985; Hawthorn 1976).

By making normative and historical explanation irrelevant to political science, the pluralists had little interest in extracting more general meaning from policy making. Any possible structural coherence of inputs or outputs was of little intrinsic interest so long as political market forces operated freely. As Goodin points out (1982, 19) the theory contained its own circularity. If the pluralist dynamic precluded the possibility of knowing the effects of our actions before the individual entered the arena (one of their favorite words), then how would one know when an increment has taken place? In this regard, the incrementalist assumptions were essential to explain how individuals regularly arrive at the best possible policy, in much the same way that materialist assumptions elevate society in Marxism. That both were thought to be uniformly constructive suggests the high price of making ahistorical theories. There was, to be sure, a small qualification made to suggest that learning by doing might help us see more general theories or lawlike propositions underlying competitive, pluralist politics. Popper, for one, thought that causal chains might appear as incremental change took place (1959, 67). From here it was only a small step to the Caiden and Wildavsky argument (1974, 309) that thinking small was the most reliable of all strategies for policy makers and to the Landau (1974) argument that redundancy is a useful device to curtail impetuous policy makers.

For these reasons, Goodin concludes (1982, 56) that incrementalism is the dominant mode of atheoretical decision making. How to accumulate the experience contained in cases about similar problems, similar political systems, or similar situations was simply irrelevant. To contrast why differing systems found different solutions was equally unnecessary, since free political competition made such differences a natural consequence. It is perhaps worth noting that the stimulus for many of the early comparative policy studies did not come from the United States, but from Europe, and did not concern the wide array of policies now commonly compared across countries but concentrated on different planning experiences. Not without a certain irony, the interest grew in the planning capacities (contrary to the pluralist logic) of European economies, where the various success stories appeared as complex case studies (Hayward and Watson 1975; Shonfield 1969). Without being nurtured by social science, interest revived, initially for economic and industrial policy making, in how microlevel behavior was influenced by—and in turn, exercised influence over—macrolevel behavior. From these and other studies, awareness spread that political systems had various forms of intergovernmental, interpersonal, and intersectoral preferences that contradicted the pluralist assumption that individual utilities explained collective behavior. From this point, it was a short intellectual step to suggest that more attention should be paid to how such connecting principles arose and acquired credibility and political legitimacy.

A second challenge arose as the early comparative policy studies revealed important differences in how various countries do the same thing. Closer examination of what Kingdon (1984) calls the "participants inside of government" and those outside "but not just looking" cast streams of light into the Eastonian black box. There was both a rediscovery of the bureaucracy (Armstrong 1973; Dyson 1980; Suleiman 1974) and behavioral comparisons of civil servants (Aberbach, Putnam, and Rockman 1981). The elaborate defense of mindless policy making became a statistical demonstration that budget growth was of little consequence (David, Dempster, and Wildavsky 1966). But policy studies were introduced through the back door of political science and again made respectable, in part, because they were shorn of the practical meanings displayed in public administration and, in part, because they were made compatible with behavioral science.

Thus, in the short space of thirty years, political science came full circle from a studied exclusion of policy making to an enthusiastic renewal of interest. As policy studies again became a legitimate concern of political science, a number of comparative studies in specific areas began to reveal deeply imbedded institutional and political differences in the policy process, in intergovernmental relations, and in government organization (Heclo 1974; Ashford 1982). Not only did the universality of pluralist decision making seem bankrupt, but the study of policy making began to invite theoretical attention. An important reason for the shift was that many of the conventional concepts of states, governments, and processes were contradicted by microlevel examinations. Ikenberry (1988), for example, shows that a presumably centralized and aggrandizing French bureaucracy responded more quickly and more effectively to the oil crisis than more loosely constructed states. Kelman (1981) shows that a more concerned and more organized Sweden had more difficulty implementing occupational safety regulations than a decentralized and indifferent United States. Vogel (1986) finds that environmental regulatory policies contradicted conventional wisdom about Britain and the United States. Ashford's comparison (1986) of welfare state policy making in Britain and France shows that the prolonged and focused welfare policies of Britain failed to solve problems that France seemed to resolve with less effort. An array of economic policy-making studies were synthesized in Hall's study (1986) of the organizational and political interdependence of policy-making institutions.

Others would no doubt summarize the disciplinary revival of comparative policy studies in different ways or with different emphasis, but by the 1980s there was an unmistakable search for new concepts and theories to fill the void between detailed case studies and the abstract models of rational decision making, conveniently disinterested bureaucracies, and mindless political competition. Perhaps because the postwar behaviorists were so firmly wedded to the individual as the only appropriate focus of inquiry, political science took much longer than economics to recognize that market restrictions and imperfections imposed major qualifications on any market theory (Olson 1965).

Contextual propositions become important to policy studies and to certain other intricate patterns of interaction and exchange, such as international political economy (Krasner 1988), because one tries to generalize about numerous levels, sectors, and organizations where there is no valid reason to assume that the rules of behavior are uniformly determined. In philosophy, the resulting problem is known as the problem of commensurability (Phillips 1975), that is, the problem of how to reconcile substantially different forms of explanation or paradigmatic perspectives. Policy studies are replete with such problems. Partly because contextual arguments have been used to defend radical paradigmatic changes in social science (Habermas 1973) as well as to deny the possibility of making radical paradigmatic change (Hayek 1955), the issue has become controversial and at times inflamed with ideological difference. At the same time, except for those closely wedded to the most orthodox view of scientific explanation—the Vienna school (Carnap 1970)—there are now sufficient philosophical alternatives in structuralism, hermeneutics, interpretive philosophy, structural anthropology, and linguistics to take the question of contextuality seriously.

Contextual statements, then, are stipulations about realities in widely different situations that enable us to extend our understanding, if not explanation (Apel 1984; Dallmayr and McCarthy 1977), to cases that escape conventional social science. As is explored more in part 1 of this volume, the use of historical explanations most clearly raises such issues, because the hiatus between levels of observation is closed to further direct observation. The translation of meanings over time always confronts the hazard of interpretation. Some areas of social explanation, most notably economics, have devised logically coherent methods to translate political and economic behavior into the same terms. Most economists use a very simple model of man, so it can be momentarily assumed within economics that rational behavior in firms, industries, and entire nations is identical. There are, of course, important reasons to doubt this is so, but a formidable body of useful economic theory has been built without calling on contextual knowledge. The justifiable notoriety of Olson's theory (1965) is based on his description of operational rules that appear to reconcile individual and collective economic behavior. Others schooled in the theory of the firm, for example, argue that the array of choices confronting complex institutions is vastly different from the simplified rules of choice that can be devised in economic organizations (March and Olsen 1975). But most postwar behavioral scientists were, and remain, highly vulnerable to radical and neo-Marxist critiques because they eschewed the analysis of collective behavior. In this sense, it is quite correct to argue that disinterest in the rules of commensurability encouraged political science to ignore collective behavior where all individual behavior could be simultaneously and accurately observed.

Context, therefore, is a conceptual device to compensate for the lack of behavioral rules and methods to compare behavior across time, space, organizations, and functions. In a word, the situations may be so different that existing behavioral methods do not apply, but at the same time there may be striking similarities and differences of behavior that we want to examine systematically. Indeed, one of the simplest forms of contextual argument in policy research is quantitative cross-national studies of decisions for which there are no clear behavioral rules to establish cross-national equivalence. British, French, and German budgeting and taxation, for example, display radically different behaviors, but the highly abstract formulations of spending decisions provided by accounting data (Cameron 1982; Hibbs 1977) can demonstrate the parameters, if not the actualities, of budget behavior.

Although they make important contextual assumptions, it is obvious that these studies are at one level of analysis, the state, and are confined to data that are intentionally standardized so as to erase major behavioral differences known to exist at the microlevel. No one, including the investigators, believes that the results of such studies say anything about the actual behavior of key political, administrative, and business actors. Indeed, as more detailed information becomes available, as was the case with recent biographical and detailed studies of the French planning process (Ashford 1987), the macroexplanation of public spending differences as reflected in national accounting data may be totally at odds with the issues and conflicts decision makers actually experience. Still, most would agree that highly aggregated structural studies detect important government differences as did similar studies of big government (Rose 1984; Rose and Peters 1978), but the apparent simplicity of aggregate data and the familiarity of the statistical methods meant that the underlying contextual assumptions were never made entirely clear. The risk is, of course, that those less sensitive to the limitations of aggregate data would make unwarranted claims about these countries being alike or different or attribute differences to underlying behavioral causes, when in fact the causes were no more than statistical constructs.

A second familiar use of contextual concepts is to link microlevel studies to institutional comparisons. The minimalist behavioral definition of institutions, the authoritative use of power, intentionally avoids differentiating institutional behavior from any other kind of behavior. March and Olsen (1983, 1984) identify more precise distinctions that might be used in a modern theory of institutions (there were numerous theories about democratic institutions in the nineteenth century), but there are as yet few policy-based hypotheses about democratic systems. Few would argue that conventional behavioral studies of party, parliamentary, and administrative behavior can be conflated to provide a more general theory about institutions as such. What does happen, of course, is that behavioral findings treat aspects of institutional behavior. Few such studies make any claim on our understanding of the content of policy making, leaving us with what Kingdon (1984, 122) calls primeval soup.

Another version of what might be called quasi-institutional theorizing from case materials is to use well-developed theories, as Hall (1989) does with Keynesian economic theory, to assess institutionalized economic behavior in complex situations. The qualification *quasi* must be inserted: first, there are obviously enormously important economic institutions that Keynesian theory leaves untouched as unrelated to economic macrotheory; second, much of Keynes's influence was felt after his death, so there are the major problems of interpreting his concepts in practice; and third, important historical differences are introduced by the timing and situations when policy makers translate Keynesian principles into public policies. These are empirical questions, to which we can bring our best historical efforts, but they are all interpretive problems of how economic institutions are defined using an analytical terminology not designed for institutional generalizations. In translating institutional behavior through abstract systems of social thought, we are at the mercy of the translators. This causes immense problems of the sociology of knowledge, most apparent perhaps in the lively debate over whether Keynes should be considered an apologist or a critic of modern capitalism (Hall 1989; Meltzer 1989; Clarke 1989; Parsons 1985; Booth 1983).

There are no clear rules of commensurability to link the macrotheory and microlevel behavior, so the contextual assumption, that Keynesian thinking characterizes most democratic economic policymaking machinery for a given (and disputed) period, is essential. This is one of the intriguing instances in social inquiry where heat may be more important than light. The dispute discloses the importance of interpretation as a prerequisite to linking macroevents and microevents. The problem is whether the hypothetical assertion of causal relations (Keynesian macroeconomics) in its application to actual circumstances produces a particular interpretation of capitalism or only of capitalism superimposed on Keynesian ideas. For this reason, contextual arguments can be accused of circularity. The contextual stipulation (Keynesian theory) cannot be totally excluded from the alleged causes of change.

Another contextual approach to the study of institutions (Ashford 1978) is to forgo the potential reification of interpreting events with disciplinary theories by using independently established institutional generalizations appropriate to a given country. There is a strategy (Anderson 1975), if not a principle, behind a procedure that sifts through social and political history of institutions and, in normative terms, the country's early choices of how to institutionalize democratic governance (Nairn 1988; Bouvier 1986; Rudelle 1986; Harden and Lewis 1986). Of course, the same problem of interpretation returns in different interpretations of historical influences and thematic consistencies but in more explicit ways than in abstract social science models. Both involve important judgments about intention and history.

The most clear-cut case, and perhaps the most persuasive one, was in Britain, where constitutional, judicial, administrative, partisan, and electoral institutions appear so well suited to adversarial politics (Finer 1975). A strong case can be made that, since the war, British policy questions have been governed by adversarial assumptions first developed in the seventeenth century (Ashford 1981). More detailed case studies of center-local politics (Ashford 1982) and social welfare (Ashford 1986) provide consistent evidence of adversarial behavior at the microlevel. This is not a functionalist argument in the sense that British jurists from Coke to Dicey set out to make but only a microlevel observation that the agencies and officials of British government have remained highly susceptible to adversarial influence for centuries. The historical and philosophical reasons are not necessarily based on policy needs or even on conscious processes of articulating British democracy (Pocock 1975) but are contextual realities that can be regularly confirmed at many levels, across many sectors, and in various kinds of institutionalized behavior within Britain. This approach to institutionalization is similar to that suggested by Krasner (1988) for transnational behavior.

The method has the virtue of arriving at institutional explanations that are unmistakably germane to the country in question, though of course subject to the charge of circularity that also arises when a macrosocial or macroeconomic theory is superimposed on microlevel experience. Depending on how one thinks theories are made, causal links may seem clearer when a macrotheory approach is applied to cases. But explicit links to institutional principles are equally available from speeches, debates, and policy materials (Hennock 1976). Explanation rests on the consistency of decision-making patterns, reinforced and often explicitly reasserted in microlevel policy making. The microlevel argument is not about some general feature of social or policy choice but is grounded in institutional, administrative, and legal conditions of exercising authority.

For these reasons, recent writing on corporatism, clientelism, networks, and linkages during the 1970s was a radical departure from behavioral requirements of the 1950s and opened the way for more ambitious studies of comparative public policy. The search for a logical explanation of how interest intermediation worked almost inevitably led back to microlevel questions concerning public policy. As these terms suggest, the first efforts were limited to the conventional social science assumptions; that is, that microlevel explanations were analogous to macrolevel explanations. Behavior that did not follow the same logic or observe the same rules was simply ignored. To return to the Keynesian illustration used above, the macroassumption was that actors in budget offices, investment banks, and credit agencies could be subsumed under an abstractly defined law of aggregate demand. In a sense, this is correct, but in terms of actual institutional behavior, thousands of agencies made decisions affecting the Keynesian model. The point is not that the hypothetical parameters of the Keynesian model are wrong but that the aggregate effect is both contextual and objective. The uniform objective effect may or may not reflect similar behavior in all the microlevel agencies. Thus, intermediation within economic policy making, for example, is not simply tracing mirror images at lower levels of decision making (or within the stated hypothetical reasons) that assume microlevel consistency with abstract theory.

These methodological problems lead to the third strategy this book is concerned with: Is it possible to devise general, possibly even lawlike, statements about microlevel policy making that might then be compared, confirmed, or denied at higher levels of institutionalized behavior? The distinction is an important one for policy studies. The aggregate-data solution, discussed above, essentially confines generalization to questions where information makes the characterization of behavior on two or more levels uncontroversial. What is left out is of secondary concern, even though these studies can reasonably claim their findings apply uniformally to all levels of behavior. Whether it explains similar or different behavior at all levels is not demonstrated. The abstract model solution is an advance insofar as it suggests that the hypothetical general law of behavior can be directly measured and is equally applicable across units, levels, and sectors. The relevant behavior is made explicit rather than implicit. But the guiding principles or rules of behavior at lower levels are still assumed to be consistent with the general theory. The third step, like earlier arguments about the independent effects of policy, is to show that features of microlevel behavior to some extent constitute, if they do not formally explain, general institutional features of the state.

The third group of comparative suggestions arises from the critique of pluralism, the search for better explanations of interest mediation, and the continued pursuit of organizational models of decision making under uncertainty. To be sure, concentrating on the microlevel in order to capture the policy-making context has certain disadvantages. For one thing, the sweeping generalizations about massive social change or pervasive economic forces (capitalist or socialist) must be forgone, at least until better ways are found to understand how officials work. For many, the sacrifice of familiar political and social concepts about class politics, electoral behavior, partisan behavior, and well-known macrosocial theories about modernization, mobilization, and protest (Ashford 1991) is asking too much. Second, at least initially, such generalizations are likely to be valid only for given institutional settings and therefore most useful for intrasystemic comparison. Again, the possibility that there are multiple forms of rationality distinguishable in the rules, procedures, and traditions of institutions contradicts the common assumption in economic and social theory that individuals are consistently maximizers and optimizers. In fact, in complex situations persons may not be consistent at all, and their inconsistencies may only become understandable in the context of institutional settings.

Third, such investigations emphasize how officials actually communicate, so there is an implicit radical implication that policy making involves advocacy. Such institutional contextual theories as policy style (Richardson 1982), organizational garbage cans (Cohen, March, and Olsen 1972; Dryzek 1983), or policy design (Anderson 1977; Alexander 1982; Linder and Peters 1988) also make few if any presuppositions about the resources, tactics, or channels through which policy makers operate. There are no agreed upon independent variables but an array of possible independent variables among which decision makers choose. They select, according to their best judgment, how to obtain a desired outcome—and, in this broad sense, are rational. But the rules of being rational, or the evidence of external influence, may not identify an outcome in a more general sense. Essentially, decision makers are advocates; perhaps they are not impassioned Habermasian communicators or driven ideologues, but, nontheless, their perceptions and behavior are governed by the best solution within given situations. Perhaps the best characterization has been provided by Sabatier (1988), who discusses "policy-oriented belief systems."

Interest in these more subjective internal characteristics of policy making also means that the functional division of labor in policy studies, the subject of the Furniss chapter, no longer works. The policy and politics book series from which this conference took its inspiration makes a similar assumption: that is, there is no reason to presume that any given policy arena necessarily takes precedence in explaining institutions and policy-making behavior. This does not mean that there are no compositions or ordering of the content of policy making but only that ordering features are not likely to be discovered by conventional hypothetical-deductive models of policy making. Policy makers work within restraints, but they are not the abstract political, economic, and social constraints common to social science theories, nor the obviously pertinent empirical questions of how general features of government relate to the amount of spending, nor the even less understood connection between abstract theories of economics, sociology, or (insofar as any comparably reliable theories exist) political science and microlevel behavior. If there is any finding of policy studies that seems incontrovertible, it is that policy makers rarely follow models, especially social science models.

The shared characteristic of these more subjective concepts of policy-making behavior is their concern to see the policy process in the eye of the beholder. To be sure, policy styles are situated within particular governing traditions and institutional frameworks, which are well known to policy makers; the garbage can does not receive information, options, and choices in a wholly random manner; and the policy design never emerges from a completely blank mind. As Farr argues in chapter 7 and Skillen in chapter 9, there are situational factors at work, as well as moral foundations at all policy-making levels. Rooted in the sociology of knowledge, shared techniques, social and economic concepts, and technological experience form part of the decisional setting for policy makers, as discussed by Wittrock and Wagner in chapter 10. At this point, the aim is only to show that the analytical choices for the comparative study of policy making are by no means limited to behavioral and quantitative techniques subsumed by political science.

As mentioned early in this chapter, the breadth of this book is intentional and will, we hope, enlarge the range of controversy and interest in comparative policy studies. The first part is in some respects the most adventurous in linking historical explanation to policy studies. History shares with policy studies the problem of evaluating intentions, and longitudinal studies of public policies by historians seem to have difficulty taking their appropriate place in enlarging the dimensions and depth of comparative policy studies. Analytical essays have been mentioned, but essentially they are illustrations of underlying issues of policy analysis that comparison might clarify. In an inversion of the usual sequence of more specific to more general, the final part of the book deals with the discipline itself, as it sifts through its findings and theories, hoping to see how, if at all, some of the traditional concerns of political science might provide guidance for new perspectives on comparative policy studies.

SOURCES

Aberbach, Joel D., Robert D. Putnam, and Bert A. Rockman. 1981. *Bureaucracies and Politicians in Western Democracies.* Cambridge: Harvard University Press.

Alexander, Ernest R. 1982. Design in the Decision-Making Process. *Policy Sciences* 14:279–92.

Almond, Gabriel, and James Coleman. 1960. *The Politics of Developing Areas.* Princeton: Princeton University Press.

Anderson, Charles, W. 1975. System and Strategy in Comparative Policy Analysis. In W. B. Gwyn and G. C. Edwards, eds., *Perspectives on Public Policy-Making.* New Orleans: Tulane University Press.

———. 1977. Policy Design and the Representation of Interests. *Comparative Political Studies* 10:127–52.

Apel, Karl-Otto. 1984. *Understanding and Explanation*. Trans. G. Warnke. Cambridge: MIT Press.

Armstrong, J. A. 1973. *The European Administrative Elite*. Princeton: Princeton University Press.

Ashford, Douglas E. 1978. The Structural Analysis of Policy, or Institutions Really Do Matter. In D. Ashford, ed., *Comparing Public Policies: New Concepts and Methods*. Beverly Hills: Sage.

———. 1981. *Policy and Politics in Britain: The Limits of Consensus*. Philadelphia: Temple University Press.

———. 1982. *British Dogmatism and French Pragmatism: Center-Local Relations in the Welfare State*. London: Allen and Unwin.

———. 1986. *The Emergence of the Welfare States*. Oxford: Basil Blackwell.

———. 1987. In Search of French Planning: Ideas and History at Work. *West European Politics* 11:150–61.

———. 1991. Bringing the Welfare State Back In. *Comparative Politics* 23:351–75.

Bachrach, Peter, and Morton S. Baratz. 1963. Decisions and Non-Decisions: An Analytical Framework. *American Political Science Review* 56:947–52.

Ball, Terence, ed. 1987. *Idioms of Inquiry*. Albany: State University of New York Press.

Beer, Samuel H. 1973. The Modernization of American Federalism. *Publius* 3:49–96.

Berger, L., and T. Luckmann. 1966. *The Social Construction of Reality*. Garden City: Doubleday.

Bernstein, Richard. 1976. *The Restructuring of Social and Political Theory*. Philadelphia: University of Pennsylvania Press.

Booth, Alan. 1983. The "Keynesian Revolution" in Economic Policy-Making. *Economic History Review*, 2d ser., 36:103–23.

Bouvier, Michel. 1986. *L'Etat sans politique*. Paris: Librairie Générale de Droit et de Jurisprudence.

Bryant, Christopher G. A. 1985. *Positivism in Social Theory and Research*. London: Macmillan.

Burns, Eveline. 1941. *The British Unemployment Programme, 1920–1938*. Washington: Social Science Research Council.

Burrow, John. 1981. *A Liberal Descent: Victorian Historians and the English Past*. Cambridge: Cambridge University Press.

Caiden, Naomi, and Aaron Wildavsky. 1974. *Planning and Budgeting in Poor Countries*. New York: Wiley.

Cameron, David. 1982. On the Limits of the Public Economy. *Annals of the American Academy of Political and Social Science* 459:46–62.

Carnap, Rudolf. 1970 (1939). Theories as Partially Interpreted Formal Systems. In B. Brody, ed., *Readings in the Philosophy of Science*. Englewood Cliffs: Prentice-Hall.

Clarke, Peter. 1989. *The Keynesian Revolution in the Making, 1924–1936*. Oxford: Oxford University Press.

Clegg, Stewart R. 1989. *Frameworks of Power.* London: Sage.

Cohen, M. D., J. G. March, and J. Olsen. 1972. A Garbage Can Model of Organizational Choice. *Administrative Science Quarterly* 17:1–25.

Collini, Stefan, Donald Winch, and John Burrow. 1983. *That Noble Science of Politics.* Cambridge: Cambridge University Press.

Crozier, Michel. 1964. *The Bureaucratic Phenomenon.* Chicago: University of Chicago Press.

Dahl, Robert. 1961. *Who Governs?* New Haven: Yale University Press.

Dallmayr, Fred R., and Thomas A. McCarthy, eds. 1977. *Understanding and Social Inquiry.* Notre Dame: University of Notre Dame Press.

David, Otto, Jack Dempster, and Aaron Wildavsky. 1966. A Theory of the Budgetary Process. *American Political Science Review* 60:529–47.

Dryzek, John S. 1983. Don't Toss Coins in Garbage Cans: A Prologue to Policy Design. *Journal of Public Policy* 3:345–68.

Dyson, Kenneth. 1980. *The State Tradition in Western Europe.* New York: Oxford University Press.

Easton, David. 1953. *The Political System.* New York: Knopf.

Eckstein, Harry. 1966. *Division and Cohesion in Democracy: A Study of Norway.* Princeton: Princeton University Press.

———. 1975. Case Study and Theory in Political Science. In F. Greenstein and N. Polsby, eds., *Handbook of Political Science.* Vol. 7. Reading: Addison-Wesley.

Eulau, Heinz. 1958. The Maddening Methods of H. D. Laswell: Some Philosophical Underpinnings. In A. Rogow, ed., *Personality Politics, and Social Science in the Twentieth Century: Essays in Honor of H. D. Laswell.* Chicago: University of Chicago Press.

Finer, Samuel, ed. 1975. *Adversary Politics and Electoral Reform.* London: Anthony Wigram.

Fisher, Frank. 1985. Critical Evaluation of Public Policy. in J. Forester, ed., *Critical Theory and Public Life.* Cambridge: MIT Press.

Forester, John, ed. 1985. *Critical Theory and Public Life.* Cambridge: MIT Press.

Geertz, Clifford. 1973. *The Interpretation of Cultures.* New York: Basic Books.

Goodin, Robert E. 1982. *Political Theory and Public Policy.* Chicago: University of Chicago Press.

Gouldner, Alvin W. 1957. Theoretical Requirements of the Applied Social Sciences. *American Sociological Review* 22:91–102.

Gunnell, John G. 1969. Deduction, Explanation, and Social Scientific Inquiry. *American Political Science Review* 64:1233–46.

Habermas, Jürgen. 1973. *Theory and Practice.* Boston: Beacon.

Hall, Peter. 1986. *Governing the Economy: The Politics of State Intervention in Britain and France.* New York: Oxford University Press.

———. 1989. *The Political Power of Economic Ideas: Keynesianism Across Nations.* Princeton: Princeton University Press.

Hansen, Norwood. 1958. *Patterns of Discovery.* Cambridge: Cambridge University Press.

Harden, Ian, and Norman Lewis. 1986. *The Noble Lie: The British Constitution and the Rule of Law.* London: Hutchinson.

Hardin, Russell. 1982. *Collective Action.* Baltimore: Johns Hopkins University Press.

Hawley, Willis D., and James H. Svara. 1972. *Community Power: A Bibliographic Review.* Santa Barbara: Clio.

Hawthorn, Geoffrey. 1976. *Enlightenment and Despair.* Cambridge: Cambridge University Press.

Hayek, F. A. 1955. *The Counter-Revolution of Science: Studies in the Abuse of Reason.* New York: Free Press.

Hayward, Jack, and Michael Watson. 1975. *Planning, Politics, and Public Policy.* Cambridge: Cambridge University Press.

Heclo, Hugh. 1974. *Modern Social Politics in Britain and Sweden.* New Haven: Yale University Press.

Hempel, Carl G. 1965. *Aspects of Scientific Explanation and Other Essays in the Philosophy of Science.* New York: Free Press.

Hennock, E. P. 1976. Poverty and Social Theory in England: The Experience of the Eighteen-Eighties. *Social History* 1:67–91.

Hibbs, Douglas A., Jr. 1977. Political Parties and Macro-economic Policy. *American Political Science Review* 71:1467–87.

Ikenberry, John. 1988. *Reasons of State: Oil Politics and the Capacities of American Government.* Ithaca: Cornell University Press.

Kelman, Steven. 1981. *Regulating America, Regulating Sweden: A Comparison of Occupational Safety and Health Policy.* Cambridge: MIT Press.

Kingdon, John W. 1984. *Agendas, Alternatives, and Public Policies.* Boston. Little-Brown.

Kiser, Larry, and Elinor Ostrom. 1982. The Three Worlds of Action: A Metatheoretical Synthesis of Institutional Approaches. In L. Kiser and E. Ostrom, eds., *Strategies of Political Inquiry.* Beverly Hills: Sage.

Krasner, Stephen. 1988. Sovereignty: An Institutional Perspective. *Comparative Political Studies* 21:66–84.

Lakatos, Imre. 1970. Falsification and the Methodology of Scientific Research Programmes. In I. Lakatos and A. Musgrave, eds., *Criticism and the Growth of Knowledge.* Cambridge: Cambridge University Press.

Landau, Martin. 1974. Federalism, Redundancy, and System Reliability. In D. Elazar, ed., *The Federal Polity.* New Brunswick: Transaction.

Lijphart, Arendt. 1971. Comparative Politics and the Comparative Method. *American Political Science Review* 65:682–93.

———. 1975. The Comparable-Cases Strategy in Comparative Research. *Comparative Political Studies* 8:158–77.

Linder, Stephen H., and B. Guy Peters. 1988. The Analysis of Design or Design of Analysis? *Policy Studies Review* 7:738–50.

Lowi, Theodore. 1964. *At the Pleasure of the Mayor.* New York: Free Press.

———. 1969. *The End of Liberalism.* New York: Norton.

March, J. G., and J. Olsen. 1975. The Uncertainty of the Past: Organizational Learning Under Ambiguity. *European Journal of Political Research* 3:147–71.

———. 1983. Organizing Political Life: What Administrative Reorganization Tells Us About Government. *American Political Science Review* 77:281–97.

———. 1984. The New Institutionalism: Organizational Factors in Everyday Life. *American Political Science Review* 78:734–49.

Meltzer, Allan H. 1989. *Keynes's Monetary Theory: A Different Interpretation*. Cambridge: Cambridge University Press.

Mills, C. Wright. 1956. *The Power Elite*. Oxford: Oxford University Press.

Moon, Donald. 1975. The Logic of Political Inquiry: A Synthesis of Opposed Perspectives. In F. Greenstein and N. Polsby, eds., *Handbook of Political Science*. Vol. 1. Reading: Addison-Wesley.

Nairn, Tom. 1988. *The Enchanted Glass: Britain and Its Monarchy*. London: Century Hutchinson.

Olson, Mancur. 1965. *The Logic of Collective Action*. Cambridge: Harvard University Press.

Parsons, David W. 1985. Was Keynes Kuhnian? Keynes and the Idea of Theoretical Revolutions. *British Journal of Political Science* 15:451–71.

Phillips, Derek. 1975. Paradigms and Commensurability. *Theory and Society* 2:37–61.

Pocock, J.A.G. 1975. *The Machiavellian Moment: Florentine Political Thought and the Atlantic Republican Tradition*. Princeton: Princeton University Press.

Polsby, Nelson. 1960. How to Study Community Power: The Pluralist Alternative. *Journal of Politics* 22:474–84.

Popper, Karl. 1959 (1944). *The Logic of Scientific Discovery*. New York: Harper and Row (Basic Books).

Richardson, Jeremy, ed. 1982. *Policy Styles in Western Europe*. London: Allen and Unwin.

Rose, Richard. 1984. *Understanding Big Government: The Programme Approach*. London: Sage.

Rose, Richard, and B. Guy Peters. 1978. *Can Government Go Bankrupt?* New York: Basic Books.

Rudelle, Odile. 1986. *La République absolu, 1870–1889*. Paris: Publications de la Sorbonne.

Sabatier, Paul A. 1988. An Advocacy Coalition Framework of Policy Change and the Role of Policy-Oriented Learning Therein. *Policy Sciences* 21:129–68.

Shonfield, A. 1969. *Modern Capitalism*. Oxford: Oxford University Press.

Suleiman, Ezra. 1974. *Politics, Power, and Bureaucracy in France*. Princeton: Princeton University Press.

Toulmin, Stephen. 1963. *Foresight and Understanding*. New York: Harper Torchbooks.

Verba, Sidney. 1967. Some Dilemmas of Comparative Research. *World Politics* 20:111–27.

Vogel, David. 1986. *National Styles of Regulation: Environmental Policy in Great Britain and the United States*. Ithaca: Cornell University Press.

Wildavsky, Aaron. 1979. *Speaking Truth to Power: The Art and the Craft of Policy Analysis*. Boston: Little-Brown.

Wolfinger, Raymond E. 1960. Reputation and Reality in the Study of Community Power. *American Sociological Review* 25:636–44.

I

IN SEARCH OF TIME

2

Historical Context and Policy Studies

Douglas E. Ashford

IN CONSIDERING the relation of historical knowledge to the analysis of public policy, it is instructive to begin by recalling how, if at all, the social science disciplines have treated history. Broadly speaking, the behavioral revolution meant that in political science and economics the presumption of rational self-interest made historical generalization and historical knowledge superfluous. There were important exceptions, such as Hirschmann (1977), Heilbroner (1963), and Gerschenkron (1943), but they were products of a European intellectual tradition where economic and political history had never been so energetically excluded from respectable social science. As time passed, economics departments had less and less use for history, even though one can still occasionally find a department with a bemused economic historian who survives more or less on collegial tolerance. Political science never embraced an impressive body of historical writing such as Commons and Beard bestowed on American economic history. The tedious necessities of large data banks not only limited study time to the available quantitative records but oversimplified the comparison of historical continuities and historical change. Only a bit more than a decade ago, I attended a conference where an analyst of French communal budgets, laboring to extend a data bank to 1871, was mystified until someone told him of the Franco-Prussian War.

Anthropology and sociology were by no means unaffected by the behavioral revolution, but their intellectual antecedents and subject matter meant that historiographic, if not genuine historical, controversies were never totally dismissed. Dealing with artifacts, remnants, and incomplete records, anthropologists and archeologists have always had to reconstruct the past with imagination as well as zeal. Though less visible now than a generation ago, anthropology and archeology has always had one foot planted in classical, humanistic learning. The relation is somewhat different in sociology, but the founders of the discipline were accomplished historians, and the discipline grew from a late nineteenth-century fascination with the "laws" of history. As Abrams writes, "In some fundamental respects the two disciplines are trying to do the same thing and are employing the same logic of explanation to do so" (1982, ix). As a result, sociology never suffered from the exclusion of history. During the 1970s, the connection between sociological analysis and history thrived, while it was virtually excluded from political science (Anderson 1974; Stinchecombe 1978; Stedman Jones 1976; Thompson 1978). The debate concerning state and society revived many traditional controversies about social history (Skocpol 1984).

This brief excursion into the history and place of longitudinal analysis in the disciplines helps us understand why, in some respects, restoring a time dimension to political science—and by implication, to policy studies—has been delayed and often resisted. In the behavioral revolution of the 1950s and 1960s, neither the remnants of historical scholarship preserved by the history of political thought nor the policy foundations of constitutional law were able to press their natural links to policy studies. Political theorists were for the most part disinclined and even disinterested, though the core problems of uncertainty, obligation, and choice that permeate official decision making are the stuff of political thought. Indeed, most of the giant figures in debates over democratic theory—Hobbes, Locke, Bentham, and Mill, to name a few—frequently gave policy advice, drafted legislation and constitutions, and were actively engaged in the policy debates of the day (Cowling 1967; Harrison 1965; Heyck 1982; Finer 1972). Legal and constitutional scholars were in some ways less harshly treated, in part because such intense issues as the civil rights movement, Vietnam, and the cold war preserved interest in the foundations of political justice. Even so, neither problem solving in the Laswellian mode nor the practical application of behavioral methods to policy issues for opinion measurement provided the grounds for the systematic theoretical integration of policy studies into politics nor for their subsequent intellectual legitimacy within the discipline.

As noted in chapter 1, behavioral politics helped revive comparative politics but did so with highly abstract theories of modernization, communication, and perception that reinforced behavioral presuppositions (Lerner 1958; Rostow 1963; Almond and Verba 1964). These studies showed little interest in internal structural relationships, such as center-periphery conflicts, or confounding social relationships, such as clientelism or corporatism. By definition, a clearly articulated macro-micro foundation, and therefore concern with contextual questions, was not only unnecessary in the pursuit of empirical knowledge but actually threatened behavioral constructs by exposing the limitations of behavioral social science. For this reason, such enthusiastic advocates of behavioral social science as Almond, Easton, and Dahl simply banished such lumpy ideas as *the state, sovereignty,* and *social class* from the vocabulary of politics. It is interesting to note that one of the most prominent early political sociologists attached to this group, Lipset, initially performed a detailed historical and structural study of the origins of Canadian socialism (1950) but later unreservedly subscribed to the behavioral model (1960), which erased time and situation as elements of human understanding. All of these dispositions were of course antithetical to the development of historically sensitive political analysis and, for reasons illustrated by the essays in part 1 of this book, erected formidable barriers between political and historical scholarship.

Perhaps the most succinct way to illustrate how historical research might contribute to comparative policy studies, both substantively and methodologically, is to examine historical writing whose relation to policy making is unmistakable. Biographies are perhaps the most important, because underscoring how uniquely placed figures manipulate authority, perceive policy choices, and use political institutions through time directly challenges behavioral assumptions. Biographies are among the richest sources of detailed, microlevel information about policy making, but they are understandably among the most confusing sources for those working with macrolevel theory. First, their interpretation rests heavily on subjective, motivational factors, which more rigorous social science, above all behavioral political science, tries to eliminate. Second, the relation of major actors to any situation is always problematical, depending on such highly variable circumstances as tactical advantage, partisan opportunity, and even chance encounters. Third, macropolitical studies often stipulate a uniformity context in order to claim equivalence in explaining how policy makers attach priorities to problems, weigh information, and manipulate the institutionalized levers of power. In sum, biographies are unique statements of famous persons and, except for the occasional moralizing and commentary, make no claim to universal or lawlike knowledge.

Against these conceptual and descriptive hazards one must also weigh the richness and persuasiveness of the various kinds of information that biographies contain at the microlevel. First, biographies help establish and clarify the institutional continuities and political decision making in a way that behavioral analysis cannot. The famous British controversy about individualism and collectivism discussed in chapter 3 by Kumar, for example, not only links political ideas to British policy making and politics but acquires validity from the remarkable array of biographical testimonials on how British institutions resisted collectivist principles. To be sure, as so effectively argued by Beer (1965), party politics acquired a consensual form in late Victorian Britain that gave British parties an extraordinary potential for policy change, but the underlying principles of British governance changed relatively little. The consistent pattern of policy-making behavior comes alive in the diverse biographies of influential Whitehall figures such as Sir Edwin Chadwick (Finer 1952; Brundage 1988); Sir James Kay-Shuttleworth and Sir John Simon (Lambert 1963); Sir Charles Trevelyan (Hart 1960); and Sir Robert Morant (Allen 1934). More recently, the semibiographical accounts of ministerial developments by policy makers such as Sir Arthur Newsholme (1925) and Sir Lewis Amherst Selby-Bigge (1927) expose the nature of British policy making between the wars. Biographies provide an invaluable test of generalizations by linking institutional behavior to larger social and political theories through time.

Biographies also provide an intimacy of detail and interaction that permit us to gauge how motivational, perceptual, and individual differences influence decision making and so provide detailed accounts of microlevel behavior in situations that are necessarily excluded from behavioral studies. Partly because of British fascination with political biography, there is, for example, an unparalleled body of biographical information for the postwar Labour party, which treats all their major decisions in immense detail: the adroit and easily underestimated Prime Minister Attlee (Harris 1982; Burridge 1985); the blunt and loyal Bevin (Bullock 1960); the whimsical but devoted Dalton (Pimlott 1985); the crafty Morrison (Donoughue and Jones 1973); the bright, ambitious young Gaitskell (Williams 1979); and the feisty, impassioned Bevan (Foot 1962, 1973; Campbell 1987). Such an array of studies may seem unwieldly, even threatening, to any systematic account of British policy making, yet these books confront us with the true proportions and the true promise of microlevel explanation. The point is not that social science has any hope of adequately dealing with so many individual and irregular differences that impinge on the policy process but that knowing of such detail produces caution in the selective use of microlevel behavior in interpreting abstract configurations of events in conventional social science terms.

Second, historical studies acquire new value as such contextual ideas as governing capacity, institutional constraint, and state formation begin to reappear in more broadly conceived analyses of politics and policy making. States, bureaucracies, and institutions are not easily circumscribed by the conventional concepts of behavioral social science. Indeed, an interesting argument can be made that clearer formulation of institutional and organizational variables is a prerequisite to the more systematic use of microlevel data in testing macrolevel hypotheses about the state, its behavior, and performance. There is, of course, an enormous body of cross-sectional information in government handbooks, guides, and indexes that have, for the most part, escaped systematic investigation because the necessary contextual and comparative framework is lacking, while their behavioral implications remain undecipherable by available methods. Historical scholarship offers an entirely different strategy, whereby microlevel institutional, administrative, and policy-making behavior over long periods can be summarized and distilled (Ashford 1978, 1986, 1989). Indicative of the force of historical analysis is the continued influence of such historically oriented institutional histories as McConnell's analysis of public and private sector decision making in America (1966), Lowi's institutional critique of interest group stagnation in America (1969), or Schattschneider's study of a semisovereign America (1960).

While it is possible that conventional macrolevel hypotheses may be disaggregated to deal with institutional comparisons through time or across sectors, the results to date are not that promising (Ashford 1991; Olsen 1988). Administrative and organizational histories are not readily translated into contextual principles linking micro- and macrolevel behavior, but many of the most successful studies—Kaufman's study (1960) of the Forestry Service, for example—acquired remarkable survival value. Though cast aside in the 1950s, administrative histories are regaining their legitimacy (White 1958; Bensel 1984; Skrownek 1982). Studies of this kind are common in Europe, which has a less hostile academic environment. There are studies of the origins of the French (Latournerie 1971) and British (Lowe 1986) ministries of labor that describe both internal negotiating behavior and structural differences of governance, which are essential to an understanding of ground rules, codes, and habits linking microlevel behavior to larger policy goals and eventually to larger theories of state and society. For those concerned with the definition and implementation of early social and economic policies, there is an enormous literature. J. Harris's study (1977) of nineteenth-century unemployment policies in Britain sheds enormous light on the implementation and organization of a fundamental welfare state policy. In some instances, such as the Macinol (1980) and Ceccaldi (1951) studies of family allowances in Britain and France, there are comparable institutional and organizational histories waiting to be interpreted (Ashford 1986). But as the chapters in part 1 show, without the contextual ideas linking historical research to macrotheory, their value will not be extracted.

There is a third category of historical writing; this writing might not only improve concepts and definitions of the state, institutions, and policy making but also raise fundamental theoretical issues of comparison. Some studies provide both macro- and microtheories by dealing simultaneously with intragovernmental policy making and the relation of policies to their social settings. As such, they provide the basis for new generalizations and suggest new hypotheses that are often more closely linked to policy making than common macrosocial or macroeconomic theories superimposed on microlevel phenomena. The advantage of such broad historical comparisons over monographical historical studies is that the historical framework is presented with microlevel evidence. There is neither the risk of treating a narrow, monographic historical study as typical when it is not, a problem that all historically minded social scientists face, nor the temptation to ignore more general questions about national, intergovernmental, and local policy making that more abstractly defined theories may ignore. For example, as provocative as some of the new international political economy analysis may be, it is difficult to link these studies to the institutional, political, and organizational differences highlighted in, for example, French (Kuisel 1981) and British (Fox 1985) studies of industrial and economic policy in the nineteenth century. The danger is that scholars may thereby be unaware that their macrotheories are quite inappropriate to the historical period.

The logic of a simultaneous cross-sectional and longitudinal comparison is pursued in more detail in the conclusion of this book but should be elaborated here to highlight the uses of history. The issue is not the more direct question of how to find good microlevel historical evidence, commonly done by extracting from monographic historical research, nor is it simply to aid the discovery of better institutional, policy-based, or organizational variables linking macro- and microlevel studies. Historians such as Kuisel are not simply presenting us with a mass of microlevel detail but also with an interpretation (a quasi theory) of the French, British, or some other economy. Rather than imposing a formal model on cross-national comparisons, as for example in the aggregate studies discussed above, these studies provide both general descriptions and detailed evidence that is integrated by the historian. There are, of course, two possible receptions to such historical generalizations. One is that the historian was unaware of missing systematic (often meaning more abstract) theory, and therefore his or her work can be freely translated into other macrolevel terms. This seems to be the position taken by Skocpol (1984).

The risk of too freely linking history to macrotheory is not only that history may be used in selective ways but that the interpretation of the historian is simply cast aside. The result is not only a rather cavalier treatment of historical explanation but perhaps greater distortion, insofar as social scientists fail to make the detailed examination of microlevel behavior on which the historical case was built.

Another and more direct way of saying the same thing is that social science should use history seriously rather than instrumentally. Obviously, the entire range of historical controversies cannot be reworked within a social science framework. Such interpretations unavoidably appear truncated and arbitrary (Skocpol 1984). Social science cannot reproduce the richness and texture of historical studies, but neither should it ignore the nuances and contradictions that historians provide at the microlevel. This is the important message of Rothstein's contribution to this volume. Marxist class theory does not fit the Swedish situation, and interesting microlevel evidence can be produced showing how the Swedes, contrary to their image as masters of harmonious and reflective agreement, skillfully manipulated policies to bind the labor movement to the party. Essentially, since the 1930s, unemployment insurance was used as an incentive to join unions. Social insurance became a policy to control union policies, both in relation to macrolevel policies on inflation, industrial relations, and labor organization but also in relation to detailed questions of union organization, collective bargaining, and union discipline. As Rothstein points out elsewhere (1985), the historical foundations for this arrangement were carefully thought through, not without some conflict, by Social Democratic leaders.

At both the macro- and microlevel, Rothstein's historical study identifies essential changes in the Swedish compromise and shows that the outcome goes well beyond the benign interpretation of received historical knowledge about Sweden. He makes clear the connection of policy-level differences, options, and choices to institutional and, by implication, social change. In other words, the historical situation provides its own interpretation rather than being forced into a particular causal model of history, used, for example, by Skocpol and her colleagues (1984 374–86).

A fourth, and in some respects the most ambitious, possibility is to treat major historical themes as theoretical frameworks and trace their own causal inferences to the microlevel. As used by Himmelfarb (1985), for example, such an exercise would be a true historical explanation of policy making rather than one adapted to contemporary hypotheses about social forces, uses of authority, or political and economic development. Instead of using history to locate causal links within the context of one country, the fourth choice uses a literal interpretation to advance a historical paradigm (essential descriptive and narrative) to provide a common theoretical foundation for both general and specific behavior.

I make a tentative step in this direction in chapter 14, which deals with an underlying constitutional dilemma of modern democratic governance, meaning the various kinds of conflicts and choices that arose as monarchial regimes gave way to democracy. The specific constitutional choices presented to Britain and France are discussed, but it may be accepted for the moment that these choices left the two countries with fundamentally different patterns of authority, in part still imbedded in the formal texts of governance and, in part, in the detailed procedures and principles of policy making. Much abstract macrotheory is concerned with only those social and economic preconditions thought essential to democratic evolution or revolution. But throughout Europe there was also an extended debate of a more purely political nature about the organization and expression of democratic values, which, through interpretation, give independent status to the principles used in the formation of modern democracies (Moon 1975; Ball 1988). In Britain, for example, these debates can be traced to the fourteenth century (Pocock 1975; Thornton 1965), when absolute monarchy came under close scrutiny and when the British system of justice was organized. While the royal prerogatives no longer exist, these historical experiences bestowed British politics with a particular set of procedures, practices, and conditions of authority that contain particular limitations and meanings for contemporary policy making and governance (Nairn 1988; Harden and Lewis 1986).

Well before Margaret Thatcher made these tendencies unmistakable, there were good reasons to think of British politics and policy making as distinctly monarchial. Moving across a number of policy areas (Ashford 1984), government procedures and practices, disclosed arbitrary controls of many kinds, which were blatantly evident in intergovernmental and territorial politics (Ashford 1982). Cast in the utilitarian mold of contemporary social science, both pluralist and Marxist, the persistence of such arbitrary, defensive practices at the policy-making level is no mystery and requires no explanation. Indeed, it is difficult to pose such problems within the framework of modern social science. But in the case of Britain, and probably of France as well (Rudelle 1986), historical policy studies bring persistent patterns of authority to the surface and link these tendencies to the specific conditions and circumstances of the exercise of power. Many historical studies of nineteenth-century British policy making (Lambert 1963; J. Harris 1977) provide extensive microlevel information on the exercise of power, the motives and perceptions of key actors, and the formulation of policies within a particular constitutional and political framework whose historical standing is well established. For Britain, and possibly for France, Germany, and Sweden, such works make it possible to link macro- and microlevel politics through time so that contemporary sectoral and cross-sectional comparisons can be tested against historical knowledge without damaging historical meanings and historical interpretations.

SOURCES

Abrams, Philip. 1982. *Historical Sociology.* London: Open Books.

Allen, Bernard M. 1934. *Sir Robert Morant: A Great Public Servant.* London: Macmillan.

Almond, Gabriel, and Sidney Verba. 1964. *The Civic Culture.* Boston: Little-Brown.

Anderson, Perry. 1974. *Lineages of the Absolutist State.* London: N.L.B.

Ashford, Douglas E. 1978. The Structural Analysis of Policy, or Institutions Really Do Matter. In D. Ashford, ed., *Comparing Public Policies.* Beverly Hills: Sage.

———. 1984. The Structural Comparison of Social Policy and Intergovernmental Politics. *Policy and Politics* 12:369–89.

———. 1986. Structural Analysis and Institutional Change. *Polity* 19:97–122.

———. 1989. L'Etat-providence à travers l'étude comparative des institutions. *Revue Française de Science Politique* 39:276–95.

———. 1991. Bringing the Welfare State Back In. *Comparative Politics* 23:351–75.

Ball, Terrence. 1988. *Transforming Political Discourse: Political Theory and Critical Conceptual History.* Oxford: Basil Blackwell.

Beer, Samuel H. 1965. *British Politics in the Collectivist Age.* New York: Knopf.

Bensel, Richard. 1984. *Sectionalism and American Political Development.* Madison: University of Wisconsin Press.

Brundage, Anthony. 1988. *England's "Prussian Minister."* University Park: Pennsylvania State University Press.

Bullock, Alan. 1960. *The Life and Times of Ernest Bevin, 1881–1960.* London: Heinemann.

Burridge, Trevor. 1985. *Attlee: A Political Biography.* London: Jonathan Cape.

Campbell, John. 1987. *Nye Bevan and the Mirage of British Socialism.* London: Weidenfeld and Nicolson.

Ceccaldi, Dominique. 1951. *Histoire des Prestations Familiales en France.* Paris: Association Nationale des Allocations Familiales.

Cowling, Maurice. 1967. *1867: Disraeli, Gladstone and the Revolution: The Passing of the Second Reform Bill*. Cambridge: Cambridge University Press.

Donoughue, Bernard, and George Jones. 1973. *Herbert Morrison: Portrait of a Politician*. London: Weidenfeld and Nicolson.

Finer, S. E. 1952. *The Life and Times of Sir Edwin Chadwick*. London: Methuen.

———. 1972. The Transmission of Benthamite Ideas, 1820–50. In G. Sutherland, ed., *Studies in the Growth of Nineteenth Century Government*. London: Routledge and Kegan Paul.

Foot, Michael. 1962. *Aneurin Bevan, 1897–1945*. London: MacGibbon and Kee.

———. 1973. *Aneurin Bevan, 1945–1960*. London: Davis Poynter.

Fox, Alan. 1985. *History and Heritage: The Social Origins of the British Industrial Relations System*. London: Allen and Unwin.

Gerschenkron, Alexander. 1943. *Bread and Democracy in Germany*. Berkeley and Los Angeles: University of California Press.

Harden, Ian, and Norman Lewis. 1986. *The Noble Lie: The British Constitution and the Rule of Law*. London: Hutchinson.

Harris, Jose. 1977. *Unemployment and Politics: A Study of British Social Policy, 1886–1914*. Oxford: Clarendon.

Harris, Kenneth. 1982. *Attlee*. London: Weidenfeld and Nicolson.

Harrison, Royden. 1965. *Before the Socialists: Studies in Labour and Politics, 1861–1881*. London: Routledge and Kegan Paul.

Hart, Jennifer. 1960. Sir Charles Trevelyan at the Treasury. *English Historical Review* 70:411–27.

Heilbroner, Robert L. 1963. *The Great Ascent: The Struggle for Economic Development in Our Time*. New York: Harper and Row.

Heyck, Thomas W. 1982. *The Transformation of Intellectual Life in Victorian England*. London: Croom Helm.

Himmelfarb, Gertrude. 1985. *The Idea of Poverty: England in the Early Industrial Age*. New York: Norton.

Hirschmann, Albert. 1977. *The Passions and the Interests*. Princeton: Princeton University Press.

Kaufmann, Herbert. 1960. *The Forest Ranger: A Study in Administrative Behavior*. Baltimore: Johns Hopkins University Press.

Kuisel, Richard F. 1981. *Capitalism and the State in Modern France*. London: Cambridge University Press.

Lambert, Royston. 1963. *Sir John Simon, 1816–1904, and English Social Administration*. London: MacGibbon and Kee.

Latournerie, Jean-André. 1971. *Le Ministère du Travail* (*Origines et Premiers Développements*). Paris: Editions Cujas.

Lerner, Daniel. 1958. *The Passing of Traditional Society*. Glencoe: Free Press.

Lipset, Seymour. 1950. *Agrarian Socialism: The Cooperative Commonwealth Federation of Saskatchewan: A Study in Political Sociology*. Berkeley and Los Angeles: University of California Press.

———. 1960. *Political Man: The Social Bases of Politics*. Garden City: Doubleday.

Lowe, Rodney. 1986. *Adjusting to Democracy: The Role of the Ministry of Labour in British Politics, 1916–1939*. Oxford: Clarendon.

Lowi, Theodore. 1969. *The End of Liberalism*. New York: Norton.

Macinol, John. 1980. *The Movement for Family Allowances, 1918–1945: A Study in Social Policy Development*. London: Heinemann.

McConnel, Grant. 1966. *Private Power and American Democracy*. New York: Knopf.

Moon, Donald. 1975. The Logic of Political Inquiry: A Synthesis of Opposed Perspectives. In F. Greenstein and N. Polsby, eds., *Handbook of Political Science*. Vol. 1. Reading: Addison-Wesley.

Nairn, Tom. 1988. *The Enchanted Glass: Britain and Its Monarchy*. London: Century Hutchinson.

Newsholme, Sir Arthur. 1925. *The Ministry of Health*. London: Putnam.

Olsen, Johan P. 1988. Administrative Reform and Theories of Organization. In C. Campbell and G. Peters, eds., *Organizing Governance, Governing Organizations*. Pittsburgh: University of Pittsburgh Press.

Pimlott, Ben. 1985. *Hugh Dalton*. London: Jonathan Cape.

Pocock, J.G.A. 1975. *The Machiavellian Moment: Florentine Political Thought and the Atlantic Republican Tradition*. Princeton: Princeton University Press.

Rostow, W. W. 1963. *The Economics of Take-off into Sustained Growth*. New York: St. Martin's.

Rothstein, Bo. 1985. Managing the Welfare State: Lessons from Gustav Moller. *Scandinavian Political Studies* 8:151–70.

Rudelle, Odile. 1986. *La République Absolue, 1870–1889*. Paris: Presses de la Sorbonne.

Schattschneider, E. E. 1960. *The Semi-Sovereign People*. New York: Holt, Rinehart, and Winston.

Selby-Bigge, Sir Lewis Amherst. 1927. *The Board of Education*. London: Putnam.

Skocpol, Theda, ed. 1984. *Vision and Method in Historical Sociology*. Cambridge: Cambridge University Press.

Skrownek, Stephen. 1982. *Building a New American State: The Expansion of National Administrative Capacities, 1877–1920*. New York: Cambridge University Press.

Stedman Jones, G. 1976. From Historical Sociology to Theoretic History. *British Journal of Sociology*, 27:295–305.

Stinchecombe, A. L. 1978. *Theoretical Methods in Social History*. New York: Academic Press.

Thompson, E. P. 1978. *The Poverty of Theory*. London: Merlin.

Thornton, A. P. 1965. *The Habit of Authority: Paternalism in British History*. London: Allen and Unwin.

White, Leonard D. 1958. *The Republican Era: A Study of Administrative History, 1869–1901*. New York: Free Press.

Williams, Philip. 1979. *Hugh Gaitskell: A Political Biography*. London: Jonathan Cape.

3

Social Thought and Social Action: The "Dicey Problem" and the Role of Ideas in English Social Policy

Krishan Kumar

> Not ideas, but material and ideal interests, directly govern men's conduct. Yet very frequently the "world images" that have been created by "ideas" have, like switchmen, determined the tracks along which action has been pushed by the dynamic of interest.
>
> —Max Weber

IT IS SOME years since John Goldthorpe urged social policy analysts to turn to sociology. There they could find theories and models of society that would enrich what would otherwise be simple historical narrative or spuriously neutral description and prescription (Goldthorpe 1964). The call has, if anything, been too well answered. Volume after volume on social problems and social policy has poured scorn on the sociological innocence of previous commentators. Following the lead given by Mills, the value premises and professional ideologies of social investigators have been put under scrutiny (Mills 1967). We have been offered conflict models, social constructionism, labeling theory, and several other sociological perspectives as the master guides to the understanding of social problems and the development of social policy.[1] Works on the ideology and the political economy of the welfare state have proliferated, suggesting the contentious and problematic status of the very concepts of welfare and the welfare state.[2]

It is interesting that Goldthorpe, in pressing the claims of sociology, effectively directs students of social policy away from history. This is ironic, in view of the fact that the specific focus of Goldthorpe's discussion is the historiography of the so-called Dicey problems: the debate, that is, sparked off by Dicey's celebrated account of the revolution in government in nineteenth-century England as set out in his *Law and Public Opinion in England* (Dicey 1962).

Dicey, says Goldthorpe, attributes developments in social policy to trends in public opinion, which were themselves ultimately derived from the thought of some famous nineteenth-century intellectual, notably Bentham or John Stuart Mill or one of their utilitarian disciples. Against this emphasis on social and political thinkers as the ultimate agencies of social change, Goldthorpe champions the work of sociologically minded historians such as Karl Polanyi, H. L. Beales, E. H. Carr, and Oliver MacDonagh. He praises them for treating the growth of social policy in nineteenth-century England as "a complex process of social change to be interpreted as an integral part of a general pattern of development of the society as a whole, rather than as the resultant simply of shifts in dominant modes of thought and belief" (Goldthorpe 1964, 46–47).[3]

Why changes in "modes of thought and belief" should be thought less sociological than other kinds of changes need not detain us here. The point is that, for all his commendation of these practicing historians, what Goldthorpe actually endorses are theoretical stances that engage least with the materials of history and that are often, in fact, profoundly ahistorical in their very principle. This is particularly true of sociological functionalism, the model that, as Goldthorpe points out, supplied these historians with their main analytical framework for explaining the growth of social policy and the corresponding growth of the nineteenth-century English state. They accounted, that is, for growing state intervention as a matter of functional necessity.

Polanyi is the best example of this. The principle of nineteenth-century society, argues Polanyi, was "the idea of a self-adjusting market"; but this implied "a stark utopia." "Such an institution could not exist for any length of time without annihilating the human and natural substance of society; it would have physically destroyed man and transformed his surroundings into a wilderness" (Polanyi 1957, 3). In the face of this threat to its very survival, market society was forced to take measures "to protect itself." The necessity and inevitability of "collectivist" action "under the conditions of modern industrial society" is proved "most strikingly" by the fact that it occurred not just in England but "in various countries of a widely dissimilar political and ideological configuration."

> Victorian England and the Prussia of Bismarck were poles apart, and both were very much unlike the France of the Third Republic or the Empire of the Hapsburgs. Yet each of them passed through a period of free trade and laissez-faire, followed by a period of antiliberal legislation in regard to public health, factory conditions, municipal trading, social insurance, shipping subsidies, public utilities, trade associations, and so on. . . . The supporting forces were in some cases violently reac-

> tionary and antisocialist as in Vienna, at other times "radical imperialist" as in Birmingham, or of the purest liberal hue as with the Frenchman, Edouard Herriot, Mayor of Lyons. . . . Thus under the most varied slogans with very different motivations a multitude of parties and social strata put into effect almost exactly the same measures in a series of countries in respect to a large number of complicated subjects. There is, on the face of it, nothing more absurd than to infer that they were secretly actuated by the same ideological preconceptions or narrow group interests as the legend of the antiliberal conspiracy would have it. On the contrary, everything tends to support the assumption that objective reasons of a stringent nature forced the hands of the legislators. (ibid. 147–48)

Essentially the procedure here is the same as in many other suspiciously circular kinds of sociological explanations. One builds a model of society (market society, industrial society) defined in such a way that the *explicandum*—in this case, social policy legislation—is seen as the inevitable concomitant or consequence of the existence and persistence of the model over time. Marxists can conjure up classes and class conflict; functionalists, as in this case, have a ready-made explanation for the countermovement of protective welfare legislation in capitalist industrial societies. It cannot really be a matter of surprise to find that all industrial societies enact an array of welfare measures since, as Goldthorpe put the functionalist case, "the creation of an effective social policy is a necessary process in an advanced society. . . . Some form of relatively extensive public provision against the disruptive, wasteful, and debilitating tendencies within industrial, and particularly capitalist, society is seen as being in some sense a functional prerequisite or imperative for the continuing existence and development of such society" (Goldthorpe 1964, 50).

Goldthorpe raises some familiar objections to this kind of functionalist explanation but only to point us toward a conflict rather than a consensus model of society. This may have the virtue of greater realism, but it, too, can easily become a substitute for the examination of actual historical cases of policy making and, especially, the observation and explanation of the differences in the welfare policies of different industrial societies. Instead of attributing social policy responses to the demands of society, one attributes them to a dominant class as part of the necessary ideological work of incorporation and the blunting or suppression of class antagonisms.[4] The motivation may be different—there social survival, here class interest—but, as so often with functionalism and Marxism, the results are strikingly similar. Once again the tendency is either to ignore or explain away historical differences as minor variations on the major theme of securing the stability of capitalist society.

Whatever insights these approaches bring to the study of social policy—and I do not deny that they may be considerable—their weakness is most apparent when we consider the varying patterns and traditions of social policy in modern Western societies. For some purposes, clearly the lofty bird's-eye view is sufficient. There are some remarkable uniformities in the response to industrialization, and much of what is best in sociology has been taken up with describing and analyzing them. Much that is at fault in sociology also has to do with the same tendency to swallow up industrial society wholesale, to iron out differences in timing and tempo, to be insensitive to the particular forms in which change takes place (see Kumar 1978). This is much more than a matter of the historian's dotting the i's and crossing the t's of the sociologist's pardonably hasty scrawl. It is indeed not a matter of a division of labor between historians and sociologists at all. Both need each other, or rather, both need to draw upon the characteristic skills and insights of each other's discipline. Historians are just as often bad sociologists as sociologists are indifferent to history.

The development of social policy in England in the nineteenth century offers us ample scope for reflecting on these questions. We have here not just an example of the formation of a particular tradition of policy, striking by comparison with developments elsewhere (see, e.g., Ashford 1986). We also have an unusually powerful and wide-ranging account, written while the experience was still fresh in the minds of observers, that boldly attempts to explain this tradition by reference to some dominant figures in English social thought. Dicey's *Law and Public Opinion in England*, first published in 1905, aimed to do two things. It sought to show that the peculiarities of the English attitude toward social policy could be traced to the persistence of longstanding beliefs about the relation of individuals to society. More radically however, and more immediately relevant to our purposes, Dicey hoped to demonstrate that social policy was the result not so much of impersonal social forces or material interests as of ideas. Quite what he—or any one else—might mean by this has not always been clear. An examination of Dicey's argument, and the possible objections to it, should help us clarify and assess this important and widely debated position.

Dicey was no simple idealist (in the Weberian sense of that term). In his endeavor "to bring the growth of English laws during a hundred years into connection with the course of English thought" (1962, x), he assumed no direct, one-to-one relation between thought and action;

certainly no direct relation between the thought of individual thinkers and legislative outcomes. He speaks of "a kind of prevalent moral atmosphere" (2) that shapes the minds of legislators in different ages and countries. Thinkers, it seems, contribute to a climate of opinion—or "the spirit of the age"—of which they are as much the creatures as the creators. Their importance is that they symbolize and, by the force of their works, further the currents of thought that otherwise remain at the level of unreflected consciousness. Their influence is always indirect, mediated by the practical concerns and political realities of the day. Even with Bentham, a key figure, Dicey refers to the effect of "Benthamite liberalism, as interpreted by the rough common sense of intelligent politicians" (xxx).[5] The public opinion that Dicey appeals to as the main source of legislation is thus a complex thing. Dicey says as much at the very outset of his work:

> It is well indeed . . . to note that the public opinion which finds expression in legislation is a very complex phenomenon, and often takes the form of a compromise resulting from a conflict between the ideas of the government and the feelings or habits of the governed. This holds good in all countries, whatever be their form of government, but is more manifest than elsewhere in a country such as England, where the legislation enacted by Parliament constantly bears the traces of the compromise arrived at between enlightenment and prejudice. (10)

What this suggests is that public opinion is an amalgam, a composite made up of the beliefs and practices of not only the thinking classes but the unthinking multitude. It is this realization that forces upon Dicey the need to make a significant amendment to his first definition of public opinion as "the wishes and ideas as to legislation held . . . by the majority of those citizens who have at a given moment taken an effective part in public life" (ibid.). This must now be accepted with "considerable reservation."

The concept of public opinion that Dicey later arrives at is sociologically richer though, by the same token, less susceptible to easy empirical investigation. It includes the ideas of the leading thinkers of the age and those of the enlightened public that has been influenced by them; but it also includes less consciously held habits of mind and heart that—even for the educated classes—qualify the pure logic of ideas and ensure that the transmission of ideas into action will always be a good deal less than perfect. Dicey's formulation now goes thus: "There exists at any given time a body of beliefs, convictions, sentiments, accepted principles, or firmly-rooted prejudices, which, taken together, make up the public opinion of a particular era, or what we may call the reigning or predominant current of opinion. . . . The influence of this dominant current of opinion has, in England, if we look at the matter broadly, determined directly or indirectly, the course of legislation" (19–20).

This more cautious statement of causal relationship must be taken with other qualifications that Dicey is at pains to make, threatening though they may be to his general position. He accepts that the influence of public opinion on legislation in nineteenth-century England was to some extent exceptional, even in English history—and certainly so when compared to countries like France and the United States, even though all three countries exhibit the same democratic tendencies of nineteenth-century civilization (7–9). He concedes—especially dangerously to his argument, some might think—that the peculiar social conditions or circumstances in which people find themselves may be the primary influence on the opinion that shapes legislation. "It is impossible, indeed, to insist too strongly upon the consideration that whilst opinion controls legislation, public opinion is itself far less the result of reasoning or of argument than of the circumstances in which men are placed. . . . Circumstances are the creators of most men's opinions" (26–27).

This point is supported with the example of the United States, where the abolition of slavery in the North and the simultaneous retention of it in the South are attributed to their different social circumstances, leading to conflicting opinions on the issue. With this concession to materialism goes a cheerful admission that real or apparent class interest—the interest of the predominant power at a given time—is often behind the laws of a country. Indeed, Dicey breezily remarks, "the connection . . . between legislation and the supposed interests of the legislators is so obvious that the topic hardly requires illustration," though he supplies that in sufficient measure (13).

Dicey's confidence in his basic position and his ability to allow what may seem damaging qualifications are due to his particular understanding of opinion and of the relation between opinion and policy. Neither circumstances nor interests are ready-made, immediately given, graspable facts; they have to be interpreted, and it is in this interpretation that the force of opinion becomes evident. Dicey quotes Hume: "Though men . . . be much governed by interest, yet even interest itself, and all human affairs, are entirely governed by *opinion*." Therefore, continues Dicey, "even . . . were we to assume that the persons who have power to make law are solely and wholly influenced by the desire to promote their own personal and selfish interests, yet their view of their interest and therefore their legislation must be determined by their opinion" (14).

The importance of this point hardly needs stressing in view of the history of the contentious concept of class interest. What, for instance, is the interest of the working class under capitalism? Is it—as the English labor movement has more or less consistently held—to better the condition of workers under capitalism, to give them a parliamentary voice, to strengthen their collective organizations, and to protect them against the uncertainties and anxieties of ill health, old age, and unemployment? Or is it—as continental labor movements have more often held—to shun bourgeois parliamentary politics, to regard trade unionism as a sham, to fear co-optation, and to organize instead as a society within a society, to intensify the feelings of worker discontent to the point, perhaps, of urging a rejection of welfare benefits as a sop and an inducement to class collaboration? The different interpretations of class interest here are as much a matter of theory as of the supposed common experiences of the Western working class and, as a matter of historical fact, have led to the quite opposed strategies of reform and revolution.[6]

The example of working class interests raises the question not just of the role of theory in social action but of the importance of differing national cultures and traditions. The reformist attitude of the English working class is evidently linked not just to a particular intellectual tradition but to a wider national history—real or putative—of gradual social change and a relatively responsive upper class. From the crucial opening of the political system that began with the 1832 Reform Act, taken with the impact of Evangelical Christianity and the still persisting tradition of Tory paternalism, English workers at the end of the nineteenth century had come to feel that their best hopes lay in working within the system of parliamentary government.

The Tory party had converted to Disraelian conservatism and sought to detach the workers from liberalism—not to mention laborism—by stressing the Tory tradition of social responsibility and the ideal of one nation. Gladstonian liberalism countered with a wide-ranging radicalization of traditional liberal philosophy that tempered its laissez-faire individualism and allowed it to lay the foundations of the British welfare state. English labor leaders were not alone in thinking that this transformation of outlook under the spur of democratic politics made feasible "the parliamentary road to socialism." That astute foreign resident, Karl Marx, also concluded that, in the conditions of English society, the gaining of the suffrage by the workers would in itself be sufficient to begin the transition to socialism. For, said Marx, in England universal suffrage means "the political supremacy of the working class" (1975, 119).

Marx held out no such hope for the workers on the continent of Europe. Here, given the political traditions and institutions of these societies, there would be no alternative to violent struggle and revolution to bring in socialism (Marx 1971, 64). Continental labor leaders in the First and Second International largely concurred with this assessment. They were impressed by the extent to which social change and reform had involved bitter class conflict and revolution. "In France," Napoleon III said, "we do not make reforms, we make revolutions." The labor movements saw themselves as the heirs of 1789, 1830, 1848, 1871. The struggle for their rights must entail not escape from that revolutionary tradition but a continuation of it. Parliamentary and reformist strategies, while possible for England and America, would in countries such as France, Germany, Italy, Spain, and Russia lead to persistent betrayal and defeat. A revolutionary stance was therefore essential. Only in Russia did this, in the end, come to anything; but Lenin was right in his protest to a French comrade in 1920 that "a Frenchman has nothing to renounce in the Russian Revolution, which only recommences the French Revolution" (quoted in Behrens 1969, 34).

It is interesting that Dicey, in opposing the view that the advance of democracy sufficiently explains the growth of collectivism, also uses the contrast of national traditions to illustrate his point. Both England and France, he argues, are democratic nations, in the sense that their governments increasingly tend toward majority rule. The natural expectation, therefore—which was certainly that of contemporary radicals such as Marx and Mill—is that legislation in these two countries will reflect that fact and will tend toward the creation of conditions of social equality. But the assumption that "there exists such a thing as specifically democratic legislation, which every democracy is certain to favour" is falsified by the experience of England and France in the nineteenth century. Democracy in England, suggests Dicey, is "tempered by snobbishness." It has "to a great extent inherited the traditions of the aristocratic government of which it is the heir." It looks back to the principles of 1688, not those of 1789, as the source of its liberties. Hence the people of England, though possessing in large measure the political power needed to effect egalitarian change, have in fact "shown no hostility to the existence either of large fortunes or of large estates." Unlike the French, they have upheld the principle of primogeniture, which maintains the unity of the large estates. They are attached to the principle of religious toleration but not of religious equality, giving to the Anglican church a constitutionally privileged place in society. Moreover, "almost alone among popular governments of the world," the English people have for most of the nineteenth century supported complete freedom of trade.

France's democracy has been actuated by quite different traditions.

It is the heir not just of 1789 but, more critically, the years of the Jacobin republic and Napoleon's empire. It is an egalitarian, leveling democracy, but one tempered by the traditions of the authoritarian state. French democracy is essentially one of small peasant proprietors, hostile alike to the large landowners and the organized working class. Though insisting on the separation of church and state, it has been largely indifferent to religious freedom and shows little regard for the right of association. In contrast to English democracy, it has been "zealous for protection" and hostile to free trade. Again, despite its dogmatic insistence on the principle of the separation of powers, its judges have far less scope for intervention in the affairs of the government and the administration than is the case in England. In all this, French democracy shows the inheritance not just of the principles of 1789 but, even more perhaps, the traditions of the centralized French monarchy as revitalized by Napoleon (Dicey 1962, 57–61; see also Gallie 1983).

In both the English and French cases, Dicey therefore concludes, we see the limitations of being guided by the formal principles of government and legislation in a society. Here, as in all cases, we must understand the spirit of the laws; we must go behind the formal principles to uncover the historical traditions that inform their interpretation and practice. Once more, Dicey is deliberately complicating the concept of opinion and its relation to legislation. Social circumstances may produce a pressure for change, but it is the governing ideas of the time that will determine how that change is understood and forwarded. Classes may wish to promote their interests, but what are their interests? There will be rival views about this, theories in contention; how classes proceed to press those interests will be partly determined by the outcome of this conflict of ideologies. But that too, as we have seen, will not be purely a matter of rational debate and intellectual conviction. The opinion that comes to prevail will be in part selected, as in a Darwinian test of fitness, by its compatibility with the traditions that have been formed by each society's history.

The simpleminded concept of ideas in command has to be rejected as much as the equally simpleminded concepts of politics or economics in command, as well as the depiction, as in the functionalist position, of an all-encompassing society that both stimulates and responds in automatic fashion. What Dicey is working toward, though he does not formulate this with any precision, is a model of social action not dissimilar to that of Weber's, quoted as the epigraph to this chapter. Ideas do not operate in a vacuum but in a complex interaction with the needs of the time. This, however, need not lead to a vacuous circularity of argument. As Weber suggests, ideas may often—like great men in history—act as switchmen, directing societies along particular tracks and guiding the material force of interests. Such a conception would be more than sufficient to establish the importance of ideas in social action. Let us then consider the specific case that is the focus of Dicey's inquiry: the role of opinion in shaping the evolution of public policy in nineteenth-century England.

Dicey, once again, seems to want to make things as awkward as possible for himself. Why, he asks, did the period of Old Toryism and legislative quiescence (c. 1800–1830) give way to the period of Benthamism and vigorous reform (c. 1825–1870)? "The answer may be given in one sentence: The English people had at last come to perceive the intolerable incongruity between a rapidly changing social condition and the practical unchangeableness of the law" (1962, 111). To this pat answer, which at first looks remarkably like a line from one of his critics, Dicey adds other hostages. He glosses the main reason for the growth of Benthamite liberalism in a number of phrases, all carrying more or less the same import: "the increasing unsuitability of unchanging institutions for a quickly developing society . . . the obvious want of harmony between the institutions and the needs of the time . . . the discord between a changing social condition and unchanging laws" (ibid., 112, 119, 123). In describing the new attitude toward parliamentary reform, he says: "In 1825, and still more in 1830, the incongruities of an unreformed Parliament had become in the eyes of many Englishmen an intolerable abuse" (117). Sensible men, Dicey sums up, had by the late 1820s come to perceive "that the state of England would soon necessitate a choice between reform and revolution" (121).

In using phrases like "intolerable abuse" and "intolerable incongruity," Dicey seems to be speaking the language of his critics. The main burden of this criticism is that Dicey overestimates the influence of thought on policy and plays down the extent to which legislation was a pragmatic response to intolerable conditions, which were plain for all to see. Dicey, says MacDonagh, is guilty "of intellectualizing the problem altogether." He attributes far too much to "political doctrine" and "trends in articulate opinion" (1958a, 56). Instead, MacDonagh offers us a model of government growth whose principal feature is an objective, more or less self-determining, process of response to what MacDonagh calls "a peculiar concatenation of circumstances in the nineteenth century" (ibid., 57).

These circumstances—actually remarkably similar to those mentioned in the same context by Dicey himself (1962 112–23)—are basically those of the Industrial Revolution and the dramatic and sometimes catastrophic changes it precipitated. Their occurrence, says MacDonagh, led to the widespread exposure of "social evils"; this led to calls for urgent remedies, and "the ensuing demand for remedy at any price set an irresistible engine of change in motion." The evils became intolerable, and "throughout and even before the Victorian years, 'intolerability' was the master card. No wall of either doctrine or interest could permanently withstand that single trumpet cry." It was clear, too, to contemporaries what form the remedies must primarily take: there must be prohibitory enactments. "Men's instinctive reaction was to legislate the evil out of existence" (1958a, 58).

In the process of legislative enactment and enforcement that followed, MacDonagh picks out several features that provided the essential dynamic of change. All are characterized by the qualities of inevitability and necessity that for him are the hallmark of the process throughout. The ineffectiveness of the first acts of legislation led to the appointment of executive officers to oversee and administer the law. This step was of "immense, if unforeseen, consequence. Indeed we might almost say that it was this which brought the process into life." The officers' investigations and revelations of failures quickly led to demands for legislative amendments. "These demands were made moreover with a new and ultimately irresistible authority. For . . . incontrovertible first-hand evidence of the extent and nature of the evils was accumulating in the officers' occasional and regular reports." The officers' "imperative demand for further legislation" was accompanied by "an equivalent demand for centralization. This, too, arose as a matter of obvious necessity from the practical day-to-day difficulties of their office."

Fresh legislation and a superintending central body being sooner or later secured, it was "gradually . . . borne in upon the executive officers" that they needed to develop a more systematic approach to administration. Single pieces of legislation and a mere increase in the number of officers was not enough. "Instead, they began to see improvement as a slow, uncertain process of closing loopholes and tightening the screw ring by ring, in the light of continuing experience and experiment." A dynamic concept of administration replaced a static one; there was "the gradual crystallization of an *expertise* or notion of the principles of government of the field in question." All this led finally to the triumph of "a new and more or less conscious Fabianism" in nineteenth-century British government that was "peculiarly modern." For MacDonagh, it is clear, the modern state is defined not so much in terms of its democratic responsiveness and responsibility as by its insulation from the anarchic public and its guidance by an elite of expert officials. This was substantially achieved in Britain, he claims, by the second half of the nineteenth century.

> The executive officers and their superiors now demanded, and to some extent secured, legislation which awarded them discretions not merely in the application of its clauses but even in imposing penalties and framing regulations. They began to undertake more systematic and truly statistical and experimental investigations. They strove to keep in touch with the inventions, new techniques and foreign practices relevant to their field. Later, they even called directly upon medicine and engineering, and the infant professions of research chemistry and biology, to find answers to intractable difficulties in composing and enforcing particular preventative measures; and once, say, ventilation mechanisms or azimuth compasses for ocean-going vessels, or safety devices for mines or railways, or the presence of arsenic in certain foods or drinks, had been clearly proved, the corresponding regulations passed effortlessly into law, and, unperceived, the ripples of government circled ever wider. In the course of these latest pressures towards autonomy and delegated legislation, towards fluidity and experimentation in regulations, towards a division and a specialization of administrative labour, and towards a dynamic role for government within society, a new sort of state was being born. (1958a, 60–61)[7]

Here is administrative dynamism indeed. And it is all of a piece with this account of autonomous government growth that MacDonagh can suggest that "in some circumstances . . . administration may be, so to speak, creative and self-generating. It may be independent, not in the sense of congealing into forms, but in the sense of growing and breaking out in character and scope. It may gather its own momentum; it may turn unexpectedly in new directions; it may reach beyond the control or comprehension of anyone in particular" (ibid., 53; see also MacDonagh 1958b). Such a Frankenstein's monster does not necessarily endear itself to all of Dicey's critics who have followed in MacDonagh's footsteps. But they too are driven to stress, not opinion and ideas, but the objective force of overwhelming circumstances in forcing reform and growth upon the nineteenth-century government machine.

So in a wide-ranging review of social legislation in Victorian England, Roberts repeatedly draws our attention to the urgency and exigency of circumstances as the principal cause of government intervention. "Conditions in the manufacturing towns demanded sanitary improvements as insistently as they did educational reforms." Most members of the governing class agreed that "these evils were intolerable and unnecessary." Health and education are major examples, but "the same response to pressing social evils led to other minor reforms—of prisons, insane asylums, private charities, railways, and merchant marine service—all of which added more central agencies to the growing administrative state." Reforms were proposed and carried through by statesmen of various persuasions "to meet the urgent problems of an industrial age, not to fulfil the ideals of a philosopher" (i.e., Bentham). The inadequacy of local government in the face of the new problems had "permitted abuses to arise which the conscience of the Victorian governing class could not endure. The only means to remedy these abuses was to empower the central government to intervene. In this ad hoc manner, and not from reading [Bentham's] *Constitutional Code*, did Parliament lay the basis for the early Victorian administrative state." Roberts writes elsewhere, "Had Bentham never written his epochal works, Victorian reformers would probably have contrived their poor laws, factory acts, and educational schemes, all fitted out with central inspectors. Such legislation was in fact a necessity, the necessity of the factory, the jerry-built town, the discontented and ignorant proletariat." The conditions of the towns led to "insistent" demands for reforms, "which brought into existence, as a sheer necessity, the Victorian administrative state." Roberts concludes: "The Victorian administrative state was a practical contrivance shaped by men of various persuasions, all of whom were disturbed at the existence of ignorance, disease, and misery in their changing society" (Roberts 1959, 203, 204, 206, 209–10; see also Roberts 1960, 27–36, 315–26).

Central to the accounts of both MacDonagh and Roberts is a denial of the importance of Benthamism as a formative influence on Victorian social legislation (MacDonagh 1958a, 65; Roberts 1960, 318). How is it then that Roberts, in reviewing the "series of momentous social reforms" that he argues had "brought about an administrative revolution" by the 1850s, can find the substance of Bentham's *Constitutional Code* in that development? What does it mean to say, as he does, that "Bentham's blueprint for an administrative state had been translated, albeit very roughly, into the reality of the mid-Victorian administrative state"? (Roberts 1959, 196; see also Roach 1978, 65). Dicey, as we have seen, was more than willing to concede the importance of social conditions and pressing circumstances in the making of Victorian social policy. But this did nothing to shake his conviction that Benthamism, as "a definite body of doctrine," had a "direct and immense influence upon the development of English law" (1962, 66–67; see also Cosgrave 1980, 182–83). What was the connection between Benthamism and the undeniable reality and urgency of "the social problem"?

Dicey's answer is partly historical, partly philosophical. He reminds us of the great fright the French Revolution gave to the English property-owning classes. Reform might give rise to great expectations, and those expectations—as Tocqueville was later to point out in the case of the French Revolution itself—could lead to revolution. Reform was therefore fraught with peril. It was by no means the automatic response of all men of good will in the face of social problems, however pressing. The landed upper class, as the struggle over the Corn Laws showed, was perfectly capable of conducting a long-drawn-out defensive campaign against formidable pressure from other classes. The fear of revolution persisted, moreover, well into the nineteenth century. European revolutions at regular intervals—1830 and 1848—not to mention "physical force" Chartism, were there to remind the upper classes that the legacy of the French Revolution was still very much alive.

There was therefore nothing natural about reform. Reformers, if they were to have any hope of success, had to couch their appeals in a manner calculated to reassure the dominant social interests. Nothing that smacked of Rousseauism or Jacobinism would do. This is where Bentham and Benthamism came in. "The teacher who could lead England in the path of reform," says Dicey, "must not talk of the social contract, of natural rights, of rights of man, or of liberty, fraternity, and equality." Bentham, with his well-known attacks on "revolutionary dogmatism" and his contempt for "vague generalities, sentiments, and rhetoric," precisely satisfied this requirement. "Even the prosaic side of Bentham's doctrines, which checks the sympathy of modern readers, reassured sensible Englishmen who in 1830 had come to long for reform but dreaded revolution" (1962, 171–72). Reformers felt, Dicey argues, that the need of the day was "thoroughgoing but temperate reform, thought out by teachers who, without being revolutionists, had studied the faults of English law, and elaborated schemes for its practical amendment. Such teachers were found in Bentham and his disciples; they provided for reformers an acceptable programme" (125).

An "acceptable programme" is not, however, just a historical requirement of the day; it is in a more general sense a philosophical requirement of all effective social action. Dicey has no need to deny that Benthamism in many ways fitted the outlook and aspirations of the English middle classes (173–75). But classes, as Marxists have often been forced to concede, do not act spontaneously. The commercial class of sixteenth- and seventeenth-century Europe might have been well situated economically and socially to make a bid for power; but as Weber shows in *The Protestant Ethic and the Spirit of Capitalism*, without the guidance of Protestant ideas it might not have seen its destiny, and its bid might have miscarried. Dicey, in an interesting footnote, says that, in fact, in seventeenth-century England, Puritanism "missed its mark." It did so because of its dogmatic "dread of arbitrary power" and its consequent inability to construct a language of practical constitutional reform. Benthamism, by contrast, provided the nineteenth-century English middle class with just that flexibility of doctrine and practicality of standard that enabled it to carry out its "pacific revolution" (170 n.2). Thus the fact that Benthamism harmonized with the needs of practical middle-class men in no way detracts from its importance. "That in 1830 the demand for reform should arise was a necessity, but a demand does not of itself create the means for its satisfaction. Had not Benthamism provided reformers with an ideal and a programme, it is more than possible that the effort to amend the law of England might, like many other endeavours to promote the progress of mankind, have missed its mark" (176).

Dicey's point would be obvious were it not for the popularity of the mechanical functionalism of MacDonagh, Roberts, Kitson Clark, and their disciples. One can argue about the precise role of individual Benthamites, such as Chadwick, Southwood Smith, and Kay, in influencing the great legislative enactments of the early Victorian period: the Factory Act of 1833, the New Poor Law of 1834, the Prison Act of 1835, the setting up of the Educational Committee of the Privy Council and its measures of 1839, and the Public Health Act of 1848. Even in these particular cases, the evidence does not all go against Dicey. In a sparkling essay, Finer, taking as his premise that "the profound influence of Bentham's arguments and models on the legislation of the nineteenth century is too well attested" to need further elaboration (1972, 11), proceeds to show in detail exactly how the Benthamites influenced members of Parliament, judges, civil servants, and what Dicey calls legislative public opinion. He concludes that, while it would clearly be absurd to claim that Benthamism was the sole influence on administrative and social reform in the first half of the nineteenth century, "in respect to India and the colonies, to penology and to health, education, and the protection of paupers and factory workers, to financial administration, fiscal policy and the machinery of central and local administration . . . Bentham's thoughts and attitudes played a predominant role" (ibid., 32).

Similarly, Parris and Hart, reanalyzing the legislation considered by MacDonagh and Roberts, try to show that Benthamism, as a body of doctrine and in the persons of particular Benthamites, was a critical influence in several of the most important social and administrative innovations of nineteenth-century government (Parris 1960; Hart 1965). On the key issue of central inspection, for example, and the appointment of central officers to supervise and enforce legislation, they rebut

Roberts's view that by the 1830s "the idea of central inspection was a commonplace" and no more than a continuation of earlier practice (Roberts 1959, 199), together with MacDonagh's contention that it represented essentially a pragmatic, learned response from the experience of previous legislative failures (MacDonagh 1958a, 58–59).

In the first place, the earlier examples cited by Roberts reveal nothing of the central control over local government that was the really controversial aspect of the 1830s legislation, beginning with the 1833 Factory Act (Hart 1965, 41–42; Parris 1960, 31). And as for learning by experience, there seems a distinct quantum jump in this ability before and after the early 1830s. As Parris says, MacDonagh's model "requires that officers should be appointed because men learnt from experience. Before 1825, men acquired the experience but did not learn from it; after 1835, they gave themselves no time to learn from experience, but appointed enforcement officers at once." Why?

> After about 1835 a demonstration effect came into existence between different branches of the central administration. The example of the first enforcement officers had set the pattern, and it became normal to appoint them simultaneously with the first incursion into a new field. . . . When other services came to be set up, they were modelled on such well-publicized exemplars as the Metropolitan Police, factory inspection, and the New Poor Law, and thus came under the direct influence of Benthamism. (Parris 1960, 32–33; see also Hart 1965, 44–45)

Cromwell adds a further dimension to the argument about the Benthamite contribution. Dicey's critics, she alleges, confuse government with social reform and are mainly concerned with refuting the alleged influence of Benthamism on the latter. They thereby ignore the possibility that Bentham's influence may have been as strong, or even stronger, in the former field. Bentham, she reminds us, was himself concerned with every aspect of government, and "one example of his influence which seems to have been ignored by all participants in the dispute was his impact on those responsible for the simplification of the mechanics of law making during the nineteenth century. New social problems involved new executive machinery, but the old organs were forced to change their ways by new pressures" (Cromwell 1965–1966, 253).

There is a further area where she hints that Benthamism may have been decisive. MacDonagh and Roberts make much of the fact that executive discretions and delegated legislation grew, as they claim, unperceived and largely contrary to the dominant laissez-faire assumptions of the period. This, Cromwell suggests, may be the wrong emphasis. "No one has yet considered the elimination of that 'anti-government feeling' so prevalent throughout the eighteenth century. This feeling was not *for* some sort of political liberty, but was *against* any sort of government interference. In many ways, it took the shape of localism and was the heritage of several centuries of dependence by the central government on justices of the peace" (1965–1966, 253). Although Cromwell herself does not offer an answer, may it not be plausibly argued that it was what Dicey called the "revolutionary principle of utility" (1962, 305), in all its forceful simplicity, that was at least partly responsible for overcoming the traditional hostility to central government? In which case, the alleged disparity between Benthamism and the growth of centralized administration may turn out to be only apparent.

We shall turn to this matter in a moment. What first needs to be said is that, whatever the force of the arguments concerning Benthamite influence in specific instances, the general importance of some such doctrines as those of Bentham cannot be doubted. On this point, Parris and Hart rightly brush aside the trivial objections of MacDonagh and Roberts that legislation was often carried through by men who had probably never read Bentham and may not even have heard of him (Roberts 1959, 205–07; MacDonagh 1958a, 65). MacDonagh, Parris says, "makes no allowance for the unconscious influence of ideas on men's minds. . . . If Dr. MacDonagh seriously contends that a man's ideas can affect the course of events only through those who have heard his name (and presumably have some knowledge of his beliefs), few indeed would be the thinkers who could be shown to have had any practical influence at all. The influence of Freud and Keynes, for example, would be factors barely worth the notice of the contemporary historian" (Parris 1960, 28–29; see also Hart 1965, 45). As Ryan observes in a related context, "the denial of a direct prescriptive influence is too easy an intellectual victory; the kind of influence which is shown not to exist is not the kind of influence anyone expected to find in the first place" (1972, 34).

The true influence of Benthamism has to be seen at another level altogether. Human beings in society act for reasons. This banality is not as empty as it first sounds. It warns us, at least, against the mechanistic psychology that assumes that a stimulus automatically elicits a response; that a problem evokes a remedy. The urgency of a question or problem does not by itself offer an understanding of it, still less a remedy; otherwise, perhaps the world would not have lived in the midst or the shadow of world war for most of this century.

In giving reasons for their actions, moreover, people draw, however implicitly or unconsciously, on some first-order theory, some conceptualization of the world within which they and their actions are situated.[8]

In nineteenth-century England, utilitarianism offered such a conceptualization. In the face of an increasing array of social problems, it provided in the form of a clear legislative yardstick—the principle of utility—a standard and a point of reference for both judging current conditions and attempting to remedy them. For, as Hart has well said, mere "intolerability" is not enough; or rather, one has to recognize intolerability before one proceeds to try to do something about it. "For actual conditions alone constitute no problem; before there can be a problem, there must be an attitude to actual conditions. People must be dissatisfied with actual conditions. And before one knows what one wants to do about the conditions, one must have some principle, or standard, or good by reference to which the conditions are judged intolerable. The Benthamites provided just such principles, standards, goods" (1965, 46; see also Parris 1960, 35–36).

Hart further points out that the MacDonagh-Roberts assumption of a consensus on the nature of social problems in Victorian England is seriously mistaken. There were profound disagreements about levels of tolerability and intolerability, often based on disagreements as to the facts of the case in question (especially in such fields as public health). "For example the hours worked in factories seemed in the eighteen thirties intolerable to many workers, whereas to Nassau Senior the long hours were practicable because of the extraordinary lightness of labour." Similarly with child labor in the mines: there were people—not all mineowners—who considered it perfectly acceptable that children should work there (Hart 1965, 49). As a result of these and many other disagreements, one cannot assume—as MacDonagh, Roberts, and Clark tend to[9]—that there was a general wave of humanitarian feeling in Victorian England that was readily responsive to the exposure of social evils. It was precisely because of the serious lack of humanitarianism in several quarters—among factory owners and the managers of mines, for instance, and even in parts of the Church of England—that the appointment of inspectors was deemed to be crucial by Benthamite reformers. Hart concludes that "in so far as social reform in nineteenth-century England is concerned, the evidence seems to suggest that most social evils were not removed without fierce battles against absurd arguments, vested interests, obscurantism and timidity, and that their removal required considerable effort and determination on the part of men . . . who realized that it was worth while making a conscious effort to control events. And in this enterprise many of them were assisted, whether they knew it or not, by Benthamism" (Hart 1965, 61; see also Henriques 1979, 262).

What this points to is the immense educative function performed by

Benthamism in nineteenth-century England. It does not matter that there were disputes about the precise meaning and applicability of the principle of utility, not even that utility sometimes failed to provide any clear answer in certain cases (education perhaps being the most notorious, as somewhat unfairly satirized by Dickens in *Hard Times;* see Roach 1978, 60–65). Rather, what was important was that, at a time when social change was especially rapid, utilitarianism provided a directly practical orientation to problems, a way of approaching them that promised some sort of tangible and manageable outcome. As Ryan says, "What was involved in accepting a utilitarian view of social and political life was the acceptance of a theoretical framework within which certain ways of describing and explaining social and political matters got to the heart of them; it did not involve the possession of answers to problems of social and political practice so much as the assurance that certain ways of posing these problems was the right way of posing them" (1972, 37).

This assurance has to be seen in the context of a society in which traditional social philosophies were bankrupt and many newer philosophies were too radical for acceptance. Burkean conservatism was as inappropriate as Chartism was alarming. But however anxious men of all parties might have been to ease the pangs of industrial society, they needed a philosophy and a program to undertake the task. Men needed, as Roberts himself admits, "to rethink the problem of government"; and, as he also admits, it was the Utilitarians alone who came forward "to offer a plan of reform both comprehensive and practical" (Roberts 1960, 28–29; see also Taylor 1972, 37; Roach 1978, 63; Perkin 1969, 286–88). One might well feel that this concession from one of Dicey's major critics is one of the best testimonies to the truth of Dicey's claim concerning the relation between Benthamite thought and legislation in the first half of the nineteenth century.

Dicey is right to see a connection between thought and public policy in nineteenth-century England. He is wrong though—or at least misleading—in his characterization of the nature of that thought and, hence, of the particular ways in which it influenced policy. As a result, he was faced with apparently contradictory developments, which he found difficult to explain.

The main difficulty comes in Dicey's identification of utilitarianism with individualism or laissez-faire. He is perfectly aware that he is not being strictly accurate in this. He goes even further. The "dogma of *laissez faire* is not from a logical point of view an essential article of the utilitarian creed." It can be granted that "the proper end of scientific legislation is to promote the greatest happiness of the greatest number," but this can as logically lead to a system of benevolent despotism as one of laissez-faire individualism (1962, 146). Nevertheless, says Dicey, "though *laissez faire* is not an essential part of utilitarianism, it was practically the most vital part of Bentham's legislative doctrine, and in England gave to the movement for the reform of the law, both its power and its character." And repeatedly in his study, Dicey makes it plain that for him individualism expresses the central contribution of Benthamism to legislative opinion. "Utilitarian individualism," he says, "which for many years under the name of liberalism, determined the trend of English legislation, was nothing but Benthamism modified by the experience, the prudence, or the timidity of practical politicians. . . . Legislative utilitarianism is nothing else but systematized individualism" (125, 147, 175).

Dicey, it is clear, is concerned not with utilitarianism as a coherent social theory but as a general philosophy, which could give reformers the necessary tools to do the job. The reformers were either practical middle-class men or they needed to appeal to such men. Among these men, as among most other groups of that time, "practical individualism was the predominant sentiment" (181). Hence, what they extracted from Benthamism was shaped by this outlook. Theirs was a "Benthamism of common sense which, under the name of liberalism, was to be for thirty or forty years a main factor in the development of English law. This liberalism was the utilitarianism not of the study but of the House of Commons or of the Stock Exchange" (170).

Utilitarianism being thus identified with individualism, Dicey was forced to argue that the decline of individualism in the last third of the nineteenth century also entailed the waning of Benthamite influence. In fact, the evidence he provides has little to do with the decline of Benthamism itself. The growth of what he calls collectivism, or loosely, socialism (64 n.), is attributed not so much to the victory of distinctively collectivist doctrines over Benthamite ones as to declining confidence in individualism. Looking back from the end of the nineteenth century, Dicey was apt to be fatalistic about this. For it is individualism, not collectivism, that is the exception to the normal rule of public policy. "The majority of mankind must almost of necessity look with undue favour upon governmental intervention." This natural bias can be counteracted only by the existence—as in England between 1830 and 1860—of "a presumption or prejudice in favour of individual liberty—that is, of *laissez faire*. The mere decline, therefore, of faith in self-help—and that such a decline has taken place is certain—is of itself sufficient to account for the growth of legislation tending towards socialism" (258).

The primary shift for Dicey is therefore the decline of individualism. The decline of Benthamism as a force is consequent upon this. But what greatly complicates this picture is Dicey's simultaneous recognition that Benthamism itself contributed to the downfall of individualism and the rise of collectivism. This is acknowledged at various points in the text but most extensively in the short chapter entitled "The Debt of Collectivism to Benthamism." Here he says, "From Benthamism, the socialists of today have inherited a legislative dogma, a legislative instrument, and a legislative tendency." The legislative dogma is "the celebrated principle of utility." The principle that legislation should promote the greatest happiness of the greatest number was bound, sooner or later, to lead to socialism. Since "in any state the poor and the needy always constitute the majority of the nation, the favourite dogma of Benthamism pointed to the conclusion . . . that the whole aim of legislation should be to promote the happiness, not of the nobility or the gentry, or even of shopkeepers, but of artisans and other wage-earners." The legislative instrument was "the active use of parliamentary sovereignty." For, once the masses were enfranchised, the Benthamite concept of "the omnipotence of Parliament" was "an instrument well adapted for the establishment of democratic despotism." Finally, the legislative tendency bequeathed by Benthamism was "the constant extension and improvement of the mechanism of government." Reformers, though generally committed to individualism, found themselves thwarted at every turn by

> the opposition or inertness of classes biassed by some sinister interest. Hence sincere believers in *laissez faire* found that for the attainment of their ends the improvement and the strengthening of governmental machinery was an absolute necessity. In this work they were seconded by practical men who, though utterly indifferent to any political theory, saw the need of administrative changes suited to meet the multifarious and complex requirements of a modern and industrial community. (303, 305–06)

Dicey himself lists the measures that, though impeccably utilitarian, show up the despotic or authoritative element in utilitarianism: "The formation of an effective police force for London (1892)—the rigorous and scientific administration of the Poor Law (1834) under the control of the central government—the creation of authorities for the enforcement of laws to promote the public health and the increasing application of a new system of centralisation, the invention of Bentham himself" (306–07).

Men of all parties, says Dicey—Whigs and Tories no less than Liberals—were so imbued with the individualism of the age that they could not imagine that these utilitarian reforms might undermine laissez-faire. Liberals were especially vulnerable by virtue of "the unlimited scorn entertained by every Benthamite for the social contract and for natural rights." As a result, unlike the case in France and the United States with their declarations of rights, liberals had no defense against the increasing encroachments of the state. "The Liberals of 1830 were themselves zealots for individual freedom, but they entertained beliefs which, though the men who held them knew it not, might well, under altered social conditions, foster the despotic authority of a democratic State" (309–10). The conclusion of this short but remarkable chapter is worth quoting at length:

> The effect actually produced by a system of thought does not depend on the intention of its originators; ideas which have once obtained general acceptance work out their own logical result under the control mainly of events. Somewhere between 1868 and 1900 three changes took place which brought into prominence the authoritative side of Benthamite liberalism. Faith in *laissez faire* suffered an eclipse; hence the principle of utility became an argument in favour, not of individual freedom, but the absolutism of the State. Parliament under the progress of democracy became the representative, not of the middle classes, but of the whole body of householders; parliamentary sovereignty, therefore, came to mean, in the last resort, the unrestricted power of the wage-earners. English administrative mechanism was reformed and strengthened. The machinery was thus provided for the practical extension of the activity of the State . . . Benthamites, it was then seen, had forged the arms most needed by socialists. (310)

There are several obvious problems with this, notably Dicey's dating of the changes. Still, it is fair to say that had he integrated this view of Benthamism with his main identification of Benthamism and individualism, there may not have been much left for his latter-day critics to cavil at. But this Dicey signally failed to do.[10] So impressed was he with the force of individualist sentiment in the middle quarters of the century, and so convinced was he of the generally individualist bias of Benthamism, that he could not see apparently discrepant phenomena as also the product of Benthamism. Thus he was forced to explain away such apparently anomalous legislation as the Factory Acts, the public education measures, and the Public Health Acts as due to countercurrents of opinion. "Tory philanthropy" was one such, and another was the current of opinion affected by the anti-individualist writing of social critics such as Southey, Arnold, and Carlyle (215–36).

More damaging to his thesis, he had to admit that collectivist or socialist measures were passed in what he himself claimed as the very heyday of laissez-faire individualism. Thus, speaking of the factory legislation of 1848–1850, he says: "The factory movement was the battlefield of collectivism against individualism, and on that field Benthamite liberalism suffered its earliest and severest defeat. . . . The success of the Factory Acts gave authority, not only in the world of labour, but in many other spheres of life, to beliefs which, if not exactly socialistic, yet certainly tended towards socialism or collectivism." This, Dicey further admits, was "at the time when the repeal of the corn laws gave in the sphere of commerce what seemed to be a crowning victory to individualism" (237, 240). Later Dicey was to concede even more. In the list of centralizing measures quoted above, which he gives in the chapter called "The Debt of Collectivism to Benthamism," it is evident that collectivist victories appeared even earlier—as early as 1829 and 1834. This was the very decade that, according to Dicey, launched the period of the dominance of individualism in legislation.

Friends and foes alike have rushed to help Dicey out of his predicament, even if only to damn him even further. The main strategy, following Dicey's not always acknowledged lead, has been to reinterpret Benthamism as a system of thought containing strong elements of collectivism as well as individualism. Actually, in a study of Bentham's thought, which Dicey briefly refers to but appears not to have fully absorbed,[11] Halévy had already argued that Benthamism rested on "contradictory principles." In economic matters, and largely under the influence of the classical economists such as Smith and Ricardo, Benthamism assumed a natural or spontaneous identity of interests, which led to an advocacy of laissez-faire. In noneconomic areas, however, and more consistently with Bentham's own teaching, his theory accepted the insufficiency of laissez-faire attitudes. Following the utility principle, the state had a right and a duty to intervene whenever it might be necessary to bring into harmony interests that needed to be artificially identified; and these were likely to be areas such as education, health, and the relief of poverty.[12] In the development of utilitarianism, argues Halévy, the doctrine of the natural identity of interests tended to submerge that of the artificial identification of interests, so leading to the common view—as with Dicey—that utilitarianism really meant individualism.

> Thus was developed in England, twenty years after Bentham's death, a new and simplified form of the Utilitarian philosophy. Disciples of

> Adam Smith much more than of Bentham, the Utilitarians did not now include in their doctrine the principle of the artificial identification of interests, that is, the governmental or administrative idea; the idea of free-trade and of the spontaneous identification of interests summed up the social conceptions of these new doctrinaires, who were hostile to any kind of regulation and law. (Halévy 1972, 514)[13]

This, however, still left the vexing problem of the appearance of a considerable amount of collectivist legislation in the very period, from the 1830s to the 1860s, that both Dicey and Halévy regard as marking the triumph of laissez-faire individualism. One recourse was to go to the other extreme from Dicey and, while accepting the influence of Bentham on legislation, to deny that Bentham was an individualist at all. "In using Bentham as the archetype of English individualism," claims Brebner, Dicey "was conveying the exact opposite of the truth. Jeremy Bentham was the archetype of British collectivism" (1948, 61). As Halévy shows, the utility principle points clearly to state intervention and thus stands directly in contradiction to the laissez-faire teachings of Smith and the classical economists.

But, says Brebner, Halévy is wrong in thinking that utilitarianism was taken over by Smithian individualism and in supposing individualism to have triumphed in mid-nineteenth century England. Benthamite collectivism was active in practice throughout this period, when individualist assumptions were said by Dicey and Halévy to prevail. There is no need to invoke, as Dicey does, some countercurrent of humanitarianism to explain this extensive state intervention. For "in practically all of its many forms it was basically Benthamite—Benthamite in the sense of conforming closely to that forbidding, detailed blueprint for a collectivist state, the *Constitutional Code,* which was written between 1820 and 1832" (1948, 62). Whatever the different social pressures and class interests behind it, "there was an astonishingly consistent inclination to resort to the Benthamite formula for state intervention." Moreover, "intervention was always cumulative, building up like a rolling snowball after 1832, whether in factories, railways, shipping, banking, company finance, education, or religion" (ibid., 64–66; see also Clark 1967, 147–62; Hume, 1967).

Brebner's provocative essay of 1948 has rightly come to be seen as an overreaction, albeit a highly stimulating one, to the Diceyan view of Benthamism. In the process of reflection since, it seems to have been generally agreed that the antithesis between collectivism and individualism in nineteenth-century England is a false one.[14] This was as true for the theory of the time as for its practice. Halévy had already pointed out that, while the classical economists placed their primary emphasis on the spontaneous identity of interests in society, they recognized that there were matters in which government intervention might be necessary. Conversely, Bentham's emphasis on the artificial identification of interests looks to an organization of government and society in which interests to a good extent are spontaneously identified. It is thus that Benthamism came to develop an affinity with democracy. Given that, as Bentham held, each individual is the best judge of his interest, the more that people are involved in government, the less need there is to legislate against minority selfishness and exploitation, since the majority will be able to judge the interests of the greatest number. It also followed that the bulk of legislation should be concerned with the freeing of the individual from as many constraints as possible, insofar as this was compatible with securing the like freedom for every other individual (Halévy 1972, 480–81; see also Dicey 1962, 158–68).

But could the individual be the best judge of his own interest if he were illiterate and ignorant? Education provides a good example of how individualist assumptions could lead to the advocacy of collectivist intervention. Mill, whose utilitarianism was in any case progressively qualified as he grew older, took the view that the state must compel parents to educate their children—if necessary, at public expense—because the cost to society of failing to do so, quite apart from other considerations, would greatly outweigh the cost of education. Parents who, being given necessary assistance, fail to educate their children "commit a breach of duty . . . towards the members of the community generally, who are all liable to suffer seriously from the consequences of ignorance and want of education in their fellow citizens." This argument from social costs was widely used, by Benthamites and non-Benthamites alike, to justify state intervention not just in education but in public health, housing, and the conditions of workers (Parris 1969, 277–79). But education could also be justified on even more narrow utilitarian grounds: the need to enable individuals to judge their best interest and so to be less in need of legislative protection or public support. As Finer says,

> Any Benthamite was automatically an educationist, since his philosophy depended on the perfectibility of society through the free play of its members' *enlightened* self-interest. . . . Education was desirable because it turned pauper children into productive citizens and prevented them from becoming permanent inmates of the workhouses; because it prevented juvenile delinquency and mendicancy; because it increased a labourer's skill, productivity, and earning power; because it prevented the growth of criminal classes; and because it led the workman to realize

> that his true interests lay not in "communism" or Chartism, but in harmony with his employers. (1952, 150–51)

The principle of utility was therefore capable of very wide deployment. It could move in both individualist and collectivist directions. The consistency was provided by the overriding general criterion, namely that all action should tend to the greatest happiness of the greatest number. To those who generally advocated a laissez-faire economy, utility justified intervention where, say, there was a danger of a producers' monopoly being established and the interests of consumers harmed. Notoriously, too, Adam Smith had justified the protectionism of the Corn Laws in the name of national defense and survival in war. It was Smith also who ascribed to government the right and duty of "erecting and maintaining certain public works and certain public institutions, which it can never be for the interest of any individual, or small number of individuals to erect and maintain," but that could clearly be held to be of benefit to all. This view allowed potentially vast scope for state intervention, and some theorists have concluded that the public corporation and the nationalized industry can be justified in its terms. And from Nassau Senior, prominent Benthamite and well-known academic advocate of laissez-faire, came, nevertheless, this unequivocal statement of belief: "The only foundation of government is expediency, the general benefit of the community. It is the duty of government to do whatever is conducive to the welfare of the governed. The most fatal of all errors would be the general admission that a government has no right to interfere for any purpose except the purpose of affording protection" (quoted in Taylor 1972, 21–22).[15]

Conversely, interventionist Benthamites such as Chadwick saw in self-interest the "spring of individual vigour and efficiency," and sought to promote it wherever possible—admittedly, by resolutely collectivist measures, if need be. And Mill, at that late stage in his life when he confessed to being converted to socialism, could still declare that "letting alone should be the general practice" and that "the burthen of making out a strong case" should rest "not on those who resist, but on those who recommend, government interference" (quoted in Perkin 1981, 63). The reaction against Dicey's interpretation of Benthamism has been so strong that it is in danger of making us forget the strong vein of individualism that ran throughout Bentham's philosophy. As Taylor says:

> No Utilitarian believed in government for its own sake. What Bentham and his followers sought was not more but better government. In pursuing the greatest happiness of the greatest number they were seeking in

> the last resort not the happiness of a collectivity but the happiness of individuals; and if this end could be achieved without the intervention of the state, so much the better. For the Benthamites even the best government was a necessary evil. (Taylor 1972, 36; see also Evans 1978, 1–18)

It is this interplay of individualist and collectivist emphases that gives to mid-nineteenth century English legislation that contradictory quality that confused Dicey and puzzled so many of his successors. It is this that makes the "mid-century dance," as Brebner puts it, "like a minuet": "Parliamentary reform in 1832, the first effective Factory Act in 1833; Peel's Budget in 1841, the Mines Act in 1842; repeal of the Corn Laws in 1846, the Ten Hours Act in 1847." Philosophical radicals of various hues were to be found in both camps, sometimes unexpectedly. "McCulloch praised the Factory Act of 1833; Macaulay and Lord John Russell successfully defended the Ten Hours bill" (Brebner 1948, 64).

One does not wish to impose too rigid a straitjacket on a complex historical experience. But it is possible to see these fluctuations as the practical outcomes of the application of Benthamite principles in differing circumstances. To the same Benthamites, the utility principle might now counsel intervention, as with the Factory Acts, and now laissez-faire, as with the repeal of the Corn Laws. With the New Poor Law of 1834, we have an interesting mixed case: a resolute act of state intervention, with central control and central inspection, aimed explicitly at increasing individual self-reliance. But to call this mixed is to speak loosely. The New Poor Law had a unity of purpose that is entirely characteristic of Benthamite thinking. State action to increase individual freedom would appear to be the most common Benthamite formula. It is no accident that the central figures behind the New Poor Law were two of the most prominent Benthamites, Edwin Chadwick and Nassau Senior. The former is generally and rightly taken to be an interventionist, the latter an individualist. But these were two sides of the same coin. In their joint influence we might say that the New Poor Law was at once the most characteristic product of the time and the most representative of Benthamite thought.[16]

The standard, in any case, was always the same: the greatest happiness principle. (As always with Bentham, it was pragmatically applied.) Benthamism, as many have noted, was not a rigid body of doctrine held by a narrowly defined sect. It embraced a spectrum of practical reformers, from willing interventionists, such as Chadwick and Kay, to passionate believers in laissez-faire, such as Joseph Hume and McCulloch—and this leaves out philosophical doubters like John Stuart Mill (Dicey 1962,

169–70; see also Mack 1955, 76–78). This catholicity of appeal should not, however, lead us to think that things would have happened much as they did in the absence of Benthamism. It is easy looking back over the record of Victorian social legislation to imagine that policies were commonsense responses to obvious needs and pressures. This would be a mistake. There are in all historical situations alternatives and options (Perkin 1969, 218–70). Material interests and the force of circumstances certainly, as Dicey readily admits, play their part in the choice of options. But he is also quite right to insist, as does John Maynard Keynes in a celebrated passage, that in the end it is opinion that rules mankind (Keynes 1973, 383; see also Keynes 1972, 277).

English historians and social theorists, following the national bent toward a bluff, no-nonsense pragmatism, have generally tended to be skeptical of the role of ideas in history. Here the influence of the Namierite school of historians has been especially significant (see, e.g., Namier 1955). In contrast to this, there have been in recent years several powerful restatements of the view that substantially endorses Wells's magisterial pronouncement that "all human history is fundamentally a history of ideas" (Wells 1920, 1:508). Some historians and social philosophers have insisted that not only are ideas formative aspects of action but that human actions may be literally inconceivable without the surrounding context of ideas (Skinner 1969, esp. 42–43; MacIntyre 1962; Freeden 1978, 245; Greenleaf 1983, 2:3–15).

Dicey, as we have seen, was aware of the care with which this position has to be understood. But his conviction, nevertheless, that ideas mattered greatly was reinforced by what he saw happening in his own lifetime. His apprehensions of the trend in social policy at the end of the nineteenth century were provoked by what he discerned as a sea change in educated opinion among the late Victorian public (Roach 1973; Cosgrove 1980, 195–228; Sugarman 1983). Opinion, Dicey was firmly convinced, was becoming collectivist, which was tantamount to socialist. The rise of the historical method, the popularity of nationalist and imperialist conceptions, as well as the spread of socialist ideas themselves, were all pushing England in a collectivist direction, as evidenced most clearly in the new liberalism of Lloyd George and Winston Churchill (Dicey 1962, xxiii–xciv, 399–465).

But was Dicey right to call this opinion and these policies *collectivist?* And was this prewar collectivism the birth pangs of welfarism, the source of the British welfare state of the post-1945 period? More important, has English social policy ever moved systematically toward the construction of a true welfare society? It is impossible here to give more than a brief consideration to these enormously complex issues. But in concluding this discussion of Dicey, some attention needs to be paid to them, for they reveal once more the vital role of ideological traditions in the social and political life of a nation. Particularly, they show the persisting strength of English individualism and raise serious questions as to the reality at any time of the British welfare state.

It is clear from our previous discussion that, for all their objections to Dicey's account of individualism in nineteenth-century social policy, most of his critics are very happy with his characterization of collectivism. Their revisionism consists of casting collectivism back into the earlier part of the century: from the post-1870 period, which for Dicey marked the rise of collectivism, back to the 1830s, which for Dicey inaugurated the period of Benthamite individualism. This is an obvious feature of those accounts most hostile to Dicey. Roberts, for instance, claims that the outlines of the British welfare state were already clearly discernible by the mid-century.

> Scarcely a single Englishman in 1833 either foresaw or desired that profound growth in the role of the central government which marked the beginning of the welfare state, and few of them, even among the Utilitarians, realized that their central government had become more paternalistic towards its subjects than any country in Europe. In 1833 the central bureaucracies of few governments in Europe did so little for its citizens as did England's. . . . Yet in 1854 the central bureaucracy of few countries in Europe did more for the well-being of its subjects than did England's and none of the governments of Europe intervened so decisively to regulate the hours of labor in factories, systematize poor relief, and promote the public health. . . . England, the historic home of Anglo-Saxon local government and the economic doctrines of Adam Smith had begun to construct a welfare state. (Roberts 1960, 315–16; see also MacDonagh 1958a, 61; Clark, 1967, 130, 162–63)

Those friendlier to Dicey on the score of Benthamite influence are nevertheless agreed, partly through their different understanding of Benthamism, that collectivism started much earlier than Dicey realized. "Dicey's erroneous beliefs about Benthamism," says Parris, "have helped to perpetuate a myth about nineteenth-century government—the myth that between 1830 and 1870, or thereabouts, central administration in Great Britain was stationary, if not actually diminishing." Instead, Parris proposes an interpretation of nineteenth-century history in which "government growth is recognized as a leading trend from 1830 onwards." *Pace* Dicey, "the nineteenth century falls into two periods only, with the dividing line about 1830" (Parris 1969, 17, 266; see also Brebner 1948, 70).

Equally striking as this consensus on periodization is that which sees a basic continuity between utilitarianism and collectivism, shown especially in the essential similarity of Benthamism and Fabianism. "What were the Fabians," asks Brebner rhetorically, "but latter-day Benthamites?" (1948, 66). Perkin calls the Fabians "the intellectual grandchildren of the Benthamites" (1969, 262). And Parris dismisses the idea that—as Dicey held—a separate philosophy of collectivism emerged after 1870. "Utilitarianism was at work throughout—'that current of thought which arises in Bentham at the beginning of the century and flows into Fabianism at its end' " (Parris 1969, 282, quoting R. A. Lewis; see also Mack 1955, 88).

What is centrally involved in linking utilitarianism, collectivism, and Fabianism in a unified tradition is the idea that the kind of social policy and centralized administration found in Victorian England was profoundly hostile to individualism and pointed decisively in the direction of the modern welfare state. This, as we have seen, is explicitly stated by Roberts. MacDonagh, too, glosses Sir William Harcourt's well-known remark, "we are all socialists now," as a clear admission of "the catastrophic and very general collapse of individualism in the last quarter of the nineteenth century." What it meant was that the traditional ruling classes were confronted "with the brute *facts* that collectivism was already partially in being and that their society was doomed to move ever further in that direction" (MacDonagh 1958a, 62–63). In this development, Chadwick is often singled out as the most representative figure, not to say its principal agent. His philosophy and practice, however thwarted by vested interests and class prejudices, clearly reveal, says Parris, a commitment to communal welfare. For Roach, Chadwick "charted a direction which was never completely lost and which has determined many of the objectives of social policy in this country during the last century and a half." Under Chadwick's influence, and whatever its imperfections, "the New Poor Law did reaffirm the principle that the state had an obligation to ensure some basic standard of livelihood for its citizens. From that concern developed most of our modern programme of public welfare" (Parris 1969, 282; cf. Roach 1978, 110, 120; Perkin 1969, 338).

It is no part of the argument of this chapter to deny this tradition of thought and practice. British welfare policy and the British welfare state are to a very great extent utilitarian or Fabian. What must be questioned, though, is the belief, clearly expressed by these writers, that such a welfare tradition has broken with the main tradition of English individualism. How far can we accept that utilitarian principles, even as reinterpreted in a full-blooded collectivist fashion, embody that commitment to communal welfare and communal growth that are intrinsic to true welfare philosphies?[17] More to the point, to what extent do English social policy and social administration over the past century and a half represent a fundamental assault on the individualist assumptions that have been the working ideology of English society for much of its history—for practically all of it, if historians such as Macfarlane are to be believed? (Macfarlane 1978).

A proper answer to these questions would take several books; let us here be brief and dogmatic. English social policy has never truly departed from English individualism. It has softened somewhat individualism's rugged edges. It has cushioned some of the more unfortunate members of society against its worst shocks. It has intervened in the interest of social peace. It has used social policy as an instrument of economic stability and growth and as support for the family and marriage. What it has not done is make that leap of consciousness, still less of practice, to the point where individual and social growth are seen as twin aspects of one process. It has generated no sense of a moral community, of "a well-founded commonsense of contributing and gaining, of pride and indebtedness, of benefits and burdens, of give and take, of power and dependency" (Skillen 1985, 14). It has remained imprisoned within the confines of a social philosophy in which the basic unit of action is the individual, and society is no more than the public structures that protect the spaces for the private interaction of individuals.

All this is of course very familiar. It is the common coin of much radical commentary on the contemporary welfare state in Britain. What is interesting, though, is how rarely this perspective is cast back onto the Victorian period of social policy. In one of those intellectual divisions of labor so familiar in academic life, social policy theorists have largely addressed themselves to contemporary manifestations of welfare policy and have left the historical aspects of their subject to practicing historians. These, for their part, have their own professional interests, particular concerns, and problematics. Most notably, so eager have they been to refute Dicey that they have made claims for nineteenth-century welfare conceptions that must, on reflection, seem highly exaggerated—certainly to anyone considering the question comparatively or in a longer historical perspective.[18] In place of the myth of individualism, which they claim Dicey has imposed on nineteenth-century social policy, they seem intent on imposing another myth, the myth of collectivism. Victorian collectivism is seen, improbably and somewhat imprecisely, as the seed of a genuine welfare state that is assumed to come to fruition—beyond their period, of course—in the twentieth century.

There are some healthy signs of dissent from what looks like a congealing into an orthodoxy. Partly, this means reasserting what is essentially a traditional view of Victorian social policy—or at least of reemphasizing certain aspects of the traditional view. Thus Taylor reminds us that "Victorian social policy was basically negative and unconstructive." The Education Act of 1870 is taken as a good example of the limits of Victorian ambition and achievement. That good Benthamite, W. E. Forster, in introducing his bill, made it plain the government's purpose was "to complete the present voluntary system, to fill up the gaps." State provision for elementary education—nothing else, of course, was contemplated—was seen as a holding operation, a stopgap necessary only so far, and for so long, as the voluntary sector found itself incapable of fully performing its task. As Taylor comments, "The Act represented the antithesis of a belief in the virtues of public education in itself." And he concludes: "There is no firm evidence here or elsewhere in the wide area touched by Victorian social policy of that positive and reaffirmative belief in the inherent desirability of communal action . . . which is the hallmark of the Welfare State" (Taylor 1972, 56–57; see also Evans 1978, 4–7; Henriques 1979, 268).

It is in any case extraordinary that historians can find the "Victorian origins of the welfare state" in a structure of social policy of which, by common consent, the New Poor Law of 1834 was the centerpiece. This is possible only by being, in a thoroughly Whiggish way, highly selective as to what we see as the essence of the New Poor Law. If we see as central the acceptance of state provision for the poor and sick—which of course was a feature of the Old Poor Law, too—or pick out the administrative innovations such as central inspection and control, we are likely to emphasize continuity between nineteenth- and twentieth-century social policy. But was this what was meant by the celebrated "principles of 1834"? Were these not rather "less eligibility" and the "workhouse test," which drove (implicitly at least) a hard and fast line between the "deserving" and "undeserving" poor? This was to have a long and famous history, especially once it was definitively articulated as the central principle of social work care by the Charity Organization Society in the 1870s (see Parry and Satyamurti 1979).

Dicey, writing with evident approval of the 1834 act, at least got nearer to its main purpose than do many of his critics. The New Poor Law, he says, "associated pauperism—a different thing from poverty—with disgrace; it revived, even among the poor, pride in independence, and enforced upon the whole nation the faith that in the battle of life men must rely for success, not upon the aid of the State, but upon self-help" (1962, 43). Finer, too, interprets Chadwick's intention in the measure as much more to do with the opening up of the labor market than with the acceptance of any specifically public welfare obligation. "The poor law administration was a machinery for enforcing competition, for creating a highly competitive labour market, and keeping it so." (1952, 475). Here too the long arm of 1834 reached well beyond the nineteenth century into our own. The New Poor Law generated such hatred towards the end of the nineteenth century that welfare provision increasingly took place outside its ambit, in new boards and ministries. But Poor Law attitudes persisted in many of the new forms, noticeably in policies toward the unemployed. Here its influence could be felt right up to the present time—indeed, especially at the present time.[19]

What is perhaps even more damaging to what has been called the Whig interpretation of the history of social policy[20] is a questioning of the novelty of the "administrative revolution" of which so much is made, not just by MacDonagh, Roberts, and Clark, but also Parris and Brebner. Administrative centralization, an evolving system of central inspection and central control of local authorities, is seen as the decisive development in the creation of a national system of welfare: a true welfare state, rather than simply a patchwork of welfare measures. In a neglected contribution to the debate, Lubenow has tried to show that

> it is not appropriate to say that the structure of government was transformed during the 1830s and 1840s from an "individualistic" to a "collectivist" system. . . . Rather than establishing a welfare state through collectivist legislation, the nineteenth-century revolution in government consisted of modifications in the administrative structure in which new structural forms were blended with the old in a kind of Victorian compromise which provided for a co-operative arrangement of central and local administrative forms. (Lubenow 1971, 10, 12; see also Moore 1976)

In the case of Poor Law administration, for instance, Lubenow shows that the central commissioners had far less power over local boards of guardians than is generally realized. Not only did the 1834 act give considerable formal powers to the local authorities, these powers were amplified by the practice of choosing local guardians from among the local gentry families, who were traditionally the dominant force in the localities. Hence, while an attempt was made to extend new bureaucratic forms, the impact was limited by the persistence of "a society which had still not outgrown the social controls indigenous to an essentially landed society" (Lubenow 1971, 40). A survey of other areas of relevance—public health, factory and railway legislation—yields the same conclusion. "Limited in objective, and tempered by centuries of preference for limited government, government growth in early Victorian Britain was restrained in scope and modest in accomplishment" (ibid., 180–81).

Perhaps even more significant than this practical limitation to administrative effort was the persistence of traditional ideologies opposing administrative centralization. Lubenow shows that it was not so much—or not only—laissez-faire theories that were the main weapons of the opponents of centralization. They drew even more upon "historical and legal assumptions and values which stressed concepts of English history, Common Law, and the English constitution." Appeals to idealized concepts of the ancient Saxon constitution, the organic society, the fight against Tudor and Stuart despotism, and the long tradition of local self-government all figure strongly in the anticentralist arguments of both Conservatives and Radicals in the debates over social policy. Like the concepts of the state of nature or the social contract in seventeenth- and eighteenth-century political thought, "the historical perspective was an alternative normative model against which contemporary institutions and practices could be evaluated and judged" (ibid., 12, 25–26, 184). It was certainly highly effective in containing the growth of government in the nineteenth century. Sutherland speaks of the "peculiarly English, negative view of the role of the state." This contrasted with contemporary opinion in France and, even more, Germany, where the expectation was that a permanent bureaucracy would be an independent positive force. In England, state intervention—as, significantly, it was usually called—was nearly always seen, by all classes, as state interference. "The state acted only when all other attempts at voluntary, local or individual action had failed" (Sutherland 1972, 10).[21]

This important stress on the longstanding ideological tradition of hostility to the state had already been anticipated by Dicey. An individualist himself, he found it easy to understand the instinctive individualism of his fellow countrymen. Benthamite individualism found a ready echo in the hearts and minds of Englishmen, he says, because "individualism has always found its natural home in England." Dicey also draws attention to "the long conflicts which have made up the constitutional history of England," and to the hatred of "the collective and autocratic authority of the State" which these conflicts engendered. Benthamism was, says Dicey,

> and was ultimately felt to be, little else than the logical and systematic development of those individual rights, and especially of that individual freedom which has always been dear to the common law of England.

> The faith indeed of the utilitarians in the supreme value of individual liberty, and the assumption on which that faith rests, owe far more to the traditions of the common law than thinkers such as John Mill, who was no lawyer, are prepared to acknowledge. Bentham is heavily indebted to Coke, and utilitarianism has inherited some of its most valuable ideas from Puritanism. This combination of innovation with essential conservatism gave to the utilitarian reformers the peculiar power which attaches to teachers who, whilst appearing to oppose, really express the sentiment of their time. (1962, 175–76)[22]

Dicey, as we know, feared that this tradition of individualism was going down under the assaults of collectivism. Most of his critics agreed with him, merely wishing to rub salt in his wounds by arguing that the pass was sold a long time ago, in the early rather than, as Dicey thought, the late nineteenth century. Both Dicey's fears and his critics' claims now seem exaggerated. Perkin identifies two forms of individualism and seven kinds of collectivism in nineteenth-century England. He points out that the differences between these were unduly accentuated for reasons of propaganda and party politics. Nearly all were, in fact, some form of individualism; they varied simply in the differing emphasis they placed on the need for state intervention to support and foster individual freedom and enterprise. In this sense, there were no fundamental differences of ideology separating Adam Smith and Jeremy Bentham, at the beginning of the century, from T. H. Green, D. G. Ritchie, and L. T. Hobhouse at the end of the century. The only radical departure came with the form of collectivism that called for state ownership of all the means of production, distribution, and exchange. Only a few fringe socialists, such as H. M. Hyndman, urged the English people to take that step. No statesman, no influential body of opinion, not even the majority of the Fabians demanded such a degree of collectivism. But the new liberalism, with its modest measures of welfare and its more forceful rhetoric of populism, scared thinkers like Dicey and Sir Henry Maine into believing that socialism was the next logical step (Perkin 1981, 62–68).

Much has indeed been claimed for the new liberalism of the late nineteenth century. It has been seen as laying the foundations of the welfare state—in thought at least, if not so clearly in practice (McCallum 1959, 75; Briggs 1961, 24). The new liberalism refers to the social philosophy of such thinkers as T. H. Green, Bernard Bosanquet, L. T. Hobhouse, and J. A. Hobson. It includes, also, the social investigations of Charles Booth and Seebohm Rowntree and the discovery of poverty as a structural problem of society rather than an individual misfortune. And it includes as well the social policies of administrators and politicians such as William Beveridge, R. B. Haldane, Winston Churchill, and Lloyd George in the Liberal governments of 1906–1914.[23]

Undoubtedly, the new liberal philosophers brought about a far-reaching modification of the laissez-faire individualism that had been the hallmark of midcentury liberalism. The key perception comes from T. H. Green and the idealists: "Without persons, no society, without society, no persons." As Michael Freeden sums up the new understanding: "Liberalism was still concerned with the optimal expression and development of the individual, but this was attainable by reflecting the scientific and ethical truth that man could only realize himself in a community" (1978, 257). This recognition gave philosophical justification to radical interventions by the state in the interest of a fuller realization of individual personality, since without other individuals (ideally, all other individuals) being given the means whereby they might realize their unique potential, the development of any one individual was likely to be stunted. Equality was therefore given its due, not in pursuit of some collectivist goal of leveling, but as an acknowledgement that it was the necessary counterpart—hitherto insufficiently stressed by liberals—to the cherished liberal principle of individual liberty. "The use of the public resources and of public power to assure a greater diffusion of educational opportunity, to control and eliminate disease, to improve conditions of work, to abolish slums, no doubt means an interference with the liberty of some individuals, but it tends on the whole to maximise liberty" (Ginsberg 1959, 7).

But this was, after all, still quite some way from that principle of collective development and communal growth that underlies most twentieth-century welfare philosophy. The new liberals remained, quite consciously and deliberately, individualists, not closet collectivists or socialists. A conceptual world separates Green and Bosanquet, not just from Marxists like Hyndman but even from the more radical Fabian wing of H. G. Wells and George Bernard Shaw. Richter's verdict on Green seems apt not just in his case but that of the majority of new liberal thinkers:

> The practical applications he himself made of [his] doctrine fell within a pattern of politics which bore little resemblance to the forces later responsible for the "Welfare State." Green and Toynbee did not argue for an extensive use of governmental action in the sphere of economic and social life. Rather they protested against the dogmatic and abstract statements of the older form of Liberalism, which seemed to imply that the government was bound to remain impotent in the face of flagrant evils. When Green spoke of "positive freedom" he did not commit himself to any use of state power beyond that in fact advocated by

> Gladstone and Bright. . . . The concept "individualism" registered the limits to which even the most advanced Liberals were willing to go. (Richter 1964, 341–42)[24]

If new liberal philosophy stayed within the limits of individualism, new liberal practice made even less attempt to break out of it. Churchill and Lloyd George were politicians before they were philosophers. The thinking behind their social policies was an eclectic blend of Greenian idealism, Bismarckian paternalism, nonconformist Christianity, and high-minded philanthropy, the whole stirred into action by a leavening of political opportunism. If, as has been claimed, they finally broke the power of the landlords in England, it was not to usher in the welfare state of the common man but to secure the predominance of the professional and commercial middle class. The most advanced measure of social policy, the National Insurance Act of 1911, broke genuinely new ground in introducing for the first time anywhere the principle of compulsory insurance against unemployment (Bismarck's measures of the 1880s had restricted themselves to sickness, old age, and invalidism). But to see this—or any other measure of these years—as betokening a move toward social democracy is stretching an already elastic term further than even it can bear (see, e.g., McCallum 1959, 75). Beveridge, the main architect of unemployment policy before 1914, was concerned—like Chadwick and Senior in 1834—with the more efficient organization of the labor market. His pet solution was the setting up of labor exchanges, which duly came in 1909. Unemployment insurance was seen as a secondary aspect of this policy, a necessary backup—restricted to certain trades with peculiar problems—to cope with short-term unemployment (Harris 1972, 211 ff.; Gilbert 1966). Neither it nor any other policies of the Liberal government pointed in the direction of a welfare state, nor were they intended to. At most, the Liberal reforms began the process of creating a social service state, one in which "limited services are provided for limited sections of the population"—that is, mainly for the poor.[25] This is a far cry from the universality of provision and equality of citizenship that are the premises of the modern welfare state.

Such a welfare state is supposed, finally, to have arrived in England after 1945. Conceived by theorists of the labor movement in the late nineteenth century, political and social realities prevented its realization until the Beveridge Revolution of World War II. After 1945, Aneurin Bevan's confident claim on behalf of the people of England—"Homes, health, education and social security: these are your birthright"—was the working postulate of all political parties. Bevan's own principal achievement, the National Health Service, was seen as the quintessential expression of the universality of the welfare state (Bruce 1968, 12; Briggs 1961, 231, 239).

This is clearly not the place to consider this claim in detail. Contemporary analyses, though, are making it plain that whatever the aspirations and achievements of the men and women of 1945, the welfare state in Britain today is in a very sorry condition indeed. Poor Law distinctions between the deserving and the undeserving poor are being reasserted with a vengeance in the field of social security and unemployment policy. The philosophy and practice of privatization are being applied to the welfare services as much as to the economy. The notion of the residuum as the basic principle of welfare is being resurrected: one set of private services for those able to afford them, another set of (markedly inferior) public services for those unfortunate remnants of the population who cannot provide for themselves. Symbolically, once more, it is the tattered condition and steady erosion of the National Health Service that provide the benchmark for the welfare ideal today (Mishra 1984; Clarke et al. 1987; Loney 1987).

Was the welfare state ever achieved in Britain? There are good grounds, of both theory and practice, for doubting it. As an influential body of opinion, English social thought has never gone beyond advanced liberalism—the social liberalism of Lloyd George, Beveridge, and Keynes. The practice has generally fallen well short even of these limited social ideals. English social policy has been at best reluctantly collectivist. Ingrained in the policies of all twentieth-century governments has been the assumption that all publicly provided services—in education, health, housing, and transport—will be, and perhaps should be, second rate. Public welfare is a regrettable necessity, provided in a spirit of charity for those unfortunates who are the casualties of the dynamic capitalist system. Public services are the second-best substitutes for the private provision of welfare, which is seen as the natural way, certainly the English way.

This deep-seated attitude, which affects practically all groups in the population, must be seen as one more expression of the curious strength of that individualist tradition of theory and practice that many have seen as marking English social development over the course of many centuries (Annan 1959; Macfarlane 1978; Marquand 1988). American observers, accustomed to an even more virulent strain of individualism, are apt to see English individualism as a mixed and moderate thing, qualified by many practices of a corporate and communal kind. This is no doubt true. But as continental traditions by comparison indicate, England certainly comes closer to the pole of individualism than that of collectivism or communalism. Dicey, whose interpretation of nineteenth-century individualism has rightly been criticized for its narrowness, nevertheless was correct in his general perception that "individualism has always found its natural home in England" and that English history has charted its course by the philosophy of individualism (Dicey, 1962, xc, 175). Certainly his own credo brings out clearly the stubborn strength of that tradition and the weight of its deposit in English thought: "A nation or a State means, conceal it as you will, a lot of individual selves with unequal talents and in reality unequal conditions, and each of these selves does—or rather must—think not exclusively, but primarily of his own self" (1962, lxxx).

NOTES

1. For helpful critical approaches and surveys, see Townsend 1976; Rubington and Weinberg 1977; Mishra 1981; Manning 1987.

2. See, e.g., George and Wilding 1976; Gough 1979; Ginsburg 1979; Room 1979; Manning 1985. For specific applications, see Navarro 1978; Corrigan and Leonard 1978; Parry, Rustin, and Satyamurti 1979; Lee and Raban 1988. For an alternative radical perspective, see Skillen 1985.

3. The works approved of by Goldthorpe include Polanyi 1957; Beales 1946; Carr 1957; MacDonagh 1958.

4. See, e.g., Ginsburg 1979; and for the problems raised by this approach, see Gough 1979, 11–15, 55–74.

5. On the indirect nature of Bentham's influence, see also Dicey's letter to Bryce, 18 August 1908, quoted in Cosgrove 1980:182–83.

6. The theoretical disputes underlying the different strategies of the labor movements in the West are well explored in Lichtheim 1966, 1970; Przeworski 1985; Gorz 1975.

7. For parallel accounts, stressing the unintended growth of the centralized welfare state, see Clark 1959, 1962, 1967; Roberts 1960.

8. See Winch 1958; MacIntyre 1962. Schutz as well as Wittgenstein stand behind this perspective; see Schutz 1972; Bloor 1983.

9. See MacDonagh 1958a, 58, 62, 63; Roberts 1960, 26–27, 88–89, 102–3, 318; Clark 1962, 177–79, 186–87, 284.

10. Lecture 9—The Debt of Collectivism to Benthamism—has all the appearance of being tacked on as an afterthought. It doesn't really fit in the main structure of Dicey's book. It is a pity that Cosgrove's biography of Dicey gives so little information on the actual composition of *Law and Public Opinion*, though Cosgrove makes clear how much in general the book differed from the original lectures, both at Harvard and later at Oxford (Cosgrove 1980, 170–71, 185).

11. Halévy's study, published in French in three volumes, 1901–1904, is footnoted by Dicey 1962, 126 n.1, 159 n.1. In choosing to regard Benthamism as the chief proponent of individualism, Dicey acknowledges the influence of Adam Smith and his disciples but argues that "in 1830 the economists and the

Benthamites formed one school" (1962, 126 n.2). It is possible that he took this view from Halévy, though it was a common enough one in Dicey's time.

12. On the need for state intervention in these and other areas of welfare, see the remarks of Nassau Senior, Chadwick, Simon, and Mill quoted in Taylor 1972, 21–23, and in Parris 1969, 273–79.

13. It should be noted that both MacDonagh and Roberts accept this characterization of Benthamism as essentially individualist in practice: MacDonagh 1958a, 66; Roberts 1959, 199.

14. See Perkin 1981; also Parris 1969, 34–37; Hart 1965, 47–48; Crouch 1967; Watson 1973; Atiyah 1979, 226–37; Taylor 1972, 11–17. For a valuable history of the concept of laissez-faire, see Viner 1960. See also Keynes 1972, 291.

15. On the classical economists and laissez-faire, see especially Robbins 1952; see also Taylor 1972, 18–26; Keynes 1972, 277–82; Kittrell 1966; Crouch 1967.

16. This is not the place for a full citation of the voluminous literature on the New Poor Law and its relation to Benthamite thought. A good recent study is Brundage 1978; see also Roach 1978, 110–20; Himmelfarb 1984, 147–76; Kumar 1984.

17. A good statement of modern welfare philosophy is Skillen 1985, esp. 3–4. See also Briggs 1961; Robson 1976; Marshall 1981.

18. On the unfortunate consequences of the lack of a long-term historical perspective on welfare, see the stimulating essay by Thompson 1986. It is precisely the historical and comparative approach that is valuable in Ashford 1986. It is a pity that, in his otherwise engaging and wide-ranging survey of the British political tradition, Greenleaf chooses to treat the nineteenth century uncritically as "the rise of collectivism." See Greenleaf 1983, vol. 1.

19. See Ditch 1987; Thane 1978, 12–19. For good accounts of the Poor Law during the nineteenth century, see Rose 1972; Fraser 1976; Treble 1983; Thompson 1986, 370–78.

20. As Briggs characterizes it: "The past was seen as leading inevitably and inexorably along a broad highway with the 'welfare State' as destination," Briggs 1961, 222. See also Thane 1978, 11. An example of such a Whiggish approach is the well-known text by Bruce 1968.

21. See also Roberts 1960, 323, 326; Thane 1978, 19; Evans 1978, 4. On working-class distrust of state intervention, see Pelling 1968; and on the individualist assumptions of late nineteenth-century trade unionism, see Currie 1979. Walter Bagehot's observation was typical of a wide range of Victorian opinion: "We look on state action, not as our own action, but as alien action; as an imposed tyranny from without." Quoted in Lubenow 1971, 184. It is interesting, though, that nineteenth-century English social theorists, including Bentham's followers, were reluctant to embrace the term *individualism* as expressive of their philosophy. See Swart 1962, 87.

22. On the strong and long-lasting individualist assumptions of the common lawyers in the nineteenth century, see Atiyah 1979, 236–67; Sugarman 1983, 108. The fundamental individualism even of paternalistic Toryism, often

said to be hostile to individualism, is well brought out in Kilmuir 1960; see also Greenleaf 1983, 2:189ff.

23. See Freeden 1978; Richter 1964; Collini 1979; Clarke 1981; Ginsberg 1959, 3–26; Weiler 1982; Hennock 1976; Hay 1983.

24. See also Burrow 1966, who shows how in the second half of the nineteenth century evolutionary theory reconstituted the elements of utilitarianism, without, however, abandoning its fundamentally individualist assumptions.

25. Hay 1983, 12, 61; Thane 1978, 15; Henriques 1979, 268. For the distinction between the welfare state and the social service state, see Briggs 1961, 222, 228. It is interesting to note that, so far from laissez-faire being killed off during the era of liberal reforms, Keynes found it still the dominant ideology of the 1920s: Keynes 1972, 277.

SOURCES

Annan, Noel. 1959. *The Curious Strength of Positivism in English Political Thought*. London: Oxford University Press.

Ashford, Douglas. 1986. *The Emergence of the Welfare States*. Oxford: Basil Blackwell.

Atiyah, P. S. 1979. *The Rise and Fall of the Freedom of Contract*. Oxford: Clarendon.

Beales, H. L. 1946. *The Making of Social Policy*. London: Oxford University Press.

Behrens, C. B. A. 1969. The Spirit of the Terror. *New York Review of Books* 27 February.

Bloor, David. 1983. *Wittgenstein: A Social Theory of Knowledge*. New York: Columbia University Press.

Brebner, J. Bartlet. 1948. Laissez-Faire and State Intervention in Nineteenth-Century Britain. *Journal of Economic History* 8 (supplement): 59–73.

Briggs, A. 1961. The Welfare State in Historical Perspective, *Archives Européenes de Sociologie* 2:221–58.

Bruce, Maurice. 1968. *The Coming of the Welfare State*, 4th ed. London: Batsford.

Brundage, Anthony. 1978. *The Making of the New Poor Law*. London: Hutchinson.

Burrow, J. F. 1966. *Evolution and Society: A Study in Victorian Social Theory*. Cambridge: Cambridge University Press.

Carr, E. H. 1957 (1951). *The New Society*. Boston: Beacon.

Clark, G. Kitson. 1959. "Statesmen in Disguise": Reflexions on the History of the Neutrality of the Civil Service. *Historical Journal* 2:19–39.

———. 1962. *The Making of Victorian England*. London: Methuen.

———. 1967. *An Expanding Society: Britain 1830–1900*. Cambridge: Cambridge University Press.

Clarke, J., A. Cochrane, and C. Smart. 1987. *Ideologies of Social Welfare*. London: Hutchinson.

Clarke, Peter. 1981. *Liberals and Social Democrats.* Cambridge: Cambridge University Press.

Collini, Stefan. 1979. *Liberalism and Sociology: L. T. Hobhouse and Political Argument in England 1880–1914.* Cambridge: Cambridge University Press.

Corrigan, P., and P. Leonard. 1978. *Social Work Practice Under Capitalism: A Marxist Approach.* London: Macmillan.

Cosgrove, Richard A. 1980. *The Rule of Law: Albert Venn Dicey, Victorian Jurist.* London: Macmillan.

Cromwell, Valerie. 1965–1966. Interpretations of Nineteenth-Century Administration: An Analysis. *Victorian Studies* 9:245–55.

Crouch, R. C. 1967. Laissez-Faire in Nineteenth-Century Britain: Myth or Reality? *Manchester School of Economic and Social Studies* 35:199–215.

Currie, R. 1979. *Industrial Politics.* Oxford: Clarendon.

Dicey, A. V. 1962 (1914). *Lectures on the Relation Between Law and Public Opinion in England During the Nineteenth Century.* 2d ed. London: Macmillan. (First edition published 1905.)

Ditch, John. 1987. The Undeserving Poor: Unemployed People, Then and Now. In Loney 1987.

Evans, Eric J., ed. 1978. *Social Policy 1830–1914: Individualism, Collectivism, and the Origins of the Welfare State.* London: Routledge and Kegan Paul.

Finer, S. E. 1952. *The Life and Times of Sir Edwin Chadwick.* London: Methuen.

———. 1972. The Transmission of Benthamite Ideas, 1820–1850. In Sutherland 1972.

Fraser, D., ed. 1976. *The New Poor Law in the Nineteenth Century.* London: Macmillan.

Freeden, Michael. 1978. *The New Liberalism: An Ideology of Social Reform.* Oxford: Clarendon.

Gallie, Duncan. 1983. *Social Inequality and Class Radicalism in France and Britain.* Cambridge: Cambridge University Press.

George, V., and P. Wilding. 1976. *Ideology and the Welfare State.* London: Routledge and Kegan Paul.

Gilbert, Bentley B. 1966. *The Evolution of National Insurance in Great Britain.* London: Michael Joseph.

Ginsberg, M., ed. 1959. *Law and Opinion in England in the 20th Century.* London: Stevens.

Ginsburg, N. 1979. *Class, Capital and Social Policy.* London: Macmillan.

Goldthorpe, John H. 1964. The Development of Social Policy in England, 1800–1914: Notes on a Sociological Approach to a Problem in Historical Explanation. *Transactions of the Fifth World Congress of Sociology* 4:41–56.

Gorz, A. 1975. *Socialism and Revolution,* trans. N. Denny. London: Allen Lane.

Gough, I. 1979. *The Political Economy of the Welfare State.* London: Macmillan.

Greenleaf, W. H. 1983. *The British Political Tradition.* Vol. 1, *The Rise of Collectivism.* Vol 2, *The Ideological Heritage.* London: Methuen.

Halévy, Elie. 1972 (1928). *The Growth of Philosophic Radicalism,* trans. M. Morris. London: Faber and Faber.

Harris, José. 1972. *Unemployment and Politics: A Study in English Social Policy 1886–1914*. Oxford: Clarendon.
Hart, Jennifer. 1965. Nineteenth-Century Social Reform: A Tory Interpretation of History. *Past and Present* 31:39–61.
Hay, J. R. 1983. *The Origins of the Liberal Welfare Reforms 1906–1914*, 2d. ed. London: Macmillan.
Hennock, E. P. 1976. Poverty and Social Theory in England: The Experience of the Eighteen-Eighties. *Social History* 1:67–91.
Himmelfarb, Gertrude. 1984. *The Idea of Poverty: England in the Early Industrial Age*. New York: Knopf.
Henriques, Ursula. 1979. *Before the Welfare State: Social Administration in Early Industrial Britain*. London: Longman.
Hume, L. J. 1967. Jeremy Bentham and the Nineteenth-Century Revolution in Government. *Historical Journal* 10:361–75.
Keynes, J. M. 1972. The End of Laissez-Faire (1926). In vol. 9, *The Collected Writings of John Maynard Keynes*. London: Macmillan.
———. 1973 (1936). *The General Theory of Employment, Interest, and Money*. London: Macmillan.
Kilmuir, Lord. 1960. The Shaftesbury Tradition in Conservative Politics. *Journal of Law and Economics* 3:70–74.
Kittrell, E. 1966. "Laissez-Faire" in English Classical Economics. *Journal of the History of Ideas* 27:610–20.
Kumar, Krishan. 1978. *Prophecy and Progress: The Sociology of Industrial and Post-Industrial Society*. Harmondsworth: Penguin.
———. 1984. Unemployment in the Development of Industrial Societies: The English Experience. *Sociological Review* 32:185–233.
Lee, P., and C. Raban. 1988. *Welfare Theory and Social Policy: Reform or Revolution?* London: Sage.
Lichtheim, George. 1966. *Marxism and Modern France*. New York: Columbia University Press.
———. 1970. *A Short History of Socialism*. London: Weidenfeld and Nicolson.
Loney, M., ed. 1987. *The State or the Market: Politics and Welfare in Contemporary Britain*. London: Sage.
Lubenow, William C. 1971. *The Politics of Government Growth: Early Victorian Attitudes Toward State Intervention 1833–1848*. Newton Abbot: David and Charles; Hamden: Archon.
McCallum, R. B. 1959. The Liberal Outlook. In Ginsberg, 1959.
MacDonagh, Oliver. 1958a. The Nineteenth-Century Revolution in Government: A Reappraisal. *Historical Journal* 1:52–67.
———. 1958b. Delegated Legislation and Administrative Discretions in the 1850s: A Particular Study. *Victorian Studies* 2:29–44.
Macfarlane, Alan. 1978. *The Origins of English Individualism*. Oxford: Basil Blackwell.
MacIntyre, Alasdair. 1962. A Mistake About Causality in Social Science. In P. Laslett and W. G. Runciman, eds., *Philosophy, Politics, and Society*, 2d ser. Oxford: Basil Blackwell.

Mack, Mary Peter. 1955. The Fabians and Utilitarianism. *Journal of the History of Ideas* 16:76–88.

Manning, N., ed. 1985. *Social Problems and Welfare Ideology*. Aldershot: Gower.

———. 1987. What Is a Social Problem? In Loney, 1987.

Marquand, David. 1988. *The Unprincipled Society: New Demands and Old Politics*. London: Jonathan Cape.

Marshall, T. H. 1981. *The Right to Welfare, and Other Essays*. London: Heinemann.

Marx, Karl. 1971. Speech delivered in Amsterdam, 8 September 1872. In S.K. Padover, ed., *Karl Marx: On Revolution*. New York: McGraw-Hill.

———. 1975. The Chartists (1852). In Karl Marx and Frederick Engels, *Articles on Britain*. Moscow: Progress Publishers.

Mills, C. Wright. 1967. The Professional Ideology of Social Pathologists. In I. L. Horowitz, ed., *Power, Politics and People: The Collected Essays of C. Wright Mills*. London: Oxford University Press.

Mishra, R. 1981. *Society and Social Policy: Theories and Practice of Welfare*. 2d. ed. London: Macmillan.

———. 1984. *The Welfare State in Crisis: Social Thought and Social Change*. Brighton: Wheatsheaf.

Moore, D. C. 1976. *The Politics of Deference*. Brighton: Harvester.

Namier, L. B. 1955. Human Nature in Politics. In *Personalities and Powers*. London: Hamish Hamilton.

Navarro, V. 1978. *Class Struggle, the State and Medicine*. Oxford: Martin Robertson.

Parris, Henry. 1960. The Nineteenth-Century Revolution in Government: A Reappraisal Reappraised. *Historical Journal* 3:17–37.

———. 1969. *Constitutional Bureaucracy: The Development of British Central Administration Since the Eighteenth Century*. London: Allen and Unwin.

Parry, N., M. Rustin, and C. Satyamurti, eds. 1979. *Social Work, Welfare and the State*. London: Edward Arnold.

Pelling, Henry. 1968. The Working Class and the Origins of the Welfare State. In *Popular Politics and Society in Late Victorian Britain*. London: Macmillan.

Perkin, Harold, 1969. *The Origins of Modern English Society, 1780–1880*. London: Routledge and Kegan Paul.

———. 1981. Individualism versus Collectivism in Nineteenth-Century Britain: A False Antithesis. In *The Structured Crowd*. Brighton: Harvester.

Polanyi, Karl. 1957 (1944). *The Great Transformation: The Political and Economic Origins of Our Time*. Boston: Beacon.

Przeworski, A. 1985. *Capitalism and Social Democracy*. Cambridge: Cambridge University Press.

Richter, Melvin. 1964. *The Politics of Conscience: T. H. Green and His Age*. London: Weidenfeld and Nicolson.

Roach, John. 1973. Liberalism and the Victorian Intelligentsia. In P. Stansky, ed., *The Victorian Revolution: Government and Society in Victoria's Britain*. New York: Franklin Watts.

———. 1978. *Social Reform in England 1780–1880*. London: Batsford.
Robbins, L. C. 1952. *The Theory of Economic Policy in English Political Economy*. London: Macmillan.
Roberts, David. 1959. Jeremy Bentham and the Victorian Administrative State. *Victorian Studies* 2:193–210.
———. 1960. *The Victorian Origins of the British Welfare State*. New Haven: Yale University Press.
Robson, William A. 1976. *Welfare State and Welfare Society: Illusion and Reality*. London: Allen and Unwin.
Room, G. 1979. *The Sociology of Welfare*. Oxford: Basil Blackwell.
Rose, Michael E. 1972. *The Relief of Poverty 1834–1914*. London: Macmillan.
Rubington, E., and M. S. Weinberg. 1977. *The Study of Social Problems: Five Perspectives*. London: Oxford University Press.
Ryan, Alan. 1972. Utilitarianism and Bureaucracy: The Views of J. S. Mill. In Sutherland, 1972.
Schutz, Alfred. 1972. *The Phenomenology of the Social World*, trans. G. Walsh and F. Lehnhert. London: Heinemann.
Skillen, Anthony. 1985. Welfare State Versus Welfare Society? *Journal of Applied Philosophy* 2:3–17.
Skinner, Quentin. 1969. Meaning and Understanding in the History of Ideas. *History and Theory* 8:3–53.
Sugarman, David. 1983. The Legal Boundaries of Liberty: Dicey, Liberalism, and Legal Science. *Modern Law Review* 46:102–11.
Sutherland, Gillian, ed. 1972. *Studies in the Growth of Nineteenth-Century Government*. London: Routledge and Kegan Paul.
Swart, K. W. 1962. "Individualism" in the Mid-Nineteenth Century (1826–1860). *Journal of the History of Ideas* 23:77–90.
Taylor, Arthur J. 1972. *Laissez-Faire and State Intervention in Nineteenth-Century Britain*. London: Macmillan.
Thane, Pat, ed. 1978. *The Origins of British Social Policy*. London: Croom Helm.
Thompson, David. 1986. Welfare and the Historians. In L. Bonfield, R. M. Smith, and K. Wrightson, eds., *The World We Have Gained: Histories of Population and Social Structure*. Oxford: Basil Blackwell.
Townsend, Peter. 1976. *Sociology and Social Policy*. Harmondsworth: Penguin.
Treble, James H. 1983. *Urban Poverty in Britain 1830–1914*. London: Methuen.
Viner, Jacob. 1960. The Intellectual History of Laissez-Faire. *Journal of Law and Economics* 3:45–69.
Watson, George. 1973. Laissez-Faire and the State. In *The English Ideology: Studies in the Language of Victorian Politics*. London: Allen Lane.
Weiler, P. 1982. *The New Liberalism: Liberal Social Theory in Britain 1889–1914*. New York: Garland.
Wells, H. G. 1920. *The Outline of History*. 2 vols. London: Newnes.
Winch, Peter. 1958. *The Idea of a Social Science and Its Relation to Philosophy*. London: Routledge and Kegan Paul.

4

Marxism and Institutional Analysis: Working-Class Strength and Welfare State Development in Sweden

Bo Rothstein

IN OCTOBER 1936, the National Union of Metal Workers in Sweden convened a conference; one of its most heated debates was about the new public unemployment insurance scheme. In 1934, the Social Democratic government passed a bill that introduced the first public unemployment insurance scheme in Sweden. Compared to other similar countries, this was a rather late effort. The scheme was, however, constructed in a special way, which at the time was called the Ghent system (from the Belgian town where the system was established in 1901). In short, the Ghent system meant that the public unemployment insurance system was not to be implemented by a government agency. Instead, the unions' employment funds would receive public grants, provided that they accepted government regulations about levels of insurance, payments, and control.

The question in the Metal Workers conference was whether the union, then the largest union in Sweden, should apply for these government subsidies to their unemployment fund and thus accept a degree of government control and regulation of their internal affairs. The majority of the union's board was in favor, because joining the scheme would be economically favorable for the union. The conference asked for a vote of the members. An intense debate followed among the rank and file, and the result of the ballot was a majority voting against joining the public insurance scheme. The same sequence of events took place at the next conference in 1939. In 1941, however, the Metal Workers conference decided to join the public scheme without a vote of the members (*Records from the Swedish National Union of Metal Workers Conference* 1936, 1939, and 1941).

This episode is a starting point to explore the relations between class formation and class power, on the one hand, and the importance of political institutions, such as public unemployment insurance schemes, on the other. There has been increased interest in the analysis of political institutions. Particularly important to this intellectual movement in social science is the treatment of political institutions as important independent variables; they are no longer seen as only something to be explained but as having an explanatory force of their own. As independent variables, political institutions are not impersonal creations, such as social structures, but are instead shaped by conscious, deliberating, and rational, humans. On the other hand, they may—for special reasons soon to be dealt with—have very different consequences than those expected by (some of) their creators. An emphasis on institutions has been put forward as an alternative to neo-Marxism, to mainstream pluralist analysis, and to public choice and rational choice theories (March and Olsen 1984; Douglas 1987; Grafstein 1988; Levi 1988; Shepsle 1987; Ashford 1986). A central empirical political event that this neo-institutionalist model is intended to explain is the development and extension of the modern welfare state (Ashford 1986).

The purpose of this chapter is threefold: first, to discuss the relation between Marxist analysis and the neo-institutionalist school; second, to put forward an explanation of the Swedish case, which is based on this analysis. This effort emphasizes the importance of understanding the politically determined nature of labor market power in explaining the relation between social classes and public policies. Third, this chapter stresses the importance of institutions responsible for the implementation of government policies to show how questions of organization have consequences outside the field of public administration.

The empirical background is the recognition that it is no longer possible to speak about the welfare state in general. Even if one can discuss different ways of measuring the degree of welfarism in modern Western welfare states, it is obvious that they differ greatly (Amenta and Skocpol 1986). The reason for choosing Sweden as a case is that this country is a very, if not the most, developed welfare state among the Western capitalist democracies. Methodologically, Sweden qualifies as the critical case in explaining why some states are more welfarist than others (Eckstein 1975).

Working-Class Strength or State Capacity?

There are, of course, many explanations for diversity in the development of the modern welfare states (Skocpol 1988). Only two explanations are considered: *working-class mobilization* and *state capacity* (Noble 1988). The first, named the power resource model, argues that the power of the working class (or class of wage earners) is the most important independent variable in explaining the differences among welfare states. The greater the organizational strength of the working class, the stronger the welfare state (Korpi 1983; Shalev 1983a, 1983b; Noble 1988). Contrary to this explanation, the state capacity model points to the different kinds of organizational forms of the state and the initiatives of state managers as most important in explaining the differences in the development of welfare states (Ashford 1986; Skocpol 1988; Weir and Skocpol 1985).

The power resource model is grounded in a special interpretation of Marxism, while the other model is more Weberian. What is important in this discussion is that this debate takes on one of the most profound and basic questions in social science—that of agency versus structure (Callinicos 1989; Mayhew 1980). The power resource model is clearly in line with a structuralist account of social change, while the institutionalist, or state, model points both to the importance of political agency and to the long *durée* of established political institutions, without explicitly confronting the dilemma between agency and structure (Skocpol 1988, 12). This chapter uses the controversy between class and state to contribute to the more general discussion about agency versus structure.

In general, there is a firm relationship between the organizational strength of the working class and the development of the welfare state in modern Western societies. The stronger the organization of wage earners, the more encompassing and generous the welfare state seems to be. Thus, the labor market seems crucial to exercising political power and to understanding social change in different kinds of welfare states. This is shown in many studies, and the facts do not need to be repeated (Korpi 1983; Hollingsworth and Hanneman 1982; Therborn 1985a; Shalev 1983b). There are indeed welfare states in countries without strong labor movements, but they are either directed at a marginal part of the population (the poor) or their general programs are not especially well funded (Esping-Andersen and Korpi 1984; Therborn 1985a). So far, the power resources model is the best description of the facts. But—and this is the problem—the model does not sufficiently explain why working classes in some countries are more strongly organized than others. The statistical relationship between working-class strength, however measured, and the extension of social policies does not say in which direction the causal link goes. At most, when discussing differences in the organizational strength of the working class in various countries, the class mobilization model points at economic forces and historical events that seem to lie outside the range of intentional political agency (Korpi 1983, 23–46; March and Olsen 1984, 735; Skocpol 1988, 11f). Thus, this is a genuine structural explanation.

Indeed, the state capacity school also recognizes the relationship between the organizational power of labor and the development of the welfare state (Skocpol 1988; Noble 1988). But they argue that important social policies in the capitalist Western states have often been carried out at the initiative of state managers or are the result of existing political institutions and thus are not to be understood as the pure results of working-class strength. Furthermore, they argue that one of the reasons why at times some working classes did not pursue demands for increased state ambitions in social policy was their lack of confidence in the state's capacity to implement these policies in an orderly way (Skocpol 1988, 14ff; Weir and Skocpol 1985). The state's capacity is said to be determined by the historical formation of the state or by the skill of state managers. The problem is that, so far, the causal link between historical state formation in the eighteenth and nineteenth centuries and actual state capacity to implement social reforms in, say, the 1930s remain unclear, as does the reason that some countries had more clever state managers than other countries.

Thus, one conclusion is that both perspectives are lacking. The power resource model does not explain why different nation-states have very different working classes, especially concerning their organizational strength. Mobilization of workers seems in this perspective to be a structurally determined process. Either working classes decide to become strongly organized, or they do not—and this is decided outside the sphere of intentional political agency. If there are any reasons given for some working classes being stronger than others, they seem to lie mainly in socioeconomic, ethnic, or religious structures (Korpi 1983, 26–43). The distribution of power resources between the social classes is made an independent instead of a dependent variable (ibid., 187). The state capacity model, on the other hand, seems to have a somewhat myopic view of the class-state relationship. In particular, they are insensitive to the fact that state capacity and policy might be deliberately constructed by political agents representing working-class parties to promote the possibilities of mobilizing workers. Why some state managers pursue social policies intended to strengthen the organizational capabilities of the working class and why some institutional arrangements are more inclined to promote other policies remain unexplained.

Recently, however, a somewhat different argument has been put forward by Skocpol (1988). Her idea is that the causal link between working-class force and social policies is not one-dimensional, but dialectical.

> Once social insurance measures were launched in Europe, trade unions and working-class-based political parties did play important roles in the subsequent expansion of coverage and benefits. Even so, the social democratic model can be criticized for downplaying ways in which state policies affect working-class organizational strength, as well as the other way around. Thus, the 1930s and 1940s constituted a watershed period in which "positive loops" between social policies and increasing working-class strength locked into place in some countries, such as Sweden, but failed through near misses in others such as Britain and, arguably, the United States. The major divergences in working-class political strength came after this watershed period, in which new policy directions were set that themselves spurred the divergences. (Skocpol 1988, 9)

In fact, this comes rather close to some of the theoretical standpoints put forward by the power resource model. Esping-Andersen, as one of the proponents of this school, argues that class power is not something that stems directly from the social structure, but that government policies have profound effects on the possibilities of mobilizing workers politically:

> Depending on its organization, scope and content, the welfare state's political effects will vary dramatically. It may introduce new divisions in the class structure, it may fragment or individuate workers, and it may unleash unmanageable and destructive equity or status conflicts. On the other hand, the welfare state may help manufacture broad class (even cross-class) solidarity and social democratic consensus. (Esping-Andersen 1985, 245)

Even the main architect behind the power resource model, Korpi, states en passant that "while the institutional structures and the state can be used to affect, e.g., distributional processes in the society, these structures also affect the way in which class-based power resources can be mobilized and are, in turn, affected by the use of power resources" (1983, 19).

Thus, looking closer, the differences between the class and the state schools of thought seem to lie more in the choice of empirical material than in genuine theoretical positions. The most profound argument about the dialectical relation between class formation and state policies is by Przeworski, who states that classes, and class power, are not just there as a result of objective socioeconomic development but that they are constantly created or decomposed by political agents, such as parties:

> If we are to draw lessons from historical experience, we can assume neither that the practice of political movements is uniquely determined

> by any objective conditions nor that such movements are free to act at will, independently of the conditions they seek to transform. These conditions constitute at each moment the structure of choice, the structure within which actors deliberate upon goals, perceive alternatives, evaluate them, choose courses of action, and pursue them to create new conditions. (Przeworski 1985a, 3)

This is a question that can only be solved by studies of concrete institutional creation and by following institutional effects on those very forces that created them, that is, by identifying what Skocpol calls loops between institutional forms and working-class mobilization (Skocpol 1988, 8; Przeworski 1985a, 66f). Thus, the main argument here is that, while people make history under circumstances not of their own choosing, the circumstances might well be of their own making.

If, then, both models state that political institutions are important, two basic questions must be answered. The first is, Which institutions are the most important to analyze when explaining working-class strength vis-à-vis welfare state development? The second is, What is it, precisely, in the operational logic of these institutions that makes them important in explaining working-class organizational strength? The answer is not given in the literature. In explaining the differences between the Scandinavian labor movements, Esping-Andersen's choice is social policy in general and housing policy in particular. Housing is, of course, important, since it can be implemented in a way that might increase or decrease conflicts between owners and renters and thus implies divisions inside the working class; but it is hard to see (and Esping-Andersen does not show) how this affects the organizational strength of the working class. Of course, no political party ought to launch policies that divide its electorate, but if this is all there is to it, then Esping-Andersen's argument is rather trivial. However, he also points to the importance of the specific modeling of policies:

> The ultimate instrument of social democratic class formation . . . is state policy. . . . It is of paramount importance for solidarity that entitlements and services be universal, generous, and attractive. . . . Social democratic class formation depends on the the eradication of differentiated entitlements, means tested and targeted benefits, individualistic insurance schemes and self-help principles. (Esping-Andersen 1985, 33)

At first glance, it seems compelling that the more universalistic and generous and the less means tested that social policies are, the more workers will support them. But it is not clear exactly how and why such a modeling of policies causes workers to join unions. Moreover, as discussed below, Esping-Andersen is wrong on two important points. First, for special reasons the institutional forms of government labor market policies cannot always evade the problems of means tests. Second, it is definitely not a hindrance for the growth of working-class organizational strength if such institutions are created on self-help principles.

Weir and Skocpol (1985, 135ff) put forward government capacity and legitimacy in general, pointing out that a state built on patronage discourages the growth of working-class organizational strength. However, it is not obvious what precisely it is about patronage that causes working-class organizational weakness. Why patronage state institutions could not be used by the working class to strengthen their organizational power is not explained. Of course, it is no use putting demands upon a government that you consider unable to implement them. On the other hand, using concurrence for a specific social policy can become a demand for total control over the implementation process.

Przeworski, who was among the first to point out the dialectical nature of the relation between class formation and political institutions, is also silent on this matter (1977, 1985a, 47–97). While emphasizing the importance of seeing political struggles as struggles about class formation as well as struggles between organized classes, he gives no clues as to how we might differentiate struggles over issues from struggles over class formation. The basic question of how government institutions and policies affect workers' preferences to engage in collective struggle is not answered. No one can disagree that "the theoretical function of class analysis is . . . to identify the objective conditions and the objective consequences of concrete struggles" (Przeworski 1985a, 81). But as with Esping-Andersen, Korpi, and Weir and Skocpol, no causal link between the institutional forms of state policy and workers' inclination to join in collective action is presented. In other words, these explanations lack a firm microrational foundation (Elster 1985).

Working-class organizational strength can be operationalized by measuring the degree of unionization (Kjellberg 1983; Wallerstein 1989). The more wage earners that organize in collective bargaining, the stronger will be the organizational force of the working class. Thus working-class strength will be most affected by government labor market policies and government institutions that affect the labor market. The reason for this seems obvious: union strength allows the working class to control the supply of labor (Offe and Wiesenthal 1980; Wallerstein 1989), and government labor market policies and institutions are thus the most important ways states can affect this control. In short, state intervention in the selling or buying of labor power, namely, intervention in the labor market, should be the primary state policy or institution to balance the organizational capabilities of workers in capitalist societies.[1]

Marxism and Institutional Analysis

In his discussion of power, Lukes (1977) argues that any social science that does not take both structure and agency into the core of their explanations does not deserve serious attention. Some variants of Marxism can rightfully be criticized for not meeting Lukes's demands. The structuralist moment has been overemphasized, leading to teleological reasoning. In some mysterious way, the (capitalist) system meets its needs through the (welfare) state, which, without any deliberating human agents, explains the functions of the welfare state. Not only is such an interpretation of Marxism unable to explain why rather similar capitalist modes of production need different kinds of welfare states, but it can be thoroughly critized on methodological grounds (Elster 1982; Giddens 1981; Mouzelis 1984). In addition to methodological criticism, there is also a question of the explanatory range of functional Marxism in explaining middle-range social change. A technological determinist interpretation of Marxism (Cohen 1978) shows how functional Marxism might explain a change from one mode of production to another. But the problem remains of explaining social change within one and the same mode of production, namely, why some capitalist systems have more powerful working-class organizations than others—and thus more developed social policies. There is no reason to believe that this is determined by the level of technological development.

Other kinds of Marxist analysis can rightfully be labeled voluntaristic; they emphasize the will of the class, or even single class agents, at the expense of the importance of social and political structures. However, the problem of agency structure is not limited to Marxist analysis but pervades all kinds of social theory. In fact, it can be argued that Marxism is a better fit than any other social theory for the rationality of agents and the institutional constraints under which rationality occurs. Thus, I agree with Mouzelis:

> If one considers Marx's work as a whole as well as the mainstream Marxist tradition, it does provide the conceptual means for looking at societies both in terms of actors' collective strategies *and* in terms of institutional systems and their reproductive requirements. This is precisely why historians and social scientists influenced by Marx's work have produced more interesting and convincing accounts of long-term historical developments than those influenced by Parsonian functionalism and other brands of non-Marxist social theory. (1988, 167)

Another and more profound problem with Marxist theory is its reductionist tendency, namely, that the economic level somehow determines political and ideological behavior. Of course, this leaves little room for a Marxist-based analysis of political institutions, their creation. and importance. But it has to be remembered that the main independent variable in the question of political power within any mode of production in Marxist theory was not the notion of forces of production but that of *relations of production* (Callinicos 1989, chap. 2). Social power, the theory says, stems not from any technological development, per se, but from the power relations in the sphere of production. The concept of relations of production is not totally economic but political as well. Obviously, the actual power in the sphere of production is not determined solely by any technological or economic structures but also by political conditions. Examples are the legal regulations of property rights, the rights and protection of wage earners to organize, the regulation of working conditions, rules about selling and buying labor power, rules about collective bargaining—in short, state labor market policies.[2] All of these matters are, and always have been, decided politically by strategically acting humans in collective struggle. The main argument is that these decisions strongly affect the organizational strength of the working class. Thus, I consider the notion of *relations of production* to be a concept about political as well as economic institutions, providing a bridge between structure and agency in Marxist social science (ibid.). This is not a minor problem because, as Levine puts it (1984, 174), "class capacities for struggle—the organizational, ideological and material resources available to class agents—are not *identical* to class interest in the *outcome* of struggles."

The weakness of mainstream Marxist analysis comes from the fact that no concept similar to that of relations of production has been developed for the analysis of political institutions (Mouzelis 1988). Some Marxists would consider such a theory a logical contradiction; if one abandons the position that the economic dominates the political, one abandons Marxism (Poulantzas 1978, 185). The problem with this position is that it takes into the conceptualization of the economy-polity relationship the very question it sets out to solve. One could of course, as Wright argues (1985, 123f), see the development of the forces of production as only setting the broad limits within which political relations can vary, but that still leaves us with a lot of unexplained variation. If an agency/structure approach justifies politically decided economic relations, there can be no reason why the same condition could not affect political or administrative relations. Mouzelis suggests that, if it is possible to speak of *mode of production*, there should also be a *mode of domination* and, consequently, relations of production that would yield relations of domination or administration. There are no reasons that structural explanations should be limited to the economic (or material) world, while agency and strategic explanations are limited to the political-institutional level (Ashford 1978). On the contrary, it is obvious that both structural restrictions or capabilities and strategically acting humans exist at both levels. To quote Mouzelis once again:

> In what sense, for instance, are military or administrative technologies less material or less limiting than economic ones? Or in what sense are structural tendencies towards state expansion or the concentration of the "means of administration" at the top less constraining than tendencies towards the concentration of the means of production? Do not the former constrain, set limits on agents as much as the latter. Any attempt to restrict the idea of structural tendencies or constraints to the level of the economy is unacceptable. . . . In all institutional spheres, one can identify structural tendencies setting more or less strict limits on agents' strategies and projects. (1984, 115)

Contrary to concepts like *relative autonomy* launched by Poulantzas (1978) to give a limited role to political dimensions, Mouzelis argues that the political level should be conceptualized in its own right and that this could be done by a development of the Marxian theory about agency/structure. As I argue above, this should not be such a difficult step if relations of production are politically and economically differentiated. It is not the level of the productive forces that forces the serf to work at the manor, but the landlord's legal rights, upheld by political and military power, to the serf's labor power. These legal rights were not given by the feudal mode of production once and for all. Instead, they varied greatly as a result of a constant political struggle between the social classes.

Political institutions are here defined as "*formal* arrangements for aggregating individuals and regulating their behavior through the use of *explicit* rules and decision processes enforced by an actor or actors *formally recognized* as possessing such power" (Levi 1988, 6). The advantage of such a definition is that it singles out political institutions from other kinds of institutions and that it clarifies the line between political institutions and social norms (Elster 1989). Thus, political institutions are deliberately created by political actors for a specific purpose (or purposes), even though their effects might be very different from those intended by their creators (March and Olsen 1984). As Levi states (1988, 2): "Individuals create institutions, which then constrain the subsequent choices of the same individuals or future generations."

It must be added that, while political institutions are deliberately created, they might be the result of unanimous decisions as well as the result of struggles and compromises between opposing agents (March and Olsen 1984). Furthermore, institutions are usually seen as constraining agents (Grafstein 1988). There is, however, no reason why institutions should not also be seen as enabling agents (Giddens 1981). As Knight puts it: "Self-interested actors will prefer institutional rules that constrain the actions of others with whom they interact. That is, they will want to structure the choices of others in such a way as to produce social outcomes which give them distributional advantage" (1988, 25). Furthermore, as Knight and also Shepsle (1987) show, there is no reason to view institutions solely as the result of the collective improvements of any general social welfare. Knight and others successfully criticize public choice theorists for doing so and for failing to "capture the conflicts that underlie the establishment of most social institutions" (Knight 1988, 1). If, as I believe, political institutions can be deliberately created, then Elster is mistaken in stating that the only social structures of any causal importance are those resulting from the *unintentional* consequences of individuals' strategic interactions (Elster 1982; cf. Callinicos 1989, 66).

As argued above, it seems that both the state and the class models recognize the importance of institutions in explaining the social policy relationship found in working-class strength. The problem is that there is, to my knowledge, no acceptable analysis of how this relation actually works. There is no study that tells us what kind of politically decided institutional arrangements makes it easier or more rational for wage earners to join in a collective struggle. It is necessary to be very precise in these matters, which means opening up the institutional black boxes to see what kind of nuts and cogs they are built with and what difference it makes. Or, as Grafstein (1988, 578) argues, "the real puzzles concerning institutions . . . are the question of detail, history, mechanism, significance and structural alternatives."

Workers' Organization and Political Institutions

Labor power is a special good. It cannot be stored and, if it is not used continuously, it is wasted. In more concrete words, unemployed time, for wage earners and society, can never be recovered. In a society where labor is treated as a commodity, the basic interest of workers is, first, to be able to continuously sell their commodity at a reasonable price and, second, to be able to exist in times when the demand for their labor vanishes (Rothstein 1987).

Why do workers join unions? According to Olson (1965), if workers act rationally, they should not join because the benefits that come from unions is a collective good. Rational workers should then prefer to become free riders, that is, to get the benefits from the collective organization of bargaining without contributing to the cost of the organization. The fact that workers historically have joined unions, sometimes on a rather large scale, is explained by Olson: some unions are able to create selective incentives that lie outside the main purpose of collective bargaining, incentives that are individual instead of collective. These incentives can be both positive and negative, both material and normative. If Olson's theory is correct, then we need to know why some unions are more successful than others in creating the necessary selective incentives. If it is in their rational interest to create such incentives, and if rational action is all that is needed to explain political behavior, then why are some unions more rational than others?

One objection to Olson's theory is that, as the social category *labor* is inseparable from its individual bearer, unions, unlike employers' organizations, must take the individual well-being of their members into account. Thus, when there is no more demand for an individual worker's labor power, unions cannot simply abandon them (which is what an employers organization would do with its members). The reason for this is that, as stated above, the main power resource unions have is their control over the supply of labor. If individual wage earners are abandoned when the demand for their labor force declines, workers will start underbidding the union-set price for work. This means that employers will be able to buy labor power at a price below that agreed upon by unions. There is no worse threat to union strength and working-class mobilization than this threat to the price of labor (Åmark 1986, Unga 1976). It is therefore of prime importance for unions to influence governments' labor market policies. If, for example, unemployment insurance is nonexistent, or if levels of insurance are too low, or if only a small part of the work force is covered by such a public scheme, then there will be a constant pressure against union control over the supply of labor. Thus, the power over the labor market, which government labor market policy always affects, is crucial to the organizational strength of unions. For this reason, unemployment insurance is more important than other social policies, such as sickness, disability, and old-age insurance, because workers in the latter circumstances do not usually have the possibility to start underbidding wages.

Let us go back to the question, Why do workers join unions? Or why are some unions more able than others to recruit and keep members? By criticizing neocorporatist theorists who argue that in some countries interest organizations, such as unions, have become compulsory organizations, Korpi underlines that in Western countries they, in fact, are not compulsory because it is rational for workers to join unions in order to further their own interests (Korpi 1983, 7–25). My argument is that what seems to be rational can be greatly affected by political institutions and policies.[3] Political institutions and policies are thus not only "intervening variables between, on the one hand, the distribution of power resources in society and, on the other hand, the pattern of outcome of distributive conflicts" (Korpi 1983, 21). Instead, they genuinely and directly affect the distribution of power resources in society.

The 1930s were a watershed for many changes in the political history of modern Sweden. As it was the first decade of unbroken Social Democratic (Socialdemokratiska Arbetarpartiet) political hegemony, there are many different interpretations of what happened. The following are some important details. The 1920s was a decade of political turbulence, massive industrial conflicts, and constantly shifting minority governments. In 1930, when in opposition, the Social Democrats launched a new program to deal with the economic crisis and the dramatic rise of unemployment. Their program to create jobs by increased government investment financed by public loans helped them with a large electoral victory in 1932. They were still, however, only able to form a minority government, but they managed, in 1933, to strike a totally unexpected deal with the Agrarian party: the Social Democrats would protect the farmers against the falling prices in the world market if the Agrarian party would support the Social Democratic party's Keynesian economic and unemployment policy. The agreement resulted in a stabilization of the political system and gave the Social Democrats the political force necessary to relieve the economic crisis and to establish political hegemony for the following five decades (Lewin 1988; Heclo and Madsen 1987; Weir and Skocpol 1985; Korpi 1983).

However, this well-known story can be differently interpreted. The following section is an analysis of how the Swedish Social Democrats, during the 1930s, created public labor market institutions and launched a labor market policy that has made it easier for unions to recruit and keep members, thus increasing the strength of the party's organizational base.

A First Step: Public Unemployment Insurance

From its very early days, the Swedish union movement, as did many other national union movements, demanded the establishment of a public unemployment insurance scheme. It was, however, not until 1934 that the Social Democrats managed to get a parliamentary majority in favor of such a scheme. This was rather late compared to other capitalist countries, such as Great Britain (1909), Germany (1927), Denmark (1907), and Norway (1906). The reason it took so long, despite the relative strength of the Swedish labor movement at the time, was not lack of government administrative capacity but the firm opposition from the Conservative and Agrarian parties to such a scheme. No less than four government commissions published lengthy studies and detailed proposals about the question before 1934, but for political reasons no final decision was taken (Heclo 1974; Edebalk 1975; Unga 1976).

Two institutional forms of public unemployment insurance were considered in the Swedish debate. One was a compulsory scheme with state administration and the other a voluntary scheme where the state would give economic support to the unemployment funds set up and administered by the unions—the Ghent system. The main reason behind the opposition from the bourgeois parties was that, while there was some support for a public unemployment insurance scheme, they considered a compulsory system too expensive. They could not accept the Ghent system because it would strengthen the unions and, as they saw it, the Social Democratic party, too (Heclo 1974, 99–105).

In order to understand the opposition against the Ghent system from the bourgeois parties, it is necessary to understand the way unemployment insurance was to be administered. Labor is a peculiar good in that it is inseparable from its individual bearer. This means that, while unemployment is definitely a macrosocial phenomena, insurance against it must operate at the microlevel, that is, it must be provided individually. The basic problem in the implementation of unemployment insurance is deciding who is to be considered unemployed and thus entitled to support. People are not just out of work, they are out of some particular kind of job in some particular geographical area. This issue also arises over the question about what kind of work, at what price, and under what conditions the unemployed should be obliged to take in order not to lose their right to support. The unions' main interests are that unemployed workers will not be expected to take jobs where there are industrial disputes or where wages are below union levels. A union might also resist forcing workers into trades that reduce its own membership.

Seen from a Marxist perspective about institutional power, the question is, Who will be given the power to answer these questions? As all workers are individuals, there must be individual judgment in each case as to what is to be called *unemployment;* that is, what is to be considered a nonsuitable job that the worker could refrain from taking and still be entitled to the insurance. These questions cannot, by the very nature of the policy, be dealt with by applying general and precise rules but have to be decided in a discretionary manner in the implementation process. In other words, an unemployment insurance scheme cannot be implemented without an individual means test (Lester 1965). For a union, it is of vital importance to get control over these decisions, as they affect the union's control of the supply of labor. It is not enough for the union to influence the enactment of the general rules, because much of the real content of such a policy will be decided at the moment of implementation (Lipsky 1980). For the individual worker, it is of equal importance to know who will have the institutional power to decide these specific matters. The reason for this is that unemployed workers, especially skilled workers, do not want to be forced to take on jobs far below their qualifications or outside their trade in order not to be deprived of support (Lester 1965).

Another vital question is, of course, whether the scheme should support unemployed workers belonging to a union that is engaged in an industrial dispute. All in all, this means state support of unions engaged in industrial conflict. Prior to 1934, the conflict about the unemployment insurance in Sweden was precisely this. The unions and the Social Democrats did not want a system in which the state could undermine union control over the supply of labor—a scheme that could force unemployed workers to take jobs at workplaces with industrial disputes. Furthermore, they were—for reasons described below—against a system where state authorities might influence the kind of jobs that workers applying for assistance should accept or otherwise lose the right to support. In particular, they were eager to prevent a system where workers could be obliged to accept jobs at wages below the level reached by the unions in collective labor agreements (Heclo 1974, 97f). On the other hand, the bourgeois parties and the employers' federation would not accept a system that strengthened unions by helping them defend their wage level, expand industrial conflicts, and recruit and keep members (Unga 1976). From the perspective of the bourgeois parties, state contributions to union-controlled unemployment funds meant state support of union organizational strength. Thus, while the Ghent system was considered the only possible system from an administrative and financial point of view, before 1934 it could not be accepted for reasons of pure class power (Heclo 1974, 94–105).

Equally important was that, if the Ghent system were to be established, it would mean that the unions would get a very powerful means of recruiting and keeping members. If the state were to provide unemployment insurance only to workers who joined a union, more workers would join unions (Heclo 1974, 73–78). During the severe crisis of the Swedish union movement after the defeat in the 1909 general strike, unions that had established their own unemployment funds managed to keep more members than unions without such funds (Edebalk 1975). This was of course a major argument against the Ghent system (Heclo 1974, 73–78). The Right also feared that union-run unemployment funds would be merged with union strike funds (Unga 1976, 112).

When the international economic crisis struck the Swedish economy in the late 1920s, unions came under severe pressure. As there was no public unemployment insurance, the temptation grew for workers to underbid union agreements. Without effective unemployment insurance, wages might be depressed. In this situation, the National Confederation of Trade Unions in Sweden (the Landsorganisationen, or LO) asked the Social Democratic party to try to make a compromise with any of the bourgeois parties to establish unemployment insurance, no matter what system. Although the unions would benefit strongly from the Ghent system, they thought it would be impossible to get the bourgeois parties to accept it. For mainly tactical reasons, the Social Democrats declared that they would accept a compulsory system, but with unstable minority governments in the late 1920s, no compromise could be reached in parliament (Heclo 1974, 94ff; Unga 1976).

After its electoral victory in 1932, the Social Democratic government still needed support from at least one of the bourgeois parties in order to pass an unemployment insurance law. The only party with whom they had any chance of making a deal on this issue was one of the two Liberal parties. This party, however, hesitated to accept any decision that strengthened the union movement, but, on the other hand, they did not want a compulsory state-controlled system because it would be too expensive and administratively complicated (Unga 1976, 98–120).

However, after failing to establish unemployment insurance in 1933, the Social Democratic minister of social affairs (Gustav Möller) struck a deal in 1934 with the Liberal party. They accepted the Ghent system with four important additions. The first was that the unions had to have their unemployment funds licensed by the state. This meant that the National Board for Social Affairs would be given the right to control the management of the unemployment funds and that the funds had to be distributed under rather tight rules. Second, the Social Democrats had to accept that nonunion workers would also be entitled to receive these funds. Third, the level of insurance was very low, and the general rules of entitlement were restrictive. Fourth, there would be no financial contributions to the scheme from employers (Edebalk 1975; Heclo 1974, 102–05). On the other hand, the implementation of the public unemployment insurance scheme was to be managed by the unions; union officials were given the power to decide what kind of work an unemployed person would be obliged to take so as not to lose the allowance; and no one would be forced to take jobs at workplaces affected by legitimate industrial disputes. Last, the Social Democratic party managed (in practice, although not in print) to provide that insured workers would not have to accept jobs at wages below the level set by unions in collective agreements (Erici and Roth 1981; Heclo 1974, 103f).

In sum, the Social Democrats greatly compromised the scale of unemployment insurance in order to institutionalize the Ghent system. When defending concessions to the Liberals, the minister of social affairs (Gustav Möller) declared that, although the scheme was not very impressive or effective, the main thing was to implant the principles, because the substance could be improved later (Parliamentary Records First Chamber 1933-47, 47f). In other words, he traded substance in policy for institutional principles. It must be added that there was intense opposition from the two communist parties, as they strongly preferred a compulsory state-administered system and the principle of universal entitlements (Edebalk 1975).

Because of the restrictions built into the scheme, few unions actually joined the system during the 1930s. As a system for helping the masses of unemployed workers during the depression, it was almost a complete failure. Of government spending on unemployment policies during 1935–1939, only 3.3 percent was spent on the insurance system (Rothstein 1982, 28). The Social Democratic strategy against unemployment was, instead, a program of massive job creation. Nevertheless, the main principles of the Ghent system were established at a substantial cost to the Social Democratic party and the union movement.

The architect behind this strategy was the Social Democratic minister of social affairs, Möller, who was convinced as early as 1926 that the Ghent system would strengthen the working class (Möller 1926). He argued that only those workers who had shown a positive interest in their well-being should be entitled to unemployment insurance. Even in public, he did not deny that this would mean that the public unemployment insurance scheme would be rather "union friendly," but according to Möller, there was nothing wrong in principle if the government supported only those workers who had taken an interest in their own and their family's well-being during hard times (Möller 1926; Unga 1976, 112). In a meeting in 1930 between the Social Democratic leadership and the central board of the trade union movement, Möller persuaded the latter that, although beset by difficulties caused by the depression, the labor movement should prefer a Ghent system to a compulsory one because it "would force workers into the unions" (quoted in Unga 1976, 118, trans. by author). In the decisive parliamentary debate in 1934 he declared:

> The voluntary system has some advantages compared to the compulsory. . . . The compulsory system works in such a way that the individual, in order to get the insurance against unemployment, does not need to bother at all about his insurance. He is by law forced into the group covered by the insurance. The voluntary system is only functional if the workers, that are threatened by unemployment, by themselves show such an interest for the insurance against this risk, that they will take the initiative to create or to join an unemployment insurance fund. (Parliamentary Records First Chamber 1934-37, 12, trans. by author)

Möller's argument about collective behavior is, of course, consistent with Olson's statement (1965, 2) that "unless there is coercion or some other special device to make individuals act in their common interest, rational self-interested individuals will not act to achieve their common group interest." It should be mentioned that Möller was not only minister of social affairs but also Social Democratic party secretary from 1916 to 1940, that is, second in rank in the party hierarchy and responsible for the party organization. As such he did not, of course, think much of workers choosing to be free riders (Rothstein 1985b).

Second Step: The Relief Works Scheme

Although public unemployment insurance was introduced rather late in Sweden, the unemployed were not left without help prior to 1934. What had been established in Sweden before then was a rather unique unemployment policy that relied on public relief works. Cash benefits were also given, not as an insurance-based right, but on a (rather harsh) means test basis. During the economic crises of the 1920s, it was generally believed that unemployment was caused by too high wages; that is, unions had been able to raise wages to unnaturally high levels (Unga 1976, chap. 10). Thus, if things were not to get worse, it was necessary for the government to pay wages for their relief works well under the union agreements.

Any government unemployment policy will, by its very nature, affect the power balance between organized labor and capital. The bourgeois parties argued that state interventions in the labor market should be absolutely neutral concerning industrial conflicts. This meant that if there was a conflict between a union and an employer (or employers' federation), the state should not support any workers, neither those actually involved in the conflict nor other unemployed workers in that trade, as this would increase the strength of the unions and thereby prolong the industrial conflict. In the Swedish case, this meant that the government agency responsible for the unemployment policy (the Unemployment Commission) could stop allowances to workers and fire workers from relief jobs if they did not accept jobs at firms where there was a conflict. For the unions, this was seen as strikebreaking arranged by the government. (Rothstein 1985a; Therborn 1985b).

Furthermore, during the late 1920s, the unions experienced problems because the state's unemployment policy undermined their local bargaining power. What happened was that local governments and other employers simply fired their whole blue-collar work force because it was possible to get their projects done as state-financed relief work projects with cheap labor. Moreover, in order to increase the downward pressure on wages, the Unemployment Commission, backed by the bourgeois majority in parliament, decided to give assistance to only about half of the unemployed. The rest had to seek assistance from the stigmatizing poor-relief scheme or start underbidding union tariffs (Unga 1976; Rothstein 1985a). Thus, prior to 1933, unemployment policy was implemented by the state to threaten the power of the labor movement in several ways. It therefore became vitally important for the labor movement to change this policy. As Unga shows (1976), these institutional circumstances, and not any new insights in economic theory, made the Social Democratic party change its labor market policy in the 1930s.

Together with a public unemployment insurance scheme, terminating the activities of the Unemployment Commission was the major union demand of the Social Democrats in the late 1920s. It must be added that, together with the threat to union organization, the very harsh conditions at the commission's labor camps made the commission generally detested by the organized working class. It is not an exaggeration to state that the commission was seen as an incarnation of the bourgeois character of the capitalist state by the working class in Sweden (Rothstein 1985a, 1985b; Therborn 1985b). Consequently, from 1922 to 1933, the commission and its policy was one of the most debated political questions in Sweden. In 1923 and again in 1926, Social Democratic minority cabinets chose to resign because they could not get a parliamentary majority to change the commission's policy forcing workers to act as strikebreakers. One of the main electoral promises from the Social Democrats in 1932 was to abolish the Unemployment Commission and to replace it with a system of ordinary government jobs at market wages—wages accepted by the unions in labor agreements (Unga 1976).

What happened in 1933, in the famous cow deal between the Agrarian party and the Social Democratic party, was that the Social Democrats were able, at substantial cost, to end the threat that the state's unemployment policy until then had posed against union organizational power. The state (the Unemployment Commission) would no longer systematically be allowed to underbid the unions in selling labor, it would no longer be able to force workers to act as strikebreakers, and it would no longer be able to deprive workers of unemployment support. Besides these changes, there was a large increase in the total spent on relief jobs. While the Social Democratic party could not get support from the Agrarian party for terminating the Unemployment Commission, they managed to withhold the major part of the money spent on public works from the commission. This money was instead directly controlled by the Ministry of Social Affairs to start a new relief work program outside the control of the commission. This difference between the two relief work policies increased after 1933 to favor the part controlled by the Ministry of Social Affairs. Finally, in 1939, the Unemployment Commission was closed down. This was "smashing the bourgeois state" in a way typical of the Swedish Social Democrats (Rothstein 1985b, 1986).

Interpretations of the 1930s

The 1930s is a watershed in the modern political history of Sweden, but there are, of course, different interpretations of what took place. The one given here is that Social Democrats, by accepting large costs in substantive gains, managed to change the institutional form of state intervention on the labor market.[4] Before the long-term consequences of these changes can be discussed, some other interpretations of the importance of the 1930s should be noted. One of the main ones is that the new policy launched in 1933 is the result not of a need to change institutional power but of new theoretical insight about government management of the economy; that is, the start of Keynesian economic policy in Sweden (Lewin 1988, 132–50; Heclo 1974; Weir and Skocpol 1985). The problem with this interpretation, besides its somewhat idealistic conception of what causes political change, is that it does not fit the actual economic operations of the state during the 1930s. First, the 1920s was a decade with more underbalanced state budgets than the 1930s. The economic effects, in Keynesian terms, were close to nil (Bergström 1969, 49; Therborn 1985b). Second, leading Social Democrats, among them the minister of social affairs, either had no understanding of Keynesian economic reasoning or did not believe in it and did not implement it during this period (Unga 1976, 157–61). The decision to pay market wages for relief jobs was not seen as a way of increasing purchasing power, because workers on relief jobs had to shorten their daily working time in order to save the government money. But by making employers pay the same per hour wage as for ordinary workers, union control of the price of labor was not threatened (ibid., chap. 10).

Another interpretation, launched by Korpi, is that the 1930s should be understood as the decade of historical compromise between capital and labor (Korpi 1983). While this is true from 1938 on, this interpretation misses the importance of earlier institutional changes. There was more than a general compromise between labor and capital: capital did not accept the unemployment insurance, the market wage level at relief works, or the changed rules for the Unemployment Commission (Therborn 1985b). Furthermore, Korpi does not show how the compromise affected the readiness of workers to join in collective action; that is, how it strengthened the organizational power of the Swedish working class. One possible interpretation is that the general compromise of 1938 between the Landsorganisationen and the Employers' Federation could also have made workers leave unions if they saw the compromise as a betrayal of genuine working-class interests.

A third interpretation, made by Therborn (1985b), argues that the Social Democratic success in the 1930s should be interpreted as a combination of tactical skill in the parliamentary arena and fortunate circumstances in the economy. The Social Democrats could float on the favorable change in the world market after 1933 and could be seen as rescuing the country from the recession. Together with the Agrarian party, the Social Democrats entered on an era that Therborn calls "popularly organized capitalism." It was not the content of the government's unemployment policy that ended the crisis but rather the more favorable position for Swedish industry in the world market due mainly to improved exchange rates. However, while there were no large economic effects of the new labor market policy, their institutional effects cannot be excluded. After all, the positive change in the world economy affected other countries, too. The substantive unimportance and the restrictive conditions of the unemployment insurance is underlined in Therborn's analysis, but no comment is made on the institutional principles and effects. The successful taming and, later, closure and replacement of the Unemployment Commission are also not mentioned.

Compared to these three interpretations, mine is definitely closer to reality. Concepts such as *Keynesianism, historical compromise,* and *popularly organized capitalism* are handy but imprecise. The advantage of an analysis of changes in institutional rules and public policies is that it is precise because the changes can be exactly identified. In this case, they are defined as a change in the power relations of government administration, that is, who wields power when the government intervenes in the labor market.

The Political Effects of Institutional Change

The result of the Social Democratic takeover in 1933 was thus twofold: the establishment of a union-administered unemployment scheme and the weakening and eventual closure of the Unemployment Commission. What have been the long-term effects of these institutional changes? Mainly for the wrong reasons, Weir and Skocpol (1985, 113) are right to state that "depression-era public policies in Sweden did greatly enhance the organizational power and solidarity of labor, thus increasing the strength of unions and the Social Democratic party." But it was not any general Keynesian policy that enhanced the organizational power of the Swedish working class, since no such policy was ever implemented, but it was the institutional changes as outlined above.

As for unemployment insurance, Möller clearly made the right prediction in 1934. Beginning in 1941, the substantive rules about levels of insurance and government contributions have been dramatically changed in favor of the unions. After 1941, unions started to join the scheme on a large scale (Erici and Roth 1981). However, there have been no major changes in the institutional principles. From equal sharing of costs, the Social Democrats have gradually changed the responsibility for costs between union members and the state so that today the government pays all the costs of the scheme (ibid., 1981; Statens Offentliga Utredningar 1987, 56). Since 1964, the bourgeois parties, together with the major business interests, have tried several times to change the institutional principles in order to diminish union power in the administration of the scheme.

It has been, and still is, a constant irritation to the Employers' Federation and the bourgeois parties that in practice there exists a direct connection between union membership and access to unemployment insurance.[5] But the Social Democrats and the unions have been able to counteract these attacks rather easily by pointing to the smooth functioning of the system and its rather low costs and lack of administrative trouble for the state. They especially emphasize the importance of union control over defining a "suitable job" and refuse to let institutional power slip out of union hands.[6] While it is formally possible to join the unemployment fund without also joining the union, in practice, unions make this difficult. In 1986, less than 1 percent of all insured employees joined only the unemployment fund (Statens Offentliga Utredningar 1987, 56). On the other hand, today all union members are obliged to join the unemployment fund (Statens Offentliga Utredningar 1978, 45).

What effect does such a system have upon the level of unionization? As shown in table 1, the five countries with the highest degree of unionization in the Western world have the same type of unemploy-

TABLE 1. Union Membership and Type of Unemployment Insurance System

Country	*Union Membership (%)*	*Insurance System*
Sweden	86	Ghent
Denmark	83	Ghent
Finland	80	Ghent
Iceland	74	Ghent
Belgium	74	Ghent[a]
Ireland	68	Compulsory
Norway	58	Compulsory
Austria	57	Compulsory
Australia	51	Compulsory
United Kingdom	43	Compulsory
Canada	38	Compulsory
Italy	36	Compulsory
Switzerland	34	Compulsory
West Germany	31	Compulsory
Netherlands	29	Compulsory
Japan	28	Compulsory
United States	18	Compulsory
France	15	Compulsory

Sources: Union membership—Kjellberg 1988 (figures for 1985 or 1986), except Australia, Iceland, and Ireland are taken from Wallerstein 1989 (figures for 1979, 1975, 1978, respectively). System of public unemployment insurance—Flora 1987 and Kjellberg 1983, except Australia (Castles 1985, chap. 3) and Iceland (Nordiska Rådets Utredningar 1984-10, 220).

Note: All industrialized countries have unions that have been free to organize since 1945, except Luxembourg, New Zealand, and Israel. New Zealand was excluded because it has, at least in some trades, compulsory union membership (Davidson 1989). Israel was excluded because its largest union is also the country's largest employer (Peretz 1979).

a. Belgium has a mixed system—compulsory insurance but union participation in the administration (Flora 1987, 776).

ment insurance system, the Ghent system, while there is no country with a union density below these five that has such an institution. It seems as if the hypothesis about the importance of union-controlled public unemployment insurance to the degree of unionization is supported. While the five countries with such a system have a mean of 79.5 percent, the others score only a mean of 38.9 percent.

When the insurance scheme was established in the mid-1930s, Sweden had a fairly high union density (Kjellberg 1983). It is thus not a uniquely strong working class that creates a Ghent system. Instead, the causal link is in the other direction. A moderately strong working class might establish such a system to enhance its future strength. It can, of course, be countered that a union that most members perceive as an insurance company is not a union based on any genuine solidarity and desire for collective action. While this probably has some truth in it, it must be added that solidarity can be affected by various outcomes of collective action. Furthermore, unions with a high membership have a better chance of promoting solidarity among their members and have the resources to make the results of solidarity known. As Elster puts it:

> Political institutions are not simply an aggregation mechanism from individual preferences to social choices. They also tend to shape and modify the individual preferences that are to be aggregated. To the extent that these effects are predictable, they should enter among the determinants of choice between alternative political systems. (1987, 84)

The ideology of collective action is, I believe, in constant need of material confirmation, and size is truly one of the most important features that makes this confirmation possible. Strength follows size follows strength in a continuously positive loop (Skocpol 1988; Olofsson 1979). If we refer again to Olson's theory, it must be added that unemployment insurance is not the only selective incentive governments can provide unions. In the Swedish case, in such laws as the 1936 Act on the Right of Association (especially its 1940 amendment), the 1974 Act on the Position of Trade Union Representatives at the Workplace, the 1974 Act on Employee Rights to Educational Leave, the 1976 Act on Joint Regulation of Working Life, and the 1977 Working Environment Act, the state has given the unions institutional power over the working conditions of the individual wage earners; so it is rather irrational, to say the least, for Swedish wage earners not to join the union (Neal and Victorin 1983; Neal 1981; Schmidt 1977). In other words, Social Democratic governments have made it worthwhile for wage earners to act collectively instead of becoming free riders. One recent such effort is the 1983 decision to free part of the union fee from taxation.[7]

If we turn to the other major institutional change, the closure of the Unemployment Commission, its long-term effects can be summarized as follows. In 1939, a totally new government labor market agency was established by Möller. The details of this process are complicated, but the main result was the erection of a government labor market agency under almost total control of the Landsorganisationen (National Organization of Trade Unions). Elsewhere, I characterize this process as the establishment of a Social Democratic cadre organization inside the Swedish state (Rothstein 1985a, 1986). Some important changes, besides the ones mentioned above, were to reject traditional Weberian-style bureaucracy based on uniform regulations and meritocratic recruitment for a much more flexible and politically oriented organization. Personnel were taken from the union movement, and union members held the majority of positions on the board. This organization, the National Labour Market Board, implemented the Swedish labor market policy (known as the Rehn-Meidner model and has thus been at the heart of postwar Social Democratic policy in Sweden (Barbash 1972; Ginsburg 1983; Heclo 1974, 136–40). It symbolizes the refusal to use unemployment as an economic means to curb inflation (Therborn 1985a). Uniquely well funded and powerful among Swedish government agencies, the board has implemented programs such as relief works, vocational training, regional industrial policy, employment exchanges, youth training, work schemes, mobility grants, and jobs for the disabled. In contrast to the Unemployment Commission, this new government agency has implemented government labor market policy in such a way as to strengthen the union movement (Rothstein 1985a, 1986).

However, one must also ask about the strength of the institutions discussed here. Between 1976 and 1982, Sweden was governed by five different combinations of three bourgeois parties; as would be expected, they tried to change both systems. However, in neither case did they succeed. Labor market policy had gained such legitimacy in Swedish political culture that it was politically impossible for the bourgeois governments to attack it openly. They started a halfhearted attack in 1981, but it was too late and too ill planned to meet with success (Statens Offentliga Utredningar 1985-7). A result of the firm institutionalization of the Labour Market Board was that the bourgeois parties (in control of the government from 1976 to 1982) fought unemployment more vigorously and successfully than many socialist or labor governments in the rest of Europe (Therborn 1985a). The reason seems to be that the institutional means for combating unemployment were well established, which implied that lowering inflation by means of unemployment was not seen as legitimate by the Swedish electorate; it was thus politically impossible for the bourgeois governments to deny the agency resources when unemployment rose.

Concerning the unemployment insurance scheme, the bourgeois parties actually initiated a commission that produced a proposal for a replacement of the Ghent system with a compulsory scheme (Statens Offentliga Utredningar 1978-45). The bourgeois government did not, however, present it to parliament. The probable reason was that union representatives in the commission were able to insist that the unions would retain institutional power over the important questions of individual implementation. One reason behind this was that the uniquely strong white-collar unions in Sweden, whose members form the electoral base of the bourgeois parties, strongly opposed any suggestion that would reduce their influence over the unemployment insurance scheme. In face of this opposition, and because of the greater costs of a compulsory system, the government gave in (Statens Offentliga Utredningar 1978-45; Parliamentary Records Labor Market Committee 1984–85, no. 11). Thus, institutions such as those discussed here can be characterized as being, to a large extent, self-reinforcing. The logic of their operations tends to strengthen those very forces that they rely on for their continued reproduction.

Of course, this is not a final test of the difficulty of changing political institutions, but it illustrates their rather persistent character and how positive loops between them and social forces might function. What they do, by and large, is to put actors in a different sort of game than they otherwise would have played and give them rational reasons to act in specific ways. Or, in Przeworski's words, the analysis of institutional creation is the answer to "how individuals under given conditions produce new conditions" (1985b, 401).

Conclusions

Transforming the Marxist analysis of power relations in the sphere of production to the sphere of administration lays bare the significance of a class-oriented analysis of political institutions. The analysis of institutional forms is a way of avoiding both structural determinist and voluntaristic traps in social science. Class-based power resources are not simply there to be exploited by political agents. On the contrary, political agents are in some cases able, by forming political institutions, to enhance the class-based power on which they build political power. In this case, however, the primary class organization, the trade union movement, did not fully realize the importance of creating new institutions. When it came to a final showdown, they traded short-term interest for long-term institutional power. For several years, from 1934 to 1941, very few of them realized the importance of joining and thus strengthening the Ghent system in order to secure long-term working-class organizational strength. Instead, it was the political wing of the Swedish labor movement, the Social Democratic party, that was the important agent. In fact, in this case, it is possible to point out the specific actor: the Social Democratic minister of social affairs. Whether he should be considered a state manager or a class agent could be discussed at length; I would suggest he was a uniquely successful combination of the two—here, as in other matters, a true designer of social structures (Rothstein 1985b).[8]

NOTES

1. The first demand from the British workers who created the First International, or more precisely the immediate reason behind the call for an International Workers Association, was to stop the import of cheap foreign labor (Collins and Abramsky 1965). See also the statement from Marx about the origins of trade unions (quoted in Elster 1985, 369).

2. See Callinicos (1989, 42f) and Elster (1985, 246, 271f) for a similar argument. In fact, Marx emphasizes this issue on several occasions, see, e.g., his comment on the importance of the legal regulation concerning the ten-hour working day in *Wages, Price and Profit* (Marx 1962).

3. Korpi's argument here is a bit strange. Workers can of course be forced by the government to join government-controlled unions. In such cases, we have corporatism in its original fascist sense. But governments can, while upholding a facade of voluntarism, make use of economic or other selective incentives to such an extent that membership is in fact compulsory. Korpi seems to forget an analogue argument that, under capitalism, it is not the law but economic pressure that forces some individuals to become wage earners. The argument presented here is simply that governments can create such economic circumstances that union membership, while formally voluntary, in fact becomes compulsory by the economic realities presented to the individual.

4. It should be mentioned that, in addition to the two institutional innovations in the labor market discussed above, there were two more of some importance. In 1935, the Social Democrats managed, by tactical skill, to prevent the passage of an antiunion labor law concerning the rights of third parties in labor disputes, despite a de facto parliamentary majority in favor of such legislation (Heclo 1974). One year later, the Social Democrats managed to put through a bill concerning the right of association, which protected union rights and the rights of workers to join unions but which left out the individual worker's protection against compulsion to join unions. Amendments to the law in 1940 protected union rights even more (Schmidt 1977).

5. See Statens Offentliga Utredningar 1963-40; Parliamentary Records Second Chamber 1964-28, 101; Government Bill 1964-115, 18; Statens Offentliga Utredningar 1971-42, 58f; Parliamentary Records 1973 motions 1825, 1827;

Government Bill 1973-56, 144, 1829; Parliamentary Records 1974 motion 133, 252; Statens Offentliga Utredningar 1978-45, 321–25; Parliamentary Records 1984–85 Labour Market Committee (Arbetsmarknadsutskottet) no. 11, 57, 1985–86 no. 11, 144. It should be added that from 1973, to deal with problems of youth unemployment, a special cash labor market support was introduced in Sweden. The reason was that unemployment started to strike young people and others who had not been able to establish themselves in the labor market and who were thus not entitled to join the union-controlled public unemployment insurance scheme. The new scheme, which was to be managed by public labor market authorities, was not constructed as an insurance scheme, and the support that people could get from it was significantly lower (less than half) compared to the union-controlled scheme. See Government Bill 1973-56; Erici and Roth 1981, 127f.

6. See Erici and Roth 1981, 120–22; Statens Offentliga Utredningar 1979-94, 289f; 1978-45, 219–28; Fackföreningsrörelsen 1973-11, 6; Parliamentary Records, Domestic Affairs Committee (inrikesutskottet) 1974-3, 17f.; Government Bill 1973-56, 144–69; Statens Offentliga Utredningar 1971-42, 103; Landsorganisationen-todningen 1988-16.

7. This could be compared to the rule decided by the Constitutional Court in West Germany that no law must give a member of an organization privileges compared to other citizens (Streeck 1981), or to recent labor legislation in Great Britain, or to U.S. labor laws.

8. It must be noted that the most radical part of the labor movement, the left-wing Socialist party and the communists, strongly favored a state-managed compulsory scheme and that the latter, in parliament, voted against the establishment of the Ghent scheme (Parliamentary Records First Chamber 1933-47, 92f, 1934-37, 54).

SOURCES

Alber, J. 1984. Government Responses to the Challenge of Unemployment: The Development of Unemployment Insurance in Western Europe. In P. Flora and A. J. Heidenheimer, eds., *The Development of Welfare States in Europe and America.* New Brunswick: Transaction Books.

Åmark, K. 1986. *Facklig makt och fackligt medlemskap.* Lund: Arkiv.

Amenta, E., and T. Skocpol. 1986. States and Social Policies. *Annual Review of Sociology* 12:131–57.

Ashford, D. E. 1978. The Structural Analysis of Policy; or Institutions Really Do Matter. In D. E. Ashford, ed., *Comparing Public Policies, New Concepts and Methods.* London: Sage.

———. 1986. *The Emergence of the Welfare State.* Oxford: Basil Blackwell.

Barbash, J. 1972. *Trade Unions and National Economic Policy.* Baltimore: Johns Hopkins Press.

Bergström, V. 1969. *Den ekonomiska politiken i Sverige och dess verkningar.* Stockholm: IVI.

Callinicos, A. 1989. *Making History. Agency, Structure and Change in Social Theory.* Oxford: Polity.
Castles, F. 1985. *The Working Class and Welfare.* Wellington: Allen and Unwin.
Cohen, G. 1978. *Karl Marx's Theory of History: A Defence.* Oxford: Oxford University Press.
Collins, H., and C. Abramsky. 1965. *Karl Marx and the British Labour Movement.* London: Macmillan.
Davidson, A. 1989. *Two Models of Welfare.* Stockholm: Almqvist and Wiksell.
Douglas, M. 1987. *How Institutions Think.* London: Routledge and Kegan Paul.
Eckstein, H. 1975. Case Study and Theory Development in Political Science. In F. I. Greenstein and N. W. Polsby, eds. *Handbook of Political Science.* Vol. 7. Reading: Addison-Wesley.
Edebalk, P. G. 1975. *Arbetslöshetsförsäkringsdebatten.* Ph.D. diss., University of Lund, Dept. of Economic History.
Elster, J. 1982. Marxism, Functionalism and Game Theory: The Case for Methodological Individualism. *Theory and Society* 11:453–82.
———. 1985. *Making Sense of Marx.* Cambridge: Cambridge University Press.
———. 1987. On the Possibility of Rational Politics. *Archives Européennes de Sociologie* 28:67–103.
———. 1989. *The Cement of Society.* Cambridge: Cambridge University Press.
Erici, B., and N. Roth. 1981. *Arbetslöshetsförsäkringen i Sverige 1935–1980.* Stockholm: Arbetslöshetskassornas samorganisation.
Esping-Andersen, G. 1985. *Politics Against Markets.* Princeton: Princeton University Press.
Esping-Andersen, G., and W. Korpi. 1984. Social Policy as Class Politics in Post-War Capitalism: Scandinavia, Austria and Germany. In J. H. Goldthorpe, ed., *Order and Conflict in Contemporary Capitalism.* Oxford: Oxford University Press.
Flora, P. ed., 1987. *Growth to Limits: The Western European Welfare States Since World War II.* Vol 4. Berlin: de Gruyter.
Giddens, A. 1981. *A Contemporary Critique of Historical Materialism.* London: Macmillan.
Ginsburg, H. 1983. *Full Employment and Public Policy: The United States and Sweden.* Lexington: Lexington Books.
Grafstein, R. 1988. The Problem of Institutional Constraint. *Journal of Politics* 50:577–99.
Heclo, H. 1974. *Modern Social Policies in Britain and Sweden.* New Haven: Yale University Press.
Heclo, H., and H. Madsen. 1987. *Policy and Politics in Sweden.* Philadelphia: Temple University Press.
Hollingsworth, J. R., and R. A. Hanneman. 1982. Working-Class Power and the Political Economy of Western Capitalist Societies. *Comparative Social Research* 5:61–80.
Kjellberg, A. 1983. *Facklig organisering i tolv länder.* Lund: Arkiv.
———. 1988. Sverige har fackligt världsrekord. *LO-tidningen* 9:15–16.
Knight, J. 1988. Strategic Conflict and Institutional Change. Presented at the

annual meeting of the American Political Science Association, Washington, D.C.

Korpi, W. 1983. *The Democratic Class Struggle*. London: Routledge and Kegan Paul.

———. 1985. Power Resource Approach vs. Action and Conflict: On Causal and Intentional Explanation of Power. *Sociological Theory* 3:31–45.

Lester, R. 1965. Unemployment Insurance. In *International Encyclopedia of the Social Science*. Vol. 16. London: Macmillan.

Levi, M. 1988. A Logic of Institutional Change. Presented at the annual meeting of the International Political Science Association, Washington, D.C.

Levine, A. 1984. *Arguing for Socialism*. London: Heinemann.

Lewin, L. 1988. *Ideology and Strategy: A Century of Swedish Politics*. Cambridge: Cambridge University Press.

Lipsky, M. 1980. *Street-level Bureaucracy. Dilemmas of the Individual in Public Services*. New York: Russel Sage.

Lukes, S. 1977. *Essays in Social Theory*. New York: Columbia University Press.

March, J., and J. P. Olsen. 1984. The New Institutionalism. Organizational Factors in Political Life. *American Political Science Review* 78:734–49.

Marx, K. 1962 (1865). *Wages, Price and Profit*. Moscow: Progress.

Mayhew, B. 1980. Structuralism vs Individualism. Pt. 1: Shadowboxing in the Dark. *Social Forces* 59:335–83.

Miller, T. 1988. Designing Social Structures. Presented at the annual meeting of the American Political Science Association, Washington, D.C.

Möller, G. 1926. Arbetslöshetsförsäkringen jämte andra sociala forsäkringer. Stockholm: Tiden.

Mouzelis, N. 1984. On the Crises of Marxist Theory. *British Journal of Sociology* 25:112–21.

———. 1988. Marxism or Post-Marxism. *New Left Review* 167:107–23.

Neal, A. C., ed. 1981. *Law and the Weaker Party*. Vol. 1. Oxfordshire: Professional Books.

Neal, A. C., and A. Victorin, eds. 1983. *Law and the Weaker Party*. Vol 3. Oxfordshire: Professional Books.

Noble, C. 1988. State or Class? Notes on Two Recent Views of the Welfare State. Presented at the annual meeting of the American Political Science Association, Washington, D.C.

Offe, C., and H. Wiesenthal. 1980. Two Logics of Collective Action. In M. Zeitlin, ed., *Political Power and Social Theory*. Vol. 1. Greenwich: JAI.

Olofsson, G. 1979. *Mellan klass och stat*. Lund: Arkiv.

Olson, M. 1965. *The Logic of Collective Action: Public Goods and the Theory of Groups*. Cambridge: Harvard University Press.

Peretz, D. 1979. *The Governments and Politics of Israel*. Boulder: Westview.

Poulantzas, N. 1978. *State, Power, Socialism*. London: New Left Books.

Przeworski, A. 1977. Proletariat into a Class: The Process of Class Formation from Karl Kautsky's *The Class Struggle* to Recent Controversies. *Politics and Society* 7:343–401.

———. 1985a. *Capitalism and Social Democracy*. Cambridge: Cambridge University Press.

———. 1985b. Marxism and Rational Choice. *Politics and Society* 14:379–410.

Rothstein, B. 1982. Från det svenska systemet till den svenska modellen. *Arkiv för studier i arbetarrörelsens historia* 23-24:3–31.

———. 1985a. The Success of the Swedish Labour Market Policy: The Organizational Connection to Policy. *European Journal of Political Research* 13:153–65.

———. 1985b. Managing the Welfare State: Lessons from Gustav Möller. *Scandinavian Political Studies* 13:151–70.

———. 1986. *Den socialdemokratiska staten. Reformer och förvaltning inom svensk arbetsmarknads-och skolpolitik*. Lund: Arkiv.

———. 1987. Corporatism and Reformism: The Social Democratic Institutionalization of Class Conflict. *Acta Sociologica* 30:295–311.

Schmidt, F. 1977. *Law and Industrial Relations in Sweden*. Stockholm: Almqvist and Wiksell.

Shalev, M. 1983a. Class Politics and the Western Welfare State. In S. E. Spiro, and E. Yuchtman-Yaar, eds. *Evaluating the Welfare State*. New York: Academic.

———. 1983b. The Social Democratic Model and Beyond: Two Generations of Comparative Research on the Welfare State. *Comparative Social Research* 6:315–52.

Shepsle, K. A. 1987. Institutional Equilibrium and Equilibrium Institutions. In H. F. Weisberg, ed., *Political Science: The Science of Politics*. New York: Agathon.

Skocpol, T. 1985. Bringing the State Back In. In P. Evans et al., eds., *Bringing the State Back In*. Cambridge: Cambridge University Press.

———. 1988. Comparing National Systems of Social Provision: A Polity Centered Approach. Presented at the annual meeting of the International Political Science Association, Washington, D.C.

Streeck, W. 1981. *Gewerkschaftliche Organisationsprobleme in der sozialstaatlichen Demokratie*. Königstein: Athenäum.

Therborn, G. 1985a. *Why Some People Are More Unemployed than Others*. London: Verso.

———. 1985b. The Coming of Swedish Social Democracy. In *Annali della Fondazione Giangiacomo Feltrinelli 1983–84*. Milan: Feltrinelli.

Unga, N. 1976. *Socialdemokratin och arbetslöshetsfrågan 1912–34*. Lund: Arkiv.

Wallerstein, M. 1989. Union Growth in Advanced Industrial Democracies. *American Political Science Review* 83:481–502.

Weir, M., and T. Skocpol. 1985 State Structures and the Possibilities for "Keynesian" Responses to the Great Depression in Sweden, Britain, and the United States. In P. Evans et al., eds., *Bringing the State Back In*. Cambridge: Cambridge University Press.

Wright, E. O. 1985. *Classes*. London: Verso.

5

The Soft State: Making Policy in a Different Context

Hans Blomkvist

OUR UNDERSTANDING of the countries of Africa, Asia, and Latin America—first as "colonies," then as "underdeveloped countries," again as "developing countries," and now as the "Third World"—has to a large extent been informed by occidental experience. Travelers, journalists, diplomats, and social scientists brought their own deeply ingrained concepts, presumptions, hypotheses—*contextual statements*—when they tried to make head or tail of these foreign lands. Usually, social scientists and political observers—Marxists and liberals alike—have assumed a Western political model when analyzing the Third World. The problem is most accentuated in policy analyses relating to the Third World. The problem is discussed by Blomkvist (1989) in relation to housing policy, by van Cranenburgh (1989) in relation to agricultural policy, and by the experienced Norwegian economist Faaland (1989) in relation to economic policy and planning in general. It is as if most writers on the policy process in the Third World had never heard of corruption, nepotism, or patronage. These rosy stories are a far cry from the harsh and self-critical words—early in his career—of India's late Prime Minister Rajiv Gandhi:

> We [Congressmen] obey no discipline, no rule, follow no principle of public morality, display no sense of social awareness, show no concern for the public weal. Corruption is not only tolerated but even regarded as the hallmark of leadership. . . . [The Congress party has] brokers of power and influence, who dispense patronage to convert a mass movement into a feudal hierarchy. (Rajiv Gandhi at the Congress centenary celebrations in Bombay, December 1985, quoted in Crisis of Confidence. *India Today*, 15 January 1986)

Instead of such candor, we usually hear of classes, parties, parliaments, policies, and trade unions whose nominal resemblance to their equivalents in Western Europe conceals more than it reveals. If my argument below is correct, it will have a profound effect on political theory and our conception of Third World politics.

At heart, my argument is that politics in many Third World countries is different from the West because it has a different genesis, a different history. Implicit in this argument is that modernization, economic development, economic dependency, and the power of the contending classes play a less significant role than historical legacy in explaining politics. I also claim that the most pivotal difference is how the state apparatus works and operates. One historian argues that the south Indian experience shows that "the pre-colonial state left an inheritance of political structures and values which continued to evolve in the new [colonial] context. This had long-term effects . . . seen in the late twentieth century across a broad spectrum of social, economic, and political activities in south India" (Price 1989a, 153). The argument, then, is this: the institution we call the state is one of the most important factors in explaining political and economic differences between the industrialized and the developing countries, and this institution has to be explained historically. Such an explanation does not rely on notions that all states develop according to the same lawlike pattern; instead, history is a process produced by the intended and unintended consequences of the actions of rational, goal-oriented individuals. "Men make their own history," Karl Marx said. "But they do not make it just as they please; they do not make it under circumstances chosen by themselves." Among the significant restraining circumstances are historically evolved state structures.

Where, then, in the state is this contrast between East and West localized? The answer, it seems to me, has to do with the way we conceptualize the state in social science; that is, as territoriality, centralization, and monopoly of violence and sovereignty. "Our consideration of states is so strongly skewed by the European absolutist experience that it has trouble even handling Western states—mostly arising out of the Anglo-American experience—that diverge on a number of the attributes encompassed by the idea of stateness" (Rudolph 1987, 734f; cf. Dyson 1980). This is not to speak of precolonial state structures in Asia, for example, which embodies political values and principles of political organization "quite different from Western models and definitions" (Price 1989a, 152). My notion is that this crucial difference is captured by the concepts of hard and soft states. Clearly, it builds on Myrdal's well-known concept (further discussed in Blomkvist 1988, 300–10); but whereas he defined soft states as those that "require extraordinary little of their citizens" (Myrdal 1968, 895f), I see them as particularistic, arbitrary, or not law-abiding states. (More on the definition below.) This is only a beginning of a more truthful, and hence more relevant, conceptualization of state, politics, and the policy process in the so-called Third World.

Only recently have scholars attempted to formulate theories and concepts more suited to an Indian ontology—in other words, to formulate an Indian "ethnosociology" (see Marriott 1989 and the other articles in the same volume of *Contributions to Indian Sociology*). That Marxism, despite its radical moorings, is not untainted by Western preconceptions is amply clear from O'Leary's (1989) excellent and merciless onslaught—theoretically and empirically—on the Marxist idea of an "Asian mode of production." In the words of Rudolph:

> Hegel, Marx and Weber understood Asian social, economic and political systems as flawed or degraded performances in a historical race in which all competitors run toward the same finish line—whether the finish line is nation-state, bourgeois capitalism, or universal rationalization. . . . But for us [today] it has become apparent that there are multiple races and many finish lines. . . . It becomes absurd to ask why Asian religions did not lead to the spirit of capitalism as we impose quotas on Japanese imports. (1987, 732)

This chapter is based on a study of politics and housing policy in the state of Tamil Nadu in India (Blomkvist 1988). Out of modesty and consistency with what has just been said, I ought perhaps to refrain from making generalizations from India to other parts of the world. But the dilemma between modesty and empiricism on the one hand and pretentiousness and generalizable propositions on the other, is nicely put—and solved—by Price: "In the face of the slow production of case studies . . . I understand there are regional variations but find strong indications that the model I present . . . is suggestive of interpretations" (1989b, 562) for other regions or countries. Simply put, extensive reading of the literature gives one a strong impression that the soft state is a phenomenon in many Third World countries. Much-needed elaborations on the soft state concept will have to wait, I think, until more research is done along these lines.

The Precolonial Indian State

What, then, are the historical antecedents of the contemporary Indian state? What were the characteristics of the premodern Indian state? As the so-called Cambridge School in South Asian historical research has emphasized, there are strong continuities from the precolonial period, via the Raj, to contemporary India. The impact of the British Raj on modern India has sometimes been exaggerated: "Many scholars in our day have tended . . . to give too much credit to the British" (Frykenberg 1981, 47). "One hundred and eighty years of British rule in India was just one of these unfortunate interruptions in our long history," wrote Jawaharlal Nehru. Frykenberg, in a historical study of Madras, says of the country around present-day Madras that it "had never known anything which might fit historic Western conceptualizations of what is known as 'State' " (1981, 6f). In another article, Frykenberg contends:

> Normally, in the West, a concentration of political power into one control system has been distinguished from the administrative apparatus through which that power was exercised. This has been especially apparent in modern and more than nominally democratic and constitutional systems, wherein power components have been elaborately organized and equipped with corrective checks, functional channels, and legitimizing symbols to prevent breakdown or misgovernment. Such neat distinctions are more difficult to apply to political institutions which existed in premodern India. . . . Precise conceptual tools for describing either political processes or entities which, when observed closely manifest themselves in bewildering patterns (now feudal, then tribal, again imperial, now regal, or patrimonial, or communal, in seemingly endless permutation and variety) *has yet to be discovered.* (1968, 107, my emphasis)

Instead of the occidental unitary state organization, which governed by abstract rules and sought legitimacy in universal ideologies such as Christendom, the dynasties in India aggregated power by means of "a simple term and its synonyms: trust, good faith, confidence, credit—feelings and convictions of human relationship which were ratified in contracts, deed, titles, treaties" (Frykenberg 1977, 126). Referring to Stein's (1977) concept of the 'segmentary state,' Frykenberg argues that "a segmented society, with segmented world-views (whether perceived as cultures, religions, ideologies, or mythic symbols), manifested itself in segmented spatial networks, and in segmented systems of authority and power" (Frykenberg 1981, 47f).

This segmentary state is inherently unstable and vacillating. Indeed, Frykenberg also talks of an "anti-state" (1968, 122). The personal links between king and senior administrators, between senior administrators and subordinate officers, between subordinate officers and district officers, between district officers and village leaders, and between village leaders and villagers were as reliable as they were unpredictable. What happened to commands passed down through this structure was not easy to perceive. Nor, possibly, was it ever intended to be otherwise:

> It is clear that, just as district officers undermined central authority, they in turn were undermined by village leaders. . . . Level by level, superiors became prisoners to those below them and risked exposure and discipline from those above them. Power became caught and tangled in the webs of village, caste and family influence. The strength of Madras Presidency was tied to the earth by countless tiny threads and was made captive to Lilliputian systems of power. (ibid., 119)

So strong were the localizing forces that the very borders between different states in the subcontinent were indeterminate. The strong position of the locality and the village lord in the Indian empires affected the way these kingdoms were run. "Concepts of universality in India were far from universally held, much less understood, and if that, only vaguely" (Frykenberg 1977, 125).

The absence of a law-governed system of authority and power—which it might be called if, following Frykenberg, one wishes to avoid the term *state*—in the traditional (precolonial) Indian society is borne out by several scholars (cf. Baxi 1986; Bayly 1971; Basham 1963). Indian political scientist Kothari remarks the occidental historical preoccupation with "creating institutions that would make man himself subject to laws, and in general producing conditions of control and predictability at all levels" (1974, 25). And he continues:

> The concern all along is to create not just a viable but an ideal social and political order. The Oriental civilizations, on the contrary, went for a minimal view of social and political order. Perfection was to be sought for the individual (and that too for the inner man), not for society. Impressed by the perennial flow of time and the fact that a particular era or social form was inevitably transient, the Oriental thinkers saw only folly in man's search for a better and still better life in society. Such an approach, on the other hand, lent too much stress on continuity, produced a cynical tolerance of inequity and injustice in social relations, and on the whole underrated the role of power and of human consciousness in moulding man's future. (ibid., 26f)

"According to Hindu political theory, . . . the primary function of the state is to maintain the social order by upholding *dharma*" (Weiner 1984, 114). And each social group, each caste, has its own dharma. Hence, "according to ancient Indian political thought, subjects do not have equal rights and duties in relation to the state. . . . Hindu theory does not confer rights on the individual as distinct from the community.

Individuals are not equal before the law, but are entitled to rights or are punished as is appropriate to the community to which they belong" (ibid., 119, my emphasis). And dharma constitutes the only limit imposed on state power according to classical Indian political thought.

It is this "extreme particularism," as Bendix (1977, 391) put it, fostered by the Hindu religion and the caste system, which was the target of Kautalya's political advice outlined in his *Arthaśastra,* of which Weber (1982a, 124) says, "In contrast with this document Machiavelli's *Principe* is harmless." In this classical Indian document on statecraft, written around 300 B.C., Kautalya's purpose is not so much practical advice on administration but rather the realization of a bureaucratic order. "What is at stake," writes Heesterman (1971, 9), "is no less than the founding of a state transcending the limitations of the tribal clan monarchy or oligarchy." But Kautalya is held back by the tribal order, which wrecks his intentions. "He wants to achieve a universalistic bureaucratic state but he is forced to work within the context of a particularistic tribal system that effectively withholds the means needed to achieve the goal" (ibid., 21). Rather than destroy the old, particularistic system, "Kautalya prefers to cumulate the old and the new without facing a decision. . . . It is this combination that seems to govern India till the present day," Heesterman (21–22) concludes.

This continuity in the political tradition of the subcontinent is also underlined by Eisenstadt. In his 1985 Stein Rokkan lecture, Eisenstadt compares the political history of Europe and India. European history has two major characteristics that persist to the present. The first is the continuous competition between different groups, strata, and elites about their access to political centers. And this multicentrism we also find in Indian history. But after capturing the center, the elites in Europe—and this is the second important characteristic—built and developed institutions. A "distinctive centre did develop within the Hindu civilization," says Eisenstadt. But—contrary to Europe—"this centre was not organized as a homogeneous, unified setting. It rather consisted of a series of networks and organizational-ritual subcentres—pilgrimages, temples, sects, schools—spreading throughout the sub-continent, and often cutting across political boundaries" (1985, 237f). Both India and Europe have a history of fragmented political power (multicentrism), but whereas Europe developed a universalistic tradition—and hence a pluralist political system—India never did. As a result, it has a fragmented political system.

In similar fashion, Saberwal (1983, 1984, 1985, 1986) and Kaviraj (1984) discuss the influence of older political institutions on contemporary Indian politics. Within slightly different theoretical frameworks, both discuss political and societal "normative orders" in Indian history. "The Indian history stands in a remarkable contrast to the European experience," says Saberwal (1985, 203). Ancient Rome's idea of constructing legal codes was carried on by the Catholic church for a millenium, providing Europe's emerging nation-states with this particular social technology. Contrary to this European experience, in India "the ethic operative behind segmental confines has tended to be particular to the segment, not general or universal. . . . Because the idea of extensively applicable imperative normative orders, effective down to particular persons, is relatively alien to our historical process, we have had difficulties both with *devising* such normative orders ongoingly and with *enforcing* them institutionally" (Saberwal 1983, 204).

The paucity of such normative orders or the particular kind of institutional power to be found in India is also emphasized, in a Marxist framework, by Kaviraj (1984). The British attempt to introduce what Kaviraj terms *modern institutions* in India was "hardly coherent." "Many of these colossal structures of colonial 'rationalism' had feet of vernacular clay," he says. "Most of the so-called rationalistic institutions were by-words in petty corruption—including the blind-folded sword-bearing justice. As social novels often point out, she could only understand English" (ibid., 227). Large areas of graft remained under the thin veneer of a Europeanized elite. The Indian National Congress never seriously raised questions of social design and the building of institutions, argues Kaviraj.

> The attitudes of Congressmen towards institutions were deeply schizophrenic. Institutions signify, in terms of choice theory, a kind of precommitment. Such precommitment can have two types of sources—first, in a calculation of interest: through the conviction that if one stuck to certain norms, even though this is constraining in an immediate way, it creates reciprocal constraints on other players. Without these, uncertainty and the attendant risks become too high. A second source could be moral commitment to a rational social order, which had to be supported, if European experience is any guide, with an intellectual tradition that analysed, in a kind of slow replay, the historical experience of each round of social conflict. That the Indian society has lacked this is perhaps best reflected in the absence of a tradition of social or political theory. . . . What is odd in this is that philosophical skills were not lacking; what was lacking was the crucial hypothesis that they could, if applied to a replay of history, lead to a more rational and controlled pursuit of political business. (ibid., 229)

This historical legacy weighs heavily on contemporary Indian affairs. In order to survive the political crises caused by Nehru's death in

1964, the electoral defeat in 1967, and the emergency in 1975, "the state elite began to seek alliances with pre-capitalistic forces on a larger scale, and lost its ability to dictate to them to a large extent, and instead began to register passively the trace of the resurgent forces in the social order" (ibid., 233). The legitimacy of institutional power was supplanted by the legitimacy of a few individuals. The socialist rhetoric celebrated triumphs: "Socialist rhetoric often gave a respectable cover for the re-emergence of an essentially pre-capitalist alphabet of social action. It looked upon impersonal rules and application of rationalistic norms with derision, as forms of bourgeois fastidiousnes" (ibid., 234).

My argument that a chasm exists between Europe and the Indian subcontinent in terms of their political and constitutional histories is not a novel argument. I merely stress contrasts between the two cultures long suggested by scholars such as Max Weber and Louis Dumont. An understanding of this legacy, however, should provide important clues to understanding twentieth-century politics in India. In the words of Saberwal:

> Seen comparatively, then, it is evident that the endowment of medieval India in cultural resources and institutional arrangements left a good deal to be desired by way of materials useable in constructing large, durable state structures. Institutions designed after Western prototypes and implanted in the modern period are not layered deep in the Indian tradition. Political actors in contemporary India are heirs, furthermore, to a variety of political traditions coming down from the precolonial period, which makes for a multiplicity of codes in the political arena. . . . Such multiplicity of codes . . . tends to exact a heavy price. (1984, 40f)

The Particularistic State

My central concepts, thus, are the *universalistic* (hard) and the *particularistic* (soft) state. The two concepts are defined as follows:

- Universalistic state: A state whose actions are ordered by rules; that is, laws or administrative regulations.
- Particularistic state: A state whose actions are ordered by something other than rules; for example, the whims of the ruler, friendship or family relations, esteem, political connections, or money (bribes).

The two concepts correspond with universalistic administration (which is synonymous with, following Weber's terminology, *bureaucracy*) and particularistic administration. It should be emphasized that these two concepts are ideal types. An ideal type, in Weber's sense, is a mental construct that "exaggerates and simplifies the evidence" in order to create "tools of analysis" (Bendix 1977, 391, 393). The purpose of constructing an ideal type is to pinpoint or highlight certain features in reality that are believed to be pivotal in explaining social phenomena and in creating a meaningful systematization from a chaos of particular events. The ideal type should not be constructed arbitrarily, according to Weber, but with "some knowledge of the historical, social phenomenon that is studied . . . through a mental 'Steigerung', a furtherance of certain elements in reality" (quoted in Petersson 1987, 28). Apart from this, the ideal type has to meet two different criteria: first, it has to be logically consistent, and second, social action should be viewed as meaningful (*sinnvoll*) action (ibid.).[1] But this mental construct should not be confused with an empirical hypothesis. The ideal type cannot, by definition, be falsified. It can only be more or less useful in ordering or interpreting reality (see also Boudon 1983; Eriksson 1979).

Evidently, our ideal types are inspired by Weber's classical discussion about bureaucracy. Our universalistic state or administration closely resembles Weber's ideal type of bureaucracy, which he characterizes as an officialdom ordered by rules and by a hierarchy, whose management is based upon written documents and whose staff is expert, works full time, and follows general rules (Weber 1982b, 196ff). Although Weber is not explicit, I think the fundamental element in his concept of bureaucracy is the notion of *rule*, "ordered by rules." Consider the following passage by Weber:

> The reduction of modern office management to rules is deeply embedded in its very nature. The theory of modern public administration, for instance, assumes that the authority to order certain matters by decree—which has been legally granted to public authorities—does not entitle the bureau to regulate the matter by commands given for each case, but only to regulate the matter abstractly. This stands in extreme contrast to the regulation of all relationships through individual privileges and bestowals of favor, which is absolutely dominant in patrimonialism, at least in so far as such relationships are not fixed by sacred tradition. (ibid., 198)

From the notion of action governed by rules follows the possibility of appealing against the decision of a lower office to its higher authority; that is, hierarchy. It also follows that management is formalized and divorced from the private sphere of the official. And, although officials appointed on personal grounds may conduct their affairs according to rules, appointment according to merit (and in the extension of merit lies training and formal exams) is more congenial to a rule-governed administration. The appointed official is more dependent on other officials—the administrative structure—than someone who is elected or someone who has purchased his office; the two latter have an autonomous position vis-à-vis the administration (cf. ibid., 201, 207). Similarly with full-time work: if an official has other incomes—and by implication, loyalties—he is less likely to comply with the formal rules of the bureau. But this requirement—like the appointment—actually tells us how dependent (ceteris paribus) the official is on his administration. In a rule-governed administration, he is more likely to adhere to rules; but, conversely, in a particularistic administration, he is less likely to adhere to rules.

Two important traits follow. One is the impersonal character of the rule-governed administration. A rule is, ipso facto, insensible and dispassionate toward the particular individual. Another characteristic is that rules can be calculated. A citizen can calculate from the rules how his case will be dealt with by the universalistic administration (assuming that the rules are not changed too often). Rules foster a "rational matter-of-factness" (ibid., 240). "Precision, speed, unambiguity, knowledge of the files, continuity, discretion, unity, strict subordination, reduction of friction and of material and personal costs—these are raised to the optimum point in the strictly bureaucratic administration" (214).

Bureaucracy corresponds, in Weber's theory of domination, to legal domination (*Herrschaft*). In this case, people obey laws because they believe these rules to be enacted by a proper and correct procedure. Weber's other two types of domination—which together roughly correspond with my concept of the particularistic state—are charismatic and traditional domination. Under charismatic domination, the governed submit because of their belief in the extraordinary quality of the specific person. Traditional domination rests upon the belief that the reign has always existed; the traditional leader commands by virtue of his inherited status. The administrative apparatus under traditional domination can ideally be patrimonial—the officials are personal retainers of the master—or feudal, where the power of the master is somewhat restrained by an oath of fealty, a kind of contract, between lord and vassal (cf. Mouzelis 1975, 15ff; Weber 1985, 124). Even though the administrative apparatus under charismatic and traditional domination resembles our particularistic state, it should immediately be emphasized that they are not identical; my concept is defined somewhat differently from and independently of Weber's. My central notion is government according to rules. It follows from this that a religiously or traditionally based authority strictly adhering to rules is, in my terminology, universalistic. Thus, and somewhat different from common usage, an administration strictly governed by the dharmic (Hindu) order, assigning specific and different rights and obligations to different castes, would be universalistic.

Before proceeding to a more detailed analysis of my central concepts, let me emphasize that the ideal types of the universalistic and particularistic states should not be confused with the concepts of either Weber or Parsons, which have inspired my work bearing similar labels. As Sir Henry Sumner Maine has remarked, "The duty of the scientific inquirer is to distinguish the meanings of an important word from one another, to select the meanings appropriate to his own purposes, and consistently to employ the word during his investigation in this sense and no other" (quoted in Williams 1975, 137f). Clearly, such an attractive term as *universalism* is used to connote many different concepts, and I can claim no monopoly on its meaning. The only important thing is to distinguish its meanings in agreement with a nominalist view of concepts. And although the different meanings of *universalism* have a family resemblance—and perhaps one could show interesting connections between them—they are different from the concept of universalism defined here. Kothari argues convincingly that, in the occidental history of philosophy, there is a connection between the search for regularities in nature (resulting in a sense of mastery over nature and, consequently, Christian mastery over other cultures—what Kothari terms *universalism*) and the search for regularities in society. The quest for laws of nature found its parallel in the quest for laws of man in political thought (posed by, for example, Thomas Hobbes).

It is not that a capacity to abstract thought was lacking in India. Instead, Kothari (1974, 24) distinguishes between two types of abstraction: the capacity to symbolize (which represents the mathematical mode of thought, with a strong tradition in India) and the capacity to generalize (which relies on empirical observation). This Western capacity to generalize led to discoveries about nature as well as to attempts to discover "a viable social and political order to minimize the capriciousness of nature and the solitariness and inherent brutality and evil in man himself . . . [and to create] institutions that would make man himself subject to laws, and in general producing conditions of control and predictability at all levels" (ibid., 25). Oriental thinkers saw only folly in this latter project (26). Schaffer (1969, 193) makes the perceptive point that the rule of ceteris paribus, which lies at the heart of science, involves overlooking many aspects of the case in hand.

My definition of the universalistic state—a state whose actions are ordered by rules—takes very little for granted. In fact, any kind of rule would qualify, no matter how inegalitarian it is or how it is skewed in favor of one particular class or ethnic group. The point is whether the state and its administration sticks to its own rules. The reader may think this definition too parsimonious. But one should, in general, include as few properties as possible in a definition; to make as little as possible "true by definition." It is often a better strategy to define less and leave more open to empirical investigation (cf. Oppenheim 1975, esp. 305ff). Aside from this general methodological recommendation, I am purposely employing a minimal definition of the universalistic state so as to be able to show the pivotal role that rules play in a state administration. The more we postulate or define, the less potent a theory is. By intentionally using a parsimonious definition, I make my explanations (provided, of course, they are correct) all the more vital and powerful.

Universal versus Particular

The central property in our ideal types is rule: a universalistic administration is ordered by rules and a particularistic administration, conversely, is ordered by something other than rules. What, then, is a rule? I realize that I am treading in a very difficult area of political and philosophical inquiry. One author says that "the question 'What is Law?' remains one of the most insistent and yet elusive problems in the entire range of thought" (Robson, quoted in Williams 1975, 134; cf. Hart 1981, 1). But, without going into a thorough analysis of the concept of *rule*, I will use the insights of others to delimit and clarify what we should understand by *rule*. First, I will explain what *rule* is not. It is not an empirical or sociological regularity, a habit or a pattern, informal social rules in the sense of rules of the game, or moral standards, even though such moral and social rules obviously exist in India.

By *rule*, I mean a (usually) written law, administrative regulation, enactment, or decree. These rules can be issued either by a parliament, a ruler, or an administration. What about an uncodified rule, an unwritten rule saying, for instance, that the first time you are charged with a traffic offense the court will let you go? Apparently the distinction between an uncodified rule and a social rule is vague and presents us with a continuum rather than a clear-cut dichotomy. The politically important feature about a written regulation is that it is undisguised and observable, not only for the ruler or the government but for the citizens as well.

From this flow two things. The first is that with a written rule you can take issue with the administration or government. On the basis of which rule is my case decided? Is my case really congruent with this particular rule? And from this follows, by social and political logic, the possibility of appeal. Second, written rules force, as it were, the system of rules to become more consistent. The character of informal, social rules make them less amenable to appeal and consistency. The important features of an unwritten rule is whether it is stated clearly and made public. The more distinctly it is formulated and the more public it is made, the more an unwritten rule resembles, and should be classified as, a rule in my sense. Another way of putting this is to use the following criterion: on being questioned, would the administrator or politician be able to formulate the (formal) rule according to how the decision was taken? Generally, this would not be the case where extralegal considerations affected the decision. Seeing, then, that decisions stemming from a distinctly stated and publicly known unwritten rule can be appealed and that the rule calls for consistency with other rules, the rule functions politically as a codified rule. On the other hand, a blurred and inconspicuous unwritten rule functions as an informal rule.

I am defining *rule* in terms of actions taken by states, rules that are applied, not rules as such. My interest is in the implementation of policies, programs, and laws—the actions taken by the administration when it, so to speak, meets the citizens. Of course, India has a constitution and a whole gamut of laws, laws that are often violated (Blomkvist 1988, chap. 8). These laws tell us relatively little about how the Indian state actually operates, since few of these laws are consistently applied. (Rubin [1987] has reviewed violations of civil rights and laws in India and the work by the People's Union for Civil Liberties to seek redress.)

A rule excludes "from practical consideration the particular merits of particular cases by specifying in advance what *is to* be done whatever the circumstances of particular cases may be" (Warnock, quoted in Marshall 1983, 188). In other words, action taken according to a rule means that similar cases are accorded similar treatment, that is, impartiality, or rule of law. The crucial principle of the rule of law is that the state may not take action on grounds that are irrelevant to the law or rule (Algotsson 1988). And a "life in accordance with rules as opposed to other standards, e.g. the *ad hoc* orders of an inspired leader, or arbitrary desires" entails, as Berlin (1956, 306) points out, a measure of equality. It is also illuminating and important, I think, to see that an applied rule is a public good in Paul Samuelson's strict sense of the word (cf. Blomkvist 1988, 216–20).

Must a rule be general to be called a rule? Can we have a rule referring to only one individual? If a rule treats all alike, what do we mean by *all*? The Christian Fifth Commandment refers to all human beings (except, saliently, in war). But, for instance, universal suffrage refers, not to all, but to all people above the age of eighteen (in Sweden). A rule granting child allowance to all people refers in fact only to those with children below sixteen years of age (again in Sweden). The rule in India reserving seats in parliament and jobs in the public sector for Harijans obviously refers only to Harijans. Or take a rule referring to people who have committed murder; obviously it applies to very few individuals. Are these last rules, since they are not general, no longer rules? Although such rules differ in terms of how general or specific their extension (domain) is, they are nonetheless rules.[2] "What is necessary is that a rule deals with a class of *cases* (whether persons, objects, or occasions)" (Marshall 1983, 184).[3]

If a rule cannot allow too little, can it allow too much? In other words, what happens if those features by which we have chosen to characterize the particularistic state are formulated as rules? A friendship, a family relationship, or a political connection forming the basis of a public decision and regulated in a law or regulation is, in our terminology, a rule. (Here, again, it is important to distinguish between formal and informal rules; I am here referring to the former.) Hence, it would belong to the universalistic state. Such rules we find in laws regulating inheritance, marriage, or a legal disqualification (challenge). But a rule stating that you must be a friend of politician x to be allocated a house is, of course, empirically highly unlikely, because the precise and crucial point about a rule is that citizens can appeal it and even change it. And this is antithetical to the particularistic politician. In the words of an admirer of the political boss Frank Skeffington, in O'Connor's (1957) novel: "The boss does not mind helping the poor—as long as he decides who are the poor." But something different happens if we formulate the whims of the ruler as a formal rule. Consider regulation by fiat or by the rule, You may do as you wish. Louis XIV's dictum "L'Etat c'est moi" is probably a good approximation of such a rule. We can conceive of a government that regulates an administration (say, in the sector of housing or health care) with the rule You may do as you wish, or Always consider the merits of the situation. Obviously, such rules would breach the notion I intend with a rule-governed, universalistic state.

How can this problem be solved? Although my problem here is conceptual, it is clear that it also has practical relevance. It is beyond the bounds of possibility to regulate every single decision in an administration; there will always remain some decisions taken according to the (fictive) rule, You may do as you wish or as you see fit. Moreover, the modern state often regulates a policy sector by means of a framework law, which we could interpret as a regulation, that says, You may do as you wish. But as long as rules are replaced by professional competence—as in medicine, engineering, and teaching—the administration covered by a framework law is regulated by professional rules.[4]

A rule declaring, You may do as you wish, may strike the reader as a typical example of a logical paradox, similar to Epimenedes' well-known liar: I am lying now. From such a proposition—congruent with Russell's paradox—we can derive its negation (if the proposition is true, it is false, and if it is false, it is true). But examined more closely, we find that from the rule, You may do as you wish, we cannot derive the negation, You may not do as you wish (or vice versa). If we instead turn to deontic logic and von Wright's (1963, esp. chap. 5) distinction between obligation norms and permissive norms, we will be able to unravel our problem. When norms are prescriptions—that is, given or issued by someone, for example, an authority—obligation norms are either commands or prohibitions. They tell us what we must do or what we must not do. A permissive prescription tells us what we may do. "Thus, what is characteristically 'permissive' about permissions would be the norm-authority's declaration of his toleration of a certain behaviour on the part of the norm-subject(s). 'Permissions are essentially tolerations,' we could say" (ibid., 90). The instance, You may do as you wish, is what von Wright calls a *strong permission*.[5] Drawing on von Wright's analysis, I call my example a *permissive rule*. In this way I supplement and extend my definition of *universalistic state:*

- Universalistic state: A state whose actions are ordered by rules, that is, laws or administrative regulations. I exclude a state ordered by too general or too many permissive rules.

A state that is ordered by too general or too many permissive rules is then, by definition, particularistic.

I have tried above to disentangle what I think are the most important conceptual problems concerning the universalistic state. The particularistic state is mainly defined negatively, that is, a state that is not ordered by rules or is breaking (its own) rules. Figure 1 relates and classifies the different types of rule breaking discussed in the literature.

Many studies of politics and society in India and similar countries have ignored—some of them despite conceding its importance—the phenomenon of administrative rule breaking. Myrdal (1968, 939) talks about a "taboo on research on corruption."[6] But this is not the only problem. There is also a prevailing vagueness surrounding the word *corruption*. Some authors equate corruption with inefficiency, others

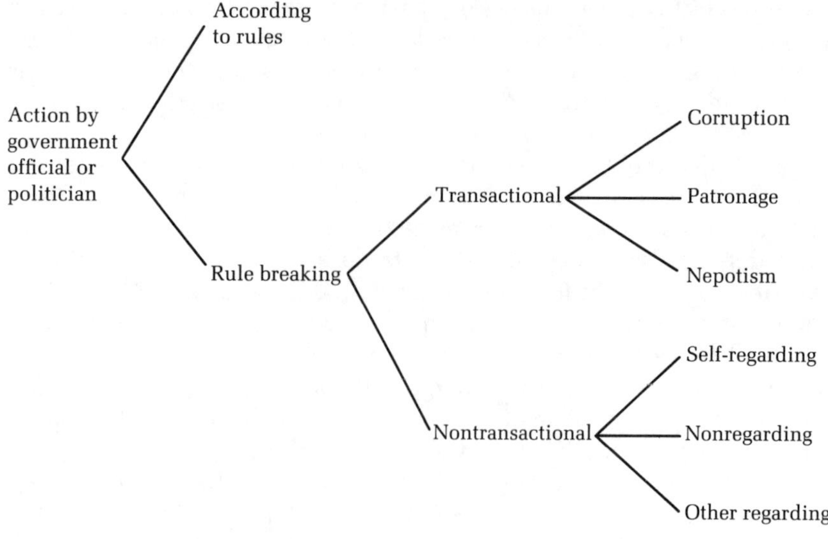

FIGURE 1: Types of Actions by Persons Qua Government Official or Politician

even include politics, in the sense of striking deals or acting strategically. One author regards this nebulousness as an advantage: "Most political scientists seem to admit implicitly that everybody knows what corruption is—which enables them to go beyond the question of definition" (Deysine 1980, 448). Myrdal (1968, 937), for instance, defines it in an exceptionally vague manner and without further distinctions (which would cover all the different actions we have classified under rule breaking plus immoral behavior): "Improper or selfish exercise of power and influence attached to a public office or to the special position one occupies in public life." Perhaps one author has a point when he says that corruption thrives because there is no agreement as to what corruption is. Several authors employ Nye's somewhat clearer definition (Nye 1967, 419). But the typology above and the accompanying definitions below are an improvement, in terms of clarity and comprehensiveness, on Nye's definitions; they attempt to clarify what we should be talking about and how the different kinds of rule breaking relate to each other.

This typology relates to (formal) rules and not to public opinion, public interest, or moral values. An action can thus be immoral without breaking any rule. A Swedish example of immoral behavior would be Prime Minister Torbjörn Fälldin's decision to start the nuclear power plant at Barsebäck, despite his promise to the contrary in the 1976 election campaign. Clearly, Fälldin did not break any rules, but he acted, according to some, in an immoral fashion by breaking his election promise. Sexual scandals in the Western world—involving politicians like John Profumo, Cecil Parkinson, and Gary Hart—are other instances of immoral but not rule-breaking behavior by politicians. And in another cultural context, acting according to (formal) rules can actually be regarded as immoral behavior. Moral or immoral behavior represents another dimension, theoretically, than action according to or not according to rules.

Similarly, my typology is not concerned with the causes or consequences of rule breaking. There are further aspects of my typology. First, it deals with public roles; that is, with persons acting in their capacity as administrator or politician—which also means that it makes no distinction between administrative and political rule breaking. Nor does it separate rule breaking at the national level from rule breaking at the local level. Second, it deals with rule breaking by actors within the state. For example, it does not refer to tax fraud by a citizen. Hence, I am discussing a particularistic state, a state that, on the one hand dissolves into society in much the same way that salt dissolves in water and, on the other hand, is capricious and sometimes quite violent. The state becomes caught and tangled in the webs of society, in the webs of village, caste, and political brokerage.

By transactional rule breaking I refer to an action involving an exchange. The administrator or politician barters a decision for support. The decision can either refer to a good—a tenement, a bank loan, or a contract—or to a license. A license can either be a permission—a trade license, a permit granted to a hawker or a shoeshine boy—or an immunity from a punishment or prohibition set down in law. Often what the client actually gets is a certain speed—the case is dealt with according to the rule book, while without the exchange, remarkable delays can occur. Fittingly, bribes are often called speed money in India. The citizen or client in their turn exchanges support.

The categories of transactional rule breaking in figure 1 are based on what the politician or administrator obtains in exchange for breaking the rule. When the support is monetary and private, I call the action *corruption*—that is, the administrator or politician sells a decision and pockets the money himself. The price of a decision can be stable, or it can fluctuate wildly, subject at times to other factors (political connections, friendship, and so forth). Johnston (1986, 466ff) calls the former "market corruption" and gives as an example black market dealings in the Soviet Union. When the support is political, I call the action *patronage*. Political support can be expressed as voting, party activism, or donations of money (for party advantage).[7] When the support is social, I call the action *nepotism*. By *social*, I refer—somewhat improperly—to social as well as ethnic, cultural, and psychological support (reverence). *Social* refers to relations of friendship, family, caste, and ethnicity.

In all three of these types of transactional rule breaking, the initiative (the suggestion to make this kind of exchange) may come from the politician or administrator or from the citizen. In the former case, I call the action *extortion*. An administrator suggesting a bribe, a policeman threatening to frame someone for a crime unless he pays him money or a "goonda" threatening to beat up hutment dwellers unless they vote for party x are all cases of extortion. Clearly, in those actions called extortion, the illegal use of violence or threats of violence may be involved. Violence serves the purpose of buttressing the bargaining position of the administrator or politician. (The actual threats or violence will often, of course, be done by henchmen.) Violence, or threats of violence, changes the utility function of citizens so that they may find that the bargain (now) is according to their preferences: they will get "an offer they can't refuse."[8]

It is in this contextual relation that we should see the "rigid and time-consuming" urban development control system in Madras in south India (cf. Blomkvist 1988, pt. 2). That the intricate rules regulating, for example, town planning are applied ineffectively means little to the actors within the state apparatus. More important is that these arduous and, at times enigmatic rules leave ample scope for transactional rule breaking. Armed with rules and possible sanctions, the state stands in a stronger position vis-à-vis the citizen. But in similar fashion, the strength of citizens' power, vis-à-vis a particularistic state, is highly varied and disparate, inviting asymmetric and unequal relationships. The greater the economic, political, or social resources one can muster, the more likely it is that one can induce the state to make the "right" decision. Whether rule breaking by the administration is intentional or not is open to empirical argument. Logically, we can conceive of either a state that lacks the willpower to implement laws coherently or a state that lacks the ability to do so. In the latter case, we are talking about a state whose central authority is not in full command of its administration.

In nontransactional rule breaking, no exchange with the citizen is involved. *Self-regarding* implies a situation where the administrator or politician uses his office to steal or embezzle, that is, *misappropriation*. This also involves the illegal use of an office to, for example, buy land in an area designated for city expansion before the public has a right to know. Self-regarding rule breaking also refers to a situation where the person assigned public power simply wishes to show this authority beyond what the rules allow him or her to do (for instance, the "police lawlessness" reported by Rubin [1987]). We may call this whims of the ruler. *Nonregarding* refers to a situation where neither the public person nor someone else is intended to benefit from the action. This can imply ignorance—the administrator is unaware of the rule—or dislike of the rule. In such circumstances, it is difficult to see how anyone benefits from the rule breaking. Last, there is *other-regarding* rule breaking, implying a situation wherein an adminstrator or a politician breaks the rule for the sake of others or for a "higher cause." Other regarding can be taken in the opposite sense: a mean cause that is, someone breaking a rule with the sole purpose of making circumstances worse for some other person. It should be added that, empirically, any particular decision can involve more than one of these actions.

The reader may think I have revealed a normative bias in favor of the universalistic, rule-governed model. Certainly, a universalistic state has advantages, which is probably already clear. But it might also, and probably does, have important drawbacks. Schaffer (1969), for instance, provides a well-informed critique of bureaucracy as an administrative model for developing countries. It is, he says, precisely the equity of the rule that leads to a "gap in perception and communication between the decisionmaker and the client of the community" (192). Like treatment for like cases means that any one bureaucratic decision maker, "however well intentioned, can see in fact only one part of what may appear to the client to be relevant and indeed essential" (193). Another disadvantageous effect of a universalistic state can be seen on a social level. Weber (1982b, 240) himself was keenly aware of "the far-reaching and general cultural effects" that the rational bureaucratic structure of domination had and would have on society. The nature of bureaucracy "develops the more perfectly the more the bureaucracy is 'dehumanized,' the more completely it succeeds in eliminating from official business love, hatred, and all purely personal, irrational, and emotional elements which escape calculation" (ibid., 216). The principle central to bureaucracy, *Sine ira et studio* (without hatred or passion), its very impersonality, "furthers the already highly developed indifference to substantive ethical and affectional values, intensifies the sense of deprivation which the disadvantaged experience in modern capitalist society" (Shils 1948, 42).

Weber's work perceptively presages the critique of the depersonalization, dehumanization, and reification of modern society, to a large extent brought about by the rule-governed state administration. In an interview, Czech playwright and political dissident-turned-president Václav Havel gave this critique:

> In my view, Soviet totalitarianism is an extreme manifestation—a strange, cruel and dangerous species—of a deep-seated problem which equally finds expression in advanced Western society. These systems have in common something that the Czech philosopher Václav Belohradský calls the "eschatology of the impersonal," that is, *a trend towards impersonal power* and rule by mega-machines or colossi that escape human control. I believe the world is losing its human dimension. Self-propelling mega-machines, juggernauts of impersonal power such as large-scale enterprises and faceless governments, represent the greatest threat to our present-day world. In the final analysis, totalitarianism is no more than an extreme expression of this threat. (*Times Literary Supplement*, 23 January 1987)

And the impersonal character of the bureaucracy, says Weber (1982b, 229), "means that the mechanism—in contrast to feudal orders based upon personal piety—is easily made to work for anybody who knows how to gain control over it." A little over a decade after Weber wrote this, Europe witnessed a draconian example of the possible consequences of a rule-governed state: the German Weimar *Beamtentum* easily turned into a tool in the hands of the Nazis and facilitated their rise to power.

The polarity of action guided by rules is action directed by the context. The credo of the context-sensitive system was formulated by the nineteenth-century poet William Blake: "One law for the lion and the ox is oppression." Ramanujan (1986) argues that context sensitivity is typical of Indian culture: "One has only to read Manu after a bit of Kant to be struck by Manu's extraordinary lack of universality." In an interesting passage, the virtues of the two different moralities are brought out:

> Universalization means putting oneself in another's place—it is the golden rule of the New Testament, Hobbes' "law of all men": do not do unto others what you don't want done unto you. The main tradition of the Western/Christian ethics is based on such a premise of universalization. Manu will not understand such a premise. To be moral, for Manu, is to particularize—to ask who did what, to whom and when. Bernard Shaw's comment, "Do not do unto others as you would have they should do unto you. Their tastes may not be the same,"—will be closer to Manu's view, except that he would substitute "natures of classes" for "tastes." Each class (jati) of man has its own laws, its own proper ethic, not to be universalized. Hegel shrewdly noted this Indian slant: While

we say "Bravery is virtue," the Hindoos say, on the contrary, "Bravery is a virtue of the Cshatriyas." (ibid., 5f)

Patrons and Clients

What is the political effect of the particularistic state? What expression will politics—the struggle for power and allocation of values—have in a society with a particularistic state? I argue below that the logical or rational strategy in these circumstances is to find an important and powerful friend, a patron. Because what is the point in fighting for general demands or policies if achievements vis-à-vis the state today are spoilt in the implementation tomorrow? And what is the point of joining or organizing an interest group if the state does not adhere in a universalistic manner to the demands posed?

But the poor are not totally devoid of power. In a pattern that totally contradicts class struggle, the poor, in a cunning way, form informal alliances with someone influential and powerful (see Blomkvist 1988, 235–40 for a discussion of the difference between clientelism and class struggle). In the public bureau, the *chaprasi*—the ubiquitous errand boy—is of central importance to the ordinary person; the *chaprasi* acts as a go-between with the powerful official, and without his services everything is likely to move much slower. Patron-client relationships are formed. In rural areas, these relationships are more likely to be affected by tradition and everyday routine; in urban areas, the patron-client relationship is less customary and more open to deliberate choice by patrons as well as clients. Many patrons compete for support in the urban arena. And even a poor and underprivileged person can be of interest to a powerful patron (cf. Blomkvist 1988, chap. 12), especially if, as in India, he has a vote.

Consider the following story related by a police official of how illegal squatter settlements in large Third world cities often emerge. "All it takes for a hut is four poles and a roof. But actually these huts are the result of long-term planning and they often involve the support of a corporation councillor or someone like that. Such a person will think, When I stand for election all the people will vote for me. And he's right in a way. If 300 huts come up, that's 300 times four or 1200 votes" (Wiebe 1981, 120f). Or the clients might even command a certain influence in their slum area, controlling a personal following or a "vote bank," the members of which are (in their turn) their clients. Patrons find these clients interesting and worthy of attention.

Certainly, these patron-client relationships are profoundly unequal;

we might call them Al Capone-type alliances. Those who control power and resources manipulate the political system as well as their friends and underdogs. Without actual rights for the citizens, the patron and the party boss can favor some people and not others—divide and rule. Attempts at horizontal organization can thus be split; through patronage, the party gains support and splits at the same time. The lack of universalism, in the sense of state power constrained by laws, gives a great amount of power and freedom of maneuver to those in control of the state apparatus.

The contradictory and chaotic character of the politics of many developing countries, which is so exasperatingly resistant to analysis using Western models and presuppositions, is actually its very essence. And the clientelistic relationships are no peripheral phenomena. On the contrary, "the patron-client exchange . . . becomes . . . central to an understanding of how at least some political systems work, constituting in some instances the most important basis of interest articulation and socio-political control" (Kaufman 1974, 285). Powell (1970, 413) provides as examples of such brokerage systems the *compadrazgo* system in Latin America, the Chinese *kan-ch'ing*, the Japanese *oyabunkobun*, the *clientela* system in Italy, the *jajmani* system in India, and the patron-client system in the Philippines. The geographical prevalence of contemporary clientelistic systems is illustrated by such works as Tarkowski (1981) on Poland, Chubb (1982) on southern Italy, and Oi (1985) on China (see also Eisenstadt and Roniger 1984 and the articles in the volume edited by Schmidt et al. 1977).

Bombay gang leader and union boss Bapu Gopal Reshim provides a colorful but not entirely untypical picture of an Indian patron. Reshim, born in 1951, grew up on the streets of Bombay and was soon involved in petty crime. His turning point came with the large textile strike in 1982–1983, when he was engaged by a Congress(I)-affiliated union to break the Datta Samant–led strike. Three years later, he lent his muscle power to one of Samant's unions, but left it when he was refused control. He then turned to the rival Congress(I)-controlled Dockyard Labour Union, where he was quickly put in charge. But the infighting between gangs and unions led to Reshim's violent death in 1987. As testimony to the popular support he had acquired, about eight thousand people attended his funeral. Both Congress(I) and the Bombay-based party Shiv Sena put up boards mourning the death of a "workers' leader." Reshim was mainly encouraged by Congress(I), and he harbored ambitions, as a representative of a new breed of gangsters, of building up "a large organisation which would have included trade unions and legitimate political activity" (Warring Underworld, *India Today*, 31 March 1987).

What do we mean by *patron-client relationship?* Kaufman's analysis is particularly useful in its brevity and clarity; he defines the patron-client relationship as a dyadic exchange distinguished by the following characteristics:

- The relationship occurs between actors of unequal power and status.
- It is based on the principle of reciprocity; that is, it is a self-regulating form of interpersonal exchange, the maintenance of which depends on the return that each actor expects to obtain by rendering goods and services to the other and that ceases once the expected rewards fail to materialize.
- The relationship is particularistic and private, anchored only loosely in public law (Kaufman 1974, 285).

In other words, it is a relationship between two individuals that is asymmetric, reciprocal, and informal; a "lop-sided friendship," as Juliana Pitt-Rivers aptly describes it, a relationship that shows "a peculiar combination of inequality and asymmetry in power with seeming mutual solidarity expressed in terms of personal identity and interpersonal sentiments and obligations" (Eisenstadt and Roniger 1984, 50). But it is important to see its basis not primarily in a value system but in a particular political situation. Hobsbawm (1953) captures this aptly in an article about the Mafia, an extreme variety of the lopsided friendship: "One should resist the temptation to link this code with feudalism, aristocratic virtues or the like. Its most complete and binding rule was among the *souteneurs* and minor hoodlums of the Palermo slums, whose conditions approximated most closely to 'lawlessness', or rather to a Hobbesian state in which the relations between individuals or small groups are like those between sovereign powers" (740).

Thus, a state unconstrained by rules, a particularistic or soft state, gives rise to a completely different policy process. With a particularistic state, the significant political struggle will be about implementation, not about policy. In the words of Scott (1969), "Between the passage of legislation and its actual implementation lies an entirely different political arena that, in spite of its informality and particularism, has a great effect on the execution of policy. . . . *influence at the enforcement stage often takes the form of 'corruption' and has seldom been treated as the alternative means of interest articulation which in fact it is*" (1142). The sensible and rational thing to do, then, is to influence not the policy or program but the implementation of the policy or program.

I have attempted to link abstract discussion about the particularistic state with a specific look at the rationality of clientelistic networks—in other words, to give microfoundations to the theory of the political logic caused by the particularistic state. How we perceive structure and rational action combining is well captured by Graziano (1976):

> This said, I maintain that in a clientelistic system *even if there are group expectations* typically clients do *not* act together for their common interests. This is not due necessarily to a lack of consciousness or to false consciousness, but often to a perfectly rational appraisal of reality. The "structure of the situation" (that is, the objective conditions and the alternative courses of action available to the actor) may be such as to persuade one to adopt a strategy of dyadic relations even though the actor is aware of operating within a system of collective exploitation. (172f)

Kaufman (1974, 286) points out that "clientelism suggests an essentially rational component in behaviors which, from other perspectives, might be viewed as extreme cases of culturally-induced irrationality." I concur with Kaufman that the models of rational behavior first developed in economics can make a particularly happy marriage with anthropological studies of micropolitics.[9] What do we mean by rational behavior? Clearly, *rational* is one of these attractive words (from the latin *ratio*, meaning calculation, or according to reason) that has taken on several meanings. Basically, the different meanings go back to Weber's distinction between *Wertrationalität* and *Zweckrationalität*—the former implying that action is motivated by a belief in the value (ethical, religious, or political) of a certain type of behavior and, as such, independent of its results. The latter implies that action is undertaken as a *means* to achieve a goal and is directed by consideration of its consequences (cf. Weber 1985, 12ff). Myrdal's (1968, 57f) postulated concept of rationality, for example, is *wertrational,* as is, the model of economic man (postulating selfishness) (cf. Elster 1983a, 10). But where I employ the term *rational,* I use it in its *zweckrational* sense. By calling an action rational, I imply "that the agent tries to do as well for himself as he can, given his beliefs about the world" (ibid., 76). Only consistency between goals and beliefs is stipulated. "Consistency, in fact, is what rationality in the thin sense is all about" (ibid., 1). Rogowski (1978) defines *rationality* thus:

> The theory of rational choice . . . rests on one and only one premise: individual conduct is wholly determined by the endeavor to relate means to ends as effectively as possible. . . . *Hence no goals that are pursued with tolerable consistency can be called "irrational"*: if a person seeks above else a life in poverty and abnegation, and if he pursues that goal consistently and efficiently, his behavior is rational in every generally accepted meaning of the term. (299)

Hence, we see that a rational action is goal orientated; nothing except consistency is claimed about the goal. It may be material or ethical, realistic or unrealistic, egoistic or altruistic.[10]

Rationality—apart from the realism in its assumption of goal-orientated behavior—also carries the beneficial methodological implication that social action must be understood as meaningful action by individuals (that is, methodological individualism). This is often a trivial postulate at the level of individual action: He carried out action *x* in order to achieve goal *y*. Nevertheless, some social scientists—often within a rational choice paradigm—have pursued precisely such kinds of studies, despite the risk of their stating the obvious and well known and ending up with near tautological or trivial explanations. Consider the critique by Indian economist Sen (1988): "The approach of 'rational behaviour,' as it is typically interpreted, *leads to a remarkably mute theory.* Behaviour, it appears, is to be 'explained in terms of preferences, which are in turn defined only by behaviour.' Not surprisingly, excursions into circularities have been frequent" (90).

The problem with the rational choice theory is actually that it explains too much. In principle, any consistent action can be explained by its *Zweckrationalität*. Popper (1972) suggests that we return to Xenophanes and reintroduce a distinction between probability and verisimilitude. "Logical probability represents the idea of approaching logical certainty, or tautological truth, through a gradual diminution of informative content. Verisimilitude, on the other hand, represents the idea of approaching comprehensive truth. It thus combines truth and content while probability combines truth with lack of content" (237). And if we aim for theories of increasing content or the growth of knowledge, "then a high probability cannot possibly be our aim as well: *these two aims are incompatible*" (ibid., 218). "Thus we accept the idea that the task of science is the search for truth, for true theories. Yet we also stress that *truth is not the only aim of science.* We want more than truth: what we look for is *interesting truth*—truth which is hard to come by" (ibid., 229). The rational choice explanation of action thus amount to a theory with high probability but low verisimilitude. And "progress in science means progress towards more interesting, less trivial, and therefore less 'probable' theories" (ibid., 236).

This critique of the rational choice theory does not make it any less valuable as a starting point for interpreting social action and constructing theories of social action. Methodological individualism claims that social action is meaningful action by individuals. But social science should not, I think, stop short at the individual level. The purpose of political science ought to be analogous to Weber's definition of sociology: "a science which attempts the interpretive understanding of social action in order thereby to arrive at a causal explanation of its course and effects," a science that seeks to unravel the "conditions of the emergence, maintenance and dissolution of social structures" (quoted in Shils 1948, 47, 46).

Individuals, not systems or structures, have goals. "Purpose is rejected at the level of the system, but not at the level of its component actors," as Coleman (1986, 1312) puts it. Preferences of actors and an assumption of rationality also serve, methodologically, to show just which structures count in peoples' lives. But individuals do not achieve their goals willy-nilly; their preferences do not come from nowhere; the formation of these preferences can be made a subject of study. People live in a social context that (presumably) influences their preferences. "What is wrong with methodological individualism," Adam Przeworski perceptively observes, "is not the postulate that collective actions must be explained by reference to individual rationality but the substantive ontology of society as a collection of undifferentiated and unrelated individuals." He calls, instead, for a perspective that sees "individuals who are embedded in different types of relations with other individuals within a multidimensionally described social structure" (cited in Katznelson 1986, 319). Our preferences are clearly not always possible to attain, and constraints of different kinds will often cripple our intentions. "The final result of political action often, no, even regularly stands in completely inadequate and often even paradoxical relation to its original meaning" (Weber 1982a, 117). Hegel calls it "the cunning of reason."

Nor does methodological individualism imply that all social states are intended by actors. These two voluntaristic fallacies—since x has intention *a*, *A* will come about, and since *A* exists, actors must have had intention *a*—are not true simply because they are common, especially in quotidian social explanations. Probably most of the social macrophenomena we may be interested in—state structures, capitalism, and colonialism, for example—were never intended by anyone. It is precisely for this reason that these macrostates are so difficult to explain. Beer (1973), in a discussion about political development in Europe, appraises this intricacy:

> The cultural orientations of modernity motivate distinctively new types of behavior. But once these floods of consequence have been sent forth into the world, they interact with profound effect on one another in ways that may be only dimly understood or *barely perceived and not at*

> *all intended* by contemporaries. The industrial revolution, the rise of the factory system, the creation of the great manufacturing city were only in part—in small part—the intentional creations of their time. (66, my emphasis)

Popper (1972, 342) argues that "*the main task of the theoretical social sciences . . . is to trace the unintended social repercussions of intentional human actions.*" But the towering problems for a theoretical social science with empirical aspirations—that is, grounded in historical and empirical data[11]—have been well formulated recently by Coleman (1986):

> But what neither Parsons nor others engaged in similar attempts seem to have realized is that the major theoretical obstacle to social theory built on a theory of action is not the proper refinement of action theory itself, but the means by which purposive actions of individuals *combine* to produce a social outcome. . . . The promise that Talcott Parsons held out in 1937 (in *The structure of social action*) of a voluntaristic theory of action has remained unrealized, and since then social theory and social research have moved along diverging paths. (1332)
>
> This micro-to-macro problem is sometimes called by European sociologists the problem of transformation. In economics, it is (misleadingly) termed the problem of aggregation; in political science, a major instance of it is the problem of social choice. It is the process through which individual preferences become collective choices; the process through which dissatisfaction becomes revolution; through which simultaneous fear in members of a crowd turns into a mass panic; through which preferences, holdings of private goods, and the possibility of exchange create market prices and a redistribution of goods; through which individuals' task performance in an organization creates a social product; through which the reduction of usefulness of children to parents leads families to disintegrate; through which interest cleavages lead (or fail to lead) to overt social conflict. (1321)

But we should beware of one problem when we use models of rationality: individuals' actual preferences need to be studied empirically. Guesswork or deduction will lead nowhere. Some social scientists (read: economists) seem to think that the content of individuals' preferences can be ascertained theoretically. Sometimes economists purporting to study economic behavior, lost in their models, remind me of the social anthropologist, Sir John Fraser, from the nineteenth century, who, asked if he had ever visited any of those tribes he was studying, quipped: "God forbid!"

Universalism Needs to Be Explained

It is not the soft state but its opposite, the rule-governed, universalistic state, that needs to be explained, the reasons being the uniqueness and the counterintuitive quality of the universalistic state. Weber (1982b, 196) observes that bureaucracy is not the historical rule but the exception, even in the massive political structures of the ancient Orient. The soft state, says Myrdal (1968, 896), "is one of the most fundamental differences between the South Asian countries today and Western countries at the beginning of their industrialization." The universalistic state in Europe is, therefore, a deviation from the norm. It is also counterintuitive, since it represents a solution to the central problem of collective action so eloquently evinced by Bardhan (1984, 69, 58f). The longer I have spent visiting and studying India and pondering its political circumstances, the more have I come to regard the universalistic state as an enigma. How did it ever come about? (cf. Blomkvist 1987).

Without doubt, this question only makes sense within a conception of political reality that denies the developmental laws or historical inevitability so ingrained in nineteenth-century social thought—whose inheritance is, today, shared equally by Marxism and economics. Boudon (1983) calls this notion the "nomological postulate," that is, the notion that all societies follow the same lawlike pattern. Apart from the theoretical arguments that have been leveled at these developmental, or stage, theories—the contention that societies are gradually climbing the staircase of history—events in the Third World have helped to put these theories in disrepute. The seizure of power by a Muslim revivalist movement in a major state in the Middle East—flying in the face of American guns and intelligence—hardly supports claims of a stage theory. Similarly, the fiercest political opposition in India during the 1980s was mounted, not by Marxist guerillas or working-class movements, nor even by a bourgeois party, but by religious revivalists in a reformist congregation from the seventeenth century, the Sikhs.

Instead of treating politics and history as processes governed by laws or inevitable stages, we should develop, for the purpose of macrohistorical comparisons and understanding, the metaphor of *game*. In his interesting paper on individuality, Minogue (1987, 6) says that "the West has *chosen* to cultivate individuality as one of the possibilities of human experience." This quotation gives us a key to the notion of *game*, because, to a certain extent, different civilizations are playing different games. This is a germane metaphor if we wish to understand or conceptualize such civilizational differences that we have discussed above. Civilization *A* is aiming to be as good as it can in cultivating individuality, whereas civilization *B* has other values. And just as one cannot judge a football player's ability by employing the values demanded of a tennis player, so one cannot judge (fairly) civilization *B* in terms of civilization *A*. Arguing that Indian civilization failed to develop universalism or a strong political center is as sensible as saying that Björn Borg failed to develop a strong right fist or a sprinting speed to match Ben Johnson. (We may ask, though, why Borg chose to play tennis in the first place.)

Now, with the help of this conception of game, we can develop a theory of how different games give rise to different institutions. The important thing about an institution is that it structures the situation: it is a prerequisite, a constraint, which we disregard only at our peril. To quote Karl Marx again: "Men make their own history, but they do not make it just as they please. The tradition of all dead weighs like a nightmare on the brain of the living."

NOTES

1. This also implies the view that individuals are acting rationally, i.e., that they are capable of divining their (socially determined) needs and acting upon them in a consistent manner. I return to this point below. Another implication—and advantage—of the ideal type is that it presupposes the methodological postulate of methodological individualism: societal macrophenomena are interpreted in the light of meaningful action by individuals. Individuals, not systems, have goals.

2. An illuminating example of how we sometimes think it is more natural and legitimate to have a more specific rule was provided in Sweden in early 1987. When it was disclosed that the Swedish immigration authorities (Invandrarverket) had refused immigrant status to Soviet Jews, a reporter asked why they did not have specific rules for Jews from the USSR (the radio program "Dagens Eko," 25 January 1987). Compare also the argument by Titmuss (1976, 118).

3. As Marshall (1983) points out, we can even conceive of a rule referring to only one individual. What we are connoting by 'rule' is also, in philosophical terminology, called an universal quantifier, expressed with the sign $\forall$. Consider the proposition '$\forall$x Good (x).' This proposition tells us nothing about how large the domain of x is. It may be that x refers to only one individual. The proposition only tells us that 'For all x, it is true that x is good.' And this proposition has the same logical structure as a rule, in our sense of the word.

4. Sverker Gustavsson has called attention to this point in personal conversation. To my knowledge, very little has been written about the bureaucratization of professions—in the sense of regulating behavior by rules—as a means of replacing state rules by professional rules in the running of state affairs. We can see such a gradual bureaucratization in the European history of professions such as law and medicine. Sometimes judges are perceived in the literature as

being, by definition, rule governed. This concept disregards the evidence of history from the Middle Ages onward. "For all their ability, learning and wisdom, English medieval judges were corrupt," says Jonathan Sumption in a review (*Times Literary Supplement*, 28 February 1986) of Ralph Turner's book on the English judiciary. Social work is an example of a profession not yet fully professionalized or bureaucratized; rules of proper professional conduct are still often ardently debated within the profession.

5. That is, "not forbidden but subject to norm." On the other hand, an "act will be said to be permitted in the weak sense if it is not forbidden" (von Wright 1963, 86). Other examples of strong permissions are, You may park your car in front of my house, Smoking allowed, You may cast a vote, or You may join a party. Of strong permissions, von Wright distinguishes between a right and a claim (ibid., 88ff).

I wish to thank Dr. Thorild Dahlquist, Department of Philosophy, Uppsala, for valuable help with this conceptual problem.

6. The word *corruption* is often used to refer to rule breaking in general; compare the definition in Black's *Law Dictionary:* "Corruption: An act done with an intent to give some an advantage inconsistent with official duty and the rights of others. The act of an official or fiduciary person who unlawfully or wrongfully uses his station or character to procure some benefit for himself or for another person, contrary to duty and the rights of others."

7. The distinction between corruption and patronage is not often drawn; but compare Shefter (1983, 460) who, following Huntington (1968), makes this distinction.

8. An actor under the threat of violence might seem to have no choice at all, but this situation can be less asymmetric, or unequal, or constraining (and hence liable to a free choice) for the actor than a situation where money is demanded. Even in situations involving violence, political force, and oppression, it is better theoretically (and more true to the facts) to perceive it in a framework where the actor has a choice. It remains for empirical analysis to judge the actor's degree of freedom—the options available to him or her and their respective costs—in a particular situation.

9. See Kaufman (1974, 303) and Barth (1959) for an early application of game theory to an analysis of an acephalous, stateless society structured by patron-client relationships (the Pathans in northern Pakistan). See also Olson (1965) in this context.

10. Sen (1983) aptly criticizes the common practice among many economists of equating preference' with egoism; an approach of "respectable antiquity" (88). Defined this way, "you can hardly escape maximizing your own utility, except through inconsistency. . . . But if you are consistent, then no matter whether you are a single-minded egoist or a raving altruist or a class-conscious militant, you will appear to be maximizing your own utility in this enchanted world of definitions. . . . This approach of definitional egoism sometimes goes under the name of rational choice, and it involves nothing other than internal consistency" (88f).

11. These problems are more complicated than in the natural sciences, precisely because human beings have intentions and can act strategically. It is, as someone put it, "like an astronomy with thinking stars."

SOURCES

Algotsson, Karl-Göran. 1988. Lagrådet, demokratin och rättsstaten (The Law Council, democracy, and the rule of law). Unpublished.

Bardhan, Pranab. 1984. *The Political Economy of Development in India.* Oxford: Basil Blackwell.

Barth, Fredrik. 1959. Segmentary Opposition and the Theory of Games: A Study of Pathan Organization. *Journal of the Royal Anthropological Institute of Great Britain & Ireland* 89:5–21.

Basham, A. L., 1963. Some Fundamental Political Ideas of Ancient India." In C. H. Philips, ed., *Politics and Society in India.* London: Allen and Unwin.

Baxi, Upendra. 1986. People's Law in India: The Hindu Society. In M. Chiba, ed., *Asian Indigenous Law.* London: KPI.

Bayly, Christopher. 1971. Local Control in Indian Towns: The Case of Allahabad 1880–1920. *Modern Asian Studies* 5:289–311.

Beer, Samuel. 1973. Modern Political Development. In Samuel Beer et al., eds., *Patterns of Government: The Major Political Systems of Europe.* New York: Random House.

Bendix, Reinhard. 1977 (1964). *Nation-building and Citizenship.* Berkeley and Los Angeles: University of California Press.

———. 1986. The Special Position of Europe. *Scandinavian Political Studies* 9:301–16.

Berlin, Isaiah. 1956. Equality. *Proceedings of the Aristotelian Society,* n.s. 56:301–26.

Blomkvist, Hans. 1987. *Democracy and State Formation: Preconditions for a Universalistic Bureaucracy: A Research Proposal.* Uppsala: Department of Government.

———. 1988. *The Soft State: Housing Reform and State Capacity in Urban India.* Uppsala: Department of Government.

———. 1989. Housing and the State in the Third World: Misperceptions and Non-perceptions in the International Debate. *Scandinavian Housing & Planning Research* 6:129–41.

Boudon, Raymond. 1983. Why Theories of Social Change Fail: Some Methodological Thoughts. *Public Opinion Quarterly* 47:143–60.

Chubb, Judith. 1982. *Patronage, Power and Poverty in Southern Italy.* Cambridge: Cambridge University Press.

Coleman, James S. 1986. Social Theory, Social Research and a Theory of Action. *American Journal of Sociology* 91:1309–35.

Deysine, Anne. 1980. Political Corruption: A Review of the Literature. *European Journal of Political Research* 8:447–62.

Dyson, Kenneth. 1980. *The State Tradition in Western Europe.* Oxford: Martin Robertson.

Eisenstadt, Shmuel N. 1985. Civilizational Formations and Political Dynamics: The Stein Rokkan Lecture 1985. *Scandinavian Political Studies* 8:231–51.

Eisenstadt, Shmuel N., and L. Roniger. 1984. *Patrons, Clients and Friends.* Cambridge: Cambridge University Press.

Elster, Jon. 1983a. *Sour Grapes.* Cambridge: Cambridge University Press.

———. 1983b. *Explaining Technical Change.* Cambridge: Cambridge University Press.

Eriksson, Gunnar. 1979. Om idealtypsbegreppet i idéhistorien (The ideal type in the history of ideas). *Lychnos,* 288–96.

Faaland, Just. 1989. Statens role i jordbruksutviklingen i fattige land (The role of the state in agricultural development in poor countries). *Forum for utviklingsstudier,* 211–23.

Frykenberg, Robert. 1968. Traditional Processes of Power in South India. In R. Bendix, ed., *State and Society.* Boston: Little-Brown.

———. 1977. Company Circari in the Carnatic c. 1799–1859. In R. Fox, ed., *Realm and Region in Traditional India.* New Delhi: Vikas.

———. 1981. The Socio-Political Morphology of Madras: An Historical Interpretation. Presented at the Seventh European Conference on Modern Asian Studies, London.

Graziano, Luigi. 1976. A Conceptual Framework for the Study of Clientelistic Behavior. *European Journal of Political Research* 4:149–74.

Hare, R. M. 1972. Principles. *Proceedings of the Aristotelian Society,* n.s. 72:1–18.

Hart, Herbert L. A. 1981 (1961). *The Concept of Law.* Oxford: Clarendon.

Heesterman, Jan. 1971. Kautalya and the Ancient Indian State. *Wiener Zeitschrift für die Kunde Südasiens* 15:5–22.

Hobsbawm, Eric. 1953. Political Theory and the "Mafia." *Cambridge Journal* 7:738–55.

Huntington, Samuel. 1968. *Political Order in Changing Societies.* New Haven: Yale University Press.

Johnston, Michael. 1986. The Political Consequences of Corruption. *Comparative Politics* 18:459–77.

Katznelson, Ira. 1986. Rethinking the Silences of Social and Economic Policy. *Political Science Quarterly* 101:307–25.

Kaufman, Robert. 1974. The Patron-client Concept and Macro-politics: Prospects and Problems. *Comparative Studies in Society and History* 16: 284–308.

Kaviraj, Sudipta. 1984. On the Crisis of Political Institutions in India. *Contributions to Indian Sociology,* n.s. 18:223–43.

Kothari, Rajni. 1974. *Footsteps into the Future.* Accra: Ghana Publishing Co.

———. 1980. Towards a Just World. Delhi: Centre for the Study of Developing Societies, World Order Models Project.

Marriott, McKim. 1989. Constructing an Indian Ethnosociology. *Contributions to Indian Sociology,* n.s. 23:1–39.

Marshall, Geoffrey. 1983. The Roles of Rules. In D. Miller and L. Siedentorp, eds., *The Nature of Political Theory.* Oxford: Clarendon.

Minogue, Kenneth. 1987. Concrete Individualism and the Classical Model. Paper prepared for European Consortium for Political Research (ECPR), Amsterdam.

Mouzelis, Nicos. 1975 (1967). *Organisation and Bureaucracy: An Analysis of Modern Theories.* London: Routledge and Kegan Paul.

Myrdal, Gunnar. 1968. *Asian Drama.* New York: Pantheon.

Nye, J. S. 1967. Corruption and Political Development: A Cost-Benefit Analysis. *American Political Science Review* 61:417–27.

O'Connor, Edwin. 1957. *Sista hurraropet* (The last hurrah). Stockholm: Gebers.

Oi, Jean. 1985. Communism and Clientelism: Rural Politics in China. *World Politics* 37:238–66.

O'Leary, Brendan. 1989. *The Asiatic Mode of Production.* Oxford: Basil Blackwell.

Olson, Mancur. 1965. *The Logic of Collective Action.* Cambridge: Harvard University Press.

Parsons, Talcott, and Edward Shils. 1952. *Toward a General Theory of Action.* Cambridge: Harvard University Press.

Petersson, Olof. 1987. *Metaforernas makt* (The power of the metaphors). Stockholm: Carlssons. The Study of Power and Democracy in Sweden.

Popkin, Samuel. 1979. *The Rational Peasant.* Berkeley and Los Angeles: University of California Press.

Popper, Karl. 1972 (1963). *Conjectures and Refutations.* London: Routledge and Kegan Paul.

Powell, John Duncan. 1970. Peasant Society and Clientelist Politics. *American Political Science Review* 64:411–25.

Price, Pamela. 1989a. Using Cultural History in Development Studies. *Forum for utviklingsstudier,* Oslo, 147–58.

———. 1989b. Kingly Models in Indian Political Behavior: Culture as a Medium of History. *Asian Survey* 29:559–72.

Ramanujan, A. K. 1986. Is There an "Indian Way of Thinking?" University of Chicago. Unpublished.

Rogowski, Ronald. 1978. Rationalist Theories of Politics: A Midterm Report. *World Politics* 30:296–323.

Rubin, Barnett. 1987. The Civil Liberties Movement in India. *Asian Survey* 28:371–92.

Rudolph, Susanne Hoeber. 1987. State Formation in Asia—Prolegomenon to a Comparative Study. *Journal of Asian Studies* 46:731–46.

Saberwal, Satish. 1983. Societal Designs in History: The West and India. Unpublished.

———. 1984. On the Social Crisis in India: Political Traditions. Unpublished.

———. 1985. Modelling the Crisis: Megasociety, Multiple Codes, and Social Blanks. *Economic and Political Weekly* 20:202–11.

———. 1986. *India: The Roots of Crisis.* Delhi: Oxford University Press.

Schaffer, Bernard. 1969. The Deadlock in Development Administration. In

C. Leys, ed., *Politics and Change in Developing Countries.* Cambridge: Cambridge University Press.

Schmidt, Steffen, James Scott, Carl Landé, and Laura Guasti, eds. 1977. *Friends, Followers and Factions.* Berkeley and Los Angeles: University of California Press.

Scott, James. 1969. Corruption, Machine Politics and Political Change. *American Political Science Review* 63:1142–58.

———. 1972. *Comparative Political Corruption.* Englewood Cliffs: Prentice-Hall.

Sen, Amartya. 1983. *Choice, Welfare and Measurement.* Delhi: Oxford University Press.

Shefter, Martin. 1983. Regional Receptivity to Reform: The Legacy of the Progressive Era. *Political Science Quarterly* 98:459–83.

Shils, Edward. 1948. Some Remarks on "The Theory of Social and Economic Organization." *Economica* 15:36–50.

Stein, Burton. 1977. The Segmentary State in South Indian History. In R. Fox, ed., *Realm and Region in Traditional India.* New Delhi: Vikas.

Tarkowski, Jacek. 1981. Patrons and Clients in a Planned Economy. In S. N. Eisenstadt and S. Lemarchand, eds., *Political Clientelism, Patronage and Development.* Beverly Hills: Sage.

Titmuss, Richard. 1976 (1968). *Commitment to Welfare.* London: Allen & Unwin.

Weber, Max. 1982a (1918). Politics as a Vocation. In H. H. Gerth and C. Wright Mills, eds., *From Max Weber.* London: Routledge and Kegan Paul.

———. 1982b (1922). Bureaucracy. In H. H. Gerth and C. Wright Mills, eds., *From Max Weber.* London: Routledge and Kegan Paul.

———. 1985 (1922). *Wirtschaft und Gesellschaft: Grundriss der verstehenden Soziologie.* Ed. Johannes Winckelmann. Tübingen: J. C. B Mohr.

Weiner, Myron. 1984. Ancient Indian Political Theory and Contemporary Indian Politics. In S. N. Eisenstadt et al., eds., *Orthodoxy, Heterodoxy and Dissent in India.* New York: Mouton.

Wiebe, Paul. 1981. *Tenants and Trustees.* New Delhi: Macmillan.

Williams, Glanville. 1975. The Controversy Concerning the Word "Law." In Laslett, ed., *Philosophy, Politics & Society.* Oxford: Basil Blackwell.

Van Cranenburgh, Oda. 1989. The African State in Crisis. Paper prepared for European Consortium for Political Research (ECPR), Paris.

von Wright, Georg Henrik. 1963. *Norm and Action: A Logical Enquiry.* London: Routledge and Kegan Paul.

II

IN SEARCH OF CONTEXT

6

Interpretive Analysis and Policy Studies

Douglas E. Ashford

ALONG WITH LAW, public administration, and philosophy, policy studies were effectively excluded from the prevailing paradigm of political science during the 1950s and even into the 1960s. In those institutions that had both political science departments and schools of public policy or public administration, relations between the two faculties often required great diplomacy. Although the interesting case of the Department of Social Administration at the London School of Economic (Donnison 1975) suggests that such tensions were by no means entirely explained by the theoretical and methodological presumptions of American behavioral science, it is also correct to argue that the behavioral paradigm defined political reality and individual reason in ways that made policy studies an unwieldy, perhaps even threatening, subject.

As outlined in chapter 2, leaders in the field of political behavior (and to a lesser extent, in the field of political sociology) were generally agreed that the philosophical, epistemological, and moral underpinnings of their view needed little further exploration. In a self-confirming way, the assumptions of liberal political thought, pluralist models of governance, and freely competitive politics implied, if they did not require, that intentional and organized intervention in the democratic process was unlikely, or at least of little consequence, in a vigorous democracy. The paradoxical result was, of course, that at the same time government itself endorsed the behavioral sciences and fostered policy studies within specific areas and for specific reasons. The Rand Corporation, for example, launched one of the most ambitious efforts to mobilize behavioral science on behalf of the cold war, much as the military had organized Stauffer, Lazarsfeld, and other early behavioralists to produce studies of military effectiveness, combat behavior, and other war-related problems. The *American Soldier* (Stauffer et al. 1950) was the launchpad for the behavioral social scientists who rebuilt American science after the war.

The history of postwar social science, then, becomes an interesting account of enjoying the best of both worlds. On the one hand, the behavioralists were well placed to fill the ranks of depleted universities and colleges during the postwar boom of higher education. Many returned to their posts enthusiastic and inspired by the generous funding and personal rewards of their wartime work. Not everything went smoothly, of course. It is understandable why the neo-Marxist refugees from the German Institute for Social Research (Frankfurt School) found themselves uncomfortable in Lazarsfeld's grimy factory in New Jersey, where wartime psychological warfare studies were being ground out. Possibly the first sophisticated policy studies group in America, Lazarsfeld's Bureau of Social Research at Columbia University, was not congenial for the critical theorists, some from choice and some from distaste, and they soon drifted away from applied social science in the behavioral mold (Jay 1986, 41–46). An intellectual milestone in setting controversial boundaries between social science and policy studies is Adorno's *Authoritarian Personality* (1950). With its heavy dose of Freudian symbolism, it drew heavy fire from the newly established behavioral social psychologists and sociologists (Christie and Jahoda 1954). The ironic, if unsurprising, result was that policy studies within the behavioral framework were no longer critical of social science theory and methods. The political scientists who came to dominate a generation of American political science were unable to engage in critical discourse and, for the most part, produced intellectual exercises for their disciples. An independent language of policy studies, distinguishable methods of policy studies, and above all, conflicting theories concerning policy formation, implementation, and results were unwelcome.

The internal harmony and intellectual consistency of prewar policy debates can be overestimated, but they serve as the background for this part of this book. Professional consensus on consensual politics was not novel. Even the discredited intellectuals who studied law and administration on behalf of the American reform movements of the late nineteenth century had bitter internal fights over the meaning of applied social and political research (Bramson 1961; Graham 1967). To take a more compelling historical example, the Edwardian reformers seem to be a coherent and enviable group of social investigators in search of a new society (Clarke 1978; Freeden 1978; Richter 1964; Collini 1979), but their zeal concealed substantial differences about the priority of English problems, the desirable nature of a more just society, and how government might best achieve these new goals. But even within the pluralist model of society and politics, the question remains why it was so easy to disassociate policy studies from politics during the 1950s and

1960s. The most persuasive answer seems that given by Hawkesworth (1988). The covering-law model, or basically the nomological deductive concept of explanation advanced by Hempel and Oppenheim, made the examination of the various contradictions, nuances, and moral dilemmas of policy choice secondary. If the political process is completely self-adjusting due to the reliable and effortless translation of competitive inputs into rational outputs within government, then the imperfections of democracy escape serious consideration.

In an illuminating chapter on institutionalized dichotomy, Hawkesworth (1988, 36–72) explains the logical and methodological consequences for policy studies of the behavioral model. The selections for this section are intended to portray some of the alternative explanations that were overlooked only a few years ago. The lawlike explanatory framework for politics meant, first, that intentions, motives, and rhetoric could be excluded. The behavioral tradition never claimed that such questions had consequences but only that such evidence was empirically irrelevant. The most obvious instance was perhaps Wildavsky's reply to the Bachrach and Baratz argument about nondecisions. If the actual consequences of not making a particular decision were empirically demonstrated, then the form of explanation was unchanged. Overlooking the empirical dilemma of how one demonstrates the consequences of decisions in counterfactual situations not only meant that the epistemology of pluralism escaped criticism but that it was made logically immune to criticism. If intentions are only meaningful when their influence is demonstrable within the behavioral paradigm, then the entire argument about the complications of subjective knowledge and its relation to politics is simply excluded. Put more simply, the pluralist paradigm made it unlikely that political science would seriously undertake the analysis of the bewildering behavior of decision makers whose behavior failed to conform to pluralist rules. Given the intricacy, confidentiality, and diversity of actual decisions, it was of course most unlikely that any investigator would have the time, energy, or inclination to replicate in behavioral terms what was already excluded on methodological and theoretical grounds.

A second consequence that Hawkesworth elaborates (1988, 78) is that it was essential to avoid the circularity of behavioral explanation under the lawlike paradigm of explanation. As many other interpretations of society and politics claim, in both theory and reality the fact-value dichotomy is by no means self-evident. By adhering to an explanatory framework that puts a premium on falsification, the behavioralists adopted an epistemological position that made empirical rejection the crucial test of reality and the sole criteria for accumulating scientific truth. Put differently, the hypothetical formulation of social science laws never claimed reliability in the natural science sense but enabled social science to impute lawlike realities to behavior. Confirming or rejecting the hypothetical law became indistinguishable from selecting hypotheses. Though it does not primarily concern this study, the result is that social science had no way of ordering independent variables in the process of scientific investigation.

The selection of independent variables (questions worth studying) was never a random choice: the long list of reputable community power studies coming from Yale shows this. But there was no way of stating why one question might be more important than another. This is, of course, the main charge of the critical theory group, though one need not accept their demanding epistemology to see the overall problem. As Farr points out in chapter 7 and as Popper (1977) discusses at length, the result is either to diminish the significance of social science laws or to confine knowledge of society to only those claims that can be falsified under existing empirical rules. The point is not so much that the epistemological foundations of this argument may be shaky (Toulmin 1958; Lakatos 1970) but that many problems involving counterfactual, problematic, and partially informed decisions are very interesting. In order to study policies, one must deal with circumstances of partial knowledge, opportunity cost, and cognitive presumptions, all of which may contradict the rules of evidence as well as the explanatory foundations for narrowly conceived behavioral inquiry.

Third, numerous philosophers of science would agree with Hawkesworth's third conclusion that "a fact is a theoretically constituted proposition" (1988, 87). To be fair, it is probably correct that even the most rigid behavioralist was always aware that many potential facts were not considered suitable for empirical investigation because they could not be confirmed or denied by the acceptable rules of verification. The result is that behavioralists claim universality under slightly fraudulent conditions. As the historical sector suggests, there are competing claims to the universality of social behavior, some arising from protest, some from moral conviction, and others from the deeply imbedded values (deep structures) of religion, ethnicity, and gender. By making explanation entirely hypothetical and counterfactual—by making hypotheses unacceptable by definition—inquiries about particularistic and irrational questions, such as historical identity, profound loyalties, and even chance encounters, were denied legitimacy in social science. The test of relevance and advocacy so ardently pressed over the 1960s had little meaning. The denial of existential universality (now revived by Geertz's deep structures), critical theory, and the renewed debate about the moral foundations of social science (MacIntyre 1971; Goodin 1988; Gutmann 1988; Gould 1988) all suggest that values have consequences and that moral consistency (conviction) can affect the real world.

A fourth consequence, which Moon (1975) points out in his discussion of interpretive theory, is that social science is confronted with numerous situations where events are loosely connected or where the causal links between remote and problematical decisions could not be predicted. His example is the cause of war, in particular World War I, which remains a mystery to many historians and social scientists. One of the interesting effects of the behavioral revolution was to assign issues of national security to the game theorists and, in line with a similar view of history, to discredit the study of diplomacy and negotiation, where all sorts of personal, momentary, and even deceptive behavior affect results. A curious consequence of the behavioral revolution is that Russian studies languished. No one could collect data on the Soviet Union, so reliance on conceptual codes, context analysis, and order of precedence at Lenin's tomb was considered a parody of social science. The few persons who actually took an interest in the internal dilemmas of the Soviet Union, such as Barghoorn (1956) on ethnic conflict, were easily marginalized, even though they raised fundamental contradictions about Marxist-Leninist theory. They continued to exist within political science departments largely because of national imperatives and the obvious realities of world politics. But explaining the Soviet Union did not cease simply because of the cold war. Causes were imputed to Russian behavior using models and theories that fell outside the realm of approved social science because of the urgency of knowing something (could one say anything?) about Russian behavior at a time when miscalculation invited world catastrophe. Unable to produce data open to direct falsification, the Kremlinologists, a fast-disappearing breed, were denigrated as low-grade social scientists.

The behavioralists had a fairly narrow concept of causation but, at the same time, never deceived those familiar with causation in natural science. The imputed similarity to natural science encased in the concept of explanation advanced by Hempel and Oppenheim, and modified by Popper, was a way of saying that the absence of empirical rejection provided grounds for cause. In this respect, the choice of terms to describe positivists is unfortunate, because in an empistemological sense they are negativists. To return to the communist example, the sudden revival of ethnic, religious, and anti-Semitic behavior in Eastern Europe provides new reasons to pause. The neutral ground of rational choice theory depends on initial assumptions of perfect information, readily formulated evaluation, and ease of communication. To accommodate these imperfections, rational choice has been qualified into virtual unrecognizable form (Downs 1957; Lindblom 1965) from its early formulation in economics. As Moon suggests (1975), incremental decision making, so fervently defended by the pluralists, presupposes that decisions (facts) could be converted into distinct and equivalent units of measurement. With the methodology in hand to make such distinctions, social science seemed a rational process. Whether this is true or not need not be decided here; the important result is that other notions of cause had no validity within the behavioral framework, and unfortunately, many lesser (imperfect) forms of causation regularly occur in making decisions.

While it will occupy part 3 more than part 2 of this book, the epistemological identification of the favored form of explanation, nomological deductive, suggests a fifth assumption of behavioral science that made policy studies less attractive to political science. As noted in chapter 2 and discussed in several essays in part 1, it is no less rational to believe that notions of reality are continually changing. The accumulation of historical experience, the advance of reliable scientific knowledge, the changing set of issues and problems, and of course, the changing preferences and utilities that democracy imposes on working governments reconstruct reality. A curious deficiency of behavioral models of humankind (and a rather menacing implication about social learning) rarely has come under full examination. Behavioralists could talk about how values were acquired, transmitted, and learned, but they could not explain where they came from. Lest this seem an invitation to teleological explanation, the question is how to test reality.

In its fundamental forms, behavioral science had perfectly good (but extremely ahistorical) explanations based on learning, reinforcement, and social conditioning, but hypothetical models have not been helpful in explaining policy-making behavior. To be sure, one can always assert that the pleasure-pain principle was at work when communities decide to dump their waste into rivers, but the same principle had curious ways of coming back to haunt officials when self-interest was transformed into disease, urban decay, and environmental destruction. Essentially, one is dealing with the limits of individual reductionism. Many issues never had a distinctly individual formulation. To put matters more bluntly, some realities are never individual choices but the result of formulating new collective values.

Although there were interesting efforts by social psychologists (Mead 1934; Festinger 1957) to deal with the nature of collectively expressed values, in its early incarnation, behavioral science had great difficulty grasping the issue of transcendent, emergent, or perpetuated values. If individual behavior is unknown or at best historically controversial, as is the case with numerous policy conditions and pressures, explanation in the formal behavioral framework is necessarily inapplicable. To be sure, sophisticated survey research and attitudinal studies can begin to construct models of how multiple realities are linked to needs, perception, and environment, but the possibility of making the detailed and repeated studies that would be needed to study the multiple situations confronting policy makers is mind-boggling—or, as Orwell suggested, and as has happily passed us by, a version of *1984*. Theories involve ontologies or basic convictions about nature. Thinking persons acting only from self-interest make self-interest indiscriminate. The behavioral model, now repeatedly compromised in hopes of preserving its initial influence, is remarkably simple. In the extreme individualist ethic (if one may use the term), reality was entirely self-defined, and self-interest was equally valid for any reality one might encounter.

Historians are, of course, a thorn in the side of strict empiricists, because they continually remind us that we have historical memories, that we substitute vague generalities for demonstrated truth, and that we often act on totally undemonstrated prejudices, assumptions, and preferences. Two of the essays in this part are illustrations of possible alternatives. The first, represented by Skillen's chapter on individualist and collectivist values in relation to the goals of the British welfare state, is both an exercise in comparative and normative theory, commonly ignored by the strict behavioralists, and a way of linking the history of political thought to framing of political questions.

Among the many neglected opportunities for the design of comparative policy studies are the numerous and controversial reexaminations of the foundations of political obligation and political morality. In an institutional context, Skillen argues that the concept of a *social citizen* was never clear in British political and social history, despite the persuasive analysis of Marshall (1950). Thus Skillen suggests that Nozick's formulation of political obligation provides an insight into the difficulties of reconciling conflicting individualist concepts of welfare, readily identified in their policy counterparts in means-tested, earning-related, and income-based social assistance, and limits the conceptual transformation of welfare states. There are now a number of works on the value structure of welfare states and welfare provision (Gutmann 1988; Goodin 1988; Gould 1988). This option emerged from our conference as one of the most attractive and provocative ways of loosening tight research designs and of confining theoretical framework to narrowly conceived behavioral and quantitative policy comparisons.

The second option, represented by Farr's situational analysis (chap. 7), is analytically quite different but offers similar ways of relaxing behavioral constraints. There is of course nothing particularly novel in suggesting that policy behavior takes place in complex settings with numerous constraints, information gaps, and political uncertainties. In rational choice theory, emerging from the pluralist-behavioral paradigm, these problems become market imperfections (Ball 1979; Moon 1975), which actors presumably rationalize for many reasons. In interpretive and critical theory perspectives, these modifications become rationalizations of weak concepts rather than reliable formulations of rational choice. In any event, policy studies are replete with situations of which we have only incomplete knowledge and where the actors themselves must be content with partial knowledge. Though of a very different kind, situational propositions work like ethical propositions to provide summaries of experience. Such summary statements are like Lakatos's discussion of "methodological falsification" in natural science, where the fact-value dichotomy is retained, while the sharp opposition of theory (hypothesis) and observation is relaxed (Lakatos 1970). Situational analysis does not confine concepts to more precise empirical theories but sees them as analytically useful devices to compress complex behavior, which might or might not involve self-interest or rational choice. The point is that, for the moment, the investigator relaxes strict empirical rules in order to proceed with the analysis of a problem that might otherwise, for both analytical and empirical reasons, be beyond reach.

In comparative politics and policy studies, there are many illustrations of how conceptual conflation, sometimes described as contextual (Ashford 1978) or structural, might be used. Bendix's account of how limited liability radically reconstructed the industrial process is one such example. In early industrial Europe, the rational foundations of economic behavior were redefined by the concept of limited liability. To be sure, behavior related to limited liability can be conflated into rational choice theory; adoption of limited liability can always be translated into rational behavior among profit maximizers. For most historical explanation, retracing the appearance of limited liability as an individual choice becomes unnecessary. In fact, most of the debates about capitalism treat limited liability in a situational or contextual way; that is, they proceed on the assumption that this new configuration of economic ideas is already substantiated and is sufficiently alike across systems so as not to require continual verification.

A limit of situational analysis, which Farr and others are quite aware of, is that there is no way to reconcile contrary results if another comparison arrives at different conclusions. To take the limited liability example, if one compares the legal foundations of economic systems, it might be crucial to assess the different results under limited liability in common and continental law (Ginsberg 1959). Comparisons of legal systems (Schwartz and Wade 1972; Teubner 1983; McAuslan and McEldowney 1985) need to examine the assumptions and processes of different ways of expressing legal rights and obligations. The object of the comparison is not the subsequent use of the principle in organizing and developing the industrial process but the expression of such rights and obligations in legal terms.

But comparative law also commonly uses contextual and situational simplifications. From at least the seventeenth century, legal systems have confronted the problem of discretionary behavior (Galligan 1986). Among lawyers, the Weberian notion, consistent with much contemporary thinking in behavioral research, discretion is subsumed within the notion of self-interest and recreational thinking. However, the foundations of democratic justice rest on the presumption that judges somehow operate without any expression of self-interest, that is, through the application of collective knowledge and agreed principles. Dworkin's study (1986) of the relation of individualism to legal principles might be thought of as a way of unraveling this complex legal issue. For the moment, all that need be said is that neither individuals nor collectivities have to resolve this controversy in order to make law a useful comparative exercise for policy studies. While it would strengthen the behavioral argument to show similar rational foundations for individual and collective justice, the two problems may also be situationally distinct.

Chapter 8 by Furniss returns to a classic controversy in social explanation, the use and abuse of functional explanations—but in a way that has particular meaning for comparative policy studies. Policies are expressions of intent, most often intentions based on certain assumptions about either the restoration of a particular state of affairs or the achievement of a new state of affairs. Functional constructs, if not functional explanations, have played an important part in many historical policy questions. For example, over many years the persuasion of the British Ministry of Education that education primarily concerned the young helps explain why the ministry resisted developing training programs for workers, which ultimately made the formation of an active labor market policy virtually impossible (McPherson and Raab 1988; Ashford 1989). Many would agree that Furniss's effort to salvage the concept of function for policy studies is, in this heuristic sense, acceptable. Whether or not functional reasoning is an adequate scientific explanation is quite distinct from the policy makers' use of function, ideas, and analogies to develop crude, causal connections when dealing with questions of enormous institutional complexity or when working with partial information.

While it would not satisfy the criteria of strict explanation, comparison provides a check against freely attributing cause to functional interpretations. Though not functional in an evolutionary or biological sense, civil servants have distinct ideas about their correct roles in advancing government policies and programs. British civil servants, for example, have very strict rules about partisan politics, reinforced by their convention of abstaining from national party politics, while French civil servants readily change administrative and partisan political roles depending on political winds and opportunities (Suleiman 1974). But the analytical issue surrounding functionalism is much older and deeper. As Furniss notes, functionalism made sense to many social and political analysts at the turn of the century largely due to a mix of moralism, evolutionary ideas, and the positivist theory closely associated with late Victorian British social thought (Freeden 1978; Clarke 1978; Read 1982) and late republican secularism in France (Logue 1983; Stone 1985). For both the liberals and Marxists of the late nineteenth century, functionalism held enormous attractions (Ashford 1986, 31–105). For Durkheim, functionalism seemed to hold the key to independently established collective values, or "social facts." It was central to Merton's thinking about the history of science (Cohen 1988) and later resolved by his famous essay on intended and unintended outcomes (Merton 1977).

For reasons laid out by Gunnell (1981), functionalism is unable to achieve explanatory status provided by the conventional rules of social science explanation. Similar reasons for rejecting functional explanation are advanced by scholars concerned with scientific explanation (Nagel 1961, 247–83) and neo-Marxist thinking (Elster 1982). This unusual consensus among social science philosophers helps us understand why other social analysts, such as Giddens (1982), have devised new ways of discussing social and political capabilities. These ideas are central to the essay of Wittrock and Wagner (chap. 10), which examines how policy makers in several countries use social science. The idea that intellectual efforts provide the introduction rather than the subsequent rationalization of social and political actions has a long and respectable tradition in social thought, perhaps most forcefully advanced by Pocock (1971) and philosophically noted in modern linguistic theory (Austin 1975; Searle 1969).

Essentially, the argument is that social science provides a language that may or may not be suitable to the needs of policy makers. A policy-related functionalism need not become mired in the sociology of knowledge (that is, why one idea proved acceptable and another did not) but concerns the context within which policy makers use ideas to focus their efforts, to build agendas, and to advance favored policy solutions. The emergence of the welfare state, for example, was accompanied by dramatic changes in official thinking that are not entirely the result of social and political forces (Ashford 1986). Important effects have linked symbols, rhetoric, and modes of discourse to macropolitical theory, but the link between ideas and policy studies has not been as well developed. In the more general setting of macrotheory, intentions, motives, and values can be dealt with in similarly generalized form, as is common in the history of ideas. But at the microlevel, considerations of intention, motive, and value generate enormous variations that make systematic study almost impossible. It is for this reason that contextual statements rooted in policy-making behavior may be important in developing skill in aggregating from cases to policy-making behavior. This part provides examples of how such contextual generalizations might be introduced in policy studies.

SOURCES

Adorno, Theodor, et al. 1950. *The Authoritarian Personality.* New York: Harper.

Ashford, Douglas E. 1978. *Comparative Public Policy: New Concepts and Methods.* Beverly Hills: Sage.

———. 1986. *The Emergence of the Welfare States.* Oxford: Basil Blackwell.

———. 1989. Death of a Great Survivor: The Manpower Services Commission in the United Kingdom. *Governance* 2:365–83.

Austin, J. L. 1975. *How to Do Things with Words.* Cambridge: Harvard University Press.

Ball, Terence. 1979. Interest Explanations. *Polity* 187–201.

Barghoorn, Frederick. 1956. *Soviet Russian Nationalism.* New York: Harcourt Brace.

Bramson, Leon. 1961. *The Political Context of Sociology.* Princeton: Princeton University Press.

Christie, Richard, and Marie Jahoda. 1954. *Studies in the Scope and Method of the "Authoritarian Personality."* Glencoe: Free Press.

Clarke, Peter. 1978. *Liberals and Social Democrats.* Cambridge: Cambridge University Press.

Cohen, I. Bernard. 1988. The Publication of Science, Technology and Society: Circumstances and Consequences. *Isis* 79:571–82.

Collini, Stephan. 1979. *Liberalism and Socialism: L. T. Hobhouse and Political Argument in England, 1880–1914.* Cambridge: Cambridge University Press.

Donnison, David. 1979. Taking Decisions in a University. In David Donnison, *Social Policy and Administration Revisited,* rev. ed. London: Allen and Unwin.

Downs, Anthony. 1957. *An Economic Theory of Democracy.* New York: Harper.

Dworkin, Ronald. 1986. *A Matter of Principle.* Oxford: Clarendon.

Elster, Jon. 1982. Marxism, Functionalism and Game Theory. *Theory and Society* 11:453–82.

Festinger, Leon. 1957. *A Theory of Cognitive Dissonance.* Evanston: Row Peterson.

Freeden, Michael. 1978. *The New Liberalism: An Ideology of Social Reform.* Oxford: Clarendon.

Galligan, D. J. 1986. *Discretionary Powers: A Legal Study of Official Discretion.* Oxford: Clarendon.

Giddens, Anthony. 1982. *The Constitution of Society.* Berkeley and Los Angeles: University of California Press.

Ginsberg, Morris. 1959. *Law and Opinion in England in the 20th Century.* Berkeley and Los Angeles: University of California Press.

Goodin, Robert E. 1988. *Democracy and the Welfare State.* Princeton: Princeton University Press.

Gould, Carol. 1988 (1944). *The Poverty of Historicism.* New York: Harper and Row.

Graham, Otis. 1967. *An Encore for Reform: The Old Progressives and the New Deal.* New York: Oxford University Press.

Gunnell, John G. 1981. Political Science and the Uses of Functional Analysis. *American Political Science Review* 62:425–39.

Gutmann, Amy. 1988. *Democracy and the Welfare State.* Princeton: Princeton University Press.

Hawkesworth, M. E. 1988. *Theoretical Issues in Policy Analysis.* Albany: State University of New York Press.

Jay, Martin. 1986. *Permanent Exiles: Essays on the Intellectual Migration from Germany to America.* New York: Columbia University Press.

Lakatos, I. 1970. Falsification and the Methodology of Scientific Research Programmes. In I. Lakatos and C. Musgrave, eds., *Criticism and Growth of Knowledge.* Cambridge: Cambridge University Press.

Lindblom, Charles. 1965. *The Intelligence of Democracy.* New York: Free Press.

Logue, William. 1983. *From Philosophy to Sociology: The Evolution of French Liberalism, 1871–1914.* Evanston: University of Illinois Press.

McAuslan, Patrick, and John F. McEldowney. 1985. *Law, Legitimacy and the Constitution.* London: Sweet and Maxwell.

MacIntyre, Alasdair. 1971. Rationality and the Explanation of Action. In Alasdair MacIntyre, *Against the Self-Images of the Age.* New York: Schocken.

McPherson, Andrew, and Charles D. Raab. 1988. *Governing Education: A*

Sociology of Policy Science—1945. Edinburgh: Edinburgh University Press.

Marshall, T. H. 1950. *Citizenship and Social Class*. Cambridge: Cambridge University Press.

Mead, G. H. 1934. *Mind, Self and Society*. Chicago: University of Chicago Press.

Merton, Robert K. 1977. *Social Theory and Social Structure*. Glencoe: Free Press.

Moon, Donald. 1975. The Logic of Political Inquiry: A Synthesis of Opposed Perspectives. In F. Greenstein and N. Polsby, eds., *Handbook of Political Science*, vol. 1. Reading: Addison-Welsey.

Nagel, Ernest. 1961. *Logic Without Metaphysics*. Glencoe: Free Press.

Pocock, J.A.G. 1971. *Politics, Language and Time: Essays on Political Thought and History*. New York: Atheneum.

Popper, Karl. 1977 (1944). *The Poverty of Historicism*. New York: Harper and Row.

Read, Donald. 1982. *Edwardian England, 1901–1915*. New Brunswick: Rutgers University Press.

Richter, Melvin. 1964. *The Politics of Conscience: T. H. Green and His Age*. London: Weidenfeld and Nicolson.

Schwartz, Bernard, and H.W.R. Wade. 1972. *Legal Control of Government: Administrative Law in Britain and the United States*. Oxford: Clarendon.

Searle, John. 1969. *Speech Acts*. Cambridge: Cambridge University Press.

Stauffer, Samuel A., et al. 1950. *The American Soldier: Adjustment During Army Life*. 4 vols. Princeton: Princeton University Press.

Stone, Judith. 1985. *The Search for Social Peace: Reform Legislation in France, 1890–1914*. Albany: State University of New York Press.

Suleiman, Ezra. 1974. *Politics and Bureaucracy in France*. Princeton: Princeton University Press.

Teubner, Gunther. 1983. Substantive and Reflexive Elements in Modern Law. *Law and Society Review* 17:239–85.

Toulmin, Stephan. 1958. *The Uses of Argument*. Cambridge: Cambridge University Press.

7

Democratic Social Engineering: Karl Popper, Political Theory, and Policy Analysis

James Farr

THE NAMES OF Adam Smith and Jeremy Bentham, John Stuart Mill and Emile Durkheim, John Dewey and Charles Merriam, Harold Lasswell and Herbert Simon suffice to remind us that we could once and can still speak of "political theory as policy analysis—and vice versa" (Goodin 1988). At the very least, we can—and in a volume like this one should—acknowledge that political theory and policy studies share a number of common objectives. Among the more important of these is to explore the *explanatory foundations* and *political implications* of various forms of policy analysis and implementation. Given the division of labor that these days seems to make ours "a discipline divided" (Almond 1990), this common objective is admittedly pursued more abstractly, textually, and historically by political theory, and more empirically, concretely, and comparatively by policy studies. But, even then, these distinctions are relative, as can be seen in the range of works represented not only by the theoretical luminaries listed above, but also by works that our discipline slots into the subfield of policy studies and policy analysis—for example, Wildavsky (1964, 1979), Jones (1975), Barry and Rae (1975), Dunn and Fozouni (1976), Dye (1978), Lindblom and Cohen (1979), Ashford (1982), Nagel (1984), Kingdon (1984), Rogers (1988), and Hawkesworth (1988).

This essay in political theory hopes to contribute to the objective it shares with policy studies by exploring the explanatory foundations and political implications of one form of applied policy analysis and implementation, namely, *social engineering*. In this context, social engineering refers to the practical (and sometimes technical) application of the theories and methods of the social sciences to social problems, usually by policy analysts who design, redesign, or maintain political institutions or public services. This understanding of social engineering draws upon the formulation made by the philosopher of science and political theorist Karl Popper (1961, 1966). But it also captures the general view of other philosophers (like Fay 1975), policy analysts (like Lindblom and Cohen 1979), legal scholars (like Pound 1922), criminologists (like Davis and Anderson 1983), and various social reformers (like the Webbs, Henry George, Robert LaFollette, Woodrow Wilson, and John Maynard Keynes).

Given, then, that social engineering is widely familiar in general terms—in political theory and in policy studies—this chapter takes as its point of departure certain prominent claims (discussed below) about its explanatory foundations and political implications. It will address—and criticize—the view that social engineering depends upon a positivist account of the social sciences, especially the view that explanations must be understood in terms of a covering-law model appropriate to the natural sciences. It will also address—and criticize—the view that social engineering necessarily commits policy analysts to a conservative, technocratic, or undemocratic conception of their public role and responsibilities. To the contrary, I hope not only to explore but also to encourage an alternative view of social engineering—and policy analysis more generally—that recognizes the *contextual* character of its explanatory foundations and advances the *democratic* character of its political implications.

In charting all this, the chapter will follow its own discursive or dialectical method inasmuch as I will engage, as theorists are wont to do, in a discourse or dialogue with the arguments of certain scientific philosophers and democratic theorists in matters that bear, directly though abstractly, upon policy analysis and implementation. In particular, I will trace out and try to develop some of the implications of the ideas of Karl Popper and his critics. Unlike many other philosophers and theorists, Popper is no stranger to students of policy analysis—whether praised or criticized, understood or not. The relevance of his thought for public life and policy analysis has been explored at considerable length (in James 1980), and this or that feature of his philosophy of science or political theory has been invoked in numerous works in policy analysis. (For a sample of recent citations and discussions, see Ashford 1978; Lindblom and Cohen 1979; Collingridge 1982; Kiser and Ostrom 1982; Paris and Reynolds 1983; Dery 1984; McCall and Weber 1984; Shortland and Mark 1985; Dror 1986; Starling 1988; Portis and Levy 1988; Eidlin 1988; deHaven-Smith 1988; Majone 1989; Dryzek 1990; as well as the introduction to this volume). Popper's ideas, furthermore, have had considerable impact on policy analysis and implementation through the independently important work of Donald T. Campbell (1988) and others.

In some of these and in other works, Popper is known, among other things, as an avowed advocate of social engineering—albeit "piecemeal social engineering" (1961, 1965). His name, along with that of Carl

Hempel, has also been given to a model of scientific explanation that depends upon the discovery and use of universal covering laws (Donagan 1964). Some have found in this model the warrant for calling Popper a positivist, which, if true, places him in a tradition known for its advocacy of applying exemplars from natural science to the social sciences and technocratic solutions to social problems. He is also often taken to be a conservative (or, as some might say, a technocratic liberal).

Some of this characterization, I hope to make clear, is misleading or false. But, mainly, it is incomplete. Closer attention to a broader range of Popper's arguments reveals a rather different configuration of views from the one that shows up in much of the theoretical and policy literature. In particular, his alternative conception of knowledge—*critical rationalism*—and his alternative model of social explanation—*situational analysis*—better clarify the explanatory foundations of social science and policy analysis. These alternatives are related to a democratic political theory that requires that social engineers and their policies be submitted to the *institutions of democratic control.* When this theory is criticized and developed, it encourages an even more *deliberative* view of democratic life, popular participation, and social engineering.

The purpose of this chapter, then, is simple. It hopes to clarify, criticize, and develop some of Popper's less frequently discussed arguments about social explanation and democratic theory in order to pursue the common objective that political theory shares with policy studies about exploring the explanatory foundations and political implications of policy analysis and, especially here, social engineering. The chapter unfolds as follows. First, it examines and criticizes the positivist model of inquiry and, especially, the covering-law model of explanation, which certain philosophers argue is conceptually connected to any conception of social engineering. Second, it articulates the claims of critical rationalism, the regulative ideal of problem solving, and the methodology of situational analysis as the most appropriate explanatory foundations for social science and policy analysis. Third, it clarifies, criticizes, and tries to develop the democratic and deliberative implications that follow from critical rationalism and situational analysis. Fourth, it summarizes the elements of what we might call democratic social engineering.

Explanation, Technical Control, and Positivism's Problems

A handbook of political theory and policy science makes this suggestion: "For a remarkably clear and insightful exploration of the abstract issue of the relationship between social theory and politics, one could not do better than Brian Fay's succinct book, *Social Theory and Political Practice*" (Portis and Levy 1988, 244). In this case, abstract issues do indeed bear upon policy analysis, as can be seen in the work of policy analysts attuned to the sorts of arguments that Fay makes (Fischer 1980; Dryzek 1982, 1990; Healy 1986; Torgerson 1986; Campbell 1988; Paris and Reynolds 1988; Portis and Levy 1988; and Majone 1989). Fay's work is reminiscent of earlier European debates (for example, Adorno 1976) but it is more directly analytical and it appeals to an Anglo-American audience more interested in the policy sciences. Fay articulates three models of policy inquiry and underscores their connections to different concepts of politics. He sketches a critical model of inquiry and defends what he calls its politics of emancipation. He articulates the communicative basis of an interpretive model of inquiry and criticizes what he calls its politics of conservatism. But he spends the greatest part of his effort (and is most successful at) detailing a positivist model of inquiry and indicting its politics of social engineering and manipulative control. We begin where he begins, namely, with positivism and especially the covering-law model of explanation, which lies behind one very important view of policy analysis and which some say must lie behind any conception of social engineering.

The covering-law model of explanation has long dominated thinking about the nature of science and policy analysis. Some even call it the received view. It originated as part of positivism's broader program in the philosophy of science. Positivism dates its ancestry at least back to August Comte (if not to Saint-Simon or Francis Bacon). Drawing upon the startling successes of the natural sciences, positivists argue that knowledge in the social realm must move beyond its previous commitments to theological, metaphysical, historical, and normative claims and investigations. They argue that there is a sharp distinction between facts and theories, and between facts and values, so that social science should be—and could be—free of values altogether. They argue that abstract and usually mathematical representations of reality are as desirable in social science as they are in physics. This encourages a trend toward modeling, especially when certain abstractions can account for large numbers of individuals, as, for example, in economics.

In our time, positivism has been associated with well-known philosophers of science like Rudolph Carnap, A. J. Ayer, Herbert Feigl, Ernest Nagel, and Carl Hempel. In the practicing social sciences, positivism (in one form or another) has found champions in the psychology of B. F. Skinner, in the sociology of Paul Lazarsfeld, in the positive economic theory of Milton Friedman, and in various forms of behavioralism in political science. For example, in a book entitled *Behavioralist Approaches to Public Administration*, Presthus says that "one of behavioralism's basic characteristics is the acceptance of logical positivism as an epistemological system. Facts, publically verifiable and sensually perceived, are regarded as the only basis of truth or reality." Behavioralism, like positivism, Presthus goes on, represents a "protest against older historical, normative, essentially descriptive kinds of analysis" (1965, 17, 19).

When it comes to the explanatory foundations of science, positivists maintain that explanations take the form of deductive arguments. The premises of such arguments must have both laws (or lawlike generalizations) and statements of initial and scope conditions. Laws themselves are the linchpin in this model of explanation, for they are alleged to provide the only guarantee for understanding general and stable patterns of social processes. More technically, laws are said to be true lawlike generalizations. The lawlikeness of social generalizations consists in several things that ensure that they are not mere summaries of accidental occurrences in the world. In particular, a law must express a genuine causal regularity, the determination of which depends upon there being a "constant conjunction" (to use David Hume's famous phrase) between two classes of events or behaviors, whether physical or social. These conjunctions may be universal or probabilistic, but they must be highly specified. That is, whether universal or probabilistic, a lawlike generalization must specify under what range of conditions it claims to hold. Furthermore, a lawlike generalization must support a set of counterfactual conditional statements that allow warranted inferences about unobserved, hypothetical, or future events or behaviors. Indeed, the future orientation reveals a key element in the covering-law model, for when used prospectively, such explanatory arguments take on the form of predictions. In short, predictions are simply the forward-looking versions of retrospective explanations. (For further discussion, see the excellent analysis in Moon 1975.)

Besides its internal coherence, this account of explanation is all the more powerful because it appears to capture the explanations that natural scientists often offer. It also holds out the key to practical action and public policy of at least *one* kind of social engineering, for lawlike explanations lay the foundation for the instrumental control of phenomena by providing the sort of information that would enable one to manipulate certain variables in order to bring about a state of affairs or prevent its occurrence. Indeed, we might say (explicitly following Fay 1975) that positivists and covering-law theorists "understand a state of affairs scientifically only to the extent that [they] have the knowledge of what to do in order to control it, and it is thus that the ability to control phenomena provides the framework in terms of which scientific explanation proceeds" (40). This is not, as Fay points out, an accidental connection. "The possibility of technical control, far from having a contingent relationship to science, is indeed part of the framework which constitutes the very possibility of scientific activity" (ibid., 39). This view was captured long ago by August Comte, himself: "From Science comes Prevision; from Prevision comes Control." Here, then, is the scientific warrant for the view of policy analysts as a class of social engineers qua technical experts. They are thought to have the knowledge—and the confidence in the knowledge—that makes the prediction and control of social processes possible.

With so much going for it, what's so wrong, one might ask, with the broadly positivist concept of science, social engineering, and technical control? Two general lines of argument seem to be warranted by the characterizations that Fay, among others, makes. The first is to suggest that it is politically objectionable. Under this view, "Science lays the basis for manipulative control" (ibid., 38). That is, the technical control of science implies a manipulative control of the citizenry. The relevant form of political association is the bureaucracy, more or less organized along the chilling lines anticipated by Max Weber. Bureaucratic organization of this sort precludes the democratic organization and communication of the citizenry. Accordingly, the positivist view of science and its accompanying concept of social engineering "seeks to destroy the claim—inherent in any sort of democratic theory" (ibid., 27–28) that "what is most significant is the involvement of the citizens in the process of determining their own collective identity" (54). It is an afterthought, perhaps, to note that this adds up to a "basic conservatism" (62).

Interestingly enough, this argument does not belabor what is objectionable about a concept of science that it alleges is undemocratic, leaving aside the rather obvious objections about manipulation and the less obvious objections about conservatism. This is probably because democratic things no longer appear to need to justify themselves. To characterize some policy or form of science as democratic is, other things being equal, to praise it; to characterize some policy or form of science as undemocratic is, other things being equal, to condemn it. In this way, democracy functions rather as happiness did in classical theories as different as Aristotle's and Bentham's. It often turns out, however, that what one means by *democratic* is rather vague; once articulated, it often proves to be contestable and partisan. Here the specter of competing concepts of democratic theory and practice raises itself.

But before this specter comes to hover over the critique of positivism and its concept of social engineering, this first general line of argument can be preempted or mooted if it can be shown that positivism (and especially the covering-law model) fails to account for the explanatory foundations of social science and policy analysis. As it turns out, this second general line of argument has received greater elaboration, allowing the undemocratic one to bolster it. Countless critics argue, quite correctly, that explanations in the social sciences have not conformed to the dictates of the covering-law model, *even when* generalizations seem available (as often they are and as often they are not). (Among these critics are Gunnell 1969; Moon 1975; Nelson 1975; MacIntyre 1983, chaps. 7–8; and Fay 1975).

In a word, social science generalizations are not lawlike. They are frequently correlational regularities which at best hint at causal actors responsible for their production. They are hedged (usually in good faith) by inexact or indeterminate modifiers like "usually," "characteristically," or "more or less." They seldom stipulate their boundary or scope with any precision. They are unsure about their counterfactual force when straying from the confirming instances that made them possible in the first place. And they hardly ever provide the gravity of assurance that makes future predictions possible. Indeed, lack of predictions has been frequently and ritually bemoaned in the social sciences for some time. So whatever the coherence and consistency of the model of explanation as a model, it has not really helped us reconstruct or understand the practice of social scientists or policy analysts.

Furthermore, even if it were a good reconstruction or understanding of practice, the model seems very removed from the kinds of tasks that social science explanations must meet. Instead of constant conjunctions and searching for laws, social scientists are (or should be) interested in actual individuals or communities of individuals that do things and act, and so cause social phenomena. In encouraging attention to laws and not to actors and actions as such, the covering-law model generally dislocates the conceptual schema appropriate to understanding politics and policy. I have in mind a conceptual schema concerned principally with rationality, intentionality, and meaning. Positivists once tried to dismiss these as "mind stuff," something to be abandoned for real things, like behavior or events that need no intentional or meaningful description. Indeed, in the name of a would-be natural science of society, they were prepared to jettison the very subject matter that made the study of politics so compelling in the first place and so intimately connected with our understanding of ourselves as agents in the world.

These criticisms seem to be eminently warranted, and indeed they have been accepted, sometimes begrudgingly, by many erstwhile positivists or proponents of the covering-law model (Ayer 1969; Davidson 1980). When taken together, these criticisms show that social engineering of the positivist kind is impossible at present or in any conceivable future. Social engineers just do not have the requisite law-governed knowledge upon which both their scientific and political bona fides are alleged to rest. And if the positivist construal of social engineering and policy analysis was the only possible construal, then there would be no social engineering and no policy analysis.

But there are alternatives, and the above criticisms require the elaboration of an alternative concept of the explanations that social scientists and policy analysts can and do offer, a requirement to which we turn in the next section. Although there are related, if competing, elaborations of such an alternative (as in Fischer 1980; Dryzek 1982, 1990; Paris and Reynolds 1983; Forester 1985; Healy 1986; Portis and Levy 1988), the one to be discussed here follows, in general outline, some of the less well-developed ideas of Karl Popper. Now, there is no little irony in this, at least in that Fay, and some of the others here cited, criticize Popper precisely for being a positivist, an advocate of the covering-law model of explanation, and a champion of social engineering. Popper does in fact champion "piecemeal social engineering," a subject to which I will return. Popper has also been credited with being the joint author—with Hempel—of the covering-law model (see Donagan 1964). Popper himself takes some of that credit, but he also says that, as far as explanation goes, "The much more important aspect of the problem is the method of situational analysis" (1976, 117).

As for positivism, it bears mentioning here that Popper has long and repeatedly denied being a positivist. His intellectual autobiography even insists on his being an early and tireless critic of positivism, especially its logical variant as espoused by the Vienna Circle. Popper says he substituted falsification for verification, clung to realism over empiricism, insisted that observations and facts were theory-impregnated, attacked the credibility of induction, praised the speculative but critical imagination, criticized the positivist account of the meaninglessness of ethical and aesthetic discourse, retained the importance of metaphysical debates in and out of science, and "fought against the aping of the natural sciences by the social sciences" (in Adorno 1976, 299). Given all this, he even once claimed to be "responsible" for the "death of positivism" (ibid., 88).

If Popper admits to being guilty of philosophical homicide, he would appear to be rather less guilty of the charge that his concept of social engineering entails a commitment to an undemocratic politics of "manipulative control." To see all of this through, we may turn in somewhat more textual detail to Popper's arguments: first to those about situational analysis, problem solving, and critical rationalism, and then to arguments concerning the politics of social engineering and democratic control.

Situational Analysis and Critical Rationalism

Situational analysis is Popper's name for his model of social explanation, though its ancestry goes back at least to Weber. It is encased in a broader philosophy of knowledge not unfairly described as critical rationalism (see Albert 1985). Critical rationalism emphasizes the imaginative employment of reason and criticism in science and ordinary life. Scientists and ordinary agents advance conjectures in the rational attempt to solve the speculative or practical problems which they face. These conjectures are then criticized and sometimes refuted when they prove mistaken or fail to solve the problems that called them forth. Thus problem solving and learning from mistakes lie at the heart of human rationality; and criticism is its principal tool.

In clear and even simple terms, Popper describes his concept of conjecture, criticism, and problem solving. It was formulated from an analysis of science as a whole, but it is clearly relevant to policy analysis, as well:

> We choose some interesting problem. We propose a bold theory as a tentative solution. We try our best to criticise the theory; and this means that we try to refute it. If we succeed in our refutation, then we try to produce a new theory, which we shall again criticise, and so on. . . . The whole procedure can be summed up by the words: bold conjectures, controlled by severe criticism which includes severe tests. And criticism, and tests, are attempted refutations. (from Magee 1971)

Indeed, Popper has given the schema of problem solving a very rudimentary formalization (1972, chap. 3; and invoked for policy analysis in Dror 1986, 141; and Starling 1988, 246–47): $P_1 \rightarrow TS \rightarrow EE \rightarrow P_2$, where P_1 is the initial problem, TS the proposed trial solution, EE the process of error elimination applied to the trial solution, and P_2 the resulting situation, with new problems. This very simple schema not only formalizes the operations involved in critical rational thinking, but also shows how scientific reasoning—and policy analysis, for that matter—are evolutionary processes. There are always problems whose solutions or failed solutions give rise to new problems. And so on and so on.

This is all a very general statement about Popper's concept of critical rationalism. It assumes different particular forms in different areas of human inquiry; and it invokes different kinds of theories and tentative solutions, depending on the problems—or, as this volume puts a related point, the cases or contexts—involved. One problem of evident importance for social scientists and policy analysts involves social situations. And "in most social situations, if not in all, there is an element of *rationality*" (Popper 1961, 140). This makes it possible to construct models of the decisions, actions, and interactions of more or less rational agents in social situations. Here is the segue from critical rationalism to Popper's alternative model of social explanation—one he takes to reveal "the most important differences" between the social and the natural sciences (ibid., 141)—namely, situational analysis. I present only a bare outline; greater details are provided elsewhere (see Farr 1985 and the literature it cites, especially Watkins 1970; Wisdom 1970; and Jarvie 1972; also see Kiser and Ostrom 1982).

Situational analysis has as its particular objective the explanation of actions undertaken or decisions made by social agents or policy makers in given concrete situations. The situational analyst will attempt to show that an action performed or a decision made by an actor or policy maker was the rational or adequate thing to do in that particular situation, when addressing that particular problem. In this way we can see how situational analysis brings together some of our fundamental explanatory concerns, mentioned earlier, with intentionality, rationality, contextuality, and meaning.

Situational analysis has two parts: the situational model and the principle of rationality. The principle of rationality, interestingly enough, puts primary emphasis not on self-interested decision making—which is the hallmark of a number of rational choice models in political science, economics, and policy analysis—but on problem solving. The ability to solve problems is the principal notion defining what we mean by a rational act or belief. Furthermore, the rationality principle of situational analysis does not have much independent explanatory power, for what it really does is to make the charitable assumption that ordinary actors are problem-solving agents. It encourages the social scientist or policy analyst to assume that actors are acting or believing rationally (and so intentionally) and then to reconstruct the situation in that light. It is a methodological postulate—a sort of searchlight principle—that directs social scientists and policy analysts in their initial inquiries. In any case, the rationality principle is certainly not a law (in the sense of the covering-law model of explanation). Now, admittedly, this is a bounded, limited, and even charitable attribution of rationality—and it has certain sympathies with a number of the arguments about incrementalism in policy studies (classically, Lindblom 1965). But, as I shall suggest presently, I prefer to emphasize what I take to be its humanistic and even democratic implications. More immediately, it clarifies the supreme importance of the other part of situational analysis: namely, the situational model.

The situational model is a detailed description of (1) the natural environment; (2) the social environment; and (3) the problem situation in which an actor defines his or her problems, and rationally tries out certain tentative solutions to them. (Here we can see how the problem schema, introduced earlier in very general terms, fits the critically rational decision processes of ordinary political actors, social scientists, and policy analysts.) Needless to say, such a detailed description of the natural and social environments, as well as the problem situation of the actors, can go in many different directions, and it can dig even deeper depending upon the problem at hand. This has certain strengths, but it also certain limits, and it would seem to put to rest any beliefs that situational understanding is ever final in some absolute sense. Situational analysis, like problem solving and science itself, is never over; it is itself "rational, empirically criticizable, and capable of improvement" (in Adorno 1976, 103). But in whatever direction and however deep we go in our attempt to criticize and improve our situational analyses of actors in social and problem-solving situations, I would like to underscore those elements that appear to have implications for describing the situation. These in turn bear upon the public image of policy analysis and the implications that can be associated with social engineering in a nonpositivist mold.

The social environment to which situational analysis refers includes the communities and institutions within which individuals frame their problems, assume their beliefs, and engage in collective actions. Thus it is essential to articulate the communities and institutions—and especially the different kinds of communities and institutions—that define the situation in a particular given context. Furthermore, how these community-based and institutionally situated individuals define or understand their own problems in their own concrete situations is descriptively essential.

In putting the matter this way, situational analysis calls attention to the meanings that ordinary actors attribute to their problems, their situations, their communities, and their institutions (Jarvie 1972). This requires, in turn, that the social scientist or policy analyst identify and appraise the situation and its problems, in large part, in the way that ordinary actors themselves do, at least initially. This generally involves using their concepts and their language when identifying a problem or when attempting to explain to actors the various alternative solutions that may be available. Indeed, it is necessary to adopt, at least initially, the actors' own concepts and appraisals of the situation, even if the policy analyst or social scientist would like to persuade actors to consider alternative solutions to their problems that they may not have imagined.

Thus the communication between the social scientist or policy analyst, on the one hand, and the ordinary individual or citizen, on the other, is crucial to the task of describing the situation and so explaining social actions and beliefs. At the same time, the adequacy of an explanation or policy position depends upon its actually being communicated to and understood by the individuals and communities involved. Communication of this sort is particularly crucial where a policy or set of actions leads to unintended (especially unwanted) consequences, the study of which makes up a good part of social science. Indeed, in terms of policy analysis, the main purpose of studying unintended (and especially unwanted) consequences is to apprise ourselves and others of the various ways in which our intended actions and decisions misfire. In this way, we can change our decisions and actions in and through the open communication between social scientists, policy analysts, and democratic citizens. At best, we can become the "conscious creators" of our society (Popper 1966, 2:94); at least, we will be better prepared to face future policy decisions and consequences.

After reading this brief outline of situational analysis, someone could point out that one implication is that explanations by social scientists or policy analysts are almost invariably *contextual* and certainly not as definitive as those of natural science, especially generalizations and predictions. Another implication is that such explanations do not radically differ in principle from those that ordinary citizens offer to themselves or to others. They too focus on individuals, communities, problems, and meanings; and they use the language of ordinary life to explain them. These things must be admitted, and they are related to the broader point that the knowledge that social scientists, social engineers, or policy analysts have is not principally different from the knowledge of ordinary individuals or citizens. Social scientists, social engineers, or policy analysts certainly have more knowledge, at least of certain things, and they usually have a greater vision of the interconnections of given situations or of the world as a whole. But such knowledge is nonetheless of the same kind, for all that.

This does not put very much in jeopardy—or, at any rate, nothing more than the misplaced hopes for a natural science of society with truly universal laws and, perhaps, the image of technical expertise and social engineering of a technocratic, positivistic kind. But we can, I think, begin to see the outlines of a different and more democratic conception of the political implications of policy analysis—and social engineering—as made possible by the concept of social science embodied in situational analysis and critical rationalism.

Social Engineering and Democratic Control

"Notwithstanding the objectionable associations which attach to the term 'engineering' "—including that it is "likely to arouse suspicion, and to repel those whom it reminds of the 'social blueprints' of the collectivist planners, or perhaps even of the 'technocrats' " (1961, 58, 64)—Popper repeatedly characterizes his concept of applied social science and policy analysis as social engineering. Given the impossibility of social engineering based on the positivist confidence of having discovered universal covering-laws on the one hand, and given the situational sensitivities of critical rationalist problem solving on the other, we are perhaps in a position to realize that the debate over social engineering may be almost entirely verbal. Indeed, Popper, or Fay, or countless other critics or partisans of social engineering might have helped the level of discussion about the political relevance of policy analysis by making much finer distinctions. Popper, for example, might have followed the lead of F. A. von Hayek and not used the term "because it is associated with . . . 'scientism' " (Popper 1966, 1:285n). But words need not—or should not—get in the way, if we are clear and make sufficient distinctions.

Recall that Fay says that social engineering is conceptually connected to technical control, and that technical control is essentially one of manipulative control—and thus undemocratic. If this is true of a positivist (technocratic or bureaucratic) concept of social engineering, is it or need it be true for any concept of social engineering, including a critical rationalist one? I think not. In showing why not, I hope to lay the basis for characterizing the more constructive—and democratic—implications of critical rationalism and situational analysis.

Popper's advocacy of "piecemeal social engineering" emerged in the 1940s in what he called his "war effort" (1976, 115). Its emergence was intended as a critique of the intellectual background of the collectivist movements of the twentieth century, going back to Marx, Hegel, and even Plato. More particularly, it was intended as a critique of what he took to be the holistic or utopian social engineering of Platonists, Hegelians, Marxists, and their modern progeny. This demonstrably political context—of nazism, Stalinism, and world war—explains the uncompromising hostility that Popper shows toward utopian or holistic social engineering (just as perhaps the political context of our period explains the hostility of some critics toward social engineering as such). Nonetheless, there is all along an acknowledgment on Popper's part of different kinds of social engineering, where the holistic or utopian kind entails wholesale social manipulation based upon the principles or blueprints of an ideal society or a totalizing policy.

The piecemeal character of social engineering has usually been discussed in policy analysis literature in terms of incrementalism (e.g., Lindblom 1965; Lindblom and Cohen 1979; Paris and Reynolds 1983); and it has been subjected to well-placed criticism, which need not be considered here. The point, for present purposes, is the political one of insisting on piecemeal interventions (given the Nazi and Stalinist background). It is also driven by a methodological conviction that piecemeal policies are not only of manageable scale and that they best fit societies whose "ideas and ideals . . . change" (Popper 1966, 1:160], but they may be subjected to criticism, "repeated experiments and continuous readjustments" (ibid., 163), if and when they turn out to be mistaken or fail to solve the problem at hand. It is of course true that there is a practical or technical character to applied science, and so to social engineering, piecemeal or not. In this sense, control (of one sort or another) will be connected (in one way or another) with the very idea of social engineering, as Fay suggests. But since the characterization of the politics of policy analysis and social engineering entirely depends upon a connection to control, one should closely attend to two features that stand out in Popper's articulation of (and indeed his use of the very word) *control*.

First, the unbridled technocratic praise of scientific control, characteristic of certain positivists beginning with Comte, is entirely absent. Indeed, caution if not vigilance is the watchword. Consider the views—expressed in 1956 but only rather recently made available—in *Realism and the Aim of Science*. These views weigh upon our understanding not only of control and its alleged scientific basis; they also weigh upon certain dangerous substantive policies that look very unpiecemeal, despite their vigorous embrace in the West, and that make Popper's words rather prescient, given the developments of the last third of the twentieth century.

> Science, one might be tempted to say at times, is nothing but enlightened and responsible common sense—common sense broadened by

> imaginative critical thinking. But it is more. It represents our wish to know, our hope of emancipating ourselves from ignorance and narrow-mindedness, from fear and superstition. And this includes the ignorance of the expert, the narrow-mindedness of the specialist, the fear of being proved wrong, or of being proved "inexact," or of having failed to prove or to justify our case. And it includes the superstititous belief in the authority of science itself (or in the authority of "inductive procedures" or "skills").
>
> The nuclear bomb (and possibly also the so-called "peaceful use of atomic energy" whose consequences may be even worse in the long run) have, I think, shown us the shallowness of the worship of science as an "instrument" of our "command over nature" or the "control of our physical environment": it has shown us that this command, this control, is apt to be self-defeating, and apt to enslave us rather than to make us free—if it does not do away with us altogether. (Popper 1983, 260)

These sentiments against the self-defeating concept of technical control and the frequent ignorance and insularity of a class of technical experts suggest one of the reasons behind the second point. Social engineering requires "democratic control" (Popper 1966, 1:124–25, 130). That is, even though social engineering presupposes the possibility of control of social processes, it must itself be controlled, since it is part of those processes, whether the engineering is piecemeal or not. And in a society like ours, this means democratic control, the control of social engineering by "democratic methods" (ibid., 159). Foremost among these methods must be counted the empowerment of ordinary citizens to have a voice—to have discursive and communicative power—in the formulation and implementation of public policy, as well as in the articulation of basic values and the redesign of institutions characteristic of a democratic polity. This is the most important implication I want to draw here about democratic control, given our circumscribed topic. So I will return to it presently, after sketching and criticizing features of the more general democratic theory that appears to lie behind it.

The control of social engineering is simply one consequence of a broader "theory of democratic control" (ibid., 124). This theory takes as its point of departure the view that democracy is simply that form of government whose leaders the people can remove without violence so that their institutions may remain. Democratic control, accordingly, requires a representative, electoral system whose basis is majority rule because such rule is "the best, though not infallible means of controlling government" (ibid., 266 n.4). It includes a system of checks and balances as well as a legal framework for the protection of certain rights, especially those of free speech, press, and assembly. It upholds reason over passion; "equalitarian and individualistic principles" (165); and toleration and reciprocity. Above all, it attempts to secure liberty, but a liberty that will not destroy itself. It requires for the well-being of its citizenry a series of economic provisions, institutions, and interventions that, for convenience, we refer to as a welfare state (Popper 1966, 2:125, 348).

In sum, democratic control is a view of the liberal democratic institutions and welfare state provisions that generally prevail at the present time and that prevailed in the 1940s in the Atlantic polities. More important, Popper defends democratic control not in terms of the "intrinsic goodness or righteousness of majority rule" or of the goodness or righteousness of the people themselves, but rather in terms of the negation of "the baseness of tyranny" (1966, 1:124). The caution and the negative formulation are further highlighted in the (Churchillian) confession that "we are democrats, not because the majority is always right, but because democratic traditions are the least evil ones of which we know" (Popper 1963, 351).

This is obviously an important and familiar concept of democracy (though there are certain novelties in its extended presentation that do not weigh upon our topic). But it also appears to be a somewhat thin concept of democracy, to use Barber's (1984) term, at least as regards its negative formulation, protective function, and institutional limitations. It might matter that we remember Popper's rather pointed and limited aims when he first articulated it—namely, to defend the liberal democratic heritage against the onslaughts of totalitarianism at a time when the resolution of world war was not at all clear. But these days we want and have the right to expect from a democratic theory much more by way of specification, not to mention vision. It should move beyond its merely negative formulation (to fight tyranny); it should help envision extrarepresentative institutions (to promote civic life). And in our time, where liberal values and representative government seem to be less fragile and threatened than they were only a half century ago, we want a more robust theory that empowers public participation or that explains in considerable detail under what (presumably very limited and special) conditions such participation must be constrained and in what ways. Nonetheless, it is a concept of democracy and of democratic control, however thin it is with respect to these things, and this concept is systematically connected with the idea of social engineering.

I wish to reemphasize the one point that strengthens the idea of democratic control vis-à-vis social engineering and policy analysis (lest it fall victim to criticisms like those of Bernstein (1978, 50–52): the requirement of popular, nonexpert participation in all forms of public discussion. Such participation is a right of democratic life. Beyond that, it is indispensable in questions about fundamental values or political goals that are not governed by expertise—and so no class of technocrats could pull rank, as it were, in such discussions. It is also essential in all questions about the redesign or adjustments of social and political institutions within a democracy. The question of *institutional* design and redesign dominated Popper's initial formulation of piecemeal social engineering (1961, chaps. 21–24). Finally, it is also essential in questions about policy analysis and implementation of even the most fine-grained kind, much less in those coarser, threatening kinds, like nuclear weapons and nuclear power. Even in arenas where social scientists, policy analysts, and social engineers may legitimately lay claim to expertise and authority, democratic involvement and control is essential. Citizens must be able to choose between competing policies, all of which presuppose scientific expertise. But they must also be able to contribute directly to the very institutions and processes of policy formation and design.

The argument for this discursive empowerment follows from the general outlines of critical rationalism. "The search for truth through free rational discussion is a public affair"; and "the tradition of free rational discussion creates, in the political field, the tradition of government by discussion" (Popper 1963, 352). Free rational discussion presupposes and underwrites other crucial political values and virtues: open access to discussion; listening to other points of view; charity and respect for other discussants; the assumption of fallibility about one's own value or policy position; the welcoming of plurality and diversity of expression; the desire for reciprocal understanding. All these show why so-called public opinion can be no substitute for free rational discussion, for it is invariably managed and promulgated by "public relations officers" in government and in business (ibid., 353).

Clearly, then, "the tradition of government by discussion" requires genuinely popular discussion, over and above the familiar discursive practices in parliaments and congresses. Rationality and the critical attitude require that all voices be heard, regardless of source or station. Since all knowledge is fallible, even so-called experts are fallible. In any case, "In spite of the limited information at their disposal, many simple men are often wiser than their governments" (ibid., 348). Let the people in their manifest diversity and plurality conjecture and refute, as befits free and critical discussion. Praising this as "perhaps the most important" of Popper's conclusions, James (1980, 68) puts the point in this way:

> The fact [is] that experts and specialists of all kinds from physicists to civil servants are not sufficient unto themselves, cannot find out the truth or lay down the law by themselves, but depend on the public at large in order to substantiate the truth and the validity of what they do, although even then there is no certainty. This is the case for democracy.

This is a much stronger concept of democracy, or contribution toward one, than the protective concept articulated above. In this instance, the political argument follows quite readily from the epistemological one—and in such a way as to empower popular voice. Magee has even argued (against Popper himself!) that critical rationalism has very "radical consequences" in that it lays "the philosophical foundations for democratic socialism" (1985, 86). The epistemological premises are here rather positive, not merely negative (in a way that qualifies Barber 1984, chaps. 3. 8). They also help to further democratize the Kantian arguments (these days much-maligned) about the political implications of the Enlightenment. In Popper's gloss, "Kant challenges us to use our intelligence instead of relying upon a leader, upon an authority. This should be taken as a challenge to reject even the scientific expert as a leader, or even *science itself*. Science has no authority. . . . It is you and I who make science, as well as we can" (1983, 260).

There is in all this a humanism and a concern with community. These are also the implications that seem to follow from situational analysis, understood as a contextual methodology of the social sciences and policy analysis. Democratic humanism is partly a consequence of the fact that social scientists who embrace situational analysis study individuals who act more or less rationally within communities that provide their lives with meaning. Gone is the search for those ineluctable laws with enormous scope and generality that are indifferent to whether their subject matter is physical or social. Occasions in which individuals can be posited in the abstract and even bloodless way characteristic of many models in (especially) political science and economics are limited. The scale, quite simply, is more human.

Moreover, there is a charitable attribution of rationality to ordinary agents, and this attribution allows the social scientist or policy analyst to reconstruct the social world and its problems as citizens themselves see or feel them to be. Charity in matters of rationality is also a principle of ordinary discourse; without it discussion could hardly proceed. And if it is true that social scientists, policy analysts, and social engineers use the very concepts and language that ordinary citizens do, at least in great measure, then the emphasis on communication and democratic discussion wins out over the technocratic emphases of more positivistic concepts of technical control and social engineering.

Democratic Social Engineering and Beyond

If terminological legislation were possible or binding, we could well call for a moratorium on the term *social engineering*, for we have surely seen how radically different the various concepts of it can be. But since the term will hardly go away, we might propose the term *democratic social engineering* to capture our sense of it. Democratic social engineering, as intimated in the above discussion, may be understood as informed by certain arguments and convictions with which we conclude.

- Social knowledge is of one piece and is best reconstructed in terms of the attempted solution of problems, the rationality of criticism, and the analysis of social situations.
- Social engineers do not have a different kind of knowledge from which citizens are exempt.
- Social engineers are fallible even in terms of their expert knowledge, and they are often insulated from criticism, as well.
- Social engineers must be controlled by citizens through a variety of familiar democratic processes.
- Citizens must not only control social engineers but also have opportunities for direct input into policy formation and design.
- Citizens must have input into and control over decisions about institutional design, redesign, and fundamental values, decisions over which social engineers can claim no special expertise whatsoever. In such cases, there are no social engineers, strictly speaking, only democratic citizens.

Social engineering need not mean what it has come to mean in some of the otherwise best theoretical literature on policy analysis. Social engineering can be methodologically and politically unfettered by the positivist and covering-law concept of social science and policy analysis, which some have permanently affixed to it. Yet it is still committed to social science and policy analysis, albeit ones that are more situationally sensitive, critically rational, and problem solving. And its idea of control can be less manipulative and more democratic. In short, the "experimenting society" of social engineers and ordinary citizens (Campbell 1988) can and should be a democratic society.

We have here before us the fundamental outline of a stronger theory of democratic discussion and of democratic social engineering. Such a theory remains to be more fully articulated, especially in terms of the practical institutions and discursive forums in which democratic citizens and democratic social engineers can actually practice "government by discussion" (some suggestions may be found in James 1980; Mansbridge 1980; Barber 1984; Forester 1985; and Dror 1986). More, in short, needs to be done as we move ineluctably "toward a technodemocratic society" (Desario and Langton 1987, 13). That more needs to be done—that more will always need to be done—follows from the situational, critical, and democratic view of social inquiry and policy analysis envisioned here.

SOURCES

Adorno, Theodor W., ed. 1976. *The Positivist Dispute in German Sociology.* New York: Harper and Row.

Albert, Hans. 1985. *Treatise of Critical Reason.* Princeton: Princeton University Press.

Almond, Gabriel. 1990. *A Discipline Divided: Schools and Sects in Political Science.* Newbury Park: Sage.

Ashford, Douglas E. 1982. *British Dogmatism and French Pragmatism: Center-Local Relations in the Welfare State.* London: Allen and Unwin.

Ashford, Douglas E., ed. 1978. *Comparing Public Policy: New Concepts and Methods.* Beverly Hills: Sage.

Ayer, A. J. 1969. Man as a Subject for Science. In *Philosophy, Politics and Society,* ed. Peter Laslett and W. G. Runciman. 3d ser. Oxford: Basil Blackwell.

Barber, Benjamin, 1984. *Strong Democracy: Participatory Politics for a New Age.* Berkeley and Los Angeles: University of California Press.

Barry, Brian, and Douglas Rae. 1975. Political Evaluation. In *Handbook of Political Science,* ed. Fred I. Greenstein and Nelson W. Polsby. Vol. 1. Reading: Addison-Wesley.

Bernstein, Richard J. 1978. *The Restructuring of Social and Political Theory.* Philadelphia: University of Pennsylvania Press.

Campbell, Donald T. 1988. *Methodology and Epistemology for Social Science,* ed. E. Samuel Overman. Chicago: University of Chicago Press.

Collingridge, David. 1982. *Critical Decision-Making: A New Theory of Social Choice.* London: Pinter.

Davidson, Donald. 1980. *Essays on Actions and Events.* Oxford: Oxford University Press.

Davis, Nanette J., and Bo Anderson. 1983. *Social Control.* New York: Irvington.

deHaven-Smith, Lance. 1988. *Philosophical Critiques of Policy Analysis.* Gainesville: University of Florida Press.

Dery, David. 1984. *Problem Definition in Policy Analysis.* Lawrence: University Press of Kansas.

Desario, Jack, and Stuart Langton, eds. 1987. *Citizen Participation in Public Decision-Making.* New York: Greenwood Press.

Donagan, Alan. 1964. Historical Explanation: The Popper-Hempel Model Reconsidered. *History and Theory* 3:3–26.

Dror, Yehezkel. 1986. *Policymaking Under Adversity.* New Brunswick: Transaction Books.

Dryzek, John S. 1982. Policy Analysis as a Hermeneutic Activity. *Policy Sciences* 14:309–29.

———. 1990. *Discursive Democracy.* Cambridge: Cambridge University Press.

Dunn, William N., and Bahman Fouzouni. 1976. *Toward a Critical Administrative Theory.* Beverly Hills: Sage.

Dye, Thomas R. 1987. *Understanding Public Policy,* 6th ed. Englewood Cliffs: Prentice-Hall.

Eidlin, Fred. 1988. Ethical Problems of Imperfect Knowledge in the Policy Sciences. In *Handbook of Political Theory and Policy Science,* ed. Edward B. Portis and Michael B. Levy. New York: Greenwood Press.

Farr, James. 1985. Situational Analysis: Explanation in Political Science. *Journal of Politics* 47:1065–1107.

Fay, Brian. 1975. *Social Theory and Political Practice.* Boston: Allen and Unwin.

Fischer, Frank. 1980. *Politics, Values, and Public Policy: The Problem of Methodology.* Boulder: Westview.

———. 1990. *Technocracy and the Politics of Expertise.* Newbury Park: Sage.

Forester, John, ed. 1985. *Critical Theory and Public Life.* Cambridge: MIT Press.

Goodin, Robert E. 1988. Political Theory as Policy Analysis—and Vice Versa. In *Handbook of Political Theory and Policy Science,* ed. Edward B. Portis and Michael B. Levy. New York: Greenwood Press.

Gunnell, John G. 1969. Deduction, Explanation, and Social Scientific Inquiry. *American Political Science Review* 63: 1233–46.

Hawkesworth, M. E. 1988. *Theoretical Issues in Policy Analysis.* Albany: SUNY Press.

Healy, Paul. 1986. Interpretive Policy Inquiry: A Response to the Limitations of the Received View. *Policy Science* 19:381–96.

James, Roger. 1980. *Return to Reason: Karl Popper and Public Life.* Somerset: Open Books.

Jarvie, Ian. 1972. *Concepts and Society.* London: Routledge and Kegan Paul.

Jones, Charles O. 1975. *Clean Air: The Policies and Politics of Pollution Control.* Pittsburgh: University of Pittsburgh Press.

Kingdon, John W. 1984. *Agendas, Alternatives, and Public Policies.* Boston: Little, Brown.

Kiser, Larry L., and Elinor Ostrom. 1982. The Three Worlds of Action: A Metatheoretical Synthesis of Institutional Approaches. In *Strategies of Political Inquiry,* ed. Ostrom. Beverly Hills: Sage.

Lindblom, Charles E. 1965. *The Intelligence of Democracy.* New York: Free Press.

Lindblom, Charles E., and David K. Cohen. 1979. *Usable Knowledge: Social Science and Social Problem-Solving.* New Haven: Yale University Press.

MacIntyre, Alasdair. 1981. *After Virtue.* Notre Dame: University of Notre Dame Press.

McCall, George J., and George H. Weber, eds. 1984. *Social Science and Public Policy: The Roles of Academic Disciplines in Policy Analysis.* New York: Associated Faculty Press.

Magee, Bryan. 1971. Conversation with Karl Popper. In *Modern British Philosophy.* London: Secker and Warburg.

———. 1985. *Philosophy and the Real World*. La Salle: Open Court.

Majone, Giandomenico. 1989. *Evidence, Arguments, and Persuasion in the Policy Process*. New Haven: Yale University Press.

Mansbridge, Jane J. 1980. *Beyond Adversary Democracy*. Chicago: University of Chicago Press.

Moon, J. Donald. 1975. The Logic of Political Inquiry: A Synthesis of Opposed Perspectives. In *Handbook of Political Science*, ed. Fred I. Greenstein and Nelson W. Polsby. Vol. 1. Reading: Addison-Wesley.

Nagel, Stuart. 1984. *Public Policy: Means, Goals, and Methods*. New York: St. Martin's.

Nelson, John S. 1975. Accidents, Laws, and Philosophic Flaws: Behavioral Explanation in Dahl and Dahrendorf. *Comparative Politics* 7:435–57.

Paris, David C., and James F. Reynolds. 1983. *The Logic of Policy Inquiry*. New York: Longman.

Popper, Karl R. 1961. *The Poverty of Historicism*. New York: Harper and Row.

———. 1963. *Conjectures and Refutations: The Growth of Scientific Knowledge*. New York: Harper and Row.

———. 1966. *The Open Society and Its Enemies*. 2 Vols. Princeton: Princeton University Press.

———. 1972. *Objective Knowledge*. Oxford: Oxford University Press.

———. 1976. *Unended Quest*. La Salle: Open Court.

———. 1983. *Realism and the Aim of Science*. Totowa: Rowman and Littlefield.

Portis, Edward Bryan, and Michael B. Levy, eds., 1988. *Handbook of Political Theory and Policy Science*. New York: Greenwood Press.

Pound, Roscoe. 1922. *Introduction to the Philosophy of Law*. New Haven: Yale University Press.

Presthus, Robert. 1965. *Behavioral Approaches to Public Administration*. University: University of Alabama Press.

Rogers, James M. 1988. *The Impact of Policy Analysis*. Pittsburgh: University of Pittsburgh Press.

Shortland, R. Lance, and Melvin M. Mark, eds. 1985. *Social Science and Social Policy*. Beverly Hills: Sage.

Starling, Grover. 1988. *Strategies for Policy Making*. Chicago: Dorsey Press.

Torgerson, Douglas. 1986. Between Knowledge and Politics: Three Faces of Policy Analysis. *Policy Sciences* 19:33–59.

Watkins, John. 1970. Imperfect Rationality. In *Explanation in the Behavioral Sciences*, ed. Robert Borger and Frank Cioffi. Cambridge: Cambridge University Press.

Wildavsky, Aaron. 1964. *The Politics of the Budgetary Process*. Boston: Little, Brown.

———. 1979. *Speaking Truth to Power: The Art and Craft of Policy Analysis*. Boston: Little, Brown.

Wisdom, J. O. 1970. Situational Individualism and Emergent Group Properties. In *Explanation in the Behavioral Sciences*, ed. Robert Borger and Frank Cioffi. Cambridge: Cambridge University Press.

8

Functionalism and Policy Studies

Norman Furniss

THIS CHAPTER explores the connections between functionalism as theory and image and the study of public policies. Given the immensity of the topic, the chance of saying anything coherent is increased by setting boundaries. The term *functionalism* is here restricted to classic formulations. At the risk of sounding hopelessly old-fashioned in these times when everyone seems to be a "neo" something, the concerns of neofunctionalism are set aside.[1] And on policies, although there are eclectic references to various policy issues, this chapter deals in a systematic way only with functionalist explanations and the development of social welfare policies in Western democracies.

Even with this narrowing of the topic, the argument of this chapter remains fairly complex. It is easy to show that functionalist explanations are not in vogue; there are many efforts to avoid the label, some of which are rather amusing. But despite these efforts, functionalist explanations and language, as opposed to the functionalist paradigm, remain omnipresent, and I argue that they will continue to persist. If this position is correct, the task then is not to banish functionalism but to identify those concerns that are potentially valuable and insightful. This chapter pursues this goal in three parts—first, through a review of classic functionalist thought starting with Durkheim; second, through a consideration of particular strengths and weaknesses of the functionalist perspective; finally, through a focus on the development of social welfare policies in Western industrial countries.

This chapter is an argument with examples; as such it falls under the generic category of essay, the general risks and potentialities of which are nicely outlined by Stannard (1977). More specifically, following David Hume, it is open to the criticism that the possibility that some future contrary example has not been foreclosed. And this is to say nothing of the likelihood that someone might advance a real counterexample. I accept these limitations; indeed I welcome the spirit that the latter problem implies. To employ the terminology introduced later in this chapter, my aim is to persuade the reader that the argument that functionalism can provide important insights warrants serious consideration.

Functionalism and the Social Science Enterprise

I begin this chapter with an intellectual stroll through the grand, if by now slightly musty and dark, corridors of functionalism. The busts of the masters—August Comte, Herbert Spencer, Emile Durkheim—attest to the heroic aspirations of the edifice. And, at least in American sociology, a generation functionalism has constituted what one might term the official paradigm of the discipline (see Gouldner 1970, 1973). As Levy (1968) summarizes: "Shorn of careless use of definitions and of teleology, structural functional analysis is simply a synonym for explicit scientific analysis in general" (22).[2]

How different matters seem today! Perhaps in reaction to the complacent certainty implied in Levy's description, to be accused of being or having been a functionalist often has become linked to a number of intellectual sins (see Gouldner 1973). And in good investigative style, the search for hidden functionalists has become a lively sport. For example, Giddens (1982) says that "one of the attractions of [Jon] Elster's article . . . is the diversity of sources in which he discovers the use of functional analysis. Some of his examples are of unlikely provenance, but perhaps for that reason are all the more telling. E. P. Thompson for instance . . . " (528).

Moreover, were the problems limited to some heretics and fellow travelers whose errors would be exposed and thus controlled, the containment of functionalism could be more manageable. But unfortunately for its critics, functionalist images have become ingrained generally in social science. As described by Giddens (ibid., 296), "The work of functionalist authors has been very important in social research precisely because it has directed attention to the disparities between what actors intend to do and the consequences which ensue from what they do. But we can identify, and attempt to resolve, the issues involved more unambiguously by dispensing with functionalist terminology altogether." He then proceeds to detail how nonfunctionalist terms can be substituted. Instead of writing, for example, that education, in a capitalist society, has the function of allocating individuals to positions in the occupational division of labor, he proposes that "in order for the occupational division of labor to be maintained, the educational system has to ensure that individuals are allocated differentially to occupational positions."

This formulation seems less than successful in beating back the contagion. What does it mean that a "system has to ensure" something or other? In short, we seem faced with a paradox. There are hardly any self-conscious, self-proclaimed functionalists anymore; the official corridors of functionalism are almost empty save for a few elderly caretakers. Yet the language and outlook of functionalism seem ubiquitous! The analogy to M. Jourdain is given a perverse twist: we are all talking functionalese without knowing it, and that is bad. If this is so, it does not suffice merely to condemn functionalism and all its works. We must attempt to understand why it is widespread and what are its at least potentially useful properties.

It seems appropriate to start these efforts historically with the emergence of functionalism as a distinct and coherent mode of inquiry in the nineteenth century. In a sociology of knowledge sense, functionalism can be seen as one of the nineteenth-century ideas described by Tilly (1984):

> In these waning years of the twentieth century, the nineteenth century also keeps its hold on many ideas about social organization. In the analysis of social change, we cling loyally to ideas built up by nineteenth-century intellectuals. Intellectuals formed those ideas in their astonished reaction to what they saw going on around them: unprecedented concentrations of population, production, capital, coercive force, and organizational power. They formed ideas treating increasing differentiation as the master process of social change, ideas of societies as coherent but delicate structures vulnerable to imbalances between differentiation and integration, and other ideas connected to them. (2)

Within these general ideas, functionalist advocates took and attempted to combine three particular tendencies of nineteenth-century intellectual thought: imagery and analogies drawn from the emerging biological sciences, a search for positive, scientific laws of human and social development, and a moral thrust that saw change as inevitable but feared its unregulated consequences. All three continue today. Again, Tilly gives a fine synopsis. There was a sense that the "social order is fragile, that differentiation threatens social order, that change is risky, that unrestrained change generates strain, violence, decay, and disintegration, that only guided and contained change leads to integration, satisfaction, and progress" (1984, 12f). Science, based on biological analogies, could provide this guidance.

These tendencies come together most completely in the work of

Durkheim, who took society as the basic unit of analysis and proceeded to investigate empirically how it worked. His investigation yielded propositions and findings that had a major impact on the discipline of sociology. In particular, his conclusions on religion's protective influence on suicide and the associated claim that Catholics commit fewer suicides than Protestants has been "touted as the closest sociological approximation to a scientific law."[3] In reaching these positions, Durkheim adopted and advanced the ideas of what Turner and Maryanski (1979) describe as the French and British traditions of functionalist analysis. From the British tradition he took the fundamental question: What is the function of a particular structure for society that encompasses the question of societal needs? What does a society have to have to survive and progress? "Durkheim's answer was clearly in the French Tradition: a society must be integrated, or reveal solidarity among its component parts. Thus most of Durkheim's work concerned the analysis of how a given structure meets the integrative needs of society" (ibid., 16f). Here we have an excellent, succinct description of the functionalist project.

Durkheim also recognized a key problem that has continually bedeviled its fulfillment: describing how a structure functions is not the same thing as describing its cause. As Durkheim puts the problem in *The Rules of the Sociological Method* (1966): "The need we have of things cannot give them existence . . . we must seek *separately* the efficient cause which produces it [a social phenomenon] and the function it fulfills" (cited in Turner and Maryanski 1979, 83). This warning is taken up later by Merton (1968), who emphasizes that functionalism is properly a middle-range strategy for theory building, a heuristic device.

In practice, however, most subsequent functionalist theorists fail to heed these admonitions and proceed directly to the assumption or proposition that function is an "*explanatory principle*" (Turner and Maryanski 1979, 84). Parsonian functionalism represents the "ultimate effort at the realization of Comte's dream that sociology would provide the basis of systematization for biology" (ibid., 70). The key question is why this causal turn was taken. If we could disentangle a pure, noncausal functionalism from the masters, then perhaps many of the difficulties later associated with the approach could be eliminated. We might, in other words, be able to extract a non-Parsonian Durkheim, just as many have claimed to liberate Max Weber from Parsons's tender but constricting embrace.

Unfortunately, the positing of a radical dichotomy between cause and function, or between cause and anything else, is not tenable in social science research. Such a distinction cannot be found in Durkheim's or

Merton's own works—which are thereby made no less distinguished. Nor can it be found in social science generally. Despite Durkheim's confident assertion that "today" (in 1895) the "law of causality" holds equally in the realm of nature and in the social world (1966, 128), in its long history sociology has managed to formulate but one self-designated "*close approximation* of a scientific law." This approximation, as noted earlier, is Durkheim's own, and it is now under severe scrutiny and attack. One must agree with the conclusion of Giddens (1976) that those who are waiting for a Newton (or a Darwin) of social science are not only like passengers waiting for a train that for one reason or another is always being postponed, they are waiting at the wrong station.

The reason is of general relevance to the contributions to this volume. And because Durkheim offers a direct introduction to the problem, a brief discussion seems warranted despite the risk of redundance. These references to causes come from nineteenth-century positivist epistemology bequeathed to functionalism, to many forms of Marxism, to behaviorism, and to other theories in which the investigator is said to stand apart from the phenomena being observed, able in principle to uncover regularities and to offer parsimonious, theoretical explanations and predictions, all of which are capable of empirical falsifiability. In *The Rules of Sociological Method*, Durkheim provides a succinct summary: "All [sociology] asks is that the principle of causality be applied to social phenomena. . . . Since the law of causality has been verified in the other realms of nature, . . . we are justified in claiming that it is equally true of the social world, and it is possible to add today that the researches undertaken on the basis of this postulate tend to confirm it" (1966, 14).

And what is this postulate? "A given effect has always a single corresponding cause." But this claim cannot be justified whatever the theoretical orientation of the investigator. Cause and effect are mixed, as are agency and structure; the "use of concepts outside of science" (ibid., 32) is inevitable. As a result, once a phenomenon has been explained or understood to our current satisfaction, we are not necessarily in a position to make predictions. The nature of this enterprise can also be seen in the manner in which the best work in social science is presented. *On Suicide* (Durkheim 1951), to cite a relevant example, is an argument. Following the useful distinction of Perelman (1979), the aim of arguments and of social science generally is to persuade. To persuade is to lead the adherent toward action, while a person merely convinced of something could remain passive.

This distinction forces us to address the nature of the social science enterprise. Is social science fundamentally different from natural science (in which passivity might be entirely warranted)? This question can be posed in another way: Is the problem of Durkheim's invocation of positivistic science that he applies positivistic norms to areas where they do not work? Or is the idea of a positivistic natural science a chimera? These questions too often are dismissed with some form of the statement that whether or not one can legitimately refer to positivistic natural science, physics being the pure form, policy analysis is a different animal. (For an instance of this deflection, see Furniss and Mitchell 1984, 28–29.) This position, while perhaps prudent, limits our ability to tease out common elements in natural and social science development and modes of inquiry.

Appropriately, given the orientation of this chapter, it was Merton who, in his Ph.D. dissertation printed in 1938, first tried to systematically link the concepts of science, technology and society (see Merton 1970). His concern was to determine "the relative amount of scientific research (in seventeenth-century England) which was influenced, directly or indirectly by socio-economic needs" (see Cohen 1988, 575–77). This concern was approached through the idea of institutional differentiation. As summarized by Gieryn (1988, 583), "To adopt the structural and functional language that has served Merton well, institutionalization is the functional differentiation of society into more-or-less independent subsystems that satisfy (again, more or less) discrete societal needs." The role of science is to extend "certified knowledge" (ibid.). Seventeenth-century England was a particularly important historical period, for it was then that, with the aid of Puritan values, science began its journey toward (relative) functional autonomy.

Merton's argument long dominated studies in the history of science, a discipline his work was instrumental in launching. This argument has been challenged by social constructionists, who maintain that science and society are linked in a far more fundamental way. (See Collins and Pinch 1982; Gieryn 1983, 1988; Latour 1987.) According to this perspective, the assumption that scientific knowledge is discrete and unique is unwarranted, because "scientific knowledge is a social construction rather than a mirror of nature; scientific facts are fabricated in laboratories and in journals, as scientists *persuade* others that their account of nature is true" (Gieryn 1988, 588; my emphasis). The scientific and social scientific enterprises become similar; more accurately, they become a wealth of competing and overlapping enterprises. And even without subscribing to the position that they are identical, it is possible, following Merton as well, to see their development and types of argumentation as interrelated.

This middle-road position seems particularly useful when we consider analogies, visualization, and images. These are essential for both social and natural science. On the latter, Miller (1978) offers this example from the development of quantum theory:

> Bohr's method to arrive at a contradiction-free interpretation of the quantum theory led him to ever deeper levels of analysis: from a purely scientific analysis, to an epistemological analysis, to an analysis of perceptions, and then to the origins of scientific concepts. A necessary prerequisite to this analysis was the acceptance of the complete wave-particle duality even though the wave aspect of matter had not yet been definitely established experimentally. For Bohr the wave-particle duality was "the central point in the whole story" because it permitted Bohr to use the symmetry of the pictures of waves and particles which are familiar from our customary intuition. Visual thinking preceded verbal thinking, and linked with visual thinking was Bohr's new aesthetic of the symmetry of pictures. (62)

Here are outlined some intriguing parallels with the enterprise of social science. Competing analogies and visualizations are basic to the structure of persuasion. Moreover, people act differently today both because of the ideas and arguments of others and because of the way, historically, individuals have managed to give them institutional representation. In this sense, past visualizations have to be taken into account by the analysts and actors who follow. This discussion permits us to make a reasoned distinction between functionalism as a paradigm based on positivist assumptions and functionalism as a set of concerns and associated language. The first must be rejected; the second warrants serious consideration.

Functionalism and Policy Studies

To summarize my argument to this point, the pervasiveness of functionalist visualizations is something to be understood, not dismissed. In their focus on institutions and patterns of social relations (e.g., networks) as nonderivative entities, functionalist images point to key variables for policy analysts. The challenge is to define their role. In his study of the politics of state intervention in Britain and France, Hall (1986) presents this problem well. He notes, as described above, that "one of the fundamental problems with functionalist theories is that they are too robust. They suggest that the state can be expected to reproduce the economic system; and Marxist variants claim that the state will act in the interests of capital. But when we compare the experience of such European nations as Britain, France, and Germany, we find wide variation in the range of policies they have adopted" (6). This difficulty is developed further later in this chapter. Hall concludes,

> Many of these problems are largely attributable to the way in which functionalist analysts reverse the priority given to institutional structures. It might be possible to identify the functions of a given institutional structure, but it is virtually impossible to derive structure from function in a systematic and non-arbitrary way. . . . Structural-functionalism only works if it gives causal priority to structure rather than to function. (7)

These concluding comments highlight the difficulty of either incorporating or rejecting functionalist imagery. It may well be virtually impossible to derive structure from function, but is it much easier the other way around? Does not the return to the notion of causal priority deflect our attention from studying the interaction between structure and function, the way one influences the other? Is the image of causal priority itself based on positivist assumptions? I will approach these issues through a discussion of the particular strengths and weaknesses of the functionalist legacy, beginning with the latter.

Because the weaknesses of the functionalist enterprise are apparent, they need be only briefly described. The ontological problem is captured in Arendt's (1959) remark that she often uses the heel of her shoe to drive a picture hook into a wall, but this use does not make her shoe a hammer. Here is not an example of confusing function with cause but of conflating what a thing does with what a thing is. This example leads to the second particular disability: functionalism has a marked disinclination to acknowledge the significance of individual or class action. Little wonder, as Elster notes (1982), that functionalism displays a fondness for the passive voice. *X* does not *do* this or that; rather this or that *is done*. Part of the reason for this downplaying of agency, as previously described, stems from the historical emergence of functionalist thought among those worried about the fragility of social order. The other part of the reason can be located in the level of analysis. And now we come to the third particular disability of functionalism.

Classical functionalist thought is focused resolutely on society as the major, if not the only, valid unit of analysis. Once again, Durkehim (1966, 17), offers a succinct argument. To be sure, he does remark that "social things are actualized only through men; they are a product of human activity." This statement, however, needs to be understood in the broader context of social phenomena; note again the biological imagery. Since social phenomena have as their essential characteristic the "power of asserting pressure on individual consciousness, it follows that they are not derived from the latter. . . . When the individual has been eliminated, society alone remains. We must, then, seek the explanation of social life in the nature of society itself" (ibid.).

But one might object that society is composed only of individuals. This objection, for Durkheim, is not telling: "In reasoning thus, it can be established that there are in the living cell only molecules of crude matter. . . . A whole is not identical with the sum of its parts." Indeed, if we "began with the individual we shall be able to understand *nothing* of what takes place in the group. In a word, there is between psychology and sociology the same break in continuity as between biology and the physiochemical sciences" (ibid., 102–04). One does not have to subscribe to methodological individualism to find problems in this position. In short, one is led away from a focus on interactions between individuals and groups, between agency and structure, between policies and politics. And, as we shall see later in this chapter, the temptation to monocausal explanations of the type suggested here is particularly great in treatments of the welfare state.

But, I would argue, this temptation is not so overpowering that all functionalist images must be avoided even if they could be. In at least four major respects, functionalism offers insights or possibilities of particular relevance to policy studies. The first involves the issue of unintended consequences stemming from the classic work of Merton (e.g., 1968). For example, it has been argued that immigration policy in the United States started as a rather straightforward effort by the dominant industrial interests to have the government regulate the flow of labor. But gradually the bureaucracy gained autonomy. (A key moment came when immigration was transferred to the Department of State, when it became a national interest.) And in the end, immigration policy functioned in ways directly opposed to the expressed interests of the groups most instrumental in its establishment.

As Fitzgerald (1987, 27) shows, "Policymaking networks were created as unanticipated consequences of the process by which public laws were formulated, and, as institutions, outlasted the temporary circumstances under which they were formed." To be sure, the idea of unanticipated consequences is not without its ambiguities. Is it functional (in the sense of system maintaining)?[4] The answer seems to vary somewhat by discipline, with sociology tending to answer in the affirmative, and with political science seeing in the idea more possibilities for political transformation. (On the general issue of functional explanation, see Noble 1984.) In either case, the image has proven remarkably fruitful, as we shall see in the next example.

Second, it is valuable to return to Durkheim's proposition that a full explanation entails a consideration of both cause and function. As Durkheim and Merton note, functionalism is unlikely to contribute much that is insightful about policy origins. Still, a functionalist perspective could well help us understand which policies survive and flourish. Public education, for example, is often described in causal functional terms; modern industrial society needs a literate, disciplined work force—therefore, public education was established. One problem with this explanation is that compulsory schooling organized by the state was instituted in central Europe well before the industrial revolution. Melton (1988) locates the origin not in the needs of society, but in the desires of state officials. In eighteenth-century Prussia and Austria, "schools became a central target of state policy precisely because they offered an instrument for exacting obedience" (xxii). Functionalism is not of much help in understanding the origin of these desires, but it provides insight into how the policies worked—which, from the standpoint of the state officials, was badly.

Melton found that compulsory school policies "were often resisted by both landlords and peasants precisely because they disrupted household production" by depleting the labor force of children (ibid., 233). In other words, the policies were not functional to the economic system; consequently, these absolutist states had trouble making them stick. And there is more. The language of instruction in the schools was the language of the local population—all the better, it was thought, to inculcate discipline rapidly. But the unanticipated consequence was an upsurge of effective national protest within the Austrian empire! "By encouraging the rise of literary vernaculars among the non-German population of the monarchy, Theresian school reform hastened the emergence of the nationalistic, anti-Hapsburg movement of the following century" (235).

Third, the ideas of Levy and others on functional prerequisites for public policies have found support. As argued by Tilton (1986), "In its quest to purge itself of the fallacies of functionalism, modern social science has eschewed virtually any sort of functional analysis. . . . The claim that *X* is an essential condition or precondition for *Y* is hard to substantiate empirically, but such claims are so important to politicians that they must be faced, for practical as well as theoretical reasons" (23–25). Tilton proceeds to outline the "essential prerequisites for the modern welfare state." One of the merits of looking at these conditions as functional requisites is that they can be considered together.

Finally, the value of functionalist ideas and imagery needs to be addressed. These can constitute both a major source of policy principles and (a related point) a major political critique. Since this position runs counter to most standard accounts (e.g., Gouldner 1973), it might be wise to begin with an analogy to pluralism, the intellectual history of which is better known in American political science. As it reached its fullest development in the 1950s in the United States, pluralist thought showed many of the same features as contemporary functionalism, not coincidentally. There was a similar conflating of origins and normal operations; class or conflict analysis was equally rejected; the status quo was celebrated as a moral good (or at least in this case, as the closest possible approximation to democracy).

Finally, there are similar claims to scientific accuracy and uniqueness, albeit those of pluralism were usually presented at a lower level of theoretical rigor.[5] Here seems a singularly unpromising place from which to launch critical observations of political or policy patterns. And yet when analysts turned their attention to the gap between how pluralist arrangements ought to work in political and corporate life and the reality of various privileged positions, the basis of a major critique was laid. The degree to which the pluralist position developed is indicated in Wildavsky's (1978) assessment of Lindblom's *Politics and Markets* as "the most intellectually interesting contribution to American radical thought since that of Randolph Bourne" (218).[6]

Although perhaps less well known, the use of functionalist ideas as critiques can be at least as powerful. An excellent example is found in the work of R. H. Tawney. (For more discussion, see Furniss [1978], from which the quotations in this paragraph are drawn.) Tawney starts with the proposition that all rights "are derived from the end or purpose of the society in which they exist." It follows, then, that a society filled with coupon clippers, idle lords, and underpaid nurses is morally skewed. It is based not on what is necessary to further social goals but on changing legal rules that themselves broadly reflect the interests of dominant social groups. In its stead must be instituted a functional society, defined by Tawney as one "which aims at making the acquisition of wealth contingent upon the discharge of social obligations, which seeks to proportion remuneration to service and denies it to those by whom no service is performed."

This type of functionalist argument could (and did) have an impact beyond that of a critique (with its connotations of practical sterility). To the extent the image of a functional society enters the policy debate, it can be important in shaping the character of new institutions. The distinction between structure and function is blurred again and in a new way. The constitution of a structure is affected by specific ideas on how it ought to function. The visualization of a functional society, in short, can be significant in the origin of policies. Functionalism becomes a tool for understanding how policies work, and functionalist images become a factor affecting their design.

Functionalism and the Development of Welfare States

In the final section of this chapter I explore the capacity of functionalism to provide insights into the development of social welfare policies in Western industrial states. This case is useful because the literature is sufficient to permit an assessment of the strengths and limitations of the functionalist perspective. The latter are immediately apparent, as we might expect, in accounts of the origins of social welfare policies. A whole line of arguments—called by Mishra (1973) the "logic of industrialism" position—on the institution of these policies in Western Europe and the United States goes as follows: Industrialization produces similar socioeconomic problems; these problems in turn produce the public policies to deal with them. These policies are needed—they are functional—therefore they occur. Policy becomes "the outcome of some demographic or economic process" (Trousdell et al., 1986, 411). Regardless of dominant groups or dominant ideologies, nations institute similar policy sequences (see Cutright 1965; Jackman 1975; and Wilensky 1975 for representative accounts).

This argument suffers from the liabilities we might expect given the evidence put forth in the earlier parts of this chapter. Empirically, the fit is very poor. As Malloy (1985) indicates, for example, we cannot explain how many Latin American nations could have instituted social insurance policies before a number of industrially more advanced states, including the United States. More generally, at the theoretical level we see a clear instance of the principle of indispensability that Merton argues against. One must conclude regretfully that Merton's strictures have had a minimal impact on much of the logic of industrialism literature.

The perspective outlined above is not confined to logic of industrialism advocates; it is also reproduced with the expected modifications in much of the Marxist literature on welfare policy determinants. (See, for example, O'Connor 1973; Gough 1979; Offe 1984.) Social policies arise to meet needs—this time the need for the reproduction of capitalist social relations; they are the "functional exigencies of the capitalist mode of production" (Offe 1984, 102). Once again, there is no room for politics, for political institutions, for political debate; regarding the last, we are told that "the history of economic theory is the history of the class struggle" (O'Connor 1981, 112). And once again there are rather frantic efforts to manipulate historical experiences to fit the requirements of monocausal, ahistorical theorizing. (For more complete discussions from different perspectives, see Skocpol 1981; and Ashford 1986, 20–29.)

Even on the matter of origins, however, many of these functionalist accounts do point to significant relationships. The logic of industrialism position admittedly has little of value to say about why welfare policies were established, but they do suggest why they stuck. In this connection, we can contrast the Prussian effort to establish compulsory schooling with Bismarck's social insurance legislation approximately a century later. Both initiatives were undertaken apart from or in opposition to existing political forces. (As Ashford [1986] comments on the latter: "By 1890 Germany built the most complete system of social insurance in the world, but democratic forces were effectively excluded" [46].) The schooling policy essentially failed, while the three compulsory insurance laws enacted under Bismarck (and consolidated in 1911 into a single national insurance code, *Reichsversicherungsordnung*) have remained the basic social welfare legislation. (For a fine account of the German system, see Alber 1986.) The reason, it is generally agreed, is that they were functional; more, they have structured subsequent patterns of social interaction.[7] Similarly, on the Marxist variant, Malloy (1985) sees social security systems in Latin America as fulfilling the function of helping to sustain capital accumulation.

In short, it is wise to abandon "big bang" notions in policy studies. As was argued earlier, one cannot isolate cause and function as discrete categories; they are structured through the interaction between state initiatives and social receptivity and reaction. In understanding this interaction, functionalism makes an important contribution to the idea of unintended consequences. I provide two contrasting examples. In much of the late nineteenth and early twentieth centuries in western Europe, trade unions began to provide unemployment benefits for their members. With the institution of the well-known Ghent system in 1901, first municipal and then central governments began subsidizing these schemes. The effects on union membership were dramatic and were particularly obvious in countries like Britain and Norway, where subsidies were not introduced in stages. In the year that subsidies were introduced (1911 in Britain and 1905 in Norway), union membership dramatically rose (by 22.3 percent in Britain and 73.3 percent in Sweden). This rise in union membership was not even necessarily the most important unanticipated consequence: subsidies made welfare matters during the 1920s not a matter for collective bargaining but a political issue.[8]

The contrast with the United States could hardly be more pronounced. In these years, American unions did not develop the benefit side of their activities; as late as 1916, only three national unions paid unemployment benefits. Consequently, even had they so desired, state and municipal governments had no union schemes to subsidize. Pension plans were instituted not by governments or by unions but by corporations. By 1928 there were 397 such plans covering 14.4 percent of the employed population and paying pensioners an average of $600 per year. (See the discussion in Mitchell 1989.) There is no evidence that corporations launched these intiatives with the aim of reducing the power of organized labor. Rather, it was government action they feared.[9] Unions were viewed far more tolerantly by the new business corporate leadership of the 1920s than they were by the industrialists who founded the National Association of Manufacturers in 1895 who had as their major goal arousing the "great middle classes to a realization of what trade-unions" really meant (see Steigerwalt 1964). Nonetheless, by superseding public provision and by making putative union schemes redundant, the impact of these corporate policies was devastating.

Perelman (1979, 208–10) offers an excellent contemporary account: As "long as anti-union capitalism depended only on force and paid a 'supply and demand' wage, the danger to unionism, while often grave, was rarely critical. . . . Unionism knew how to handle situations under the 'old' capitalism. But this 'new' capitalism which fights unionism with a far-sighted 'preventive' method rather than with the old 'remedial' one leaves it stunned and bewildered." That strikes and membership declined was less significant than the unanticipated consequences for policy orientation. Instead of working with governments or public institutions, unions had to turn to corporations for effective welfare collaboration. The American Federation of Labor outlined the parameters of such a deal in 1925 with its new wage policy, based on the corporate ideology of cooperation and service. Why, it was asked somewhat plaintively, have company unions when an AFL union can prove as loyal and more productive?

The advantage given corporate leadership from this unanticipated development can be brought out in the context of a study by Griffin et al. (1989) on class conflict and market distribution in capitalist democracies since World War II. They find that social democracy has reduced political power imbalances between capital and labor and has conferred other benefits—in particular, reduced unemployment. At the same time, however, labor in social democratic countries is less militant. And militancy "directly builds unions" and "strengthens the market efficacy of those unions." In sum, labor in social democracies "simultaneously has been empowered and weakened" (62). From this perspective, we can see that labor in America in the 1920s got the worst of both worlds: militancy was foresworn, and there were no political gains either.

The distinction between origin and operation is further clouded with the reintroduction of the issue of how functionalist images helped shape the ideas behind social welfare provision. One can distinguish two types: Swedish and British. In Sweden, within the Social Democratic party—and therefore generally within the government—there has been the tradition of seeing property as a bundle of rights, which can be disaggregated and reconstituted in ways consistent with public purpose. The title of the book by Adler-Karlsson, *Functional Socialism* (1969), captures this position well. Those rights that are functional in private hands should remain there; those that are not should be subject to public regulation or control. In practice, this has meant a switch from socializing "the commanding rights of industry" to organizing a more equal distribution of services. The reason is plain: capitalism was extraordinarily effective at producing wealth; in this area it was functional. What was needed—and was recognized as early as the 1930s by leading Social Democratic theorists and ministers (the two categories were not distinct)—was a socialization not of production but of consumption. (For a discussion of this point, see Tilton 1989.)

The British experience is more difficult to describe, in part because the connections between social theorists and the Labour party and between the Labour party and political power are much more tenuous. Some insight, however, can be derived from a review of the position of Tawney.[10] As mentioned earlier, Tawney (1920) launched a powerful critique of capitalism from a functionalist position overlaid with ideas of stewardship and Christian service. This critique is unsparing. "The will to economic power," Tawney argues, "if it is sufficiently single-minded, brings riches. But if it is single-minded it destroys the moral restraints which ought to condition the pursuit of riches. . . . It divorces gain from service, and justifies rewards for which no function is performed" (33). Here is a spirit very different from that articulated in functional socialism. Production is not seen as a property right that can be disentangled from consumption and left to perform useful functions. The issue is much more basic and involves nothing less than the replacement of an acquisitive society with a functional society, which "would honor, even in the person of the humblest and most laborious craftsman, the arts of creation" (35).

What are the policy implications? The major point is that they are far less easy to identify than in the Swedish case. One can infer a disinterest with creating more wealth to distribute and a focus on "the humblest," on poverty, as the concern of welfare policy. This is a noble concern; it is presented well by Dr. Johnson, who observed to Boswell that, while "gentlemen of education were pretty much the same in all countries, the condition of the lower orders, the poor especially, was the true mark of national discrimination." This focus on the poor has remained at the center of the British welfare state (see Furniss and Tilton 1977, 94–121). But it is not particularly a social democratic concern; more concretely it offered little guidance to Labour party leaders interested in designing new policy initiatives after 1951.

These insights need not be totally retrospective; functional perspectives might offer some ways of organizing discussion of possible evolutions of welfare policies. The recent panacea of privatization is one example. As I noted earlier, the United States has a long tradition of private welfare provision. Some of the implications for the relative power of social groups are worthy of note; I propose that a shift from public provision will bring (as in America in the 1920s) further pressure on organized labor to change the content of its proposals and demands. More broadly, the fit between welfare policy, social needs, and the political system becomes a central concern. Writing at the beginning of Margaret Thatcher's government, for example, Ashford (1981) states that "the British political system may be unable to accommodate what is in many ways its most creative achievement, the welfare state itself" (24). In this case, it may be the welfare state that will have to go or be altered in a functionally more congruent way.

The possibility of a change in the welfare state is increased when, in addition, there are tensions between the welfare state and social needs. Again, Britain offers the most obvious case. As summarized by Marshall (1981) the (British) welfare principle aims "to provide not what the majority want but what minorities need" (126). Given this principle, it is quite correct that "the normal process of political and industrial democracy is out of harmony with the spirit required for taking policy decisions at operational level in the field of welfare" (109). In brief, one can project troubled times for British welfare policy that is not functional at either the political or at the societal level. I also suggest that, to the extent that liberal reformers in the United States also focus on poverty as the evil to be cured, they will face similar difficulties. In the absence of a welfare ethos of the kind that facilitated the establishment of the British welfare state after World War II, it is extremely doubtful that proposals to end poverty (as opposed to those aimed to temper those aspects most obvious to the middle class) will be instituted, let alone develop.

Despite my efforts to restrict the scope of this essay, what began as a rather leisurely stroll through the foyer of functionalism, with time to cast a critical yet respectful gaze at the busts of the masters, has ended in a rather hurried exit via the halls of policy relevance. This tour reflects something of the potential strengths and limitations of the functionalist enterprise. Its domain is immense. It has something to say about almost everything. The question is whether it has something important to say about a discrete set of issues.

The argument of this chapter is that it does have something important to say. To begin with, the functionalist perspective, if creatively employed, can identify relationships that previously have been explored only haphazardly. One example is Merton's linkage of science and society. Moreover, these linkages are pursued with sufficient analytical rigor to permit the development of alternative positions. As has been shown, the idea of institutional differentiation is basic to the development of the social constructionist critique. This is not the same as subscribing to Popper's criterion of falsifiability. Social science advances through the consideration of competing images but only if the images are sufficiently clear to permit us to see what they are. Gieryn (1988, 585) uses a different metaphor. Social constructionists are looking in a different direction, but that they are able to see at all results from standing on the shoulders of giants. We find many similarities in our review of the literature on the welfare state. To be sure, the logic of the industrialism-functionalism school has many disabilities. But the best work (Offe 1984; Wilensky 1975) is presented in a way that furthers the articulation of competing explanations.

Beyond this general point, one can identify four specific ways in which functionalism defined as a set of concerns and associated language can make a major positive contribution to policy analysis. The first is the image of unanticipated consequences. The second is an insight into why some policy initiatives are more likely than others to be institutionalized. The third is the concept of functional prerequisites, which is also developed in historical and institutional terms. The final is the contribution to the construction of policy principles, as described, for example, by Anderson (1979). Perhaps the most controversial argument is that these contributions can be used in policy analysis without signing onto functionalism as an intellectual project. The nature of social science inquiry does more than warrant, the eclectic consideration of images, it mandates it. In this orientation, functionalism can play a vital role.

NOTES

I want to express my appreciation to Alfred Diamant, Anne Figert, Keith Fitzgerald, Larry Griffin, Jeffrey Issac, Bernice Pescosolido, Simon Reich, David Robertson, and Timothy Tilton for their help in bringing more coherence to the argument. Special thanks to Douglas Ashford both for organizing the conference, at which an early draft of this chapter was presented—and for his detailed and thoughtful comments at every stage of this project.

1. A good introduction to these concerns is provided by Alexander (1985). The title of the first chapter—The Practical Groundwork for Critical Theory: Bringing Parsons to Habermas (and Vice Versa)—indicates why it is prudent to defer addressing them. In this chapter, Sciulli (1985) argues that "Parsons's collegial form is, ultimately, Habermas's communication theory and standard of procedural reason" (44).

2. This official paradigm was fostered by close professional linkages. Most of the major architects of the functionalist approach in the United States—Parsons, Merton, Kingsley Davis, Levy himself—were associated with Harvard either as students or teachers.

3. The quotation is from Pescosolido and Georgianna (1989, 34). The use of the term *scientific law* to describe Durkheim's contribution has been advanced by Merton (1967) and Johnson (1965), among others. For a more extended discussion, see Pescosolido and Georgianna.

4. This question was posed by Simon Reich in a review of this chapter.

5. Polsby (1963), for example, concludes *Community Power and Political Theory* with the hope that "as students become increasingly concerned with satisfying the demands of scientific method and theoretical relevance in the conduct of their research, their results become more amenable to meaningful summary, and we may therefore reasonably expect the early formulation of provisional theories of community power which correspond more closely to the facts of the world around us" (138).

6. Why Bourne is cited is a bit unclear, since his critique is essentially cultural. One could also cite Walzer (1983) as a more general normative statement of a critical position that is basically pluralist. For an excellent argument that pluralism cannot change its spots, see Manley (1983).

7. To be sure, this insight cannot be attributed to all members of the logic of industrialism school. In his insistence on dating the German constitution to 1949, for example, Jackman (1975) obscures all historical continuities. For a discussion, see Coughlin and Armour (1980).

8. Again, we should not fall into a monocausal trap. This opportunity was

realized much more in some countries than in others. See the discussion in Furniss and Mitchell (1984).

9. That this fear was not confined to America is shown in the work of Katzenstein (1985). In Switzerland (which provides a good comparison with the United States), for example, he finds that the 1935 peace agreement between the employers' association and the metalworkers' and watchmakers' union was agreed to by the employers "to forestall further government intrusion in the private sector" (147).

10. Ashford has described Tawney as the main idea man in rebuilding the Labour party before the war (personal communication). For an overview of Labour's thinking, see Addison (1975).

SOURCES

Addison, Paul. 1975. *The Road to 1945*. London: Jonathan Cape.

Adler-Karlsson, Gunnar. 1969. *Functional Socialism*. Stockholm: Prisona.

Alber, Jens. 1986. Germany. In Peter Flora, ed., *Growth to Limits: The Western European Welfare States Since World War II*. Vol. 2. Berlin: Walter de Gruyfer.

Alexander, Jeffrey, ed. 1985. *Neofunctionalism*. Beverly Hills: Sage.

Anderson, Charles. 1979. The Place of Principles in Policy Analysis. *American Political Science Review* 73:711–23.

Arendt, Hannah. 1959. *The Human Condition*. Garden City: Doubleday.

Ashford, Douglas. 1981. *Policy and Politics in Britain*. Philadelphia: Temple University Press.

———. 1986. *The Emergence of Welfare States*. Oxford: Basil Blackwell.

Cohen, I. Bernard. 1988. The Publication of *Science, Technology and Society:* Circumstances and Consequences. *ISIS* 79: 571–82.

Collins, Harry, and Trevor Pinch. 1982. *Frames of Meaning: The Social Construction of Extraordinary Science*. Boston: Routledge.

Coughlin, Richard, and Philip Armour. 1980. Methodological Issues in the Comparative Study of Social Security. *International Review of Modern Sociology* 10:25–48.

Cutright, Phillips. 1965. Political Structure, Economic Development, and National Social Security Programs. *American Journal of Sociology* 70:537–50.

Durkheim, Emile. 1951. *On Suicide*. New York: Free Press.

———. 1966 (1895). *The Rules of Sociological Method*. Glencoe: Free Press.

Elster, Jon. 1982. Marxism, Functionalism and Game Theory. *Theory and Society* 11:453–82.

Fitzgerald, Keith. 1987. *Immigration, the State, and the National Identity*. Ph.D. diss., Indiana University.

Furniss, Norman. 1978. Property Rights and Democratic Socialism. *Political Studies* 26:450–61.

Furniss, Norman, and Neil Mitchell. 1984. Social Welfare Provisions in Western

Europe. In Harrell Rodgers, ed., *Public Policy and Social Institutions*. Greenwich: JAI.

Furniss, Norman, and Timothy Tilton. 1977. *The Case for the Welfare State*. Bloomington: Indiana University Press.

Giddens, Anthony. 1976. *New Rules of Sociological Method*. London: Hutchinson.

———. 1984. *The Constitution of Society*. Berkeley and Los Angeles: University of California Press.

Gieryn, Thomas. 1983. Boundary-work and the Demarcation of Science from Non-science. *American Sociological Review* 48:781–95.

———. 1988. Distancing Science from Religion in Seventeenth-Century England. *ISIS* 79:582–93.

Gough, Ian. 1979. *Thc Political Economy of the Welfare State*. London: Macmillan.

Gouldner, Alvin. 1970. *The Coming Crisis of Western Sociology*. New York: Basic Books.

———. 1973. *For Sociology*. New York: Basic Books.

Griffin, Larry, et al. 1989. National Variation in the Context of Struggle. *Canadian Review of Sociology and Anthropology* 26:36–68.

Hall, Peter. 1986. *Governing the Economy: The Politics of State Intervention in Britain and France*. New York: Oxford University Press.

Jackman, Robert. 1975. *Politics and Social Equality*. New York: Wiley.

———. 1980. Socialist Parties and Income Inequality in Western Industrial Societies. *Journal of Politics* 42:135–49.

Johnson, Barclay. 1965. Durkheim's One Cause of Suicide. *American Sociological Review* 30875–86.

Katzenstein, Peter. 1985. *Small States in World Markets*. Ithaca: Cornell University Press.

Latour, Bruno. 1987. *Science in Action*. Cambridge: Harvard University Press.

Levy, Marion. 1968. Functional Analysis. *International Encyclopedia of the Social Sciences* 6:21–29.

Malloy, James. 1985. State and Social Security Policy and Crisis. In Camelo Mesa-Lago, ed., *The Crisis of Social Security and Health Care*. Pittsburgh: University of Pittsburgh Press.

Manley, John. 1983. Neo-Pluralism: A Class Analysis of Pluralism I and Pluralism II, *American Political Science Review* 77:368–83.

Marshall, T. H. 1981. *The Right to Welfare and Other Essays*. New York: Free Press.

Melton, James Van Horn. 1988. *Absolutism and the Eighteenth-Century Origins of Compulsory Schooling in Prussia and Austria*. Cambridge: Cambridge University Press.

Merton, Robert. 1967. *On Theoretical Sociology*. New York: Free Press.

———. 1968. *Social Theory and Social Structure*. New York: Free Press.

———. 1970. *Science, Technology and Society in Seventeenth Century England*. New York: Harper and Row.

Miller, Arthur I. 1978. *Frontiers of Physics: 1900–1911*.

Mishra, Ramesh. 1973. Welfare and Industrial Man. *Sociological Review* 21: 535–60.

Mitchell, Neil. 1989. *The Generous Corporation*. New Haven: Yale University Press.

Noble, James. 1984. Marxian Functionalism. In Terrence Ball and James Farr, eds., *After Marx*. Cambridge: Cambridge University Press.

O'Connor, James. 1973. *The Fiscal Crisis of the State*. New York: St. Martin's.

———. 1981. Accumulation Crisis. *Contemporary Crises* 5:109–25.

Offe, Claus. 1984. *Contradictions of the Welfare State*. Cambridge: MIT Press.

Perelman, Chaim. 1979. *The New Rhetoric and the Humanities*. Dordrecht: D. Riedel.

Perlman, Selig. 1944. *A Theory of the Labor Movement*. New York: Augustus M. Kelley.

Pescosolido, Bernice, and Sharon Georgianna. 1989. Durkheim, Suicide, and Religion. *American Sociological Review* 54:33–48.

Polsby, Nelson. 1963. *Community Power and Political Theory*. New Haven: Yale University Press.

Rodgers, Harrell, ed. 1988. *Beyond Welfare: New Approaches to the Problem of Poverty in America*. Armonk: Sharpe.

Sciulli, Robert. 1985. The Practical Groundwork for Critical Theory: Bringing Parsons to Habermas (and Vice Versa). In Jeffrey Alexander, ed., *Neofunctionalism*. Beverly Hills: Sage.

Skocpol, Theda. 1981. Political Responses to Capitalist Crises. *Politics and Society* 10:151–201.

Stannard, David. 1977. *The Puritan Way of Death*. New York: Oxford University Press.

Tawney, R. H. 1920. *The Acquisitive Society*. New York: Harper and Row.

Tilly, Charles. 1984. *Big Structures, Large Processes, Huge Comparisons*. New York: Russell Sage.

Tilton, Timothy. 1986. Perspectives on the Welfare State. In Norman Furniss, ed., *Futures for the Welfare State*. Bloomington: Indiana University Press.

———. 1989. *The Political Theory of Swedish Social Democracy*. Cambridge: Oxford University Press.

Trousdell, Elizabeth, et al. 1986. Organizing Principles and Issues in the Welfare State Literature. In Norman Furniss, ed., *Futures for the Welfare State*. Bloomington: Indiana University Press.

Turner, Jonathan, and Alexandra Maryanski. 1979. *Functionalism*. Menlo Park: Benjamin-Cummings.

Walzer, Michael. 1983. *Spheres of Justice*. New York: Basic Books.

Wildavsky, Aaron. 1978. Changing Back. *Yale Law Journal* 88:216–20.

Wilensky, Harold. 1975. *The Welfare State and Equality*. Berkeley and Los Angeles: University of California Press.

9

Welfare Ideologies and State Policies: British Oppositions

Anthony Skillen

IN CLASSES on moral and political philosophy, I am fond of asking my students to think about cases such as the following:

- You are on a country road driving home to keep a dinner appointment. Suddenly, at an intersection, you are approached by two despairing men. "Can we use your car? There's been a gas explosion in our home. Two people are badly injured—they need to be got to hospital." "Sorry," you reply, "I'm late for an appointment." Failing with further pleas, the two men pull the door open, push you out, and drive off to get their injured friends.
- You have just finished twenty brisk laps in the hotel swimming pool when you see your little sister on a poolside seat looking miserable and in need of attention. You are going to her side, when suddenly (it's always *suddenly!*) two boys, before running off, throw another small child in at the deep end, where she splashes about helplessly. A large man turns to you: "You can swim, I can't—save my daughter!" You tell him you are attending to your sister and turn away. He grabs you violently. "Get in there and don't come out until you bring my child to safety." You obey him.
- You belong to a rare blood group. There is a knock on the door. It is your doctor, looking worried. "There's been a car crash. An old man needs blood. We don't have his type. You're the only one I know who can help!" "That's your problem, doctor. In the words of the old song, 'I've got troubles of my own,' " you say. The doctor then summons two powerful men.

The question here is: Were the agents of those in need morally entitled to use force? For what it's worth (and in the context of a book whose theme is differences in policy perceptions, it seems to me worth a lot), I get a slight majority who say no. However we may condemn your selfishness as the driver, the swimmer, or the blood groupie, and however we may understand the feelings of the coercers, their forcing you to the rescue was unwarranted, a violation of your individual right to do as you want as long as you do not harm or interfere with others—to mind your own business. So many say.

The liberal principle thus formulated differs importantly from that of John Stuart Mill's *On Liberty.* Mill's principle includes the phrase "to prevent harm to others," and it is certainly the case that the coercive agents are interfering to that end. Oddly enough, people are still surprised by Mill's position. In the introductory chapter, he writes:

> There are also many positive acts for the benefit of others which he may rightfully be compelled to perform; such as to give evidence in a court of justice; to bear his fair share of the common defence; or in any other joint work necessary to the interest of the society of which he enjoys the protection; and to perform certain acts of individual beneficence, such as saving a fellow-creature's life, or interposing to protect the defenceless against ill-usage, things which, whenever it is obviously a man's duty to do, he may rightfully be made responsible for not doing. A person may cause evil to others, not only by his actions, but by his inaction. (1962, 136–37)

With the last sentence, then, Mill assimilates the idea that a person may be coerced if he harms or threatens to harm others with the idea that he may be coerced if he fails to help others. In each case he "causes evil." This claim about causation might be thought to be the decisive one—if *A* causes *B*, *A* is causally responsible for *B*.

But my students argue over whether the selfish driver, swimmer, or blood groupie can properly be said to be a cause of the sufferer's plight. What counts for us as a cause, then, far from determining what we hold people responsible for, depends in part on a background of expectations and requirements we have of people—on what they are (deemed) responsible for. If we were required and expected to pick up hitchhikers, our failure to offer someone a ride might be agreed to have "caused" their late arrival with the same force as today we speak of bus failures "causing" such things. What we call a cause, then, is shaped by what we think ought to be expected and by what is expected. The intractability of that issue, then, is a symptom of the problem, not its solution. After all, even if most of the students accepted that the selfish swimmer couldn't have been charged with murder, they could hardly deny that he or she was in a position (easily) to cause the drowning child to survive, a long-winded way of saying "to save it." And so the dispute is back to the beginning.

What I then do is to sketch putatively analogous rescue situations, some of which involve victims of hunger or oppression in other parts of the world, some of which involve the needs of strangers in their own country, needs that rescuers might meet either directly through voluntary work or indirectly through voluntary payment to a charitable institution, such as Oxfam or the Salvation Army, or compulsory taxes imposed by the welfare state.

The welfare state, then, is like the helpless father of the drowning child. He (it) can do nothing unless he (it) obtains and redirects capacities to where they are needed. Because people can't, it seems, be expected or trusted to offer the needed help voluntarily, he (it) has to compel the necessary action. The selfish swimmer and the others are outrageous because they refuse to help in the face of urgent need and with little trouble or risk to themselves. These analogies can be developed. Thus for example, we could envisage swimming pool systems in which a voluntary contribution or a compulsory levy supports a lifeguard. Not only will there be arguments pro and con, this scheme entails a certain pool culture, in terms of which arguments pro and con will be framed: So we all just forget about each other in the pool and leave it to the guard? Great! The whole spirit of the pool is going to disappear! Wait and see! Well, wait and see how this affects the children's safety!

The welfare state, as we know it, operates through compulsory taxation, whereby resources to meet needs are extracted and transferred. Through this process, we are forced to render benefits, including rescue, which are spread among indeterminate recipients. These recipients include equivalents to the drowning child, as well as to ourselves in sickness, study, unemployment, or old age. Taxes, then, impose no concrete or particular duty; I do not even have to seek a job to receive some benefit. Nor do I have to assist anyone in particular. Yet I think Nozick (1974, 169) correctly connects being taxed with forced labor. A critic might reply that you are not forced to labor at all, let alone to labor for the state's coffers. But Nozick is right to the extent that, for any officially recognized work you do, a proportion of that is work for the state coffers. The implication is also right, though Nozick would not like this, that the general compulsion to work is a real one—an alternative to poverty. Now we have seen that the intuition that we can be legitimately forced to do things for people is shared with many of my students by John Stuart Mill. Why should it not be legitimate not only to tax people so that they work abstractly for the good of others, but to oblige them to work concretely for the good of others? If, in other words, you accept the legitimacy of welfare taxation, why do you object to compulsory welfare work?

Beveridge's Giant Model

In September 1989, Charles, Prince of Wales, gave notice of a scheme under his patronage for all young people in the United Kingdom to be encouraged and financially maintained to undertake three months' work serving the community. From small beginnings, this army would, for example, work with the sick and the aged and would repair damage to the environment. The prince told of the "giant raspberry" his scheme had for years received "from John O'Groats to Lands End." Now he was able to speak as chairman of a committee with senior members of all political parties, trade unions, and businesses—the idea's time had come. And so, it seems, it has. The prince's theme was of community, of citizenship, and of the lack of vehicles for reinforcing or expressing their values. He pointed, on the one hand, to "the damage done to the sense of community within society by a social philosophy too narrowly based on individualism." On the other hand, he criticized the welfare culture, which teaches us either to reluctantly pay out taxes or to passively depend on state officials to cater to our needs. The former thrust was derisively rebuffed by Rupert Murdoch's *Times*. The prince had, the editor said, turned away from the necessary "race for personal success" and "scramble for lucrative jobs" to a Boy Scout vision not "fit for a prince" in its scarcely veiled hostility to the values of Margaret Thatcher's government (*Times*, 5 September 1989).

Yet the prince's substantial criticism of the welfare state and his endorsement of the voluntary principle were in terms that would be expected equally to meet with a defensive riposte from the left. After all, voluntary community service looks like a low-cost rival to statutory professional provision. Does this mean that the welfare state's time has passed even in the minds of those most likely to defend it? If we look to the ideological origins of the British welfare state, to the time when its time had come, we get a different sense of its root values than its bureaucratic fruits would lead us to expect. Beveridge wrote in 1942: "A revolutionary moment in the world's history is a time for revolutions!" He proclaims three principles: first, the new order to emerge from the war would serve all, not merely "sectional interests"; second, the national insurance scheme is "part only of a comprehensive policy of social progress, the others being Disease, Ignorance, Squalor and Idleness"; and third, "the state in organizing security should leave room and encouragement for voluntary action for each individual to provide more than a minimum for himself and his family" (1942, 6).

We now tend to think of the welfare state as the provider for especially needy and dependent people ("the residuum") and for especially needy and dependent times in citizens' lives (childhood, sickness, old age). But as was implied in Archbishop Temple's talk of transition from a "power" to a "welfare" state, the founding vision is of a whole order—of the universal welfare of citizens as part of a state, not simply subjects of its institutions (Birch 1976, 3). Whatever else might be implied by the word *paternalism*, Beveridge accepts the term, at least in the sense that the state is obliged and committed to provide the bases of human existence to its members, just because they are its members, and not in response to market demand, sectional power, or deserts. But it is Beveridge's second principle that sketches the context of the specific proposals of the social security provision. Indeed, only by seeing the welfare state in terms of an attack on all five giants" (Beveridge 1943, 43) do we get a proper appreciation of its political and ethical claims—and of the shortfalls in the delivery of its promise. Beveridge looks forward to a national health scheme, "preventative, curative and palliative," to the development of educational institutions for adults as much as for children, and to a "revolution in housing" and town planning. But these attacks on the giants of want, disease, ignorance, and squalor rest on an attack on idleness: "The largest and fiercest of the five giants and the most important to attack. If the giant Idleness can be destroyed all the other aims of reconstruction come within reach" (ibid.).

Idleness, then, was to be the welfare state's prime target. To bear in mind this supply-side emphasis on work is to get a measure of the conceptual slippage that occurs when we think of the welfare state, not as an organized ecosystem, a circular flow, but as the great provider doling out goods to dependent and abject subjects, seen as disgustingly grateful (servile) or disgustingly ungrateful (scrounging) receivers. This drip-feed model draws us into conceptualizing as central what is secondary in Beveridge's vision—a division of society that compares burdened contributors to reluctant blood donors (Titmuss 1978). Though a mandarin to be sure, Beveridge foresees a world in which, broadly speaking, contributors and burden sharers would be coextensive with beneficiaries. The state's role is to orchestrate and provide infrastructure for the interflow, within a commonwealth, of things that the market mechanism does not, at least by itself, allocate adequately. We are a far cry here from the conceptual framework of Merle Haggard's "I ain't never been on welfare" boast in his song "Working Man's Blues."

It is common for welfare state operations to be described as mechanical—as inhumane state machinery. Such a picture is scarcely corrected by adding to it a full-employment policy. But when we look at Beveridge's ideas about idleness, we get a measure of the ideal ambitions of the British welfare state and of why it captured the imagination of a British public patriotically inspired by war. He writes: "So long as the community leaves the search for employment to individuals it must put pressure on them to continue the search—by giving public relief only under harsh, degrading or otherwise repellent conditions." Such harshness, he observes, must ultimately fail, as the unemployed—like the errant schoolboy, the prisoner, or the vagrant—get anesthetized and accustomed to their condition and so become indifferent to the goad. The solution, he thinks, to end miserly state policing and tormenting of the unemployed and destitute is satisfaction from work itself. Beveridge rejects political economy's axiom of the universal aversion to labor: "The feeling of not being wanted demoralises. . . . The people employed below their capacity are the unhappy ones" (1943, 84).

> Idleness is not the same as Want, but a separate evil, which men do not escape by having an income. They must also have the chance of rendering useful service and of feeling that they are doing so. This means that unemployment is not wanted for the sake of employment, irrespective of what it produces. . . . Employment which is merely time-wasting, equivalent to digging holes and filling them in again, or merely destructive, like war or preparing for war, will not serve that purpose. Nor will it be felt worth while. It must be productive and progressive. (Beveridge 1944, 20)

The state's function should be "to protect its citizens against mass unemployment as it is now the function of the State to protect the citizens against attack from abroad and against robbery and violence at home" (ibid., 29).

Work, then, is a fundamental condition of mutual service that makes for social fellowship. It is a basic dimension of full citizenship and, as such, a basic right. Contrary to the Keynesian ideas that had come to dominate, full employment is, in Beveridge's eyes, not merely a means to consumption-led growth. He considers work and wages part of the community's underpinning, Hence the passionate conclusion: "We shall be united in combined attack on tyranny and savagery abroad and on Want, Disease, Ignorance, Squalor and Idleness at home. Let us become united now for total war and for a peace different from the last peace at home and abroad" (1943, 52). Unity within the welfare state, then, is not to be mechanical or coerced but based on a sense of fellowship reinforced with a material and institutional base. Beveridge has neither a laissez-faire nor a *laissez à l'Etat* mentality. He has a positive moral aim. "There should be something in the daily life of every man and woman which he or she for no personal reward or gain, does ever more consciously as a mark of the brotherhood and sisterhood of all mankind . . . as a member of a community, as a member of the nation, as a member of the brotherhood of man" (ibid., 38).

So, as the third principle states, Beveridge does not envisage the welfare state as an alternative to personal charity, fellowship, or responsibility. Rather it is to provide an infrastructure and embodiment of these qualities. He is struggling to secure the foundations of reciprocity and community that would remove the fear and jealousy, the poverty and ignorance that he thinks kept British subjects at each other's throats. "Man is a spirit, not an animal." Hence sufficiency and security will not sap his enterprise, humanity, and responsibility. It will, on the contrary, allow them to flow (ibid., 90 ff).

Beveridge's liberal vision was hinged first to the pragmatic politics of Churchill's war government. As Titmuss (1963) puts it in his essay on war and social policy, welfare policies were "determined by how far the co-operation of the masses is essential to the successful prosecution of the War" (76). The Beveridge report was received as a promise of a society worth fighting for. The 1944 Education Act, the 1946 National Health Service Act, the 1946 Children's Act, the Town and Country Planning legislation of 1948, nationalizations of essential but unprofitable industries (steel, railways, coal), full-employment strategies, the whole Butskellite apparatus, though disowned as a travesty by Beveridge in 1953, seemed to establish a consensual if watered-down and compromised version of his vision.

Margaret Thatcher's Great Vision

> The moral fibre of our people has been weakened. A state which does for its citizens what they can do for themselves is an evil state; and a state which removes all choice and responsibility from people and makes them broiler hens will create an irresponsible society. In such an irresponsible society, no one cares, no one saves, no one bothers—why should they when the state spends all its energies taking money from the energetic, the successful and the thrifty to give it to the idle, the failures, and the feckless. (Boyson 1971, 5)

Thus wrote a future minister in the Thatcher government. He went on to celebrate the "free man's independent provision" for himself, his family, and also for the recipients of his charity, by which he "grows in stature by his free gift." At the end of a decade of Thatcherism, such themes recurred. In a riposte to the left-wing *New Statesman* of 29 April 1988, Home Secretary Douglas Hurd set out in opposition to the passive inhabitant of the welfare state, an ideal of the active citizen: "If there is one lesson which socialism has taught us it is that governments cannot legislate for neighbourliness . . . the modern socialist notion that it is more virtuous to lie back and be taxed than to work hard for yourself and your neighbour."

A month later, in a widely reported speech to the General Assembly of the Church of Scotland, Margaret Thatcher addressed these themes "personally, as a Christian" and as the prime minister of a state that is "Christian" through heritage and constitution:

> Most Christians would regard it as their personal Christian duty to help their fellow men and women. . . . "If a man will not work he shall not eat," wrote St. Paul to the Thessalonians. . . . What is certain, however, is that any set of social and economic arrangement which is not founded on the acceptance of individual responsibility will do nothing but harm. . . . We simply cannot delegate the exercise of mercy and generosity to others. . . . Intervention by the State (which must, however "ensure" through laws that no-one is left without sustenance, help or opportunity) must never become so great that it effectively removes personal responsibility. . . . There is little hope for democracy if the hearts of men and women in democratic societies cannot be touched by a call to something greater than themselves. (Raban, 1989, 9, 12, 14, 19)

So the state pulls back from choosing to replace the choice of charity and responsibility in order to leave it to the deeply rooted, best instincts and convictions of the people, which need to be rooted in and nourished by the Christian faith: "Political structure, state institutions, collective ideals are not enough. *We* parliamentarians can legislate for the rules of *law. You* the Church can teach the life of faith. For when all is said and done, a politician's role is a humble one" (ibid., 19). In this vision, the welfare state is not wholly disowned. We are not in the world of Nozick (1974), who concludes that "the state may not use its coercive apparatus for the purpose of getting some citizens to aid others" (ix).

The welfare state, then, has a legitimacy at the minimal level, given the absolute impossibility of all people relying on their families or friends in time of need. But the Thatcherite critique, familiar to those on the other side of the Atlantic, focuses on both the supply and demand dimensions. Given human nature, its sinfulness if you like, many will shun the tasks imposed by God's curse on Adam and hence make infinite demands, provided these are unconditionally met. The welfare state, therefore, encourages idleness, fecklessness, and failure. Thus does Thatcher endorse the Pauline injunction—if you will not work, you will not eat.

There is ambiguity here. When state welfarism is under attack, provision for the needy tends to be castigated, to be the artifical milk by which the nanny state fosters a dependency culture among its recipients. Yet the cardinal place allotted to personal, voluntary, or private charity raises the question of whether, at the receiving end, there is any inherent attribute demarcating good dependency from bad dependency. It would hardly be an advertisement for voluntary charity that its undependability and scarcity prevented dependency, so that scarcity of supply is a virtue in this area! We need to look elsewhere, and arguably we can find a legitimating picture.

Perhaps bad dependency is bad because, experienced as a right enshrined in law, it is taken for granted. Good dependency, however, is good because it is recognized as something to which one is not entitled but for which one ought to feel grateful. This putative gratitude could be said to have two dimensions: one, it is an intrinsically appropriate feeling that justly locates the donor-recipient relationship in the sphere of supererogatory charity rather than required justice. And two, it consequently acts as a check on the recipient's potentially infinite demand for care, attention, and material things by marking an awareness of the labor, sacrifice, and costs of service. After all, a mark of the ingrate is greed! So might the picture be painted.

The free gift is "the exercise of mercy and generosity to others," the hard work for your neighbors. It is clear that just as the welfare state is held to undermine personal responsibility among its clients, so it is accused of destroying both responsiveness and responsibility among those whose taxes fund its services. The welfare state, in other words, destroys the civic virtue of charity by replacing the choice to help with the requirement to lie back and be taxed so that the state can do the good. And so, while civic-minded and especially Christian citizens of means should seek wealth, should multiply their talents, precisely in order to confer bounty on others—"the spiritual dimension," says Thatcher, "comes in deciding what to do with one's wealth" (Raban 1989, 13)—the welfare state forcibly takes income that might be charitably disposed away from the wealthy, encouraging—instead of a class of altruistic good samaritans—a class of frustrated, resentful, and incentiveless taxpayers. So we have at one end a culture of greedy, dependent idleness, at the other end a culture of narrow tax evasiveness and meanness. And thus a picture is developed of a society caring because it is capitalist. The invisible hand supports the hand of pity extended to the poor, while, by contrast, the all-too-visible hand of the state causes the hand of pity to atrophy. And so the state, beyond providing a minimum, stays out of the picture except, at least in Britain, for propping up the church, which is charged with watering the necessary roots of a religious faith whose fruits are acts of charity.

Thatcher's problems here are old ones. From the days of Mandeville, Ferguson, Maine, Smith, and Hume, it has been recognized that, as a system based on and promoting self-interest, capitalism (1) requires stringent limits on the disincentive of charitable provision and (2) tends in any case to promote a culture of mutual indifference, where, as Ferguson (1966) puts it, the "bands of affection" being broken, civil man tends to "deal with his fellows as he does with his cattle or his soil—for the sake of the profits they bring" (19, 34). In this world, charity is a dubious and fragile virtue. Moreover, given that Thatcherite rhetoric emphasizes the relative virtue of the wealthy over the "idle fecklessness" of the "failures" (how else justify their poverty save through their defect), charity itself takes on the familiar mark of moral superiority, making its exercise one of enhancing moral stature and, by the same token, of humiliation for the less than grateful recipient. So, even if, contrary to fact, it flows freely and evenly in a capitalist culture, it would have a bitter taste. Yet, for all that, without a dimension of charity, Thatcherism stands as the ideology of the haves, leaving the have-nots without political obligations, since they are without material indebtedness.

Alienation and the Mode of Welfare Production

The Beveridge model for the welfare state is an ideal expressing the will of citizens, voters, and taxpayers for sufficiency and security not only for themselves but for all—welfare state *as* moral community. I have outlined the conservative retort: people freed from the state's compulsions will take more responsibility for their own well-being and will be spontaneously more responsive to the needs of others. The welfare state needs bringing down to size, not just because it is a tax disincentive to private gain, but because it is a block to responsible citizenship. These two wagons, amply open to reinforcement and decoration, collide in the night of mutual hatred and incomprehension.

There is, I want to argue, an individualism common to the "wet" (soft) and "dry" (hard) positions on this issue. I also want to argue that rhetorical and ideological counterblastings in this area represent inevitable ambiguities in social policies of industrial urban societies. I want further to suggest that, for all the recent talk of citizenship and civic virtue, insufficient attention is paid to the conditions under which such notions can tackle the issue of social welfare. Whether the active concept of citizenship that I argue to be necessary—a concept more binding than that envisaged in Prince Charles's proposals—could get off the political ground is a further question, (which, encouraged by the fate of his giant raspberry, I leave aside). Consider the following situation that came to light in 1984. It is a typical atrocity story of the welfare state as we know it.

A Liverpool man, already known to be under police suspicion for a similar offense, sexually assaulted his mentally handicapped new foster child. A social services official was interrogated on the BBC as to how such a man could have been given the care of a foster child. The embarrassed official, under fire from all the nation's media, made the point not only that this man was, in other respects, an excellent foster parent, but that it is almost impossible to find families who will foster handicapped people. Now, whereas this statement incurred public derision, the official had a point. Thousands of handicapped people in Britain, out of sight and mind, live in conditions far worse than this unfortunate child. How can the community be outraged by the failure of the officials? They are operating under conditions where the community's caring capacity is so feeble as to fail to provide sufficient foster parents, so that a sexual pervert is the alternative to no one to care for a child in need of much more special attention than most of us.

How, on the the other hand, can the public official bemoan this lack of community involvement, when the culture of the welfare state makes care the business of the state and none of our business except as it consumes our taxes—so that, as Boyson says, "No one cares"? The example is of a kind of mutual buck-passing between state and society typical of the welfare state. On the one hand, it is itself an expression of a caring society, freely voted for from altruistic motives and a rejection of the callous and whimsical ways of free-market capitalism, where the hindmost are the devil's takings. On the other hand, mocking Beveridge's wartime vision, the welfare state seems to draw up into itself institutions, networks, and mutual-aid values that nourish and protect human welfare. Thus we complain about the state's failures to do in our name things we have ceased to think of as anything to do with us at all. So, as Hurd says, we pay our taxes so that officials will think about such things. But just because we therefore do not think about them, we begrudge the tax man his due, and so services wither.

There is, in other words, a dialectic of self-destruction in the welfare state. Its very existence and survival testifies to the conviction that membership in society, analagous to membership in a family, is grounds for expecting a start and support in life. To be denied this, to be abandoned to one's fate, is to be released from the obligations of citizenship as from the obligations of one's parents. This sense of belonging, membership, fellowship, and common citizenship is not adequately represented by talk of rights, even though rights are entailed insofar as state laws and machinery are required to protect them. Yet the welfare state seems to undermine the very sentiment of the moral community of which it is the expression. It depends, in opposition to its dismantlers, on precisely those communal attitudes that it undermines. The welfare state is sustained through compulsory income deductions from people, the taxpayers, who, by the same token, are left to mind their own business and pursue their own interests. Their citizenship obligations are thus extracted by force and are discharged by state officials. There is an utter separateness between my felt interests and the interests that I compulsorily and indirectly support, even when those interests are my own—when the grumbling taxpayer becomes the hospital patient.

State welfare service personnel (the caring professions and their supervisory bureaucracies) thus become our agents (and, as a teacher in a state-funded university, I am such an agent). It is they who have traditionally professed and cultivated professional ethics of service, of dedication to something other than their pay packet. But this service ethic—among, for example, teachers, nurses, ambulance attendants, and fire fighters—has historically received a cynical and ironic reward—low pay, which is at once the badge of "Christian dedication" and the index of popular neglect and presumption.

But this sacramental dimension of welfare state work has always coexisted with another dimension—that of a job or career, with associated pay, status, and power. In other words, welfare workers are themselves members of the taxpaying public. As employees, they necessarily form a typical interest group, with positions to protect. Hence, they may (often at the cost of undermining their reputation and self-image as self-sacrificing servants of the public) act in a manner typical of an industrial interest group—by going on strike, for example. As an added irony, this perceived abandonment of their vocation reduces their work to ordinary jobs either filled by public service personnel or, more appropriately, contracted out by the state to the private sector, so that market disciplines will more efficiently and cheaply produce what the service ethic is allegedly failing to produce. So the market's hand is found pawing the welfare state's once pure body.

Servants of the welfare state are also authoritative officials. Their position entitles them to intrude in, interrogate, interfere in, and control the lives of the subjects (now often called *clients*) with whom they deal. The powers of welfare state workers over the lives of the recipients of welfare (the *delivery end*, in the new market vocabulary), are frequently alienating, humiliating, infantilizing, and disabling. All this might be true of private charity, but private charity can be rejected without having the police at one's door. So the welfare state's workers are in a complex position that is reflected in their own miserable familiarity with burnout. So the welfare state not only alienates its contributors from its recipients, it alienates both from itself.

Beveridge's principle solution to all this is the abolition of unemployment, the universal availability of real work, the consequent establishment of the nation as one of mutual contribution, and the destruction of the fundamental human division that the welfare state, as we have come to know it, scarcely touches. But despite his idealism, Beveridge, it seems to me, is too mechanical in his thinking. For, if middle-class taxpayers resent their contributions to the welfare state, even though countless studies show they are its most adept beneficiaries, why should the alienation, resentment, and irritability that I have outlined disappear? I began with Prince Charles, and I would go back to his stress on caring work as the direct expression and reinforcement of societal bonds.

No society can be just or humane when its institutions do not promote among its members a sense of contributing and gaining, of pride and indebtedness, of benefits and burdens, of give and take, of power and dependency, of community, justice, and freedom. The state form of welfare provision, funded through taxation and compulsory insurance, tends to block and atrophy a society's capacity for more direct, mutual, and common responsibilities and concerns. The alternative to statism is not pure Christian charity decorating pure capitalism but a form that, while not doing without either the state or the market, opens up space for, supports, and institutionalizes networks of cooperation and responsibility. It is cant to speak for example, of returning mentally ill or handicapped people to the community, for, unless we adopt a social Darwinist view that early death is fitting for the unfit, we must make sure that handicapped people, released from institutions, have a real community that can and will give care and support.

Any modern society's members are strangers to one another, but through active and cooperative contact, through direct, initially domestic, and local experience, people can discover and appreciate their own and others' talents, needs, and limits. Unless we can develop institutional forms that foster rather than atrophy bands of affection among strangers, unless we go beyond the present mix of mothers, markets, and ministries, we shall travel further down the path strewn with breakdown, poverty, and cynicism. As there is no acceptable alternative to it in some form, we need to develop models of the state in which community resources and initiatives are represented and fostered.

At this point Prince Charles steps in: with the cooperation of schools and firms, and with government financial support, young people will be encouraged to engage, for three months of their lives, in community work. Whereas Thatcher appealed to the churches to supply the spiritual motivation to charity, Prince Charles actually wants the state to take a lead in getting young people to learn about their fellow citizens' needs by spending time meeting those needs. But why should this be a merely optional matter? Why, should it be something that awaits one's sixteenth birthday and takes up only three months? Why should this sort of work not be deemed part of one's duties as a citizen? Why, given that its requirements need take up only a relatively small part of one's time, would that obligation or compulsion (perhaps with a punitive tax sanction) entail anything but an acceptable limit on freedom? Why, given the spontaneous idealism of children and the absurdity of their spending so much time stuck passively in schools absorbing little moral education, should not civic virtues be taught through practice from an early age?

It seems to me that the answers to these questions, taken in the abstract, are as compelling as the answer that the father had the right to make you rescue his drowning daughter. But the mixed response to that question, the widespread individualism that would place the right of minding one's own business above the necessity of helping others, indicates the wisdom of Prince Charles's moderate proposal for a voluntary and modest commitment. My argument is couched in terms of the conditions of social solidarity, consensus, and responsibility. If the welfare state is criticized for undermining the acceptance of its own legitimacy, then imposing a system of compulsory social service that would, in our present climate, be regarded as oppressive is not the solution. Rather, if Prince Charles's project becomes reality, perhaps it would encourage a shift in moral culture, so that mutual aid becomes a normal expectation demanding full institutional support. Then maybe we can begin to talk about the welfare state without embarrassment or irony.

NOTE

This chapter has been developed from my address to the British Society for Applied Philosophy, which was published in the society's journal in 1985. Of related interest are my articles "Flew on Russell on Nozick on Justice," *Journal of Applied Philosophy* 7 (1990), 87–90; and "Active Citizenship as Political Obligation," *Radical Philosophy* 58 (1991), 10–14.

SOURCES

Beveridge, William. 1942. *Report on Social Insurance and Allied Services.* London: HMSO.

———. 1943. *Pillars of Security.* London: Allen and Unwin.

———. 1944. *Full Employment in a Free Society.* London: Dickens.

Birch, R. C. 1976. *The Shaping of the Welfare State.* London: Longman.

Boyson, R. 1971. Farewell to Paternalism. In R. Boyson, ed., *Down with the Poor.* Churchill Press.

Ferguson, Adam. 1966. *An Essay on the History of Civil Society.* Edinburgh: Edinburgh University Press.

Hurd, Douglas. 1988. Citizenship in the Tory Democracy. *New Statesman,* editorial. 29 April.

Mill, John Stuart. 1962 (1859). *Utilitarianism.* London: Fontana.

Nozick, Robert. 1974. *Anarchy, State and Utopia.* Oxford: Basil Blackwell.

Raban, Jonathan. 1989. *God, Man and Mrs. Thatcher.* London: Chatto and Windus.

Times (of London). 1989. Editorial. 5 September.

Titmuss, Richard. 1963. *Essays on the Welfare State.* London: Allen and Unwin.

———. 1978. *The Gift Relationship.* New York: Vintage.

10

Policy Constitution Through Discourse: Discourse Transformations and the Modern State in Central Europe

Björn Wittrock and Peter Wagner

POLITICAL SCIENCE is often defined in terms of its focus on the study of policy processes. The causes and consequences of policies have been assessed and evaluated. The problems of policy planning, implementation, and evaluation have been subjected to an ever increasing stream of studies. The informational bases of policy processes have been brought into focus by knowledge use studies pinpointing both the relatively rare occasions when clearly identifiable research products have been fed into policy planning processes and the much more common phenomenon of unforeseen and unplanned partisan uses of research (Weiss 1991; Wittrock 1991). This burgeoning field of research has, however, also brought forth, as a major conclusion, the notion that the most important effects of disciplined discourse are indirect and long-term; that discourse serves an enlightenment function rather than an engineering one, and that it reshapes the fundamental conceptual grasp of reality on the part of the general public and policy makers alike and thereby opens up, or forecloses, whole avenues of action.

This may also be expressed as a basic notion that policies are not so much "influenced" by findings and facts but rather premised on a vast range of discursive rules that define domains of reality and relevant parameters for effective intervention—that is, not only the processes of policy making have to be studied but also policy constitution through discourse. Thus in every polity there will be a set of standard operating procedures for making and shaping policies in institutional terms. There will, however, also be more or less predominant, more or less embattled domains of discourse that serve as tacit backdrops for every such policy process and course of action. The rules of this domain of discourse define the field of policy intervention and the range of proper policies. They are both enabling and constraining and decisively delineate the range of options open for policy agents at any time while not preprogramming policy processes that in themselves are neither deterministic nor arbitrary.

This chapter will elaborate the idea of how policy constitutes discourse by comparing Sweden, Germany, and Italy in three broad domains of discourse during the development of the modern nation state—namely, in the late nineteenth century and early twentieth century, in the period of the transition from a traditionally restrained constitutional state to an interventionist early corporatist state. It will conclude with an overview of some major developments in "the age of the great programs," that is, the age of expanding public policy programs and interventions across the board in the 1960s and 1970s.

Recent years have seen a stream of studies with texts, rhetoric, and discourse as their focus. Often these studies are premised on what, for want of a better term, may be labeled an equally fashionable and idealistic ontology of signs—or sounds—bereft of any cognitive content or at least of any ascertainable relations to a nonlinguistic universe. The scholar's task is not to unmask but to deconstruct and reconstruct inherent ironies and layer upon layer of meanings. Without access to an extradiscursive vantage point from which discourses may be assessed in terms of their *horribile dictu* correspondence to the causal powers operating in reality, such analysis constitutes an endless glass bead game or a sophisticated tour through a house of mirrors and horrors with no emergency exit.

Our focus on the relationship between developments of discourses and institutions, that is, between types of argumentation and vehicles for the mobilization of resources, or (to use a familiar political science idiom) between ideas and power, should make it abundantly clear that we do not work within the confines of such postmodernist discourse analysis and deconstruction. Nor do we feel that either the traditions of more narrowly conceived Foucaultian structuralism, conceptual history, or Skinnerian political philosophy are appropriate to the task at hand. These ideas leave little room for any theory of human agency, they risk giving the concepts a self-perpetuating essence and moving force, and they risk focusing on microintentional events at the expense of a study of macroinstitutional change. These are the broad and exaggerated indications of a point of departure.

We have outlined our analytical framework elsewhere for the study of the emergence and transformation of the discourses of modern social science (Wagner and Wittrock 1987, 1990a, 1990b, 1991a, 1991b; Wagner 1990; Wittrock and Wagner 1990; and Wittrock et al., 1991). The term *discourse* is then clearly preferable to another such as, say, *discipline* precisely because one of the major transformations of texts and talk about society is the transformation from a predisciplinary type of ameliorative-associational social study to a disciplinary form of knowledge.

Discourse is a more generic and historically appropriate term because it gives proper weight to the social character of social knowledge. Thus it highlights the fact that we are dealing with a form of communicative action that involves reciprocity and interaction. It is reasoned in the sense that it relies on an ability and willingness of participants to supply, if need be, reasons for statements and standpoints. Finally, it is also recessive in the sense that social discourse is, in Giddens's terminology (1984), the reflexive monitoring of social reality. Not only does discourse draw on terms and notions prevalent in social life itself, but also its concepts may enter that reality and fundamentally affect its self-conception. Classical examples, sufficiently separated in time to make the point, are the notion of sovereignty in the early modern state and of Keynesian economic theorizing in the modern welfare state.

The emergence and transformation of social science discourse argues that the sociology of science should be linked to scientific and intellectual history and to social theory. In this respect we have tried to demonstrate how these transformations can be fruitfully understood with the help of a type of analysis, discourse structuration, that gives weight to sociopolitical traditions and to the respective institutions that underpin and help reproduce these traditions. Furthermore, it is a type of analysis that focuses on actual human beings propounding and perpetuating different intellectual projects, establishing discourse coalitions under historically, but not arbitrarily, changing states and political organizations.

Our focus in this chapter is different. It is not so much a question of analyzing the transformations of the discourse per se but rather of trying to demonstrate (or at least indicating) how discourse may conceptually constitute broad parameters of political action and policy. This type of analysis may yield far more powerful results in the policy sphere than much traditional research on ideology or knowledge use in which the notion of enlightenment is a vague metaphor for conceptually structuring principles. We shall briefly outline our notion of policy constitution, which to our knowledge has not been used before but is related to ideas recently proposed by James Farr (1989).

State-Centered Societies in Transition

In the history of industrialization and state building, most central European nations differed considerably from Western countries that have often served as the model for political debate, namely, England, France, and the United States. Sweden, Germany, and Italy were latecomers to industrialization compared to western Europe and even North America, and thus to democratization. Central European countries were state-centered, a feature they shared with France but not with England and the United States. Central Europe had a tradition of state centrality and absolutism with a much weaker emphasis on liberalism and representation than in the Western nations. In the late nineteenth century, central Europe experienced rapid economic and political transformations. Once the industrialization process gained momentum and released political forces that threatened autocratic political systems, the first stumbling steps towards parliamentary democracy could be made. In Germany and Italy, this process followed the consolidation of the nation state.

In Sweden, the parliamentary reform of 1866 ended four centuries of four-estate representation and replaced it with a bicameral system with basically universal and equal male suffrage for the second chamber. Far from ushering in radical reform policies, the new system strengthened broadly conservative coalitions of the landed aristocracy and well-to-do farmers, urban nationalists, and monarchistic forces, including the central bureaucracy. Universal and equal suffrage to Parliament for men and women was not achieved until after World War I. Throughout the first decades of the twentieth century, there were harsh industrial clashes, most dramatically seen in the long drawn-out general strike of 1909 and ending with the defeat of the trade unions. The subsequent deep crisis of the labor movement continued throughout the 1920s.

Germany's development in the same period has often been captured by the term *Sonderweg*, an equally characteristic and ill-fated combination of rapid economic progress and retarded political reforms (Blackbourn and Eley 1984; Kocka 1988). Much of the discussion of this road to modernity has, however, assumed that the relevant comparison is with parliamentary England and postrevolutionary republican France. However, compared to developments in many other countries in central Europe and possibly Japan, the German road may not be special but an infelicitous variation of a more general theme. The development of Germany, Italy, and Sweden in the late nineteenth and early twentieth centuries poses a particular challenge. Not only did these three nations develop swiftly but also they shared a number of characteristics that have been invoked in efforts to account for "the German disaster," national socialism and all its murderous consequences (Meinecke 1945). There is a dramatic divergence of ideas between the extreme

German *Volksgemeinschaft* (people's community), corporatist intervention enforced by terror and a full-blown warfare state, on the one hand, and the mildly paternalistic Swedish *folkhem* (people's home) and consensus-oriented corporatism of a social democratic welfare state. Italian fascism is in an intermediate position. In accounting for this divergence, scholars have pinpointed three crucial constellations of social phenomena in the Swedish case.

First, in Sweden there was a basis for a broad coalition of urban and rural liberal forces and a rapidly growing labor movement. Until the end of World War I they were effectively linked in a continuous struggle for parliamentary democracy and in opposition to lingering royal prerogatives. Second, the long and largely unbroken tradition of substantial local self-governance provided a political foundation for radical reform and mass democracy without threatening the orderly conduct of social affairs as they had traditionally been handled and perceived. Third, there was a fundamental choice among leading employers and industrialists to opt for compromise and accommodation rather than for all-out conflict. Even at such times as the victory for the employers in the 1909 general strike, such a strategy might have appeared possible and promising for hard-liners in the conservative camp.

These socioeconomic factors alone, plausible though they may be, cannot account for the historical divergence of Sweden from other central European states. In particular, they do not shed light on the discursive underpinnings of these paths. The constitutive features of a policy can be outlined against the backdrop of discourse practices that supply the systemic rules for delimiting domains of action and basic parameters for policy formulation and choice.

Divergence of Discourse in Newly Industrialized Nations

In Germany, Italy, and Sweden there was a basic concern for the transformation of the modern nation state in the wake of major social transformations. In these processes three broad realms of scholarly discourse were particularly significant: historical-philosophical discourse, economic discourse, and legal-administrative discourse.

In the last sphere, there is a basic parallel of discursive developments between Germany, clearly providing the exemplary contributions, and Italian and Swedish legal-administrative scholars. The transition is from Savigny's historically oriented legal scholarship to the emergence of an all-encompassing, internally consistent, and self-contained legal framework in the works of Gerber and Jhering, to the legal positivism of Laband (Wagner 1990; Sundell 1987; Ashford 1986). One should stress, though, that both the intellectual originality and discursive hegemony of legal positivism was much stronger in Germany and Italy than in Sweden. This difference is related to the specifics of nation building in those two countries. It can, therefore, be used to show that the emergence and evolution of discursive systems are intimately related to state developments. Three aspects can be distinguished.

First, the legal scholars who elaborated this system were fully aware that its evolution was premised on the creation and consolidation of a united German Reich. The only social meaning was to systematically spell out the detailed relations between the various legal traditions in the individual principalities. Such systematization might translate into real legal coordination. Only if the plethora of minor states formed part of one single political entity could they serve as the formal basis for a coordination of rule systems. This was made explicitly clear by Gerber and in the writings of his Italian counterpart, Orlando.

Second, in the newly created German nation state, a Prussian-based civilian and military bureaucracy effectively served as the key coordinating social factor. Such effects were anticipated in the creation of the Italian national administration, based on highly formalized and centralized rules of the Napoleonic type. In the Second Reich and the Italian kingdom, there were substantial regional and local differences in heritage, customs, and culture that effectively prevented anything like a traditional civil community or a modern civil society from serving as the major cohesive element in the new state. Unification had to be undertaken by a formally constituted section of society, the administrative apparatus. This apparatus acquired cohesion and competence through a comprehensive system of rules. Legal positivism provided such regulation and devised the university training required for its proper application and mastery (Dyson 1980).

Third, legal positivism projected the image of an exemplary modern state, ideally ordered and rationally interlinked. This state, no matter how much it might be based on "blood and iron" or on political clientelism, was an archetypical legitimate political order. The whole realm of legal-administrative discourse in Germany, including the so-called state sciences, came to be deeply influenced by this root model. As a consequence, there was little hope for an empirically oriented, non- or antilegalistic turn in the development of the state sciences. In Italy, the divergence between the "real country" and the "legal country" was more obvious to intellectuals than in Germany. Some attempts were made to develop an empirical administrative science or political science based on the concept of political class to analyze the relation of the ruling elite to wider society. By the turn of the century, however, these discourses had given way to the legal approach.

The Swedish developments, however, were characteristically different. Even if Swedish legal discourse was largely modeled on German developments, a traditional social cohesion defined independently of formal and recently reconstructed legal-administrative state machinery was sufficiently strong to prevent discursive hegemony for legal theorizing in the Swedish context. In fact, public debate and literary life in late nineteenth-century Sweden, Strindberg's novels being one instance, ridiculed the legalistically inclined bureaucracy. In short, an ideological legitimation of the Swedish version of a *Beamtenstaat* had been supplied by the idealistic and hierarchical philosophy of the so-called Boström school (Nordin 1981).

This school, and Boström himself during the time as the private teacher of the princes, held almost total sway over Swedish philosophy for more than sixty years. A course in philosophy was compulsory for future civil servants, and the hierarchical world view was strongly promoted. By the turn of the century, however, this school was clearly losing its grip, even within traditionalist academia, and it was soon also to lose its privileged position in the academic curriculum. In this situation there was a real possibility for other discourses on society and the state to assert themselves. At least three alternative discourses were continuously reproduced in institutions of higher education. First, basically by coincidence, within economics a generation of theoretically brilliant, internationally oriented and socially and politically engaged scholars (among them Knut Wicksell, David Davidsson, Eli Heckscher, and Gustav Cassel) within a generation changed the position of Sweden on the intellectual map from peripheral laggard to front-runner second to none in economics. These developments laid the foundations for the later prominence of the so-called Stockholm school which exerted decisive intellectual and political influence in the 1930s (see, for example, Hansson 1986; Petersson 1987; Wadensjö 1987).

Second, demographic and statistical research suddenly rose to prominence. The immediate reasons were widespread concerns about the consequences of continued mass emigration, a problem perceived as a deadly threat to the very survival of the nation. A government commission set up to investigate the causes and consequences of emigration and a prominent statistician and demographer, Gustav Sundbärg, came to occupy the key role. Sundbärg, who had previously pioneered historical demographic research on Sweden's population dating to the mid-eighteenth century, monitored the production of an impressive range of reports detailing every conceivable aspect of the migrations. Despite the deep conservatism of Sundbärg himself, he pinpointed the negative effect of the late expansion of Sweden's economic infrastructure and of delayed popular participation in governance. His work underscored the need for political reform in turn-of-the century Sweden and helps explain the subsequent rapid development of reform efforts.

Third, partly out of the old discipline of state science a new discourse on state politics and administration emerged, still carrying the traditional label of state science but essentially being a precursor of the modern disciplines of government or political science. On the eve of Sweden's momentary rise to great power in 1622, Uppsala University had resurrected the study of politics and subsequently opened new approaches to the discipline of history. The key representatives of this resurrected discipline were leading intellectuals in turn-of-the-century Sweden. In scholarly terms they tried to promote research that might be characterized as a combination of contemporary history, constitutional theory, and a broadly conceived sociological understanding of social change—for example, the works of Fahlbeck at Lund or Boethius at Uppsala, both of whom received their basic training in history. Rudolf Kjellén, first professor of government and geography at the new university college in Gothenburg and later the successor of Boethius at the Skytte chair at Uppsala, was by far the most original of the turn-of-the-century Swedish state scientists. His writings are a persistent critique of the limitations of both historical and legal scholarship.

The background to this critique was Kjellén's need to understand the real workings of an ever more interventionist state beyond just tracing its historical roots or its formal framework. Out of this critique grew a comprehensive research program that might be characterized as a plea for a institutional and policy-oriented analysis of the modern state. One aspect was the analysis of natural resources and the geographical and physical conditioning of political activities. Today this side of Kjellén's research program earns recognition among many Third World scholars as a precursor to their own efforts. It is also the aspect of his work that gave him prominence and notoriety in the interwar years as the father of geopolitics and the inspiring mind behind the activities of Haushofer and his colleagues in the Third Reich.

As policy intellectuals, Boethius, Fahlbeck, and Kjellén were all conservative members of Parliament and intensively active in the public debate. In the political struggle of this period over parliamentary democracy, they all reinforced the antiparliamentary defense of predemocratic constitutional monarchy. In the case of Kjellén, resistance to parliamentary democracy went far beyond the bounds of traditional conservatism. When the introduction of the method of crude numerical majorities seemed inevitable, he advocated a form of corporatism to mitigate the worst effects of parliamentary government. Their influence and visibility was clearly greater than that of their economics colleagues, of whom Wicksell, the theoretically most original, consistently supported radical critics of the established order. Other prominent economists, such as Heckscher and Cassel, persisted in a liberalism that turned out to be equally incompatible with the nationalistic ambitions of predemocratic Sweden and with the interventionist plans of later social democratic Sweden.

In the German context, the continued hegemony of legal positivistic theorizing about state and governance was paralleled by an intellectual rupture that fundamentally affected the future course of the two key disciplines economics and history in Germany and in the rest of the world. This was the so-called battle of methods (*Methodenstreit*) which raged between representatives of the previously predominant historical school in economics and the other social sciences. It basically divided the most influential policy intellectual organization of late nineteenth-century Germany, the Association for Social Policy (*Verein für Sozialpolitik*) from marginal economists and their new, more rigorous theory. This scholarly struggle and its outcome was a key theme in most social sciences in turn-of-the-century European academic life (Wagner 1990; Swedberg 1990). Thus Weber's scholarly endeavors were in a sense a heroic effort to straddle the two strands in this protracted and immensely divisive conflict. The long-term outcome of this battle, the separation of marginal economics from the other social sciences, had three crucial implications.

First, the intellectual foundations of institutionally entrenched, historically oriented, socioeconomic studies of contemporary society were being eroded at the precise moment when similar activities were first emerging in Sweden. Second, the intellectual victory of marginal economics, decisive though it came to be in the long run, still required intellectual consolidation and defense in universities and government. As a consequence, economics developed theoretically but had a relatively late and limited impact on policy. Third, the intellectual predominance of two rigorous and formally coherent discursive systems, legal positivism and marginalist economics, exerted a strong influence on other disciplines. Clearly sociological theorizing of the Weberian type, broadly historical and comparative yet theoretically informed and empirically oriented, was much less congenial to such a rigorous model than the formalistic, "pure" behavioral sociology which emerged as a strong contender for sociological supremacy in interwar Germany.

In the case of economics, Italian developments paralleled German ones but showed even sharper contours. In the 1880s, a "battle of the two schools" evolved in which the historical economists were the policy intellectuals siding with an interventionist and protectionist elite of policy makers opposing a small group of marginalist economists. The latter tried to preserve the purity of their theorizing against the practical considerations of their opponents. Some of them, like Pareto, Pantaleoni, and later Einaudi, were recognized for their intellectual contributions (Schumpeter 1954), but they remained completely uninfluential in terms of economic policy making (Gioli 1990).

Thus, despite a wide range of similarities in industrial, institutional, and intellectual development, at a crucial juncture in the development of the predemocratic central European nation states, discursive developments in Sweden, Germany, and Italy drastically diverged in their application. The combined effects of these developments and of parallel political and institutional changes stand out as better explanations of intellectual changes than the standardized accounts in terms of "separate" roads, or worse, "national souls" or characters.

Political Evolution of Industrial Societies: On the Road to Radical Reconstruction

The radical shifts in policy and politics in the wake of the world depression of the late 1920s and early 1930s have been the object of an endless stream of analyses. Their major discursive underpinnings were, for example, analyzed in studies of the interlocked transformations of economic policy and economic theory (Coats 1981; Hall 1989; Weir and Skocpol 1985; Wadensjö 1987). Some of these studies, especially that of Wadensjö, reconstruct the changes, in almost laboratory fashion, with a step-by-step analysis of how fundamental changes in economic thought eventually brought out gradual but dramatic changes in public policies. These studies make it clear that the impact of policies varied greatly across countries (Weir and Skocpol 1985). They also show, however, that both the strengths or weaknesses of the theoretical tradition were as influential in shaping policy as were the institutional characteristics of the political system.

Because the German marginal economists were forced to wage a protracted battle with the still strong historical school, they were forced into a stance that left relatively little room for revisionist thinking (Wagner 1990). Though simplified, this relationship captures some of the differences between the situation in Germany and Italy, on the one hand, and Sweden or Britain on the other. In the latter case, the transformation of economic discourse opened new avenues of economic policy intervention and helped to make economists key policy intellectuals. At least in societies with a strong humanistic tradition in the universities, policy intellectuals had generally been historians and philosophers during most of the nineteenth century. The main intellectual spokesperson for the national and liberal movements in Italy and Germany, for instance, was the "political professor" in such disciplines. Where it occurred, the rise to prominence of the new economists displaced historical-philosophical scholars as propounders of a comprehensive world view or as makers of a modern national identity. This role was handed over to the lay life world philosophers of the Spenglerian type, while academic philosophy developed into an increasingly sophisticated technical and analytical exercise or else into hermeneutically constituted philosophical systems that were prohibitively opaque to the real world.

Similarly, in most countries historical research reached a level of technical complexity in the treatment of different documents and sources that acted as a barrier to the fast and easy translation of history into policy conclusions or the political language of real politics. This situation, however, did not preclude both historians and philosophers from exerting an important indirect influence on both intellectual and political developments. In Scandinavia, for instance, the conception of an ever existing tradition of popular participation in governance (*folkhem*) in practice reinforced a Scandinavian self-image in ways totally at odds with German national socialism, which claimed that the "people's community" was an authentic continuation of Teutonic-Nordic past.

The discursive contrast is even greater in societies where policy-oriented economic and social science did not arise or remained weak because historians and philosophers held key positions in the interpretation of society. This was most clearly the case in Italy, where Benedetto Croce's idealism remained culturally hegemonic throughout the first half of the twentieth century. Even his main adversary during the fascist period, Giovanni Gentile, was a philosopher of a similarly idealist orientation. Croce remained distant and critical, while Gentile was minister of education and the quasi-official ideologist of the Italian state.

More profoundly and more immediately relevant to policy, however, was the discursive restructuring of the borderline between legal-administrative and philosophical discourse. In Germany, legal positivism, far from losing discursive hegemony with the fall of imperial Germany, survived in a new shape in the Weimar Republic (Heun 1989). The notion was that the administrator was the servant of the state by way of mastering an exceedingly elaborate, conceptually highly structured and interlocking system of rules. The prime principle of state reason was beyond question and could serve equally well as the administrative ideology in Germany's republican or imperial incarnations. More moderate representatives of legal positivism—Hermann Heller being the most prominent—made an effort to reconcile this formalistic framework with the social policy needs of Weimar. In Italy, Santi Romano tried to move legal positivism to an analysis of the "crisis of the state," while trying to safeguard the theoretical framework.

In the extreme version expounded by the most brilliant advocate of legal positivism, Hans Kelsen, these concerns were pushed to the side. The value and legitimacy of legal positivism in democratic perspective was perceived to reside precisely in its comprehensive nature and in subordinating the bureaucracy to the new democratic political power of republican government. In Kelsen's words, the notion that every state is a constitutional state could help to persuade remnants of the imperial bureaucracy to grudgingly accept the supremacy of republican government, but it could equally well justify obedience to any other state power no matter what its characteristics. In terms of administrative practices, however, civil servants throughout the Second and Third Reichs and Weimar continued to be trained in the tradition and practices of legal positivistic thinking.

However, in the interwar period legal-positivism was attacked by legal and state theoreticians, most prominently by Carl Schmitt who argued that it neither contained any notion of the political element proper, nor could serve the purpose of underpinning radical policy changes based on legally unconstrained friends and foes. Schmitt argued that the "technocratic" state theory of legal positivism presupposed "decisionistic" state theory. Such ideas were spearheaded by scholars who broke new ground for a strong interventionist state with little regard for legal subtleties. This radical decisionism could potentially help support the policy practices of the new warfare-welfare state of German national socialism.

In Sweden, new policy interventions to combat unemployment and to spur economic growth also laid the foundations for an extensive welfare system that had to come to terms with the legal-administrative basis for state actions. In practice, charting new policy interventions had to be premised on a new understanding of the limits and the legitimacy of a radically increased scale of activity. In a first such expansion, policy making shifted to a cadre of politically loyal and committed experts as well as the traditional legally trained bureaucracy (Rothstein 1986). Especially during the war years, pervasive corporatist administrative arrangements were introduced and were extended to the lowest level of local government. All relevant social interests were secured for the successful implementation of the policies of the wartime economy (Friberg 1973).

This dramatic shift in administrative practices drastically diverged from previous wartime experience and from interwar policy execution by a still fairly traditional state bureaucracy. As in Germany, this shift involved an attack on previously dominant legal-administrative discourses. Spearheading this attack was the so-called Uppsala school of antimetaphysical philosophy with Axel Hägerström as the undisputed leading figure. Hagerström posited an insurmountable difference between fact and value statement that denied any truth content or cognitive meaning to the latter. He also had a deep interest in legal philosophy, a field in which he gained two prominent adherents, Wilhelm Lundstedt, a law professor at Uppsala and for many years a social democratic member of Parliament, and Karl Olivecrona, a law professor at Lund. The Hägerström school also clearly influenced important policy intellectuals such as the economist Gunnar Myrdal, possibly the leading social democratic intellectual of the time, and the political scientist, Herbert Tingsten, an extremely active participant in public debates and in the postwar period editor-in-chief of Sweden's most influential daily newspaper (Källström, 1986).

The new form of legal-administrative discourse attacked both natural rights theorizing and legal positivism, both of which were deemed metaphysical. For example, under natural rights doctrine in the regulation of property, persons could claim to be exempt from intervention on a priori grounds. Under legal positivism, an abstract state provided the ultimate rationale and premise of a complex corpus of legal rules to prevent intervention. Legal realism bluntly declared that the extent and degree of political intervention was a matter of political convenience that could not be circumscribed a priori by an abstruse system of self-proclaimed rights or abstract state entities. Since value statements were, furthermore, nothing but the expression of emotive states and lacked cognitive meaning, the theoretical result is a system in which political acts of will generate their own legitimation. Of course, in the framework of the Uppsala school, acts of will were constituted to be benign welfare policies rather than the more sinister versions discursively supported by Schmittian decisionism.

Discourse Coalitions and Radical Rationalism

In central Europe, World War I ended the period of preparliamentary political rule and of precorporatist (although increasingly interventionist) governance of the economy (Winkler 1974). However, it did not usher in any single continental European model of modernity but rather a multiplicity of efforts—some socialist, some liberal, and some fascist in nature. In an age of increasing state economic intervention and weakened traditional patterns of political and social authority, finding a new path was essential. In some European countries, such as Sweden, the whole period from the early 1920s to the early 1960s can be seen as a long transition, sometimes continuous, but in most countries discontinuous and at times violent. The transition was from a relatively loose, often inadvertently progressive, linkage between state and economy and between state and society toward the undisputed hegemony of one particular model of managing the links in an age of economic growth and growing public programs (Katznelson 1991). By 1960 a radically rationalistic and interventionist welfare state had clearly moved beyond the cautious model of macroeconomic management inherent in the classical Keynesian program.

In most of central and western Europe, the decade after World War II was a period of reconstruction and recovery under political regimes pursuing economically liberal policies. Under these circumstances, there was neither a need nor an urge for a restructuring of knowledge to help underpin vastly expanded public policy programs. Much the same holds true for the United States, where the wartime experiences were being converted into the "policy sciences" (Lasswell and Lerner 1951). The effective use of these new types of instrumental knowledge did not occur until they were moved out of think tanks, such as Rand, and into the command posts of the Kennedy administration and, subsequently, of the Johnson administration in the War Against Poverty and in Vietnam.

In much of western and central Europe, the 1960s was also a period when new political majorities came to power and embarked on ambitious programs of policy reform and public sector expansion. This was equally true of West Germany as of Italy and Great Britain. Even in France this was a period of major efforts in social and economic modernization and policy innovation. In all these cases, reform policies involved ambitious initiatives to tap new forms of knowledge, normally with the eager backing of reform-oriented social scientists who saw a long-awaited chance to promote policies they embraced while simultaneously and finally securing a place for their disciplines. All this was made easier by the rapid expansion of higher education in the 1960s. Of course, there had been a strong affinity between the discourse of leading scholars and policy makers in previous periods, but the terms and conditions of such interactions new tended to change dramatically.

First, the nation state building processes of the late nineteenth century and the concomitant efforts to solve social questions had rested on a thematic affinity between the discourses of scholars and power holders. More intense and immediately policy-oriented forms of interaction tended to occur in clearly circumscribed spatio-temporal settings. Parliamentary and government commissions became the archetypical institutional medium for such interactions (Wittrock et al. 1991). After 1918 the reconstruction of the European states and their policies introduced more permanent state and semipublic institutional arrangements for the production and use of policy-relevant knowledge. Perhaps the most typical of such new institutions were the economic survey institutes set up in a number of countries and widely used in the wake of the Marshall Plan after the Second World War. In many countries, such as Sweden, medium-term economic forecasting was not performed by a permanent planning secretariat in a ministry but in ad hoc commissions made up of both academics and politicians. In the mid-1960s there was a dramatic growth of such planning in Europe as well as in the United States.

From then on a plethora of units for planning, research, analysis, and evaluation were set up in all minor ministries and government agencies in Western Europe and North America. This shift was premised both on the introduction of new techniques for policy analysis, programming, and budgeting and also on a new doctrine of science and technology policy planning which, with slightly different names, became the dominant presence in almost all OECD states (OECD 1971) and which aimed systematically to apply all types of knowledge across the whole spectrum of public programs. The need for such a systematic planning of future research and development was felt more strongly because public programs extended to more and more sectors of social life and ever further into the future. There occurred, in other words, a secular shift from temporary and ad hoc types of interactions to continuous and comprehensive ties between the administrative-political realm and the academic-scientific one. It is important to see that this shift was not subjecting academic autonomy to political needs but rather indicated an important change in the institutional terms of interaction (Elzinga 1985; Gibbons and Wittrock 1985; Torstendahl 1991; Wagner and Wittrock 1991b).

Second, shifting political institutional linkages had a correlate in the changing institutional position of social science discourse itself. On the one hand, the reform policies of the 1960s and early 1970s coincided with a major expansion of higher education in Europe. In many countries for the first time, this permitted social science disciplines to get a firm footing within academic institutions. It may well be argued that only in this late postwar period did pragmatically professional social scientists of the type that had prevailed in the United States since the turn of the century predominate in Europe (Wagner, Wittrock, and Whitley 1991). However, both higher education institutions and scientific activities at large were much more tightly regulated and monitored by administrative-political controls than before. These new gains for social science were far more precarious than some of the Faustian proponents of the reform coalitions may have envisaged at the timc. This became even clearer in some countries, such as Britain and Denmark, where during the 1980s new conservative governments actively broke up old reform coalitions and from a position of power, started renegotiating what was left of the old tacit contracts between policy makers and scholars.

The second element of the shift in institutional location of discursive debate was equally far-reaching. In the late nineteenth and early twentieth centuries, ameliorative-associational types of social inquiry were gradually replaced by disciplinary and university-based discourses that secured institutional protection for their own reproduction. Whereas the interwar development of new types of policy-oriented nonuniversity research institutes had not deeply affected the previous secular trend, the shift in the 1960s and 1970s did. True enough, the highly instrumentalist, (not to say technocratic) conception of the production and use of knowledge was premised on an equally instrumentalist conception of the policy process. Ordinary social scientists supplied the planning machineries with discursive fuel, and the high-level scientists were the princely advisors at the pinnacles of power whose wisdom and directives flowed down a well-ordered hierarchy to be translated into beneficial social change at the end of the process.

Not much later, and maybe not too surprisingly, it turned out that the "planning objects" and their "environments" were not impassively filled as new directives from the high-level "planning subjects." Abstract "policy domains" were actually filled with human beings perfectly capable of thinking, talking, and acting on their own initiative and even able to get their own "counterexpertise" to meet the claims of the officially designated planning overlords as their advice was translated into policies. So instead of a scientifically governed hierarchical policy process there was an unanticipated but irreversible pluralization of expertise (Wagner 1985). Soon this process spread from the sphere of public decisions to every walk of life, and not least to markets and commerce—fields that tended to offer much richer (and quicker) rewards than painstaking scholarly work in the unevenly and normatively guided university departments. Moreover, European universities were easy and obvious victims of the budgetary squeeze of the 1970s and 1980s. So discourse on society was not so much moved out of academia; it was to be found in all types of institutional settings, most of them detached from traditional scholarly standards.

Third, the institutional diversification of planning meant not only the construction of numerous and impenetrable of bodies consulting, advising, and studying social phenomena in more or less elaborate terms, but also that the cognitive core of disciplinary programs was directly affected by multiple external interests and demands. An inevitable indeterminacy characterized judgements on discourse regulation, sometimes been called "epistemic drift" (Elizinga 1985). If pushed to an outer, postmodernist limit, the situation makes everything possible since there are no extradiscursive instances or practices that might assist in the difficult choice between an infinity of rhetorical figures in society conceived as text and talk. If such a position is taken seriously, we are no longer dealing with epistemic drift but are on an epistemic roller coaster where fragments of sounds and words swirl by. Unfortunately, this viewpoint can help us understand neither the world nor scientific practices as socially constructed. The new constructs appear meaningless since they are not premised on any clear postmodernist or positivist ontology. They rather abandoned the search for mechanisms and causal connections change and simply examined a thin layer of appearances or linguistic blurbs (Outhwaite 1987; Bhaskar 1989).

In this perspective, the real challenge is to elaborate an analysis of policy processes (and indeed of society) that takes language and power, argument and force, communication and institution equally seriously. The study of policy constitution through discourse—and the concomitant analysis of discourse structuration—aims at such an analysis. We have tried to show that it yields an understanding of the shaping of basic policy options in three central European state-centered societies which is more powerful than the alternatives of either a traditional functional-evolutionary analysis or a purely textual or linguistic study of practices with no links to the institutions that ultimately perpetuate and reproduce these practices.

SOURCES

Ashford, Douglas E. 1986. *The Emergence of the Welfare States.* Oxford: Blackwell.

Bhaskar, Roy. 1989. *Reclaiming Reality.* London: Verso.

Blackbourn, David, and Geoff Eley. 1984. *The Peculiarities of German History.* Oxford: Oxford University Press.

Coats, A. W. 1981, ed. *Economists in Government.* Durham, N.C.: Duke University Press.

Dyson, Kenneth H. F. 1980. *The State Tradition in Western Europe.* Oxford: Robertson.

Elzinga, Aant. 1985. Research, Bureaucracy, and the Drift of Epistemic Criteria. In *The University Research System. Public Policies for the Home of Scientists,* ed. Björn Wittrock and Aant Elzinga. Stockholm: Almqvist and Wiksell.

Farr, James. 1989. Understanding Conceptual Change Politically. In *Political Innovation and Conceptual Change,* ed. Terence Ball, James Farr, and Russell L. Hanson. Cambridge: Cambridge University Press.

Friberg, Lennart. 1973. *Styre i kristid: studier i krisförvaaltningens organisation och struktur.* Stockholm: Allmänna Förlaget.

Gibbons, Michael, and Björn Wittrock, eds. 1985. *Science as a Commodity.* Harlow: Longman.

Giddens, Anthony. 1984. *The Constitution of Society.* Cambridge: Polity.

Gioli, Gabriella. 1990. The Teaching of Economics in Nineteenth-Century Italy and the Characteristics of its Institutionalization. In *Discourses on Society: The Shaping of the Social Science Disciplines,* ed. Peter Wagner, Björn Wittrock, and Richard Whitley. Dordrecht: Kluwer.

Hall, Peter. 1990. *The Politics of Economic Ideas.* Cambridge: Cambridge University Press.

Hansson, Björn A. 1986. *The Stockholm School and the Development of Dynamic Method.* London: Croom Helm.

Heun, Werner. 1989. Der staatsrechtlich Positivismus in der Weimarer Republik. *Der Staat* 28:377–403.

Källström, Staffan. 1986. *Den gode nihilistan: Axel Hägerström och striderna kring Uppsalafilosofin.* Stockholm: Rabén & Sjögran.

Katznelson, Ira. 1991. In *Social Knowledge and the Origins of Social Policies,* ed. Dietrich Ruesschemeyer and Theda Skocpol.

Kocka, Jürgen. 1988. German History before Hitler: The Debate about the German *Souderweg. Journal of Contemporary History* 23:3–16.

Lasswell, Harold, and Daniel Lerner, eds. 1951. *The Policy Sciences.* Stanford: Stanford University Press.

Manicas, Peter T. 1987. *A History and Philosophy of the Social Sciences.* Oxford: Basil Blackwell.

———. 1990. The Social Science Disciplines: The American Model. In *Discourses on Society: The Shaping of the Social Science Disciplines,* ed. Peter Wagner, Björn Wittrock, and Richard Whitley. Dordrecht: Kluwer.

Meinecke, Friedrich. 1946. *Die deutsche Katastrophe.* Wiesbaden: Brockhaus.

Nordin, Svante. 1981. *Den Bostromska skolan och den svenska idealismens fall.* Lund: Doxa.

OECD. 1971. *Science, Growth, and Society.* Paris: OECD.

Outhwaite, William. 1987. *New Philosophones of Social Science: Realism, Hermeneutics and Critical Theory.* London: Macmillan.

Petersson, Jan. 1987. *Erik Lindahl och Stockholmsskolans dynamiska metod.* Lund: Lund Economic Studies no. 39.

Rothstein, Bo. 1986. *Den socialdemokratiska staten.* Lund: Arkiv.

Schumpeter, Joseph A. 1954. *History of Economic Analysis.* New York: Oxford University Press.

Swedberg, Richard. 1990. The New "Battle of Method." *Challenge,* January–February:33–38.

Torstendahl, Rolf. 1992. Transformations of professional education during the nineteenth century. In *Fact and Idea in the European and American University Since 1500,* ed. Sheldon Rothblatt and Björn Wittrock. Cambridge: Cambridge University Press.

Wadensjö, Eskil. 1991. The Committee of Unemployment and the Stockholm School. In *The Stockholm School of Economics Revisited,* ed. Lars Jonung. Cambridge: Cambridge University Press.

Wagner, Peter. 1985. De la "scientification" de la politique à la pluralisation d'expertise. In *Situations d'expertise et socialisation des savoir,* ed. CRESAL. St. Etienne: Dumas.

———. 1990. *Sozialwissenschaften und Staat. Frankreich, Italien, Deutschland, 1870–1980.* Frankfurt/M: Campus.

Wagner, Peter, and Björn Wittrock. 1987. Social sciences and societal developments: The missing perspective. Berlin: WZB papers.

———. 1990a. Analyzing social science. On the Possibility of a Sociology of the Social Sciences. In *Discourses on Society. The Shaping of the Social Science Disciplines,* ed. Peter Wagner. Björn Wittrock, and Richard Whitley. Dordrecht: Reidel.

———. 1990b. States, Institutions and Discourses. A Comparative Perspective on the Structuration of the Modern Social Sciences. In *Discourses on Soceity. The Shaping of the Social Science Disciplines,* ed. Peter Wagner, Björn Wittrock, and Richard Whitley. Dordrecht: Reidel.

———. 1991a. Social Sciences and the Building of the Early Welfare State. Towards a Comparison of Statist and Non-Statist Western Societies. In *Social Knowledge and the Origins of Social Policies,* ed. Dietrich Rueschemeyer and Theda Skocpol.

———. 1991b. Epistemic Drift or Discourse Structuration. Transformations in the Societal Position of the Social Scientists. In *Intellectuals in the Welfare State,* ed. Ulf. P. Lundgreen and Thorsten Nybom. London: Jessica Kingsley.

Wagner, Peter, Björn Wittrock, and Richard Whitley, eds. 1990. *Discourses on Society. The Shaping of the Social Science Disciplines.* Dordrecht: Reidel.

Weir, Margaret, and Theda Skocpol. 1985. State Structures and the Possibilities for "Keynesian Responses" to the Great Depression in Sweden, Britain, and the United States. In *Bringing the State Back In,* ed. Peter B. Evans,

Dietrich Rueschemeyer, and Theda Skocpol. Cambridge: Cambridge University Press.

Weiss, Carol H. 1991. Policy Research: Data, Ideas, or Arguments. In *Social Sciences and Modern States,* ed. Peter Wagner, Carol Hirschon Weiss, Björn Wittrock, and Hellmut Wollmann. Cambridge: Cambridge University Press.

Winkler, Heinrich August, ed. 1974. *Organisierter Kapitalismus.* Göttingen: Vandenhoeck und Ruprecht.

Wittrock, Björn. 1991. Social Knowledge and Public Policy: Eight Models of Interaction. In *Social Sciences and Modern States: National Experiences and Theoretical Crossroads;* ed. Peter Wagner, Carol Hirschon Weiss, Björn Wittrock, and Hellmut Wollmann. Cambridge: Cambridge University Press.

Wittrock, Björn, and Peter Wagner. 1990. Social Sciences and State Developments. In *Social Science, Policy, and the State,* ed. Stephen Brooks and Alain G. Gagnon. New York: Praeger.

Wittrock, Björn, Peter Wagner, and Hellmut Wollmann. 1991. Social Science and the Modern State: Policy Knowledge and Political Institutions in Western Europe and the United States. In *Social Sciences and Modern States: National Experiences and Theoretical Crossroads,* ed. Peter Wagner, Carol H. Weiss, Björn Wittrock, and Hellmut Wollman. Cambridge: Cambridge University Press.

III

IN SEARCH OF AGENCY

11

Political Science and Policy Studies

Douglas E. Ashford

THE SUBTLE reorientation of policy studies, often propelled by the anomalies and contradictions produced by comparative policy studies, has shifted from what academics should do with their knowledge of policy to what academics need to know about policy makers. In its more extreme formulations, the notion of agency arises from criticisms of conventional social science in interpretive and critical theory. The ambiguities that both schools of thought see in a close adherence to a nomological-deductive explanation tend to break down the rigid lines between fact and value and to soften the polarized meaning of rational and irrational behavior. Without our entering into the philosophical implications of these positions, some of which have arisen in previous chapters, we can see that the concept of agency stresses emergent patterns of behavior and a redefinition of objective reality. Rather than concentrating on particular hypothetical constructions of events, we shift the emphasis to reality testing and, eventually, to concern with major transformations in institutions, societies, and cultures.

Taylor, a leading exponent of interpretive theory, says, for example, that to have a theory is to engage in applied social science. With the domain of social interaction, theory transforms "its own object" (Taylor 1983, 74). This is of course very close to what policy studies and traditional public administration aimed at doing for many decades; these areas of inquiry simply had no philosophical justification in the eyes of behavior social science. A major conclusion of this book is, of course, that within the behavioral model of humans and social science, policy studies would never be able to discover such a justification.

The aim of this part of the book is to come full circle, that is, to return to the prevailing notions of political and social inquiry, to examine the recent history of conceptual and theoretical history of the discipline, and to uncover, if possible, how policy analysis might be, as it were, integrated into political science (and presumably other social sciences) rather than be treated as a misguided offspring or a slightly embarrassing vestige of an earlier age. To do so means returning to an evaluation of how the prevailing concerns, possibly the dominating theories, of political science connect with policy studies and, more generally, with comparative policy studies. As should be apparent to the reader, it is not possible to recapitulate the erosion of the narrow empirical model that inspired political science over much of the 1950s and 1960s. But this was basically a model of systemic political action, closely aligned with an economic model of equilibrium, that saw political inputs and political outputs as interconnected through the black box of government. Though not often discussed, there was of course a more general theory—even metatheory—at work, which implied, if it did not claim, that inputs and outputs were ultimately translatable, that is, that the utilities suggested in elections were in some sense reproduced in the utilities represented by government actions. That such a monumental assumption could remain unchallenged for nearly twenty years is one of the mysteries of social science.

On the demand side, the rational model of voting behavior was absolutely basic. Rather like the very similar preoccupations of neo-Marxists with the collapse of working-class solidarity, the collapse of rational voting constituted a mortal blow to the entire edifice of calculated political behavior. The decline of the rational voting model has been chronicled elsewhere (Goodin 1982) and so needs no repetition here, but the destruction of the notion that government somehow acted as the free marketplace of individual preferences had devastating results, especially for policy studies. The marginalization of policy studies was largely justified by the claim that the electoral process was a reliable way of transmitting aggregated utilities to government. Nonvoting was of course always an uncomfortable contradiction, because it suggested that many voters did not believe what many academics had spent years trying to demonstrate. Downsian "intelligence of democracy" was, by implication, either an intellectual subterfuge about what might happen in the best of all possible worlds (a kind of behavioral analogue to the proletarian revolution) or an impossible dream. For any observer, there were just too many elections in which mandates, platforms, and goals were discarded neglected, or cynically pushed aside.

In chapter 12, Rockman links voting behavior to a careful critique of how the systemic idea of inputs break down and, more important, how this breakdown opens the way for a policy analysis of the democratic process. Rather than take the more obvious course of the neo-Marxist or the neoconservative, both of whom in their own eschatology propose radical changes in linking demands to government performance, Rockman adheres to the empirically relevant literature while asking provoking questions. In posing what he terms "sociological" objections to Down's rational voter model, Rockman does not avoid the challenge of deep social cleavages, ideology, and clientelism to the presumably free marketplace of ideas that is supposed to exist in the electoral process. In doing so he raises the question of whether such subjective issues indeed have the same epistemological status of so-called rational voting. Like the pluralists who preceded them, or perhaps actually accompany them, the scholars of rational voting assume that the behavioral epistemology of being rational and irrational is wholly reliable. Even if not practiced, there is the temptation to believe that, if only all voters would be rational—that is, would act on demonstrated knowledge in the rational mode—then voting could accurately reflect preferences; there would be a sort of momentary reality that government would then accurately translate into goods and services. The fact that, even if achieved, such a representation would be only momentary is conveniently overlooked.

From this perspective, the ensuing controversy over strong and weak parties is an interesting analogue to the controversies over interest intermediation described in the introduction to part 1. The odd aspect of the parties argument is that it is never quite clear whether conventional social science is arguing for a strong party system, which presumably could impose its will on government, or a weak party system, which would reflect more transitory shifts in popular preferences and, assuming similarly responsive government machinery, would then more nearly fulfill the aggregated utility preferences. It is for this reason that Rose (1980), a political scientist very sensitive to policy studies, paradoxically argues that the British party system is weak (141), an argument in direct conflict with Beer's (1965) highly respected historical argument that the British party system is strong because it can more readily arrive at a social consensus than most other party structures. Though sensitive to policy studies, Beer is making an assumption about parties that is consistent with the rational voting model of elections. Rose and Beer are talking about different things. Rose is concerned with the ability of British parties to extract from Whitehall those changes that it promised, while Beer has in mind a more general issue—how parties reconcile social conflicts and differences to make stable government possible. Achieving one does not necessarily preclude the other. Missing in both equations is some way of estimating the readiness and ability of governments to actually produce those goods and services that the weak or the strong party system elicits from voters. This is of course the neglected task of policy studies.

Even in some of the more recent state-society analyses, there is the implicit assumption that, were parties able to firmly grip the levers of government through such devices as strong planning agencies, central economic planning, and well-disciplined civil services (Weir, Orloff, and Skocpol 1988), the various failures of American government might be avoided. Rockman makes a strong contextual argument that in fact American parties, contrary to the European image, more accurately reflect demands. For the left, Reagan may not be the best of examples, but he was nonetheless, in Rockman's words, a "radical assertion" made possible by American party and electoral politics. This of course does not respond to the query from the left concerning the American failure to assemble a social democratic alternative (Katznelson 1978), or the inability of the United States to make a radical redistribution of power among levels of government (Skrownek 1982). Though Rockman does not press his case this far, the possibility that Americans are content with the radical initiatives they have made (and they are not negligible in the field of environmental, occupational safety, and mental health policies, to name a few) may not be a minor accomplishment. The American welfare state, for example, may seem less effective than the British or Swedish models, but it has made some gains others have not while working within a set of rules and procedures that would have stalled most European welfare states (Lockhart 1989).

In the face of growing evidence of weakened party machinery and lower party membership, Rockman's reassessment of party politics and policy making is persuasive. There is a certain paradox in the concern among some students of American politics and policy (Weir, Orloff, and Skocpol 1988) that American parties should be more disciplined and more uniform, even though, for example (1) the German Social Democrats are losing votes to the Greens in part because of their inability to forge a convincing environmental policy, (2) the British Labour party needed nearly a decade to reconstruct itself in a form that might persuade British voters it could manage the declining economy, and (3) the French Socialists find themselves under attack by the left wing of the party for not more aggressively pursuing socialist objectives. All these trends suggest that issue politics has gained importance, and to that extent, comparative policy analysis has an opportunity to directly relate its results to party politics.

In both Europe and the United States, theories of party politics have until recently been most often derived from the Downsian notion of the rational voter. But recent studies of party politics suggest that the simple systemic linkage from party to legislation to implementation does not hold. As Rockman notes, and as many critics of democracy forget, policy making does not end with legislation. As Rockman puts it, why should we expect the entire system to jump to the party bark? The disjunction between policy studies and party politics may not be that they are different phases of an abstract chain of events, but that policies relate differently to partisan politics within such a chain of events known abstractly as the political system.

The intriguing possibility of more realistically linking policy studies to party politics and elections rests on the formulation of a better theory of policy making as much as it does on reworking macrolevel theories of parties and elections. Even if the concept of rational choice prevails in party and electoral analysis (where it may be most persuasive), there is no reason to assume that, in the intricate, interdependent world of policy making, parties can ever again regain their overall powers of supervision, accountability, and concern that was common in the nineteenth century. Indeed, there is ample evidence that the more disciplined and more programmatic parties of Europe never exercised the kind of broad control that is imputed to them. Rothstein's work on the Swedish Social Democrats, part of which is given in chapter 4, is one such demonstration that rests on a carefully done historical case study of policy making.

It can also be shown that the British Conservative party was seriously confused and badly divided over social legislation in the 1930s (Lowe 1986). Thus, well-constructed case studies are critically important in revising our concept of party politics, and as Rockman notes, much of the confusion that exists may actually arise from the tendency to select the most controversial decisions for case studies, thereby heightening both ideological difference and partisan motivation beyond that which legislators normally experience. In this perspective, case studies may have contributed to the distortion of party politics, on the one hand, by persuading the left that strong parties could behave more programmatically and, on the other hand, by persuading the right the strong parties could more energetically recast policy making. Relieved of rational choice theories, policy studies may build a concept of policy making that more accurately reflects how policies themselves interlock and interdepend on partisan politics.

Such an interpretive reconstruction of cases does not mean a revival of a convergence theory of democratic political behavior (Freeman 1975)—something like the "end of ideology" theses of the 1950s—nor does it mean that the critical role of free parties in setting agendas must be replaced by the more pessimistic, neo-Marxist interpretations of democratic politics. The problem is of a different magnitude: how to imagine a modern democratic state, with its immense burden of problem solving, monitoring, and evaluation, working within a democratic framework. In its largest sense, the problem is truly interpretive or contextual insofar as the framework within which such larger questions might be raised has yet to be devised. Policy studies have an important role to play in such an enterprise, but their ability to do so depends on considerable, if not radical, revision of many basic political science concepts. Rockman's evaluation of the party literature seeks new ground for the use of comparative policy studies and, by implication, new ways for the aggregation of microlevel experience into macrolevel findings that would assist in the construction of a policy-based political science. There are undoubtedly other crucial questions to be asked about underlying structures and relationships in the modern states. The two singled out for this essay are a reexamination of the foundations of bureaucratic influence and the nature of constitutional power.

In the early part of his chapter on bureaucracy, Peters outlines the theory of bureaucracy that, largely due to Weber's influence, was subsumed into the theory of rational descision making. Indeed, despite the extensive writings showing that Weber himself had deep misgivings about the powers assigned bureaucracies and about the German bureaucracy itself (Mommsen 1974; Mommsen and Osterhammel 1987), the logical consistency between Weber's thinking about administrative behavior and behavioral macrotheory, both rooted in assumptions about rational behavior, leave little room for argument. The truly devastating attack came from Simon (1947) many years ago but was conveniently put aside by a political science discipline intent on imprinting the nomological-deductive model in social science. Simon's alternative is easily misunderstood, for he does not attempt to break out from the main behavioral paradigm of the time but does attempt to reconstruct its assumptions so that organizational complexity is compatible with the individualistic rationality on which most macrotheory of the time is based (ibid.; March and Olsen 1976). Compared to Olson's (1965) ingenious effort to make the irrationalities of collective behavior consistent with macroeconomic theory, Simon's efforts were more fundamental and more radical, not because he departed from individualistic assumptions, but because he showed that within organizations individual and collective reason did not necessarily contradict. However one may assess Simon's importance in the history of social science, there is no doubt that he revolutionized thinking about bureaucratic behavior and opened the way for March, Cyert, and Olsen to rebuild theories of collective behavior.

This background may help place Peters's contribution in context and also reveal how possessive the behavioral constructs had become by the 1960s. For whatever reasons, Simon rarely appeared at political science meetings after the 1960s, and the new macrotheories took little interest in what was inside the black box of government. In retrospect, it is easy to see how the attacks on bureaucratic government during the 1960s, while by no means directed against such a formidable opponent as Simon, were efforts to validate a primitive concept of individual rationality as the only reliable foundation of generalizations about government and policy making. The famous Pressman-Wildavsky study of implementation (1973), for example, had no difficulty showing that, when millions of dollars move through an intricate and barely understood chain of political and administrative actors, the outcome has very little resemblance to the initial intent. The study is especially relevant to present concerns because it suggests, on the one hand, that all the irrational elements between Washington and Oakland might be removed and, on the other hand, that the initial intent as described in law should be an accurate representation of how the money was made available to Oakland. Given its immense popularity among political scientists of the time, there is perhaps no more dramatic illustration of how the rational model of man was elevated into an attack on government without examining the internal assumptions and logic of policy analysis.

In his sketch of the differing assumptions of policy analysts and public administration, Peters puts his finger on one of the major contradictions of policy studies during the 1960s and 1970s. Policy studies cannot defend the assumption that groups are utility maximizers or that organizations are politically neutral. As Peters notes, this means disregarding either the organizational complexity that masks self-interest or the policy-making role that civil servants clearly assert for themselves. In this light, much of the postbehavioral inquiry into interest mediation as a form of organizational complexity (Mayntz and Scharpf 1975), policy networks, and policy communities takes on new meaning. These efforts might be seen as quasi-contextual concepts seeking resolution of an inner contradiction in policy studies. In the development of policy studies, these efforts were a prelude to finding a valid foundation for comparative policy studies. In effect, policy analysts chose to work with a self-denying rule that either made their work highly suspect or greatly oversimplified policy making. In both instances, an understandable reluctance to break with the methodological norms of behavioral political science made policy studies irrelevant. It is for this reason, as presented in the introduction to part 1, that interpretive theorists argue that all social science is, in some sense, applied—that is, that it cannot arbitrarily exclude the perceptions, motives, and knowledge of the policy maker. In a more extreme formulation, all social science must be applied, that is, it must state the desired outcomes to make social science into a guide to political action.

As the Peters and Rockman essays indicate, political science has never fully succeeded in excluding contextual knowledge. Both the variety of adjustments to the rational voting model and the obvious contradictions of value-free administrative behavior seriously challenges conventional social science. But as suggested in the introduction to part 1, until recently, political science has rejected contextual inquiry, and historical interpretation has survived because of early debates within economics, sociology, and anthropology (Abrams 1982; Stedman Jones 1976; Nadel 1957). Concern with contextual concepts does not imply mindless or relational social science, as is sometimes asserted in defense of hypothetical methods, but more careful attention to those historical, motivational, and ideological presumptions that are made in social and political action. To claim that one cannot analyze society or politics in the absence of such assumptions is not simply to trash conventional social science but only to deal more explicitly with those issues that the nomological-deductive model puts beyond our grasp. While this may be perceived as a dilution of scientific method, it is neither intended to be such an attack nor does it presume that conventional behavioral knowledge is in some sense untrue or unreliable.

As illustrated in chapter 14, it may be no more than an attempt to bring back into policy analysis well-known historical and philosophical debates such as the origins of the British, French, and American constitutions. Constitutions are not only texts in the hermeneutic sense, but also exceedingly complex and at times obscure statements about a nation's past, the limits of political action, and the values that underlie political choices. Constitutional questions almost necessarily involve contextual interpretation because, as Ball and Pocock (1988) note, constitutions express "principles of early modern politics in early modern language" (9). As Stourzh (1988) points out, the term *constitution* was not that common when constitutional democracy was first imagined; it more nearly corresponded to the constitution of government or, simply, government itself (37). The problem arises, as one of the foremost analysts of the British constitution writes, because it is "hard to find any theoretical limit to the number and variety of contexts in which a past historical action may be situated for purposes of interpretation" (Pocock 1988, 56). As a result, the rules of interpretation and variety of contextual interpretations should be under constant review. It is of course precisely this critical exercise of the imagination that the more extreme behavioralist eschews.

My constitutional argument in chapter 14 singles out a particular but common issue in the early growth of constitutional government: how to describe and, in most instances, to circumscribe royal prerogatives. Relying on interpretive and historical studies of the British and French constitutions, it is clear that these two countries, and likely most others, carried on lively and protracted debates over how such prerogatives or discretionary authority might be integrated into constitutional government. It is in this context that constitutional interpretations become crucial for policy studies, because the formulas, practices, and legal foundations devised to resolve this dilemma of governance not only became basic constitutional tenets of each country but had direct bearing on what kind of government and administration might be constructed. In Britain, Parliament, and through Parliament, cabinet government, became the primary check against the abuse of discretionary powers, the various writs and petitions being alternative but less-used ways of checking excess power. This meant that, as government developed modern activities, the ability of the British government to state explicitly the limits and procedures for the use of arbitrary powers operated under a narrow constitutional limit, one that could only be qualified by calling into question the entire constitutional structure. This helps explain why the most stable parliamentary system of nineteenth-century governance was so loath to reform local government (Ashford 1982), was slow to develop a merit-based bureaucracy, and had little choice, compared to other governments, but to assign ministers draconian powers over the administration of social questions, labor relations, and public safety.

Consistent with most nineteenth-century interpreters of the British constitution and numerous developments in British government and administration since the turn of the century, the use of discretionary powers has always posed difficult, if not insoluble, constitutional problems. Such an argument is not simply historical hindsight, since no claim is being made that the many situations where this occurred are in fact all linked directly to the ancient constitutional debates, nor that the causes of these various dilemmas in constitutional interpretation are identical. The argument is only that, because discretionary choices are remarkably similar over an extended period and under such a wide variety of circumstances, a more persuasive explanation than ordinary self-interest in the behavioral mode is needed. Put directly, in Britain, discretionary powers posed constitutional dilemmas, which were most often settled by assigning extraordinary powers to ministers and relying on the ancient checks of the British constitution, which were barely accessible to the common citizen. The policy consequences are described in the following chapters and are much like those described by Harden and Lewis (1986), Nairn (1988), and McAuslan and McEldowney (1985) in applying the British constitution to policy problems.

SOURCES

Abrams, Philip. 1982. *Historical Sociology.* London: Open Books.

Ashford, Douglas E. 1982. *British Dogmatism and French Pragmatism: Center-Local Relations in the Welfare State.* London: Allen and Unwin.

Ball, Terence, and J. G. A. Pocock, eds. 1988. *Conceptual Change and the Constitution.* Lawrence: University of Kansas Press.

Beer, Samuel H. 1965. *British Politics in the Collectivist Age.* New York: Knopf.

Freeman, Gary. 1975. National Styles and Policy Sectors: Explaining Structured Variation. *Journal of Public Policy* 5:467–96.

Goodin, Robert E. 1982. *Political Theory and Public Policy.* Chicago: University of Chicago Press.

Harden, Ian, and Norman Lewis. 1986. *The Noble Lie: The British Constitution and the Rule of Law.* London: Hutchinson.

Katznelson, Ira. 1978. Considerations on Social Democracy in the United States. *Comparative Politics* 10:77–99.

Lockhart, Charles. 1989. *Gaining Ground: Tailoring Social Programs to American Values.* Berkeley and Los Angeles: University of California Press.

Lowe, Rodney. 1986. *Adjusting to Democracy.* Oxford: Oxford University Press.

McAuslan, Patrick, and John F. McEldowney, eds. 1985. *Law, Legitimacy and the Constitution.* London: Sweet and Maxwell.

March, James G., and Johan P. Olsen. 1976. *Ambiguity and Choice in Organization.* Bergen: Universitetforlaget.

Mayntz, Renate, and Fritz Scharpf. 1975. *Policy-Making in the German Federal Bureaucracy.* Amsterdam: Elsevier.

Mommsen, Wolfgang J. 1974 (1959). *Max Weber and German Politics, 1890–1920.* Trans. Michael S. Steinberg. Chicago: University of Chicago Press.

Mommsen, Wolfgang J., and Jurgen Osterhammel, eds. 1987. *Max Weber and His Contemporaries.* London: Allen and Unwin.

Nadel, S. F. 1957. *Theory of Social Structure.* London: Cohen and West.

Nairn, Tom. 1988. *The Enchanted Glass: Britain and Its Monarchy.* London: Radius.

Olson, Mancur. 1965. *The Logic of Collective Action.* Cambridge: Harvard University Press.

Pocock, J. G. A. 1988. States, Republics and Empires: The American Founding in Early Modern Perspective. In T. Ball and J.G.A. Pocock, eds., *Conceptual Change and the Constitution*. Lawrence: University of Kansas Press.

Pressman, Jeffrey L., and Aaron Wildavsky. 1973. *Implementation*. Berkeley and Los Angeles: University of California Press.

Rose, Richard. 1980. *Do Parties Make a Difference?* Chatham: Chatham House.

Simon, Herbert A. 1947. *Administrative Behavior: A Study in Decisionmaking Processes in Administrative Organization*. New York: Macmillan.

Skrownek, Stephen. 1982. *Building a New American State: The Expansion of National Administrative Capacities, 1877–1920*. New York: Cambridge University Press.

Stedman Jones, Gareth. 1976. From Historical Sociology to Theoretical History. *British Journal of Sociology* 27:295–305.

Stourzh, Gerald. 1988. Constitutions: Changing Meanings of the Term from the Early Seventeenth to the Late Eighteenth Century. In T. Ball and J.G.A. Pocock, eds., *Conceptual Change and the Constitution*. Lawrence: University of Kansas Press.

Taylor, Charles. 1983. Political Theory and Practice. In Christopher Lloyd, ed., *Social Theory and Political Practice*. Oxford: Clarenden.

Weir, Margaret, Ann Orloff, and Theda Skocpol, eds. 1988. *The Politics of Social Security*. Princeton: Princeton University Press.

12

Parties, Politics, and Democratic Choice

Bert A. Rockman

THE LINK BETWEEN parties and public policies is inescapably of foremost importance to democratic politics. Yet, the nature of this linkage is exceptionally complex and does not easily yield to simple and all-encompassing theories. Notwithstanding the importance of political parties for democratic choice, the connection between those choices and policy outcomes is certainly considerably less than transparent.

This chapter explores many of the factors impeding a straightforward connection between party and policy, examines the relevance of research perspective to the answers one is likely to obtain about the connection of parties to policies and, finally, evaluates the role of political parties as mechanisms for democratic choice in a context of many factors influencing policy choice and implementation. While simplistic notions of party command are largely irrelevant, more limited but empirically adequate conceptions of the role of parties in making policy are necessary. When such conceptions are considered, parties well may be regarded as vital instruments of democratic policy choice.

The first part of this chapter sets forth the contradictory images of parties as policy makers and lays out an inventory of conditions influencing the ability of parties to be policy makers. The last condition raises the issue of uncertainty between policy and outcome.

The second section deals broadly with the matter of party cleavages—the consistency and adaptability of party positions, the role of parties even in a "weak party" state such as the United States, and the role of analytic approach in evaluating the relevance of parties to policy choice.

In the conclusion, contradictions between durability in power and the ability to emit clear policy direction are discussed. Despite numerous complications to any simple theory of party control over policy, I argue that parties remain key actors in a process of democratic control over policy choices.

Parties and Policies—Where Do We Begin?

The primary vehicle for the organization of policy conflict in democratic states is the political party. Parties organize supporters, contest elections, and seek (usually) to gain office. Presumably, one of the essential reasons why they perform these functions is to influence the policies that governments choose. Not surprisingly, any set of organizations reputed to perform activities as central as these ought rightly to attract a great deal of attention from professional students of politics and government. For these reasons, political parties have indeed occupied a primary role in modern political science.

The Contradictory Images of Parties

The roles played by parties, however, are beset by contradictory images. On the one hand, from the perspective of public choice, they are reputed to make only those policy choices and promises that will maximize responsiveness to voters (especially the alluring median voter of spatial models) and, thus, enhance their prospects for electoral success (Downs 1957). On the other hand, from the perspective of political sociology, parties also organize cleavages, ideologies, and constituencies and, in this sense, constrain their opportunities for maximum electoral adaptability. This perspective, in fact, has also been modeled in the public choice mode (Aldrich 1983). From this we can conclude that parties are presumed to do a great many contradictory things.

To the extent that parties are median-vote chasers, it is unlikely that in governing they will deviate significantly from the status quo. Incrementalism and centrism are polarities. Alternatively, to the extent that parties are ideologically driven and programmatic, they may (1) have their opportunities for governing reduced, because they fail to gain needed electoral support, and (2) be unable, because of limited support, to implement their programs in office. In stark form, the question is whether the struggle for political power through the modern democratic device of the political party is simply an unprincipled effort to gain and maintain the perquisites of office (as much public choice theory implies) or whether its purposes are to gain advantage for a given set of policy preferences.

The simple question of what parties can actually achieve in power is not, in fact, so simple to answer. A wide variety of factors influences the party-policy nexus. I begin here with merely a set of building blocks, but not a theory.

MOTIVES. We must begin with what it is that parties, more specifically party leaders, want to do—a matter I have just discussed. In vastly simplified form, we may think of parties as vote maximizers or program emphasizers. In the former role, parties are best viewed as agents of popular majorities; in the latter, they are best viewed as risk takers and opinion mobilizers. Typically, when parties assume the latter role, they intend to depart from the status quo. Whether their intentions bear fruit depends, however, upon many other factors.

ORGANIZATION. Among a variety of organizational characteristics that parties may possess, one set has to do with their relative cohesion. In this regard, parties may be fractionalized, factionalized, or, more rarely, centrally unified. Fractionalization often is the result of fragmented authority structures and federal systems. Under these conditions, parties may be better organized around a subnational territory than at the national level. It is fair to say that the American parties, at least until very recently, have been characterized by their internal regional differences and by the relative strength of their local and state organizations rather than by that of their national organizations. This sort of fractionalization probably means that parties carry more influence locally or regionally than nationally, but ironically, local and regional issues may be less likely to evoke cleavages as strong as those at the national level. And where there is local or regional one-party dominance, cleavages are more likely to be organized within the dominant party than between parties.

Factionalization typically requires a unitary system, in contrast to fractionalization. Some parties are notorious for their factionalization, a characteristic of the major Italian and Japanese parties, especially the Christian Democrats in Italy and the Liberal Democratic party in Japan. Whether factions are inhibiting or facilitating in regard to policy impact probably depends upon their institutionalization and the mechanisms employed for arriving at agreements. It is evident, though, that no factionalized system can be self-sustaining without some payoff for the factional followers. Thus, one would anticipate that factionalized parties are especially likely to be proponents of pork barrel politics and particularistic and divisible benefits.

Parties are always less internally unified than is implied by the imagery of a mobilized cadre organization. Democratic parties typically unify more around issues than organizational doctrines. Thus, despite the relatively weak organization of American political parties at the national level, this deficiency did not prevent them from addressing in the 1830s and 1840s (and also the 1980s) national issues in a remarkably cohesive way (Silbey 1967). In sum, the organizational characteristics of parties are not deeply fixed.

POWER STATUS. The ability of any given party to successfully put forward its manifesto or program depends upon its position relative to other parties. Is it in the situation of being a majority party government? If so, then the next question is whether the contents of the manifesto are, in fact, feasible. Aside from the Westminster model, however, parties mostly find themselves in coalition situations. Such coalitions may be formal, as in parliamentary systems, or informal (divided government, cohabitation), as in presidential systems.

In coalitions involving a senior (big) and junior (small) partner, the small one often exercises pivotal influence. Thus, small parties are in an ideal situation when they are situated between two large parties opposed to one another. The Free Democratic party in Germany has been a continuous coalition partner since 1969 and has played an outsized role in regard to foreign and economic policy. Similarly, in Israel, the religious bloc (which does not sit astride the major contenders so much as along an intersecting dimension) has had, in spite of the bloc's small parliamentary size, continuous influence over religious and educational policy since the founding of the state. Although larger and less distinctly influential, the confessional coalition in the Netherlands has maintained a prominent role in Dutch government despite its dwindling share of the popular vote. Being a pivotal minority in a coalition government where the dominant partners can change, consequently, puts the smaller pivotal parties in the position to colonize particular sectors of government and, thus, to play a very large policy-making role in the affected areas.

Another vitally important feature of a party's power status is its durability in government. The remarkable durability of pivotal parties in alliance with a senior coalition partner gives such parties, as noted, significant influence, if not outright control, over particular policy domains. Yet, a dominant coalition partner can be expected to exercise far more extensive influence when it also carries with its status an expectation of its durability as the primary governing partner. The Japanese Liberal Democratic party, and earlier the Swedish Social Democrats and the Norwegian Labor party have occupied such positions at the national level. Finally, when a single party is continually returned to office in a majoritarian position, it is obviously best situated to pursue its objectives, subject only to its own internal differences. Majorities, naturally, are most easily formed when the number of competing parties is small. A two-party system necessarily creates a governing majority. Yet, a competitive majority two-party system may well contain within it elements of a a long-term equilibrium of party alternation (Stokes and Iversen 1962).

POLITICAL CIRCUMSTANCES. While a party's power status may be regarded as an endogenous element in its exercise of policy influence, the political circumstances influencing its status position can be regarded as an exogenous element. A number of writers have touched upon change within the electorate itself as one such exogenous factor. In the American context especially, the language of alignment, realignment, and dealignment is used to describe such changes and the energies these shifts may either bestow upon or detract from the party system (Burnham 1969; Brady 1978; Beck 1979). Others have talked about the related concept of political time and the notion that regimes go through natural if lengthy cycles of revitalization and devitalization, until they eventually are supplanted by alternative regimes and different policy premises (Skowronek 1988). By influencing the power status of parties, these conditions also influence the available opportunities for certain sets of policy ideas. The stream of policy ideas may run independently of the flow of political party power (Heclo 1974; Kingdon 1984), but parties are often the vehicle through which ideas from the policy stream are put into practice (Aberbach and Rockman 1990).

Popularly perceived crises represent a type of exogenous political condition with potentially very different results for the role of parties. On the one hand, crisis conditions can lead to strong political changes, as apparently occurred at the onset of the New Deal. The elections of 1930 signaled a shift in national political party dominance for the next two decades. In this sense, crisis produces *agenda change*. Alternatively, crisis conditions sometimes can lead to the development of grand coalitions, which, strictly speaking, produce nonpartisan government. In this particular conception, crisis may produce, from a partisan standpoint, *agenda constraint*.

POLICY STATUS. Policies, like decisions, are not discrete acts but constitute, instead, a vector space of continuous choices. So conceived, the policy universe, as Hogwood and Peters (1983) imply, may have finite rather than ever expanding properties. Choices made earlier constrain choices made today. Well-established policies tend to resist being disestablished. Policies that prove most resistant are not always, despite the popular lore, the ones protected by a subgovernmental apparatus. Instead, they are likely to be programs that are well established and broadly popular, carrying with them universal benefits—pensions and health care, for example. Such policies, of course, typically constitute the vast proportion of nondefense and noninterest expenditure commitments in national budgets. In general, parties tend to resist frontal assaults on policies such as these because of the obvious political costs. The preferences of party politicians are to expand these benefits once the programs are established and prove to be popular.

Yet even here, indirect tinkering of a contracting nature does come about. By changing the nature of health care financing, for example, even such popular programs as medicare in the United States have capped costs by, in essence, rationing care. More of this, to be sure, has been done to the medicaid program, which is a nonuniversalized and less broadly popular program of medical care for the low-income population. User costs have also increased. It is possible that these outcomes would be inevitable given budgetary constraints and increases in health care costs. But such restrictions are the product as well of a political ideology to reduce the public sector. Nonetheless, in general, the influence of parties over policy is likely to be greatest in domains less crowded by existing policy. This influence is likely to be least when existing policies are well established and popular.

POLICY OUTCOMES. Parties can help mold policies, but policies do not always mold outcomes. Much foreign and defense policy, for example, is predicated on guesses as to how others will react. Indeed, foreign policy in general presents problems of measuring what, in fact, *policy* is—problems that are sufficiently complex by themselves that they must be clarified before one can even address questions of impact and its measurement.

In macroeconomic policies, fiscal, tax, and monetary interventions can produce some distinctive outcomes—for example, the size of the structural deficit or the likely level of interest rates. Nevertheless, the view that complex processes such as macroeconomic fortunes can be readily tinkered with and manipulated has receded in the post-Keynesian environment. Even socialists in Western states have become sobered. Economies have become intertwined and increasingly less subject to the pull of national policy. Policy remains national, while capital is international. And even within the realm of national influences, the capacity to control rests increasingly upon accurate and refined economic indicators, such as the money supply. The reliability of such indicators, in fact, has become more uncertain in the face of growing technical complexity in the recording of economic transactions.

Consequently, the measurement of party influence on outcomes is at best a highly imperfect guide to party differences with respect to policy choices (Rose 1980). There are many reasons why outcomes, especially those involving complex processes, may vary relatively little with changes in party control. Certainly, some of these have to do with compelling systemic forces that narrow the effective range of policy choice for whatever party is in office. Some have to do with the relative inefficacy of policy choice itself. Chad, for example, cannot simply will itself, given its limited endowments, to be economically developed. As well, some reasons have to do with the problems of measuring the effects of policy. Literature on the political-business cycle originally made influential by Nordhaus (1975) and popularized by Tufte (1978) focuses not merely on the assumption that politicians intend to produce good times for electoral gain but also on whether the instruments they choose (when they do choose) are capable of achieving the results they are presumed to desire (Golden and Poterba, 1980).

Parties and Public Policy

My intent here has been to produce a set of building blocks with which to think about the remarkably complex relationship between political parties and public policy. No theory has been produced from this exercise; and producing such a theory is unlikely until we begin to specify particular pieces of the policy puzzle and subject them to empirical testing. Of course, such specification first requires that policies be distinguished from outcomes. Second, it requires that types of policies be distinguished with regard to their complexity, instrumentation, and institutionalization. One obvious proposition is that it is easier to change direction in matters influenced by words or postures than in those influenced by laws, programs, and an organizational apparatus. A nation's foreign policy, hence, is probably more subject to party-directed change than its social policies, but there has been a truly stunning absence of work across comparative policy domains that would allow us to test such a notion. Third, we need to ask what aspects of policy parties can have influence over. The traditional view is that parties symbolize policies, while the administrative apparatus realizes them. While this perspective is not entirely untrue, it is overblown. In this regard, I note the rapidly burgeoning literature in the United States on the issue of political control over implementation and administration (Miller and Moe 1983; Moe 1985; Weingast and Moran 1983; McCubbins and Schwartz 1984; Aberbach 1987). Clearly, implementation is not wholly outside the sphere of party politics, and I suspect that while the American case exaggerates these tendencies, it is probably not fundamentally idiosyncratic.

The relation of political factors—leadership strategies, organizational characteristics, power status, and political conditions—to the actual role played by parties in policy making is important, but not simple, to understand. Part of the problem lies in defining what policy making is. Policies and the process of policy choice are neither well bounded nor discrete. Policies are not concrete or static. They are equilibrium outcomes—some stable, some unstable—reflecting a continuous and iterative process. This lack of boundedness is at the heart of our bewilderment about the relation between party and policy.

All analytic distinctions are, of course, artifices. And without such artifices, we are entrapped within a seamless web, unable to say much that is intelligible. So, no matter how resistant the subject of policy making is to being cut into analytically discernible pieces, doing so constitutes a necessary route to making headway.

In the following section, I examine the ambivalent views that political scientists take toward the policy role of parties. In my conclusion, I come back to two issues, namely, durability in power and governing style.

Do Parties Matter?

Like most seemingly simple questions in political science, the one implied in the heading above leads to no uniform answer—sometimes even from to the same political scientist. For example, in 1974, Richard Rose published an exquisitely well-balanced volume on the pitfalls and benefits of party government, eventually finding the need for political and policy direction to be sufficiently important so as to override his concerns about other potential defects of party government. Yet, only half a dozen years later (1980), he concluded that, while British parties, indeed, had followed the expected doctrines of party government, they were not nearly so strong a force in policy direction as might have been anticipated.

I cannot do better here than to quote Rose himself on the nature of the difference parties have made for British government:

> Yes, parties do make a difference in the way Britain is governed—but the differences are not as expected. The differences in office between one party and another are less likely to arise from contrasting intentions than from the exigencies of government. Much of a party's record in office will be stamped on it by forces outside its control. British parties are not the primary forces shaping the destiny of British society; it is shaped by something stronger than parties. (1980, 141)

In short, parties do matter in the sense that they articulate the demands of different constituencies and bring different intentions about policy to bear on government. Such differences often make a difference in what government does, especially in those policy domains unburdened by an extensive inventory of precedents or in those domains less subject to larger countervailing forces. Powerful intentions, however, often are reversed by even more powerful systemic constraints. The income and tax policies initiated by the Socialists in France in 1981–1982 were limited and altered by the threatened flight of capital. Similarly, the vast increases in military expenditures in the first years of the Reagan administration were later offset by vast decreases that resulted from the large budget deficits produced by tax reductions and the consequent targeting of the military for disproportionate spending reductions.

Most important, Rose's analysis suggests that, while British parties tend to act consistently on their principles, party principles are not rigidly fixed. A party's positions at any given time reflect adaptations based on perceived failures and successes of earlier programs, sometimes including those that are part of its own past record. Thus, in the 1972 election year, Republicans and Democrats bid up the price of indexing social security adjustments—a program perceived as successful but that Republicans once firmly opposed. Equally, the same reasoning applies to perceived policy failure. This helps to explain why in 1981 after Reagan's victory over Carter, the partisan switch of the Senate, and other assorted humblings of the Democratic party, the Democrats, in spite of their doubts, bid up the price of the Reagan tax reduction proposals by throwing indexation into the package—a maneuver that the Reagan administration happily accepted and proceeded to bid up yet further (Aberbach and Rockman 1985).

The notion of adaptive principles also helps to explain why it is that in the United States, Democrats now frequently articulate positions that sound more like those of Taft Republicans (expressing concerns about budget deficits and foreign interventions), while Republicans of the Reaganite persuasion often sound like Democrats who once governed (budget deficits are not themselves so bad; it's the impact on economic growth that's important, etc.). *Parties, in other words, are both principled and opportunity seekers.* The images, while distinct in the abstract, are not wholly conflictual in practice.

Whatever the party programs, however, the outcomes of complex processes are not easily manipulated. As Rose (1980) demonstrates, the basic contours of economic performance and of aggregate government functions are not severely affected by oscillations in policy, even though as the political-business cycle literature suggests, there may be short-term effects. Part of the reason for this lack of impact is plain ignorance. Many, if not most, policy interventions in complex processes are mere guesses. Another part of the reason is that interventions are often watered down to provide momentary adjustments but are insufficient to affect secular trends. A further part of the reason has to do with the first, namely the influence of exogenous and unknown factors that can counter policy interventions. These include the basic systemic parameters that constrain policy choice and certainly limit policy impacts. In sum, making policy does not lead to remaking the world, in spite of the enthusiasms of party ideologists.

Differences in Ideology and Behavior

There are obviously several different levels of analysis at which one can deal with the question of party differences. The first, and generally the most powerful, is that of attitudinal differences over issues. Although factors in the political environment can soften or intensify the magnitude of cross-party cleavages in political attitude and behavior, the single best predictor at any time to an individual's political attitudes and behavior is that individual's party membership. This is particularly true among those most attentive to politics, and especially so among the even more rarified stratum of political and public officeholding elites (Putnam 1976).

Because of the absence of formalized party discipline, the American case allows us to see dramatically just how important party is to ideological differences toward policy. Poole and Rosenthal, for example, observe the remarkable polarization between the American congressional parties, a view that is supplemented also by examinations of party activists (Miller and Jennings 1986) and administrative elites (Aberbach and Rockman 1990). Essentially, these analyses have drawn attention to the powerful role of political parties and the distinctiveness of their positions. Analysts differ as to what forces have been pushing that change. Examining elite attitudes, Miller and Jennings (1986) and Aberbach and Rockman (1990), for example, emphasize the rightward shift of the Republicans, while Poole and Rosenthal (1984), examining congressional votes, stress a leftward movement on the part of the Democrats.

The data clearly show, however, that in the supposedly weak-party politics of the United States, the ideological visions of elites have grown more distinctive by party, and there is now clear evidence that at least legislative behavior has similarly become more distinctive along party lines, despite the numerous incentives in the American system to behave in a constituency-particularistic fashion. Thus, Poole and Rosenthal (1984) note that "two senators from the same state and party tend to be very similar. In contrast, senators from the same state but from different parties are highly dissimilar" (1061). The policy implications that Poole and Rosenthal draw from this are that the parties now possess nonoverlapping support coalitions and have equal probabilities of being elected. Consequently, there is a strong party-policy relation. But when this is accompanied by a high turnover of party in office, what they call a "ping-ponging" effect takes place. Strong initiatives are thus displaced by strong countermeasures. The result, of course, may be that parties have little net effect over policy, but that simply may be due to a failure to sustain political control. To be sure, Rose (1974) notes this as a potential defect of party government.

My emphasis here is mainly on the American case, and there are good reasons for this. U.S. parties reputedly have been catchall parties organized only vaguely around broad constituencies and with few mechanisms to enforce cohesion. The implication, therefore, is that the parties are more interested in votes than in policies. The evidence is not wholly consistent with this view, however. The differences between the parties, at least in basic perspective, are currently very strong. Party cohesion in legislative activity is stunningly high for a system in which there are few costs for a legislator to deviate from the party line. In other words, even in a relatively weak party system such as that in the United States, parties have represented basic issue conflicts with considerable consistency and coherence, though the issues by no means remain perfectly stable.

There are still important questions to be answered. First, is the present high level of party conflict merely a temporal phenomenon? The answer to this question is partly yes and partly no. It is yes in the sense that from time to time the temperature of party conflict rises (and thus also lowers), and these fluctuations have to do with the often related phenomena of highly divisive issues coming to the political forefront, of new coalitions forming within the parties (the exodus of cold warrior Democrats to the side of the Republicans reflects this), and the leadership style within the parties. In the United States and Britain under Reagan and Thatcher, the leadership was committed to radical goals. Although President Reagan's style was softer than Prime Minister Thatcher's, the Reagan agenda was equally radical. And while the American system hinders radical accomplishment, it certainly does not impede radical assertion. Assertion is transformed into accomplishment during moments when the American system operates much like a majority party government system, as it did in 1981.

As for the no part of the answer to whether the magnitude of party difference is only a temporal phenomenon, it is well to recall that, although other pressures normally impinge upon the ability of the parties to articulate and to enact their legislative goals, party conflict still commands center stage, still accounts most strongly for both electoral and legislative behavior, and still divides elite opinion more powerfully than anything else. Unlike most other political democracies, parties in the United States do not always monopolize either the debate or the action over policy, even within the overt political arena. But relatively few issues get far without eventually being articulated within the party framework. Of course, some issues have become either depoliticized or politicized along lines other than party. The favored position of Israel in American foreign policy in the Middle East exemplifies such transpartisan issues, as does social security, wherein each party wants to avoid political risk.

While specific proposals are the product of many and various agents—interest groups, bureaucrats, executive politicians, and individual legislators—parties articulate mostly policy frameworks. It is at the level of policy framework, therefore, that the magnitude of disagreement tends to be especially strong. Thus, even in the less-polarized times of the early 1970s, for example, surveys of elites in the American executive branch reveal that only 16 percent of Republican executive elites favored a more interventionist state in social and economic affairs, while 73 percent of the Democrats did (Aberbach and Rockman 1976). Over the years, these figures have slid rightward, toward favoring smaller government, but party differences remain at least as powerful (Aberbach and Rockman 1990).

A second, and probably more fundamental, question, however, is to what extent these overt party divisions actually bear on policy. There is no simple answer to this, because there is no simple answer to what the term *policy* means (Hale 1988). Certainly, a great deal depends upon the role that overt political processes play in policy making—whether these are regarded as mere rhetorical exercises in political dramaturgy or, instead, arenas for providing directions, signals, and sometimes even precise controls over what is to be done and how laws are to be administered. It is certainly the case that, in the United States, one important consequence of political polarization with divided government is that the overt political processes have become increasingly significant in the formulation of very detailed policy guidelines. That, admittedly, is partly a function of American institutions, especially the extremely powerful role played by an independent legislative authority.

In regard to this question, one's methodological approach is profoundly important as to how one sees parties in the policy process. If one looks principally at political cleavages, particularly from a historical or political-sociological standpoint, the role of political parties, particularly as gatekeepers of policy ideas, will loom fairly large. On the other hand, two other types of investigation as to the determinants of policy will tend to diminish the apparent influences of party: (1) cross-national analyses of quantitative measures of outcome change or of expenditure commitment and (2) intensive case analyses of the evolution of policy within specific domains. It will be useful to examine a few specimens of each type of inquiry.

Cleavage Structure and Political Change

"Breakthrough" politics, producing a surge of policy change, is, by definition, a relatively rare phenomenon, typically arriving at the crest of broader political change. Often this occurs after deeper changes have taken hold in society. In electoral party politics, this phenomenon typically is known as the cycle of political realignment. Such political changes are of striking importance, however, only if they can be related to equally fundamental changes in policy. Indeed, realignment does tend to have significant legislative impact, at least for a while. Brady and others have observed enhanced party cohesion and party voting during such periods, a general sharpening of party-based political cleavages, and the emergence of new policies and issue structures (Brady 1978; Ginsberg 1972, 1976; Ferguson 1983). In modern times, policy ideas originally promoted elsewhere await opportunities such as these to come to fruition in the form of legislation. The postwar Attlee government in Britain and the Great Society programs of Lyndon Johnson exemplify this open window. Even though the parties themselves may not have been the primary incubators of policy ideas, they are the primary vehicles for bringing them to expression. The so-called supply-side theory, for instance (a fiscal revolution written on a napkin), was promoted by intellectuals loosely associated with the Republican party in the United States, but supply-side ideas needed a ripened set of political circumstances to be molded into public policy.

In these episodic periods of policy surge, what we see primarily is the passage of a government program in the form of statutory law. What is more generally neglected in focusing on the passage of laws, if for understandable technical reasons, are some of the other aspects of policy—administrative implementation, counterpressures for change, reevaluations, and changes in goals. That is because, if one may paraphrase a well-known American baseball player-philosopher, policy isn't over even when it's over. Policy, after all, is the equilibrium result of successive iterations; legislation most often establishes a policy framework, but policy simply does not end at that point.

Consequently, policy change is associated with political change. But focusing on that alone generally will not tell us much about how policy ideas emerge, how policy goals may be displaced or implemented, how potentially countervailing reactions may be mobilized, or how the policy framework may become institutionally embedded and normatively accepted and, hence, resistant to change (Rockman 1984).

Aggregate Analyses of Party Influence

Aggregate analyses of public policy tend naturally to look at those elements of policy that are most susceptible to quantification. These normally are expenditures used as indicators of policy effort. Expenditures in the aggregate can conceal a great many things. But in the broad area of social security policies, they are likely to be good indicators of what the outcomes look like. Sweden, for example, with a very large social security sector and a very high marginal tax rate also has a low level of income inequality (Verba et al. 1987).

In Wilensky's (1975) effort to model determinants of welfare state expenditure across the industrialized democracies, he employs elite ideology as a variable representing differences in party position regarding income redistribution, the welfare state, and the tax load. Given the level of aggregation at which Wilensky's model operates, the party differences (elite ideology) variable explains virtually none of the variance in welfare state expenditure. Explanations of welfare state expenditure, in fact, derive from inertia and demographics. Inertia is reflected in the age of the social security system—the longevity of which also works to incrementalize additions in benefits. Demographics are reflected in the age of the population over sixty-five—a sector of the population that both collects almost all the pension benefits and receives a disproportionate share of the medical resources. In the face of these compelling forces, party ideologies fail to influence overall expenditure commitments. What this really says, of course, is that when policies are highly institutionalized, have formulated payment benefits, and have a population-induced demand profile for their consumption, party differences wash out as significant determinants of the overall standardized expenditure levels.

But this misses several important points at which parties are important. First, only a few programs, usually widely popular, influence the overall welfare expenditure effort. These programs contain the self-triggering characteristics noted above. Consequently, when only expenditures are examined, the overall effort is not highly influenced by partisan politics. If parties influence welfare policies at the margins of expenditure, (the controllable or discretionary portion), however, they can have a major impact on stipulating eligibility, delivery, and intended targets of welfare services or payments. The Thatcher and Reagan revolutions did not put a dent in overall expenditures, but each government had reallocated the nature of its effort and made it more difficult for some groups to get benefits. Each also had tried to tinker with the tax system in ways that would affect, even if moderately, income distribution and inequality. From the standpoint of overall expenditure, of course, such policies are marginal, but to the affected populations, they are often central.

Furthermore, emphasis on cross-sectional explanation of a highly aggregated expenditure profile tells us little about whether or not parties were critical to the organization of the policies or to debates surrounding their formulation. Nor can cross-sectional aggregate analysis address changes in rates of expenditure effort. In larger-scale comparisons of the sort Wilensky has undertaken, inertia appears inevitable and demography appears as destiny. But that is because, at this level of aggregation, and with a static focus, political factors are relatively unimportant (Fried 1976).

Party structure assumes greater importance in another Wilensky study (1976)—one that examines the determinants of tax backlash among a number of OECD countries. Here, Wilensky emphasizes the age of the party system as a determinant of welfare state tax backlash. The age of the party system is an indirect determinant and is strongly linked to the visibility of taxes, which, in turn, provides the final and strongest direct link to welfare state tax backlash. Theoretically, the older the party system, the less clearly linked it is to corporatist mechanisms for arriving at decisions. Presumably, such mechanisms help to syndicate political risk and reduce political reaction to the welfare state tax explosion.

Wilensky's analysis here, however, fails to take into account ideologies, for the key obviously can be found in the range of agreement and disagreement between political parties in various countries. As Verba et al. (1987) show, Swedes disagree about the appropriate level of equality, whereas Americans disagree about the welfare state itself.

Case Studies of Policy Making

Case studies of policy making deemphasize the role of parties in the process mainly because they tend to focus on issues that rarely are decidedly partisan. Additionally, they tend to focus within the organizational structure of government, not on the party system as such. Bureaucrats, interest groups, and idea entrepreneurs (sometimes a part of each of the first two groups) become the actors of particular importance. Many of the questions that naturally flow from intensive examinations of policy making focus on organizational issues, participatory scope, the role of institutional structure or interest arrangements in decision making, the place of ideas in stimulating policy change, and the displacement of goals. My point is not that these issues are unimportant; it is that focusing on them tends to ignore or downplay the role that parties play in policy making. That is a natural, not a conspiratorial, result.

While aggregate analyses deal at a level so broad that the influences of party on policy are masked, case studies tend to focus on those policies or aspects of policy making in which the party role is relatively weaker. Such emphases are also implicitly linked to notions of issue opportunities and idea entrepreneurship (Kingdon 1984; Heclo 1974; Derthick and Quirk 1985). Issues that are mostly nonpartisan to begin with, however, do not always remain that way. The great push for environmental regulation throughout the 1970s, for example, was born in a relatively nonpartisan atmosphere, but once in place, it did not stay nonpartisan for long. The issue, in fact, became redefined as political agendas changed—from the idea of protecting the environment to the idea of reducing the costs of regulation and freeing productive forces from presumed paralysis. When the debate sharpened, environmental regulation frequently became partisan. The sequence often occurs in reverse order, too. Previously highly partisan issues such as social security, for example, become essentially nonpartisan by virtue of their institutionalization and popularity.

The role of parties in policy making, then, depends on what one sees, which is partly a function of how one chooses to see. And depending upon how one chooses to see, the party role is either large or small.

Conclusion—Durability, Command, and Osmosis

It is clear that the impact of parties on policy has a great deal to do with their longevity in government. As noted, even durable junior partners in a coalition can be highly influential, especially in proportion to the vote they receive and the seats they hold. But longevity of tenure for a dominant party is crucial to its ability to influence policy over the long run and to institutionalize it. A dominant one-party government, even more so, can operate unimpeded by party turnover in office. Thus the Swedish government under the long dominance of the Social Democrats produced policies on the issue of housing more consistent over time with previous decisions than those produced in Britain, where the parties held more strongly polarized positions and also alternated in power more frequently (Headey 1979).

Were everything as straightforward as this, simple propositions about the durability and the party policy nexus would be easier to generate. Unfortunately, everything is not so straightforward. The long tenure of a single party is not a simple determinant of policy effects, at least if we think of policy in the form of a programmatic agenda. The long reign of the democratic Left in the Scandinavian countries consummated the social welfare state and pushed into other areas of social change before being temporarily ousted in the 1970s. On the other hand, neither the Christian Democrats in Italy nor the Liberal Democratic party in Japan have been especially programmatic; indeed, to a considerable degree, the LDP has resisted programmatic thrusts in social policy—although, of course, this too is a policy. Both parties seem to have adapted as much as they have led.

None of these cases, including the Scandinavian ones, readily fit the idealized concept of the Westminster model of party command. This idealized concept, which is popular among some American commentators (Burns 1963: Cutler 1980), assumes that the majority party's bark should cause the rest of the system to jump.

Some of the pieces of the party policy puzzle lie in party organization. Other pieces are to be found in party support coalitions and their eventual deterioration over time. Factionalized parties are likely to emphasize political payoffs and the pork barrel and are likely to avoid decisions that might disrupt the mechanisms for internal conflict mediation. Such parties often are composed of very heterogenous support coalitions, elements of which are potentially in conflict with one another. The Japanese LDP, for example, is supported by business, rural landholders, and the urban bourgeoisie. The interests of the farmers often conflict with those of the urban middle classes, whose high cost of living is partly a subsidy to both the farmers and export-oriented business.

Esping-Andersen's (1985) very interesting book on the realignment of political forces in the Scandinavian countries indicates, however, that political decomposition is a virtual inevitability as the fabric of the social structure changes. These shifting social forces require the parties to forge alliances around stable and more marginal elements of support. The key to the greater success of the social democratic movements in Sweden and Norway than in Denmark apparently has been the ability to forge class alliances and avoid policies that would sharpen cleavages. In other words, support coalitions that keep dominant parties in power for lengthy periods of time also eventually constrain the party's abilities to lead public policy in directions that lack broad support. Setting the political foundation for acceptance of new policies is an important function of parties operating in a consensual yet directional style. Durability is important to the development of such a style but is no guarantee of it.

An additional piece of the puzzle is much neglected—namely, party principles. To a considerable degree, it has been the parties of the Left that have articulated a vision of the future and the programmatic means by which to achieve it. Thus, to the degree that we associate policy with use of the state as an instrument for goal achievement, it is natural that left-wing parties appear as policy parties. Conservative policy making is less programmatic, more likely to emphasize maintenance and social harmony values, and more likely to be linked to the needs of capital. Occasionally, by virtue of their use of the state or their deployment of experts to guide the state, rightist governments also appear to be policy activists. In this regard, the Gaullist governments and that of Giscard appeared to be policy active (although none of this was much dictated by parties per se).

The notion of party command tends to dominate the imagery of party influence over policy. This can be misleading, because, over long periods of time, parties in government are also in an osmotic condition, influenced as well as influencing. They do affect the governing environment around them, and, when in power long enough, they also define the expectations of other institutional actors in the system. But equally, parties are also influenced by the institutional structures around them. Long-term responsibility makes shirking more problematic. It provides sobriety and usually a better understanding of the functions of others in governing.

But alas, here too, no simple propositions emerge. Some parties in power a long time, such as the Christian Democrats in Italy, failed to enjoy good relations with the bureaucracy, despite the fact that, in the 1950s, when this party had unquestioned political hegemony, the bureaucracy largely acted as its political tool. In Sweden and Japan, relations have been more cordial—partly a function of the historically esteemed status of the bureaucrcy in each country and the emphasis on consensual deliberation in governing. Nonetheless, the instincts of party politicians and bureaucrats are fundamentally different. The ruling Liberal Democratic party in Japan may compartmentalize these instincts to some degree by granting considerable discretion and autonomy to the vital economic and trade ministries while using some other ministries to enhance the political pork barrel (Aberbach et al. 1990).

Longevity, then, provides parties with considerable policy opportunities—if they are so moved and if they can effectively shape the expectations of others involved in governing. But longevity is never assured, at least in truly democratic systems. And opportunities enhance but do not guarantee, policy success. Support bases erode. Exogenous events often block policy intentions from being fulfilled. Other parties may or may not be able to position themselves as plausible alternatives. A world of increased interdependence, as well, means lessened policy autonomy within states and probably a more homogeneous response, across states and across parties, to similar conditions.

Like human appetites, policy appetites are governed by a realistic schedule of priorities arrived at, if not a priori, then a posteriori. There are things that parties would like to do; there also are things that parties must do. When parties cease being governed by what they like to do, they lose their vision, their message, and ultimately, their constituencies. But when parties cease doing what must be done, they lose elections and their claim to govern. Exigencies do muffle policy response and, in that regard, we would be well advised to examine the systemic sources of these exigencies. At the same time, ceteris paribus, parties do define policy differences, and these differences are not trivial. The differences, of course, are not always locked into the same position. If they were, parties would be unable to adapt to changes in society. Above all, they would be unable to govern. Still, policy is influenced by many hands. Parties are one set—an important but not exclusive set—in influencing the policy equilibrium.

To conclude, parties account for a great deal less than their most fervent advocates hope. Yet, efforts to account for policy without reference to parties mislead. Even though not all issues can be placed within a framework of party conflict, the most central ones can. For the most part, the most consistent, if not always the most directly involved, players in the policy game are the political parties. My supposition is that we are likely to know more about policy agendas and choices by knowing the positions of the parties than by knowing any other datum. If this is so—and I think it is—then this vehicle for organizing political choice and policy framework is a superbly democratic instrument.

SOURCES

Aberbach, Joel D. 1987. The Congressional Committee Intelligence System: Information, Oversight, and Change. *Congress and the Presidency* 14:51–76.

Aberbach, Joel D., and Bert A. Rockman. 1976. Clashing Beliefs within the Executive Branch: The Nixon Administration Bureaucracy. *American Political Science Review* 77:974–90.

Aberbach, Joel D., and Bert A. Rockman. 1985. Governmental Responses to Budget Scarcity—the United States. *Policy Studies Journal* 13:494–505.

Aberbach, Joel D., and Bert A. Rockman, with Robert M. Copeland. 1990. From Nixon's *Problem* to Reagan's *Achievement*—The Federal Executive Reexamined. In *Looking Back on the Reagan Presidency*, ed. Larry Berman. Baltimore: Johns Hopkins University Press.

Aberbach, Joel D., Ellis S. Krauss, Michio Muramatsu, and Bert A. Rockman. 1990. Comparing Japanese and American Bureaucratic Elites. *British Journal of Political Science* 20:461–88.

Beck, Paul Allen. 1979. The Electoral Cycle and Patterns of American Politics. *British Journal of Political Science* 9:129–56.

Brady, David W. 1978. Critical Elections, Congressional Parties and Clusters of Policy Changes. *British Journal of Political Science* 8:79–99.

Burnham, Walter Dean. 1969. *Critical Elections and the Mainsprings of American Politics*. New York: Norton.

Burns, James McGregor. 1963. *The Deadlock of Democracy: Four Party Politics in America*. Englewood Cliffs: Prentice-Hall.

Cutler, Lloyd N. 1980. To Form a Government. *Foreign Affairs* 59:126–43.

Derthick, Martha, and Paul J. Quirk. 1985. *The Politics of Deregulation*. Washington, D.C.: Brookings.

Downs, Anthony. 1957. *An Economic Theory of Democracy*. New York: Harper and Row.

Esping-Andersen, Gøsta. 1985. *Politics Against Markets: The Social Democratic Road to Power*. Princeton: Princeton University Press.

Ferguson, Thomas. 1983. Party Realignment and American Industrial Structure: The Investment Theory of Political Parties in Historical Perspective. *Research in Political Economy* 6:1–82.

Fried, Robert C. 1976. Party and Policy in West German Cities. *American Political Science Review* 70:11–24.

Ginsberg, Benjamin. 1972. Critical Elections and the Substance of Party Conflict: 1844–1968. *American Journal of Political Science* 16:603–25.

———. 1976. Elections and Public Policy. *American Political Science Review* 70:41–49.

Golden, David G., and James M. Poterba. 1980. The Price of Popularity: The Political Business Cycle Reexamined. *American Journal of Political Science* 24:696–714.

Hale, Dennis. 1988. Just What Is a Policy Anyway? and Who's Supposed to Make It? A Survey of the Public Administration and Policy Texts. *Administration and Society* 19:423–52.

Headey, Bruce. 1979. *Housing Policy in the Developed Economy: The UK, Sweden, and the U.S.* New York: St. Martin's.

Heclo, Hugh. 1974. *Modern Social Policies in Britain and Sweden*. New Haven: Yale University Press.

Hogwood, Brian, and B. Guy Peters. 1983. *Policy Dynamics*. New York: St. Martin's.

Kingdon, John W. 1984. *Agendas, Alternatives, and Public Policies*. Boston: Little, Brown.

McCubbins, Matthew D., and Thomas Schwartz. 1984. Congressional Oversight Overlooked: Police Patrols versus Fire Alarms. *American Journal of Political Science* 28:165–79.

Miller, Gary, and Terry M. Moe. 1983. Bureaucrats, Legislators, and the Size of Government. *American Political Science Review* 77:297–322.

Miller, Warren E., and M. Kent Jennings. 1986. *Parties in Transition: A Longitudinal Study of Party Elites and Followers*. New York: Russell Sage.

Moe, Terry M. 1985. The Politicized Presidency. In John E. Chubb and Paul E. Peterson, eds., *The New Direction in American Politics*. Washington, D.C.: Brookings.

Nordhaus, William D. 1975. The Political Business Cycle. *Review of Economic Studies* 42:169–90.

Poole, Keith T., and Howard Rosenthal. 1984. The Polarization of American Politics. *Journal of Politics* 46:1061–79.

Putnam, Robert D. 1976. *The Comparative Study of Political Elites*. Englewood Cliffs: Prentice-Hall.

Rockman, Bert A. 1984. *The Leadership Question: The Presidency in the American System*. New York: Praeger.

Rose, Richard. 1974. *The Problem of Party Government*. New York: Free Press.

———. 1980. *Do Parties Make a Difference?* Chatham: Chatham House.

Silbey, Joel H. 1967. *The Shrine of Party: Congressional Voting Behavior, 1941–52*. Pittsburgh: University of Pittsburgh Press.

Skowronek, Stephen. 1988. Presidential Leadership in Political Time. In Michael Nelson, ed., *The Presidency and the Political System*, 2d ed. Washington, D.C.: Congressional Quarterly Press.

Stokes, Donald E., and Gudmund R. Iversen. 1962. On the Existence of Forces Restoring Party Competition. *Public Opinion Quarterly* 26:159–71.

Tufte, Edward R. 1978. *Political Control of the Economy*. Princeton: Princeton University Press.

Verba, Sidney, Steven Kelman, Gary R. Orren, Ichiro Miyake, Joji Watanuki, Ikuo Kabashima, and G. Donald Ferree, Jr. 1987. *Elites and the Idea of Equality: A Comparison of Japan, Sweden, and the United States*. Cambridge: Harvard University Press.

Weingast, Barry, and Mark Moran. 1983. Bureaucratic Discretion or Congressional Control: Regulatory Policymaking by the FTC. *Journal of Political Economy* 91:765–800.

Wilensky, Harold L. 1975. *The Welfare State and Equality: Structural and Ideological Roots of Public Expenditures*. Berkeley and Los Angeles: University of California Press.

———. 1976. *The "New Corporatism," Centralization, and the Welfare State*. London: Sage.

13

Public Policy and Public Bureaucracy

B. Guy Peters

TO UNDERSTAND the sources and meanings of public policy in contemporary democracies, we must first understand the organizations and the organizational networks within which those policies are developed. The major actors in most public policy choices are organizations. Organizations are, of course, composed of individuals, but policy making can be more easily understood by beginning at the organizational and institutional level rather than the individual level (Campbell and Peters 1988; see also Timsit 1987). This is true at the formulation stage of the policy process (Bryner 1987) but may be even more important as policies are implemented and then evaluated.

When analytic attention is focused on organizations, distinctions among various stages of the policy-making process (Jones 1984; Peters 1986; Hoppe, van de Graaf, and van Dijk 1987) are less clear. Those stages remain useful primarily for the analytical purpose of describing what steps must be taken in developing any policy. A good deal of the policy literature focuses on the connection between formulation and implementation. Organizations that implement programs almost inevitably consider new approaches to problems in their policy area, just as organizations charged with formulating policies must have some concept of the manner in which programs should be implemented (Hogwood and Peters 1983). As a result, activities of most policy-making organizations are too closely intertwined to be neatly separated into phases.

A conceptualization that links policy formulation and its actual practice is closely associated with the "garbage can" model of choice (Cohen, March, and Olsen 1972) but is also associated with other ideas about the developmental relation between policy ideas and policy action (Linder and Peters 1987, 1988; for a more extreme vision of the argument, see Wildavsky 1979; Dery 1984). Rather than being made at one time, policies evolve through a continual interaction between the intentions of formulators and the outcomes produced by implementation. This interaction occurs primarily within organizations; without an understanding the internal dynamics of the organizations, a good deal of understanding of policy making is lost.

Unfortunately, there is increasing separation between policy analysis and the study of public (and private) organizations. This separation can be seen in scholarly disciplines, scholarly organizations, and in much of the policy analysis literature. Organizations appear in this literature, if at all, as utility-maximizing clichés of themselves, rather than as complex institutional actors with numerous goals, both individual and collective. Few formal models of policy making accommodate the complexity that organizational realities introduce into decision making. Further, policy models rarely are capable of accommodating the diverse organizational interactions typically involved in a single policy choice (Hanf and Scharpf 1978; Franz 1985). Descriptive approaches to policy making (Heclo 1978; Jordan 1981) include a more complete constellation of organizational forces surrounding policy making. These policy networks exist between organizations in government and private sector organizations (Laumann and Knoke 1987), and they also exist within government itself. In the case of networks within government, organizations with complementary or competitive programs are decisive elements of the policy-making environment for any one organization (see Peters 1988).

On the other hand, much of the study of public organizations and public administration does not adequately conceptualize the policy-making role of organizations. In the case of most public administration literature, there is a continuing normative influence by scholars who argue for the separation of policy and administration. This includes both practitioners who may not want their policy ideas trampled upon by the bureaucracy and academic followers of major theoreticians whose analytical frameworks call for the separation of these two sets of actors. Many policy analysts seek to avoid organizations because of the complexities they introduce, while students of public organizations frequently prefer to avoid thinking about the policy roles of organizations. This is, in part, the function of their normative views, but it is also an unwillingness to dive into the complexities of policy making. The tendency to avoid the policy-making role of public organizations may be accentuated by the trend toward managerialism in the roles given civil servants by their political masters (Aucoin 1988). For whatever reasons, this analytic separation is not conductive to the development of a complete and nuanced understanding of public policy or the process by which it is created.

The condition of the literature linking organizations to policy is not, however, entirely bleak. For some years, scholars (for example, Appleby 1949) have linked the elements of the old dichotomy. They point out that the intellectual forebears who developed the separation arguments did not themselves make the separation as strongly as their disciples (Page 1985; Doig 1983). More recently, a return to an interest in the state as a focus of inquiry in political science requires a greater consideration of the role of the public bureaucracy in defining policy interests (Duvall and Freeman 1983; Poulantzas 1978). Likewise, the new institutionalism in political science (March and Olsen 1984) places institutions in a central position, with the public bureaucracy and the organizations it comprises being dominant examples. The movement of the discipline of political science away from the excesses of the behavioral revolution has helped to restore the bureaucracy to a central role in political inquiry and to force a consideration of its link to public policy. That change may require, however, models that explain the role of bureaucracy in policy making that meet the canons of social scientific respectability, while retaining sufficient contact with the reality and complexity of policy making. This is no easy task.

However, significant problems remain in linking policy and organizations. As Gray (1988) has emphasized in a review of two books about bureaucracy and policy, the linkage of the two is a "nagging question." It is nagging, not only because it has not been solved, but because it is so central to contemporary government. More than ever, governments are composed of organizations, and despite the attempts of political leaders to downplay the contributions of their civil servants, most policy making is done in the civil service. Further, as Gray points out, there is still a dearth of systematic analysis of the role of bureaucracies in making policy. There are a number of interesting descriptive analyses of the role of bureaucracies in individual countries (Suleiman 1984; Gray and Jenkins 1985; Mayntz and Scharpf 1975) but substantially less in the way of systematic analysis and theory development. Such an exploration must be comparative if it is to contribute to theoretical developments in this area.

Bureaucracy's Role in Policy Making

Once the basic problem is laid out, the difficult question is where to begin in expanding our understanding of the role played by the public bureaucracy in policy making in contemporary governments. Governments have been struggling with the empirical and normative question of the role of the bureaucracy in policy making for years. It still requires, however, the development or utilization of different approaches that permit systematic analysis of the role of bureaucracy. Where can those approaches come from?

The Old Masters

One obvious place to begin our quest for understanding is with the old masters of this field—Weber and, for Americans, Woodrow Wilson. Both explicated concepts of public bureaucracy but with a definite normative intent. For Weber that purpose was to point toward a pattern of development leading toward the rational-legal bureaucracy as a superior means of organizing the affairs of state and toward rationality and legalism as the source of authority in society. Weber's ideal-type methodology (Giddens 1971) used the "perfect" case as a standard against which to compare any real-world administrative and political systems. Weber did not expect the emergence of the perfectly rational-legal authority structure in society nor any bureaucratic organization that might embody all its many subconcepts (Udy 1958). Further, he did not himself posit the inevitability of bureaucratic dominance (*Beamtenherrschaft*) over policy, as have some of his commentators and presumed followers. His understanding of politics and society was too subtle and nuanced for such a unidirectional view (Portis 1986; Mommsen and Osterhammer 1987). Weber's ideas of bureaucracy did, however, admit the possibility of such dominance, and statements such as "everyday rule is primarily administration" (Weber 1972, 126) made such dominance appear probable. The model remains, however, a useful point of departure for analysis and, at least in the minds of some, represents a superior means of organizing the state.

In order to understand Weber's applicability for approaching the characteristics and role of the public bureaucracy in contemporary government, Page (1985) disaggregates the concept of bureaucracy and then examines the component parts in France, West Germany, Britain, and the United States. The fundamental finding is that bureaucracy is a crucial policy-making institution in all these governments, if not always in the ways envisaged by Weber. Page is concerned about the possibilities of a more pluralistic democracy functioning effectively in contemporary, bureaucratically dominated, political systems. All the trappings of bureaucratic power anticipated by Weber may not be in place, but the power does appear to be so.

For Americans, Woodrow Wilson is a more accessible figure than Weber as a formulator of ideas about the relation of politics and administration. Writing in the tradition of the American reform movement that sought to minimize political tampering with policies, Wilson argued for the separation of politics and administration. He was not, however, attempting to apply good democratic principles but rather arguing the need to allow professional administrators more latitude for independent action (Doig 1983). Unlike subsequent politicians who have commented on the obstructive or destructive actions of their civil servants, Wilson wanted to remove amateurs from central roles in order to allow the professional civil service sufficient latitude to make government work effectively. In Wilson's concept of good government, the public interest was not to be found through elections and partisan political institutions, but rather it would emerge through efficient management and the public bureaucracy. While Page wonders if bureaucratic government would allow sufficient public involvement, Wilson regarded the public as better served if they, their representatives, and especially their interest groups could be separated from most actual policy making.

Many scholars and politicians following Weber and Wilson have been less sanguine about the capabilities of the public bureaucracy or have been more concerned with other aspects of political democracy. Thus, many of those who discuss the separation of politics and administration tend to do so from the perspective of preventing bureaucratic dominance. Even these early writings, however, seem to be fighting a rearguard action to stop the almost inevitable bureaucratization of the policy-making process. Rarely do these authors disparage the capabilities of the bureaucracy (unlike more recent politicians), but instead they argue on a normative basis for the proper role of democratically elected political officials (Hyneman 1950).

The Administrative State

Without attempting a complete history of public administration, the next major group of theorists that must be mentioned in connection with bureaucratic power over policy comprises those who have developed the concept of an administrative state and have expressed concern about the role of democracy within such a state, be it Western and industrialized or not (Mosher 1968; Redford 1969; Waldo 1948; Marx 1957; Wilson and Dwivedi 1982; Dwivedi and Jain 1985). These scholars rarely deal with specific policy issues or, indeed, with any systematic analysis of the policy process. They do, however, document very fundamental changes in the conduct of public affairs in their governments.

These authors share a common concern with the increasing capacity of the public bureaucracy to shape policy. Indeed, the term *administra-*

tive state implies that the bureaucracy has become capable of dominating and shaping the bulk of activity that occurs in contemporary government and, in doing so, shapes the nature of the state itself. As with the old masters, the concerns of the scholars of the administrative state are at once empirical and normative. They document the manner in which the role of the bureaucracy has been expanded, including a number of very subtle means. Further, they discuss the implications of the changing role of the public bureaucracy for government and the public. Similar to Wilson's analysis, they are not entirely negative about the growing power and influence of the bureaucracy. This should perhaps be expected, given that they come largely from public administration, but it is still interesting, given the outcry of politicans, journalists, and some members of the public about these changing constellations of power.

The most interesting of the many contemporary discussions of the administrative state is Yates's book *Bureaucratic Democracy* (1982). Yates argues that American democracy represents a compromise between two ideals: pluralist democracy and administrative efficiency. Historically, these two elements have been traded off in a number of ways to produce the complex and somewhat incoherent system of American government. In the era since the New Deal, the president and the executive bureaucracy have become the dominant value. The search for efficiency, through the Brownlow Commission, the Hoover Commission, and even the Grace Commission, and through mechanisms such as PPBS (planning, programming budgeting system), MBO (management by objectives), and ZBB (zero-based budgets), among others, has been a major and recurring activity of government. Thus the principal task facing the U.S. government is ensuring the accountability of the bureaucracy to democratic control (Gruber 1987; Mashaw 1983) while at the same time preserving its capacity to make appropriate decisions. Yates identifies some problems of accountability, but those problems remain largely unsolved.

Implementation Research

After Pressman and Wildavsky (1974) "discovered" implementation, that concept has had a substantial impact on thinking about the role of public administration and its impact on public policy. At least one school of implementation scholars, largely European (Hjern and Hull 1982; Hanf and Hull 1982; Hanf and Toonen 1985; but also see Elmore 1980), argues that policy making is best understood from the bottom up, that is, from an understanding of the implementation that occurs at the very lowest levels of organizations. They argue that if the policy selected is not compatible with values and desires of the lowest levels of the organization, or perhaps even with those of clients, then the policy is doomed to failure from the outset. In such a view, implementation (and hence the perspectives of the public bureaucracy) offers the best guide to policy formulation.

A number of normative, and even empirical, reservations about the bottom-up perspective on policy making and implementation have been expressed (Linder and Peters 1987; Sabatier 1986; O'Toole 1986). However, implementation research has pointed out several important ways in which the public bureaucracy influences policy, even through the daily exercise of routine administrative functions. First, this literature emphasizes that policy is what actually happens, rather than a nominal program written on a piece of paper. Implementation and the actions of even the lowest echelons of public organizations define the substance of policy. A number of studies demonstrate the power of seemingly menial positions in public agencies (Almond and Lasswell 1934; Lipsky 1980; Prottas 1979; Goodsell 1976), but the implementation perspective highlights bureaucratic power and points to patterns of systematic application of organizational power in government. Further, the implementation approach emphasizes the importance of a suitable administrative structure for carrying out a stated policy. This aim is not that the administration's needs and motives should determine policy choice (as more extreme versions of implementation studies argue) but rather that the two components of policy should be closely linked (Hoppe, van de Graaf, and van Dijk 1987).

The problem with implementation studies is that, after having asserted that implementation is important, there is little to add (Sabatier 1986; O'Toole 1986; Linder and Peters 1987). Implementation research points to enduring truths about the power of the lower echelons of public organizations but appears to make little other intellectual contribution. Interestingly, the one approach to implementation labeled the "horrors of war" elsewhere (Linder and Peters 1987), which has the fewest intellectual pretentions of any approach, ultimately may be the most useful for a systematic analysis of the influence of the public bureaucracy over policy. This approach catalogs the numerous impediments that governments (comprising both elected and career officials) face (Hood 1976; Pierce 1981) when attempting to put their programs into effect. It therefore relates to studies of party government that document the numerous impediments that elected political leaders face when putting their programs into effect (Rose 1974; Katz 1987; Castles and Wildenmann 1986). In both instances, the majority of the impediments arise within the bureaucracy itself.

Although certainly not identified as implementation research per se, several European (largely French) organizational sociologists have sought to understand the distribution of power within organizations and networks of organizations. Crozier (1964, 1979; Crozier and Friedberg 1980) is prominent among these, but others such as Dupuy, Worms, Grémion, and Thoenig are also significant. Like at least some of the implementation scholars, these find bureaucratic power (in terms of the capacity to resist formalized authority) residing in many echelons of organizations, rather than being concentrated at the top. This leads them to view the dynamics of organizations in a manner more similar to that of the bottom-up view of implementation.

Crozier and his followers provide an interesting counterpoint to other students of public administration in France, where the power rests at the apex of organizational pyramids—the *grands corps* (Suleiman 1974, 1978, 1984; Kessler 1978). The Crozier school further stands in contrast to those who argue that bureaucratic power is centralized; in the Crozier system, the "periphery is central." While those at the top of organizations exercise great and visible power, including power in society, Crozier and others point to the extent to which that power is limited by characteristics of French society and the unwillingness of many in the organizations to accept political authority (Crozier 1964, 214–17). Thus, we see much of the same contrast we have seen between the top-down and the bottom-up schools of implementation studies. The contrast is between those who perceive power as being exercised through formal structures, with an expectation that orders will be followed, and those who perceive even organization members at the bottom of the pyramids as having substantial power, if only to avoid the control of those at the top. In such an organizational and cultural system, public administration is truly "shattered" (Dupuy and Thoenig 1985).

What distinguishes Crozier and his school of administrative studies from bottom-up implementation scholars is the normative element. Crozier appears to have a top-down normative concept about organizational decision making, yet he understands that the actual functioning of organizations may be different. The organizational question that arises in this approach is how to design organizations that can function effectively in a world with contrasting or even contradictory demands of centralization and decentralization, authority and discretion. One answer is that they cannot be designed, if logical consistency is a criterion. Another answer might be that the world of implementation is tension ridden everywhere and not just in France. Organizations often confront a number of competing and conflicting demands, and they must develop their own means of resolving the contradictions that arise.

Public Choice

Another theoretical approach linking public organizations to public policy has been advocated by scholars enamored of economic models of political and organizational life. These scholars are most commonly characterized by the work of Niskanen (1971) and the numerous followers of his basic approach (Borcherding 1977; Orzechowski 1977). Many of the empirical and theoretical problems associated with this approach have been analyzed elsewhere (Peters 1988; Hood, Huby, and Dunsire 1984; Cullis and Jones 1984; Sigelman 1986; Bendor 1989). Public choice remains, however, one approach for a systematic understanding of the role of the public bureaucracy in policy making.

The public choice approach argues that the role of bureaucracy is dominant, especially in determining the growth of public expenditure. Further, it argues that bureaucratic agencies should be capable of deceiving or outmaneuvering their political sponsors and of commanding substantially more resources than they actually need to complete their missions. In this approach, policy is not itself the end of the decision-making process, but rather it is a means to the end of bureaucratic expansion and self-perpetuation. Expansion may serve the interests of the organization (Downs 1967), or the interests of the managers (Niskanen 1971), but growth will be the objective. In this approach, policies are means of justifying budgets, and policies will be selected to maximize those budgets. For example, it is assumed that, left to themselves, the bureaucracy will always propose labor-intensive programs as a means of maximizing both its employment and its budget (Orzechowski 1977; Dunleavy 1985).

As with the implementation studies, however, once that assertion has been made, where can we go next—if anywhere? What comparative predictions are there to be made using this approach that could not be made from other approaches? The predictions might be that, in situations in which the sponsor is capable of more independent judgment, the capacity of organizations to expand at will is diminished. However, the model was developed for the United States with an autonomous and well-staffed legislature (Ripley and Franklin 1987). If the model works in the United States, despite the objections, one could only assume that it would work elsewhere (Hood, Huby, and Dunsire 1984). The models of bureaucratic power that have been developed in this tradition do not appear sufficiently nuanced to permit meaningful comparative analysis.

Empirical Approaches

In addition to analytical exercises in theory construction about public bureaucracy and the formulation of public policies described above, there are important empirical studies of administrative elites. This work is best typified by Aberbach, Putnam, and Rockman (1981) and their appraisal of the perceived roles of bureaucrats and politicians in making policy. Heclo's (1977) study of the "government of strangers" in Washington is based on rather similar means of approaching the role of career civil servants in the policy process (see also Olsen 1983; Anton 1980; Eldersveld, Kooiman, and van der Tak 1981; Krauss and Muramatsu 1984). Although based less directly upon empirical research, Nakamura and Smallwood (1980) and Peters (1987) are concerned with many of the same issues of the relationship of career civil servants and politicans. All this corpus of writing has identified two crucial sets of actors in the policy-making process and has sought to understand how they interact. They all ask the implicit, if not explicit, question of who really has the power as policies are made.

These empirical studies have made a very significant contribution to the analysis of the policy-making process in industrial democracies, but they share some inherent weaknesses as well. They have not demonstrated directly how career and political officals function together in making policy—they only show what each thinks its (and the other group's) appropriate roles are. The degree of conformity of these roles (see Searing 1988) is important for the functioning of democracy, but we are left with little information on what actually happens. The work describes, in very interesting and important ways, individuals and their beliefs, but it does not describe systems of interaction and policy making nearly as well. We may assume that the individuals in question will behave in manners consistent with their attitudes, but decision making in complex situations may involve such complex and crosscutting motivations that any simple attitudinal system may not be a good predictor.

In dealing with decision making within a complex organizational context, with multiple actors and multiple motives, we may have some idea of how upper echelons of organizations perceive their roles but have much less information about the lower, implementing echelons. No one study, especially one employing the rather extensive interviews involved in the elites' approach, can hope to do everything. This comment is intended to point to work that remains to be done rather than to any significant deficiencies in what has already been done. Acquiring the methodology and the access to get at interaction directly is difficult but crucial for understanding how power is exercised.

Bureaucratic Government Revisited

While the above discussion may appear highly critical of several approaches to the study of bureaucracy and policy making, the purpose is more constructive. The intention is not only to point out what the existing literature does but also to point to unanswered questions concerning the relation between public bureaucracy and public policy. Again, there is ample descriptive material, but there does appear to be a dearth of systematic analytical and theoretical work to organize the findings. In particular, we do not have a framework with which to assess our understanding of the contributions of bureaucracy to policy.

Some of my own earlier work attempted to push this inquiry ahead. Since "The Problem of Bureaucratic Government" was written in 1981, the manner in which government is conducted in many industrialized democracies has changed substantially. This is most obviously true on the surface, when dramatic announcements about policy change are made (although the reality is rarely as dramatic as the announcements). It is, however, also true of the manner in which government is managed and of the role of the permanent civil service in government (Aucoin 1990). Changes in the bureaucracy are likely to be much more enduring than the more mutable changes in budgets or programs. Indeed, it might be argued that, in the 1980s, some leaders have made changes in the machinery of government in their countries that will be difficult to erase over several decades. Given that these changes are intimately connected to political power and the ability of an elected government to influence policy more effectively, they may not be undone in the visible future.

Both the programmatic and more enduring administrative changes in government have been brought about by the representatives of a new wave of ideology in democratic governments. While most of these new ideologues are from the political Right—Reagan and Thatcher as the prime but not only examples—some are from the political Left. Both extremes have, however, sought closer control over government and to break the consensus over the "mixed economy welfare state" that has characterized public policy in industrialized democracies since the end of World War II. Further, justifications for departures from the status quo were phrased more in ideological than in pragmatic terms: policies were justified by their simply being right. Perhaps even more than previous governments, these leaders viewed the public bureaucracy as resistant to change and the imposition of a new policy agenda. Hence, the public bureaucracy was a force that had to be conquered or contained if the new agenda was to be implemented.

The Basic Model

The basic model used for understanding the possibilities of bureaucratic government is derived from Rose's (1974) analysis of the possibilities of party government. Rose is concerned with the ability of elected politicians (in Britain) to influence policy once in office. This in turn implies that voters have some influence over the policies that they actually "consume" after an election. If democracy works, then the policies adopted by a government must bear some resemblance to those the voters thought they were "buying" in an election. Rose's analysis is not very sanguine about the capacity of elective governments to produce the changes they argue for in their platform. This was, however, written before Margaret Thatcher came to office and proved capable of adopting and implementing most of the policies she said she would, to the amazement of most and the dismay of many. Even she, however, was incapable of implementing all the fundamental changes she and some of her advisors apparently would have liked (Rogaly 1988).[1]

It is especially interesting that Rose finds the public bureaucracy to be a major impediment to elected officials seeking to supply a particular brand of governance to its public. In Britain, to a greater degree than in other countries, a small number of elected officials confronts a large, well-educated, experienced, and well-entrenched civil service. Ministers have found it difficult to alter the path on which those permanent officials have set policies. This leads to the question of whether the country is governed by the bureaucracy rather than the elected officials—a question that is reinforced by both serious and humorous commentaries on the civil service (Lynn and Jay 1984, 1987; Hennessy 1989). The same sort of questions arise concerning the powerful role of the public bureaucracy in policy making in many other democratic political systems. Thus, there is an important question about assessing bureaucratic government in Britain or in any other political system. That assessment includes both the reality of the claims of bureaucratic dominance over policy and some idea about what the policies adopted by a bureaucratic regime would look like.

Many of the same questions that might be asked concerning the capacity of a political party to supply governance might be asked of the public bureaucracy. Few declarations of constitutional change are likely to emerge from the depths of office buildings on Whitehall, Independence Avenue, or Karlavagen. Rather, the question is the capacity of the bureaucracy to impose its own values and ideas on policy in the face of contrary pressures from elected officials and, to some degree, from the public. The absence of an electoral basis is both a strength and a weakness for the bureaucracy in their endeavors. It reduces their legitimacy in a democratic government but gives them stability and immunity to some pressures. Bureaucratic dominance over policy would not come through one decision but rather through the gradual accretion of power and policy-making authority.

A bureaucracy is not by any means a unified or coherent institution. In most industrialized countries, it is an aggregation of the many organizations contained within the public sector. These organizations and their members rarely act in concert about any policy issues, with the possible exception of issues that affect their own pay and perquisites. The ideas and values that bureaucratic organizations advocate tend to be specific to their own policy areas rather than sweeping ideologies about policy in general. The fundamental feature of any bureaucratic government would probably be the absence of coordination among policies—government by "non-consensual directions" (Peters 1981, 82). Further, the confrontation of those many and disparate policy ideas contained within bureaucratic organizations with more ideologically conservative governments in the 1980s has served as the leitmotif for both policy and institutional change in many governments. In many industrialized societies, the old conflict of "red versus expert" has been transformed into "blue versus expert," but the same institutional dynamics of conflict over decisional authority remain. There is still the conflict between those who want to impose a more ideological conception of good policy on government versus those who desire to deal with policies on a narrower technical basis.

Bureaucratic government does not imply constitutional change or declaration of victory. Rather, it implies that the principal moving force in government and policy is not parliaments and political executives but the career civil service. The business of elected governments continues, although parliaments are reduced to "the process of mere registration" of the decisions that have been made elsewhere (Grosser, quoted in Dogan 1975). The technical content of policy and the sheer volume of decision making that modern governments face limit the capacity of these governments to govern effectively. The time and energy required for mass politics, as well as the increasing trivialization of politics by the mass media, may further inhibit the capacity of parliaments and prime ministers to govern. Bureaucratic dominance over policy may emerge simply because of the incapacity of other institutions to control and govern. If we can assume that, for the moment, this occurs, then the question becomes: What would such a government do, and what would be the implications?

The model of bureaucratic government that I posit (again derived from Rose) contains six fundamental elements. To supply that commodity called governance to its society, a bureaucracy

(1) must formulate policy intentions for enactment in office;

(2) must support those intentions by statements of "not unworkable" means to the ends;

(3) must have some competition over the allocation of resources;

(4) must be in sufficient numbers in the most important positions in the regime;

(5) must have the skills necessary for running large, bureaucratic organizations; and

(6) must give high priority to the implementation of the policies designed to reach the stated goals.

Policy Intentions

The first thing that any actors must do if they are to govern is to know what they want to do; the statement of goals is a crucial, but often an overlooked, component of the policy process. Goals do not come out of the ether but are derived from the ideas and experience of the key actors who must posit them. In this case, we are concerned with the manner in which goals arise within the public bureaucracy. As implied above, goal statements likely to emanate from the bureaucracy will be narrow and partial and will tend to be confined to a single policy domain. This is in contrast to the political exposition of goals in terms of encompassing ideologies that speak to a number of different domains and concerns.

Bureaucratic policy intentions may be of two sorts: soft and hard. Soft intentions are the tendencies of organizations to attempt to continue doing what they have been doing and to defend the status quo against possible attacks. This defense need not be entirely sloth or self-interest, but it may be based on a sincere belief that the status quo represents the best way of addressing the narrow policy problem. On the other hand, hard agency ideologies are those that contain the agency's ideas about change and seek to significantly alter the nature of policy in their area of government. These ideologies, although concerned with change, are rather narrowly defined and are concerned with specific policy issues.

As in the garbage can model of organizational choice (Cohen, March, and Olsen 1972), goals are defined by practice, rather than policy making being determined by goals. In such a setting, what is, is good, not only because of the human need to justify one's own choices and one's work with more than practicality but also because of political pressure from clients. Clientele pressure may be transmitted through legislative and other political actors with a stake in the continuation of existing programs. The problem that this soft version of agency ideology encountered in the 1980s was the reassertion of broader ideologies by political leaders and an increasing willingness of politicians to engage in conflict with existing organizations over goals. While a spirited defense of the status quo may once have been sufficient to ensure an agency's survival and prosperity, a more ideological age creates a need for stronger assertions of the utility of programs and the logic and values justifying them. The continuing struggles of the National Health Service in Britain, for example, represent a conflict of an ideology about the best (most humane) way to deliver medical care against an ideology of market provision of services for which that is possible.

Some changes in both institutional politics and the policy environment have made the assertion of soft agency ideologies less successful for agencies. First, there has been a growing tendency of political leaders to employ their own loyalists to run public organizations rather than rely on careerists or, at a minimum, to use a litmus test on careerists for their political and ideological reliability, if they are to be given significant responsibility. The politicization of the civil service appears to have become virtually a worldwide phenomenon (Meyers 1985), even in societies that pride themselves on an impartial and virtually apolitical civil service (Ridley 1985). There may be many impediments to the outsiders being effective in these organizational settings, but it is difficult for the organization to continue to put forward status quo arguments and policies when the leadership of the organization has announced an intention to change programs. In France, for example, the new Socialist elite that came to power with Mitterrand sought to change policies in fundamental ways and sought more direct involvement in those changes (Stevens 1985).

A second point is that the policy communities that surround most public programs and organizations are now sufficiently broad to include advocates for almost any policy position. Further, those advocates will have suitable professional and academic credentials to manage or advise a policy-making organization. Heclo (1978) first pointed to the rise of issue networks and the rusting of the old iron triangles. In place of insulated and tightly linked arrangements, a variety of loosely coupled policy communities containing a number of experts, often with diverse views concerning the policy sector, have arisen. Especially important in the United States has been the rise of right-wing think tanks such as the Heritage Foundation and the Cato Institute, which provide a very different kind of advice than is provided even by moderate Republican sources such as the American Enterprise Institute. There have been some parallel developments, at least in Britain (for example, the Adam Smith Institute). Groups with status quo orientations no longer dominate these communities, and the communities are more open to new concepts and ideas. Policy communities may be built by policy entrepreneurs, who have particular visions of the future of policy to sell to the public and politicians (Marmor with Fellman 1986; Lewis 1984). This then allows politicians to pick and choose expert advisors and advocates to an extent not possible previously and to break the monopoly of the agency over advice and policy ideas. In this setting, there need be no real contest between ideological commitment and expertise; the question becomes merely which experts to select.

Another manner in which the iron triangles have been rusting has been the development of a multiplicity of interest groups with divergent ideas about specific policies. This is in contrast to the domination of a policy area by a single-interest group—usually one associated with the agency and its soft agency ideology. This development is associated with that of alternative sources of expertise, but these interest groups do not go away even if their members are not appointed to leadership positions in an agency. The array of groups surrounding a policy may include policy-specific groups as well as general public interest groups that speak to a variety of topics (McFarland 1983). Further, while some of the most obvious examples of public interest groups are American, this is a general phenomenon. In most industrial countries, the bureaucracy has a more difficult time doing what it has always done without challenge (OECD 1983). Interest groups not associated with the agency may advocate alternatives to the status quo and be willing to circumvent existing agency relations in order to have their views enter the policy process. They therefore are a major challenge to agencies and to the continuation of their existing policies.

Policy networks surrounding agencies include other parts of the bureaucracy as well as interest groups. One of the dangers in a government dominated by bureaucratic agencies is that the proliferation of programs and organizations will produce incoherence and overlapping.

One means of attempting to counteract this tendency is the development of advisory committees and procedures that include representatives of other agencies. For example, advisory committees for ministries in the Scandinavian countries include representatives of other ministries (Johansen and Kristensen 1982; Olsen 1983). Likewise, the elaborate layers of coordinating structures in French government (Fournier 1987) check the tendency of bureaucratic agencies to pursue their own vision of the public interest.

Finally, the slowdown of economic growth in most countries of the industrialized world affects the ability of organizations in government either to advocate new programs or to continue to promote their old programs as before. In several countries, this slowdown interacts with changes in the ideology of the political leadership to produce resistance to new programs and to foster attacks on many existing programs. In these settings, its mere existence is no longer a sufficient justification for the continuation of a program. Some agencies attempt preemptive actions by deciding what they can afford to cut and then cutting it before worse cuts are imposed. Other agencies ask for more money, thinking that being refused counts as accepting cuts. Whatever strategies agencies adopt, the status quo is rarely an alternative.

Not Unworkable Means to the Ends

The point in the policy-making process where the bureaucracy is most capable of influencing and controlling oucomes is in determining whether policy will achieve the ends. Even if outsiders are able to contest the substantive expertise of the bureaucracy, they are unlikely to be able to contest their mastery of the procedures of government. Procedure, however, may not be as clear a handmaiden of the bureaucracy as it once was. First, many procedures are linked to specific policy goals, and if those goals are declared invalid, then so too are the procedures and the power they imply. For example, in a government intent on the privatization and deregulation of a good deal of existing public activity, the procedures that enable the public services to function become unnecessary. Worse yet, those procedures become symbolic of the (putative) inefficiency and intrusiveness of the public sector. As governments become interested in privatization and deregulation (Ascher 1983; Savas 1987), then procedures may become a millstone around the neck of the bureaucracy and reduce rather than enhance their influence in government.

The recurrent theme of efficiency in government is associated with the new emphasis on privatized mechanisms for service delivery and on making government operate more like the private sector (Allison

1986). Schemes for improving the quality of management in government threaten the position and influence of the public bureaucracy. The primary threat is that public agencies will no longer be able to use procedures to preserve and enhance their own policy choices. Rather, they may have to de-emphasize their concerns for deliberation and appropriate consideration in favor of more streamlined procedures. Whether those procedures actually produce better policy (however that may be defined) is problematic, but what does appear certain is that it will be more difficult for the civil service to hide behind procedures to get the policies they want.

In addition to devaluing some existing procedural corridors for action, a number of new procedural remedies have been introduced to convert the senior civil service from policy makers and policy advisors into mere managers. The most obvious examples are the United Kingdom's Financial Management Initiative and its sequel, Next Steps. These programs of the Thatcher government would have had senior civil servants responsible for cost centers in government, with their principal task being to manage budgets rather than to prepare policy advice for ministers (Richards 1987). Thus an alteration of procedure would have a significant impact on the authority of the bureaucracy.

In a more fundamental sense, the procedural powers of bureaucracies over individuals have been opened to greater political and public scrutiny, again depriving the bureaucracy of powerful instruments of control. This is especially important if we look at policy making from the implementation, or street-level, perspective and use what actually happens to individual cases as the measure of government policy. With the implementation of greater procedural safeguards and, consequently, with less latitude for action, the relative powers of the bureaucracy have been diminished substantially. Likewise, increasing statutory requirements for public participation in policy decisions expose the decision premises of bureaucracies to public scrutiny (DeSario and Langton 1987).

Finally, procedures with which public bureaucracies are comfortable are relatively clearly defined and permit limited discretion. Workers in public organizations, like workers in almost any organization, want to exercise their judgment and make decisions. On the other hand, inadequate guidance in decisions threatens many people, especially when making decisions about matters that deeply affect clients. The difficulty for an increasing number of bureaucratic agencies is that their policy problems are no longer so readily defined and conceptualized. As a consequence, legalistic procedures become inadequate or counterproductive (Lerner and Wanat 1983). Many problems confronting governments—drugs, poverty, global environmental degradation—do not have easy procedural solutions. Procedure may be, rather than a source of power, a source of error and misinterpretation, and it may expose bureaucracies to abuse rather than generate support.

Competition Over Resources

Competition in party government is competition to gain and retain office. Competitors in bureaucratic government already are in office and are unlikely to lose it. Their competition is for the resources to carry out programs and perhaps also to increase budgets and personnel. While the simple-minded ideas of bureaucratic expansion for personal gain implied in the public choice literature on bureaucracy is doubtful (Niskanen 1971), still there is an important element of bureaucratic resource competition. That competition may be over resources, or it may be over legislative authority to become involved in a particular policy area, perhaps at the expense of another organization. Competition may be motivated by personal gain or by a sincere desire to serve clients. In any case, there is a competitive dynamic in public bureaucracy, and competition affects the characteristics of public policy.

Competition among government agencies can produce substantial negative consequences. One of these is central to public choice arguments about bureaucracy: competition will produce unplanned and uncontrolled growth in public expenditure and public employment (Borcherding 1977).[2] The other substantial evil that can result is incoherence among government programs. Such incoherence may be a dominant feature of governments with a strong bureaucratic element in their decision making. Given that there are few decision rules by which to eliminate organizations in government (as there are for politicians through partisan elections), organizations tend to persist, even in the face of substantial competition (Kaufman 1976; Casstevens 1980; but also see Nystrom and Starbuck 1981; Peters and Hogwood 1988). If so, then some public organizations that are in direct competition with one another may well survive and even flourish. Although the organizations are, in principle, competitive, they may insulate themselves through responsibility to different budget committees or different ministries and therefore be able to survive. The overall collection of organizations that survives competition, and the policies they represent, may appear inconsistent to the outside observer.

Incoherence in the public sector is not in itself evil. It may merely signal the responsiveness of government to the multiple and competing demands in its environment. In a large and complex democracy, voters rarely have monolithic interests, and the existence of multiple organizations with competitive and even inconsistent programs may represent a triumph of democracy rather than a failure. Further, some commentators on bureaucratic systems with competition regard that competition as a positive feature, permitting the airing of different views and the consequent development of a more desirable policy mix (Pempel 1982, 1984; Johnson 1982). A permissive view of competition is not, however, shared by many contemporary conservative politicians, who consider much of what transpires in the complex public sectors to be wasteful and undesirable. Nor is it considered positive by some political theorists, who desire greater guidance and control over policy.

Bureaucratic competition emphasizes the conflict between central political control (and associated political ideologies) and bureaucratic discretion, which characterizes much of contemporary bureaucratic politics. Even the structured competition in Japan (Pampel 1984) appears to allow substantial latitude to agencies to pursue their own goals, albeit within the context of central budgetary guidelines and perhaps some general policy direction. When more ideological politicians have taken power, they have attempted to reduce the latitude of organizations to pursue their own goals. Further, when those politicians have been of the political Right, they often have attempted to eliminate any apparent redundancies. The result has been a less favorable climate for bureaucratic competition. Further, if we return to the democratic justification of incoherence and redundancy in public policy, it would appear that the new ideologues of the Right and the Left have been willing to make the tough redistributive decisions (if sometimes from the poor to the rich) that previously were eschewed in favor of serving all major groups.

Although centralization and suppression of competition were the responses of the political leaders of the 1980s, a contrary position was to decentralize government rather dramatically and to allow competition for programs that had been government monopolies. By forcing programs to be private or quasi-private, governments acted on an assumption that competition produces better services at lower prices. The resultant competition cannot really be called bureaucratic, but it certainly does place programs that had been, or could be, in government agencies in a situation of competing for funds, clients, and even personnel.

Political actors entering government in the 1980s introduced procedural mechanisms to reduce some of the growth effects of bureaucratic competition over budgets. Although the mechanisms vary (Tarschys 1985), they share a common commitment to exercising control over budgeting, limiting total spending, and at times forcing a reexamination of decisions already taken through conventional procedures. These procedures, in turn, severely constrain the capacity of bureaucratic agencies to use the budgetary process as a locus of competition. In the 1980s, agencies had difficulty maintaining their real expenditures, much less being able to expand their activities.

Thus the concept of bureaucratic competition may be anathema for politicians attempting to gain greater control of the public sector; bureaucratic competition can result in higher expenditures and waste. Allowing competition to determine allocations may reduce the control that politicians seek, whether that control is for ideological purposes or simply to reduce expenditures. On the other hand, once institutions are in place, it is difficult to restrain the competition. It is more difficult to unmake clients than not to make them in the first place. Likewise, it is more difficult to dismiss employees than not to hire them. Although the ability of public organizations to preserve themselves is often overstated (Peters and Hogwood 1988), the persistence of organizations is nonetheless an important constraint on the ability of political leaders to impose their own priorities and to control the public sector. For many politicians, the easiest thing to do has been to allow organizations to continue but to exist in a more competitive, quasi-privatized environment that places managerial pressures on them that could not have been imposed readily in government.

The Incumbency of Positions

The fourth criterion for effective government is that there must be sufficient personnel, with the appropriate skills, to make policies and to make them effective. In the model of party government, this is problematic. Even in the United States, which moves more people in and out of government than most (Heclo 1988), changing governments only involves several thousand people. Those several thousand are expected to control several million career employees. It would follow then that, in a model of bureaucratic government, the number of persons involved in governance is no problem. That, however, is not entirely the case. Numbers are not sufficient to govern, and those who would exercise policy control must have the requisite skills for policy management if what is desired to happen is to happen.

Pressures for reforming government in the 1980s tended to alter the balance of power between political and administrative officials. First, there was a declining number of permanent civil servants with important policy posts, as governments recruited loyalists to fill what they considered crucial positions. The generalist career manager may have had his or her skills devalued as partisans were recruited and placed into positions that careerists occupied previously. For example, in France, during the first years of the Mitterrand presidency, the *grands corps* were virtually excluded from ministerial positions and ministerial cabinets—positions they had come to frequent, if not dominate, during Gaullist governments (Stevens 1985; Cohen 1981; Wright 1974). Likewise, the Thatcher government employed greater numbers of externally recruited policy advisors in place of civil servants, and German governments recruited outsiders (including *Land* civil servants) into senior government posts (Derlien 1988; Katzenstein 1987). In general, control and centralization tendencies associated with the return to ideological argument and management in government are associated with a declining positional advantage of civil servants in policy making in most governments.

Associated with the tendency of political leaders to employ external recruits in decision-making positions in government has been the development of institutions and procedures limiting the capacity of civil service careerists to exercise any substantial control over policy decisions. One means for counteracting the centrifugal tendencies associated with bureaucratic control over policy is to place these bureaucracies under strong central agencies (Campbell and Szablowski 1979), which ensure that policies in line with the wishes of the central political authorities are carried out. Central control may be financial, as with the Treasury in Britain and the Office of Management and Budget in the United States. Central control may affect personnel and personnel policy, sometimes to the point of controlling the expansion of public employment (Muramatsu 1988). Further, politicians may attempt to strengthen central clearance of legislation to prevent agencies from pushing their own agendas legislatively—something obviously more important when there is an independent legislature and strong legislative committees, as in the United States. Finally, some central agencies can be dismantled if it is felt that they are too sensitive to outside demands. For example, Prime Minister Thatcher terminated the Civil Service Department and later placed its functions in the Management and Personnel Office within the Cabinet Office. Even if there were no ostensible reduction in the decision roles and powers of the civil service, organizational changes such as these could produce a substantial reduction of the real power of the civil service.

Finally, the changing nature of expertise and its distribution has affected the capacity of administrative agencies to dominate policy. One characteristic of bureaucracies that has been important to their role in policy making has been their control over information. For many policy areas, government and especially its bureaucracy have had a virtual monopoly of information and were virtually monopsonistic purchasers of some types of expertise (e.g., meteorology and nuclear fuels). The knowledge market has now become much more pluralistic, both inside and outside government, with the result that the expertise of agencies, as well as their policy judgments, are likely to be challenged. Further, procedures allowing or demanding greater openness—public inquiries, open hearings, *remisser,* environmental impact statements—in decision making have subjected what might have been internal decisions of agencies to greater public scrutiny and even rejection (DeSario and Langton 1987). Counterbureaucracies were developed within government, and even legislatures with little history of independent research and judgment have counterattacked against the bureaucratic control of policies (Ashford 1981, 44–47). In short, even policy making about highly complex and technical subjects has lost its exclusivity and has become open to a range of actors.

The Possession of Managerial Skills

The fifth requisite for any group attempting to exert influence over policy is to be able to manage the organizations responsible for policy and to be able to put policy into action. Politicians have been found to be exceptionally lacking in this capacity in a number of settings, at least when compared to their civil service counterparts. However, when compared to some absolute scale of managerial ability rather than just to politicians, the career civil service at times also has been found wanting. In fact, one standard complaint about the civil service (usually with some implicit or explicit comparison to management in the private sector) is that they are inefficient and bound up in many of the commonly cited managerial dysfunctions of government. These dysfunctions have been encapsulated, at least in Washington, by the phrase "fraud, waste, and abuse."

One solution offered by many of the new ideologues for the problems they have perceived in the public sector has been to place a greater emphasis on the managerial role of the civil service. This was both to reduce fraud, waste, and abuse and to reduce the policy advisory role of the civil service. While easy to implement at one level, these managerial initiatives have been far from successful in eliminating the policy-making powers of the civil service. First, management has always been a central role for the civil service, despite its policy-making influence, and if used properly, management can be anything but policy neutral. Management can, in fact, determine the content of policy. Further, decoupling management from policy advice may give the civil service more independence in day-to-day management issues than they might have had when they were more closely linked with the policy-making machinery.

Second, few civil service employees actually favor fraud, waste, and abuse, and many believe these problems result from the actions of their political masters. Thus, orders to attack the evil triumvirate may provide the civil service with the desired latitude to weed out programs it considers undesirable. At this point, we encounter the fact that the civil service is far from monolithic, and one person's efficiency is another person's waste. Providing an administrative authorization to attack problems, however, may enhance rather than diminish the power of those administrators.

The emphasis of some administrative reforms on the outputs of public service may perversely assist those seeking to preserve their powers and programs. If we begin with an assumption that much of the value of public sector output is not readily measurable (Byatt 1977), and that the measurement of the value of almost all of the output will involve heroic assumptions about markets and the pricing of services, then a whole new administrative and managerial jumble has been created. Even rather dull civil servants could devise measurement devices by which their programs would look good, since they have an understanding of the calculations required. Thus, placing an emphasis on producing more bang for the buck may, in essence, give a good deal more bang to civil servants.

Just as some governments have sought to overtly politicize their civil service, or at least the upper echelons, some attacks on the civil service have had the same unintended effect. This has been most noticeable in Britain, where the abrogation of a pay system linking civil service pay to private wages, the rescinding of union rights at the Government Communications Headquarters, and the general denigration of the civil service pushed the civil service away from the Conservative government. One would not expect strong support for a Conservative government from lower-echelon civil servants, but the level of hostility of most public service unions was probably unprecedented, as was the increasing commitment of elite unions (the First Division Association in particular) to the trade union cause and, thereby—implicitly—to the Labour party.

In addition to full-scale privatization of public functions, some public functions are delivered by quasi-public organizations (Barker 1982; Salamon 1981) or through partnership arrangements between the public and private sectors. Politicians of the ideological Right desire to limit public expenditure and to disguise (if not actually reduce) the power of the public sector in most modern economies and societies. These arrangements may reduce public expenditure, but they also may have rather perverse effects if another political goal is limiting the relative powers of civil servants. The negotiation and management of quasi-public arrangements is complex—usually substantially more complex than straightforward service delivery through public organizations (Kettl 1987). Their continuity and their understanding of the procedures and legalities of the public sector place the civil service in a powerful position in devising and manipulating these innovative arrangements. As more and more service delivery involves the coordination of organizations delivering complementary if not competitive services, there is an increased need for the managerial skills of career civil servants, as well as for their ability to negotiate lasting arrangements among organizations that will persist after any single government has left office.

Implementation as a Priority

Implementation gives the civil service direct impact in defining and controlling public policy. Even if one does not adopt the more extreme bottom-up views concerning implementation (Elmore 1980; Barrett and Fudge 1981), the delivery of services is crucial for specification of policy. The policy of the street may well be different from the policy assumed by policy makers (Lipsky 1980; Prottas 1979), but the policy of the street is the policy that really matters to the public.

Political attacks on the policy-making power of the civil service have been concentrated on the power of the senior civil service. Control over the implementation process is perhaps too massive and complex a task for partisan control from the center, or policy centralizers may simply not perceive the utility of exercising control over the lower echelons of organizations. This oversight then leaves a substantial amount of policy-making power still in the hands of the career civil service. This does not imply that political attempts to limit the powers of the senior civil service have all been for naught, because it is unlikely that all echelons in the organization were in agreement on prior policies. Implementation of policy may be as much out of the control of organizational superiors with a powerful senior civil service in control as it is when those civil servants have had their wings clipped.

The implementation process becomes problematic when, as often happens, it depends upon subnational governments. Even if it has charge of its own machinery in central government, a centralizing political regime will find it difficult to impose control over local authorities.

This is true even in political systems that appear, on the surface, to be highly centralized (Crozier and Thoenig 1976; Jones 1988). Political considerations, as well as differences in perspective on policies at different levels of government, limit the capacity of central governments to impose their authority through implementation. The Conservative government in Britain fought prolonged, costly battles with its local authorities, and regional and local governments in many countries often implement programs as they see fit (Keating 1988). In short, central-local relations serve as yet another factor limiting the capacity of a centralizing regime (or the senior civil service in such a regime) from getting its own way with public policies.

For the centralizers of the political Right, implementation has been a somewhat less vexing problem than it might be for politicians who have more positive agendas. Given that a great deal of what was desired by the Right was to do less, and to force government to do less simply by reducing the amount of money available, the desired program changes have been relatively simple to implement. Further, some program changes, such as rolling a series of categorical grants into block grants, avoid a number of possible barriers to implementation; the aim is to allow local authorities greater latitude to make their own decisions about program priorities. Thus, implementation, oddly enough, is less of a concern for Conservative governments, that should expect to face a hostile civil service, than it might be for a government with a more activist agenda. One might expect implementation to become more difficult as bureaucracies become increasingly professionalized and have their own policy priorities. While the relationships between conservative political leaders and career civil servants have been far from perfect, the more ideological regimes (of the political Right, at least) have encountered somewhat less difficulty with implementation than might have been imagined, largely due to the negative nature of their agenda and the minimalist design of many of their programs.

Summary

The role of the public bureaucracy is a distinguishing feature of contemporary government. The massive increases in the number and complexity of government functions since the end of World War II, or even since the mid-1960s, have generated demands for governance that could be met most readily through an increased capacity in the public bureaucracy. The development of the public bureaucracies in most industrialized democracies has been associated with the development of the welfare state and the mixed economy, and bureaucracies have been the principal instruments for both formulating and implementing those programs. In the contemporary welfare state, the public bureaucracy has achieved an importance that few of the major theoreticians of public administration, or of democratic government, could have imagined or condoned.

The image of government by bureaucracy, rather than through democratic institutions, has been raised as a real possibility for industrial democracies. The volume and complexity of the decisions modern governments must make appear to require permanent and technically competent policy makers rather than the amateur and often unstable governments produced through the political process. A number of governments in the 1980s sought to reverse the expansion of the public sector and the powers of the bureaucracy. These governments used a conservative, antistate ideology to justify their actions and can be seen as new ideologues gaining power in what had been assumed to be a technocratic age. Further, there has been at least one example of a socialist government forming after a long period of conservative rule and applying an equal (if different) ideological thrust to government. The resurgence of ideological concerns in government has produced a demand for reduced bureaucratic prominence in government. Interestingly, both Right and Left express concern about the bureaucracy and its policy preferences, with the Right assuming that the bureaucracy advocates spending programs, and the Left assuming that the bureaucracy is hopelessly conservative and tied to the status quo. Both may be correct.

Despite the political pressure to minimize the policy-making role of the bureaucracy and maximize the role of true believers, the public bureaucracy remains in a powerful policy-making position. That power may simply be a prerequisite of effective government in contemporary society. The real question for elected politicians may be how to blend the need for professional competence and predictability with their own mandates for policy change. By reexamining an earlier discussion of bureaucratic government, this chapter has intended to explicate some of what happened in the 1980s and, thereby, to identify some of the limits of partisan control in bureaucratic government. The mix between these two elements will greatly determine the future of democratic governance.

NOTES

1. In many instances, it appears that Friedrich's Law of Anticipated Reactions was in effect, and more radical reforms were kept off institutional agendas in favor of more moderate, albeit substantial, changes.

2. Here I do not refer to the growth of the public sector per se as a negative consequence, only to the unplanned and incoherent growth in expenditures that appears to result.

SOURCES

Aberbach, J. D., R. D. Putnam, and B. A. Rockman. 1981. *Bureaucrats and Politicians in Western Democracies*. Cambridge: Harvard University Press.

Allison, G. T. 1986. Public and Private Management: Are They Fundamentally Alike in All Unimportant Respects. In F. S. Lane, ed., *Current Issues in Public Administration*. New York: St. Martin's.

Almond, G. A., and H. D. Lasswell. 1934. Aggressive Behaviors by Clients Toward Public Relief Administrators. *American Political Sciencc Review* 28:643–54.

Anton, T. 1980. *Administered Politics: Elite Political Culture in Sweden*. Boston: Martinus Nijhoff.

Appleby, P. H. 1949. *Policy and Administration*. University: University of Alabama Press.

Ascher, K. 1983. *The Politics of Privatisation*. London: Macmillan.

Ashford, D. E. 1981. *Policy and Politics in Britain: The Limits of Consensus*. Philadelphia: Temple University Press.

———. 1982. *Policy and Politics in France: Living with Uncertainty*. Philadelphia: Temple University Press.

Aucoin, P. 1988. Contraction, Managerialism and Decentralization in Canadian Government. *Governance* 1:144–61.

———. 1990. Administrative Reform in Public Management. *Governance* 3: 115–37.

Barker, A. 1982. *Quangos in Britain*. London: Macmillan.

Barrett, S., and C. Fudge. 1981. *Policy and Action*. London: Methuen.

Bendor, J. 1989. Formal Models of Bureaucracy: A Review Essay. In N. Lynn and A. Wildavsky, eds., *Public Administration: The State of the Discipline*. Chatham: Chatham House.

Borcherding, T. E. 1977. *Budgets and Bureaucrats: The Sources of Government Growth*. Durham: Duke University Press.

Bryner, G. C. 1987. *Bureaucratic Discretion*. New York: Pergamon.

Byatt, I.C.R. 1977. Theoretical Issues in Expenditure Decisions. In M. V. Posner, ed., *Public Expenditure: Allocation Among Competing Ends*. Cambridge: Cambridge University Press.

Campbell, E. C., and B. G. Peters. 1988. *Organizing Governance: Governing Organizations*. Pittsburgh: University of Pittsburgh Press.

Campbell, E. C., and G. Szablowski. 1979. *The Superbureaucrats: Structure and Behaviour in Central Agencies*. Toronto: Macmillan of Canada.

Casstevens, T. 1980. Birth and Death Processes of Government Bureaus in the United States. *Behavioral Science* 25:161–66.

Castles, F. G., and R. Wildenmann. 1986. *Visions and Realities of Party Government*. Berlin: DeGruyter.

Cohen, M. D., J. G. March, and J. P. Olsen. 1972. A Garbage Can Model of Organizational Choice. *Administrative Science Quarterly* 17:1–25.

Cohen, S. 1981. Le Role du Secretaire Générale de la Présidence de la République. In F. de Baecque and J.-L. Quermonne, eds., *Administration et Politiques sous la Ve République*. Paris: Presses de la Fondation Nationale des Sciences Politiques.

Crozier, M. 1964. *The Bureaucratic Phenomenon*. Chicago: University of Chicago Press.

———. 1979. *On ne Change pas la Société par Decret*. Paris: Grasset.

Crozier, M., and E. Friedberg. 1980. *Actors and Systems*. Chicago: University of Chicago Press.

Crozier, M., and J.-C. Thoenig. 1976. L'importance du système politico-administratif territorial. In A. Peyrefitte, ed., *Décentraliser les responsabilités? Pourquoi? Comment?* Paris: Documentation Française.

Cullis, J. G., and P. R. Jones. 1984. The Economic Theory of Bureaucracy, X-Inefficiency and Wagner's Law. *Public Finance/Finances Publiques* 39:191–201.

Derlien, H.-U. 1988. Reprecussions of Government Change on the Career Civil Service in West Germany: The Cases of 1969 and 1982. *Governance* 1:50–78.

Dery, D. 1984. *Problem Definition in Policy Analysis*. Lawrence: University of Kansas Press.

DeSario, J., and S. Langton. 1987. *Citizen Participation in Public Decision Making*. New York: Greenwood.

Dogan, M. 1975. *The Mandarins of Western Europe*. New York: Wiley.

Doig, J. W. 1983. If I See a Murderous Fellow Sharpening a Knife Cleverly. . . . *Public Administration Review* 43:292–304.

Downs, A. 1967. *Inside Bureaucracy*. Boston: Little, Brown.

Dunleavy, P. 1985. Bureaucrats, Budgets and the Growth of the State: Reconstructing an Incremental Model. *British Journal of Political Science* 15:299–320.

Dupuy, F., and J.-C. Thoenig. 1985. *L'Administration en Miettes*. Paris: Fayard.

Duvall, R. D., and J. R. Freeman. 1983. The Technocratic Elite and the Entrepreneurial State in Dependent Development. *American Political Science Review* 77:569–87.

Dwivedi, O. P., and R. B. Jain. 1985. *India's Administrative State*. New Delhi: Gitanjali.

Eldersveld, S. J., J. Kooiman, and T. van der Tak. 1981. *Elite Images in Dutch Politics*. Ann Arbor: University of Michigan Press.

Elmore, R. F. 1980. Backward Mapping: Implementation Research and Policy Decisions. *Political Science Quarterly* 94:601–16.

Fournier, J. 1987. *Le travail gouvernemental*. Paris: Dalloz.

Franz, H.-J. 1985. Interorganizational Arrangements and Coordination at the

Policy Level. In F. X. Kaufmann, G. Majone, and V. Ostrom, eds., *Guidance, Control and Evaluation in the Public Sector.* Berlin: deGruyter.

Giddens, A. 1971. *Capitalism and Modern Social Theory.* London: Cambridge University Press.

Goodsell, C. T. 1976. Cross-Cultural Comparison of Behavior of Postal Clerks Toward Clients. *Administrative Science Quarterly* 21:140–50.

Gray, A. 1988. Bureaucracy and Political Power. *Political Studies* 36:131–34.

Gray, A., and W. I. Jenkins. 1985. *Administrative Politics in British Government.* Brighton: Wheatsheaf.

Gruber, J. E. 1987. *Controlling Bureaucracies: Dilemmas in Democratic Governance.* Berkeley and Los Angeles: University of California Press.

Hanf, K., and C. Hull. 1982. The Implementation of Regulatory Policy: Enforcement as Bargaining. *European Journal of Political Research* 10:159–72.

Hanf, K., and F. W. Scharpf. 1978. *Interorganizational Policymaking: Limits to Coordination and Central Control.* Beverly Hills: Sage.

Hanf, K., and T. A. J. Toonen. 1985. *Policy Implementation in Federal and Unitary Systems.* Dodrecht: Martinus Nijhoff.

Heclo, H. 1977. *A Government of Strangers.* Washington, D.C.: Brookings.

———. 1978. Issue Networks and the Executive Establishment. In A. King, ed., *The New American Political System.* Washington, D.C.: American Enterprise Institute.

———. 1988. The In and Outer System: A Critical Assessment. *Political Science Quarterly* 103:37–56.

Hennessy, P. 1989. *Whitehall.* London: Secker and Warburg.

Hjern, B., and C. Hull. 1982. Implementation Research as Empirical Constitutionalism. *European Journal of Political Research* 10:105–15.

Hogwood, B. W., and B. G. Peters. 1983. *Policy Dynamics.* Brighton: Wheatsheaf.

Hood, C. 1976. *The Limits of Administration.* New York: Wiley.

Hood, C., M. Huby, and A. Dunsire. 1984. Do British Central Government Departments Measure Up to the Budget/Utility Theory of Bureaucracy? *Journal of Public Policy* 4:163–79.

Hoppe, R., H. van de Graaf, and A. van Dijk. 1987. Implementation Research and Policy Design: Problem Tractability, Policy Theory, and Feasibility Testing. *International Review of Administrative Sciences* 53:581–604.

Hyneman, C. S. 1950. *Bureaucracy in a Democracy.* New York: Harper.

Johansen, L. N., and O. P. Kristensen. 1981. Corporatist Traits in Denmark, 1946–76. In G. Lehmbruch and P. C. Schmitter, eds., *Patterns of Corporatist Policymaking.* London: Sage.

Johnson, C. 1982. *MITI and the Japanese Miracle.* Stanford: Stanford University Press.

Jones, C. O. 1984. *An Introduction to the Study of Public Policy.* Monterey: Brooks/Cole.

Jones, G. W. 1988. Central-Local Government Relations in Britain. *Governance* 1:162–83.

Jordan, A. G. 1981. Iron Triangles, Woolly Corporatism, or Elastic Nets: Images of the Policy Process. *Journal of Public Policy* 1:95–124.

Katz, R. 1987. *Party Government: European and American Experiences*. Berlin: deGruyter.
Katzenstein, P. J. 1987. *Policy and Politics in West Germany: The Growth of a Semisovereign State*. Philadelphia: Temple University Press.
Kaufman, H. 1976. *Are Government Organizations Immortal?* Washington, D.C.: Brookings.
Keating, M. 1988. Regional Policy in France, Italy and Spain. *Governance* 1:184–204.
Kessler, M.-C. 1978. *La Politique de la Haut Fonction Publique*. Paris: Presses de la Fondation Nationale des Sciences Politiques.
Kettl, D. 1987. *Government by Proxy*. Washington, D.C.: Congressional Quarterly Press.
Krauss, E. S., and M. Muramatsu. 1984. Bureaucrats and Politicians in Policymaking; The Case of Japan. *American Political Science Review* 78:128–46.
Laumann, E. O., and D. Knoke. 1987. *The Organizational State: Social Choice in National Policy Domains*. Madison: University of Wisconsin Press.
Lerner, A. W., and J. Wanat. 1983. Fuzziness and Bureaucracy. *Public Administration Review* 43:500–09.
Lewis, E. 1984. *Public Entrepreneurship: Toward a Theory of Bureaucratic Political Power*. Bloomington: Indiana University Press.
Linder, S. H., and B. G. Peters. 1985. From Social Theory to Policy Design. *Journal of Public Policy* 4:237–59.
———. 1987. A Design Perspective on Implementation Research: The Fallacy of Misplaced Precision. *Policy Studies Review* 6:459–75.
———. 1988. Implementation as the Source of Policy Formulation: When Rather than Whether? International Review of Administrative Science 55:631–52.
Lipsky, M. 1980. *Street-Level Bureaucracy: Dilemmas of the Individual in Public Services*. New York: Russell Sage.
Lynn, J., and A. Jay. 1984. *Yes, Minister*. London: BBC.
———. 1987. *Yes, Prime Minister*. London: BBC.
McFarland, A. S. 1983. Public Interest Lobbies and Minority Faction. In A. J. Cigler and B. A. Loomis, eds., *Interest Group Politics*. Washington, D.C.: Congressional Quarterly Press.
March, J. G., and J. P. Olsen. 1984. The "New Institutionalism": Organizational Factors in Political Life. *American Political Science Review* 78:734–49.
Marmor, T. R., with P. Fellman. 1986. Policy Entrepreneurship in Government: An American Study. *Journal of Public Policy* 6:225–54.
Marx. F. M. 1957. *The Administrative State: An Introduction to Bureaucracy*. Chicago: Rand McNally.
Mashaw, J. L. 1983. *Bureaucratic Justice*. New Haven: Yale University Press.
Mayntz, R., and F. W. Scharpf. 1975. *Policymaking in the German Federal Bureaucracy*. New York: Elsevier.
Meyers, F. 1985. *La Politisation de l'Administration*. Brussels: Institut International des Sciences Administratives.

Mommsen, W. J., and J. Osterhammer. 1987. *Max Weber and His Contemporaries*. Boston: Allen and Unwin.

Mosher, F. C. 1968. *Democracy and the Public Service*. New York: Oxford University Press.

Muramatsu, M. 1988. Recent Administrative Developments in Japan. *Governance* 1:469–78.

Nakamura, R. T., and F. Smallwood. 1980. *The Politics of Policy Implementation*. New York: St. Martin's.

Niskanen, W. 1971. *Bureaucracy and Representative Government*. Chicago: Aldine-Atherton.

Nystrom, P., and W. Starbuck. 1981. *Handbook of Organizational Design*. New York: Oxford University Press.

OECD (Organization for Economic Cooperation and Development). 1983. *Consumer Politics in OECD Member Countries*. Paris: OECD.

Olsen, J. P. 1983. *Organized Democracy*. Oslo: Universitetsforlaget.

Orzechowski, W. 1977. Economic Models of Bureaucracy: Survey, Extensions and Evidence. In T. E. Borcherding, ed., *Budgets and Bureaucrats: The Sources of Government Growth*. Durham: Duke University Press.

O'Toole, L. J. 1986. Policy Recommendations for Multi-Actor Implementation: An Assessment of the Field. *Journal of Public Policy* 6:181–210.

Page, E. C. 1985. *Political Authority and Bureaucratic Power*. Brighton: Wheatsheaf.

Pempel, T. J. 1982. *Policy and Politics in Japan: Creative Conservatism*. Philadelphia: Temple University Press.

———. 1984. Organizing for Efficiency: The Higher Civil Service in Japan. In E. N. Suleiman, ed., *Bureaucrats and Policymaking*. New York: Holmes and Meier.

Peters, B. G. 1981. The Problem of Bureaucratic Government. *Journal of Politics* 43:56–82.

———. 1986. *American Public Policy*. 2d ed. Chatham: Chatham House.

———. 1987. Politicians and Bureaucrats in the Politics of Policymaking. In J.-E. Lane, ed., *Bureaucracy and Public Choice*. London: Sage.

———. 1988. *The Comparative Study of Public Bureaucracy*. Tuscaloosa: University of Alabama Press.

Peters, B. G., and B. W. Hogwood. 1988. The Death of Immortality: Organizational Change in the US Federal Bureaucracy, 1933–1982. *American Journal of Public Administration* 18:119–33.

Pierce, W. S. 1981. *Bureaucratic Failure and Public Expenditure*. New York: Academic Press.

Portis, E. B. 1986. *Max Weber and Political Commitment*. Philadelphia: Temple University Press.

Poulantzas, N. 1978. *State, Power, Socialism*. London: New Left Books.

Pressman, J. L., and A. Wildavsky. 1974. *Implementation*. Berkeley and Los Angeles: University of California Press.

Prottas, J. M. 1979. *People Processing: The Street Level Bureaucrat in Public Service Bureaucracies*. Lexington: Lexington Books.

Redford, E. S. 1969. *Democracy in the Administrative State*. New York: Oxford University Press.

Richards, S. 1987. The FMI. In John Gretton and Anthony Harrison, eds., *Reshaping the Public Sector*. New Brunswick: Transaction Books.

Ridley, F. F. 1985. Politics and the Selection of Higher Civil Servants in Britain. In F. Meyers, ed., *La Politisation de l'Administration*. Brussels: Institut International des Sciences Administratives.

Ripley, R. B., and G. A. Franklin. 1987. *Congress, the Bureaucracy and Public Policy*. 4th ed. Chicago: Dorsey.

Rogaly, J. 1988. Mrs. Thatcher Knows How Far Is Too Far. *Financial Times*, 22 April.

Rose, R. 1974. *The Problem of Party Government*. London: Macmillan.

Sabatier, P. 1986. Top-Down and Bottom-Up Approaches to Implementation Research. *Journal of Public Policy* 6:21–48.

Salamon, L. 1981. Rethinking Public Management: Third-Party Government and the Changing Forms of Government Action. *Public Policy* 29:255–75.

Savas, E. S. 1987. *Privatization: The Key to Better Government*. Chatham: Chatham House.

Searing, D. C. 1988. Roles, Rules and Reasons: A Little Political Behavior for the New Institutionalism. Presented at the annual meeting of the Midwest Political Science Association, Chicago.

Sigelman, L. 1986. The Bureaucrat as Budget Maximizer: An Assumption Examined. *Public Budgeting and Finance* 6:50–59.

Stevens, A. 1985. *L'Alternance* and the Higher Civil Service. In P. G. Cerny and M. A. Schain, eds., *Socialism, the State and Public Policy in France*. London: Frances Pinter.

Suleiman, E. N. 1974. *Politics, Power and Bureaucracy in France: The Administrative Elite*. Princeton: Princeton University Press.

———. 1978. *Elites in French Society*. Princeton: Princeton University Press.

———. 1984. *Bureaucrats and Policy Making*. New York: Holmes and Meier.

Tarschys, D. 1985. Curbing Public Expenditure: Current Trends. *Journal of Public Policy* 5:23–67.

Timsit, G. 1987. *Administrations et Etats: Etude Comparée*. Paris: Presses Universitaires de France.

Udy, S. H. 1958. "Bureaucratic" Elements in Organizations: Some Research Findings. *American Sociological Review* 23:415–18.

Waldo, D. 1948. *The Administrative State*. New York: Ronald Press.

Weber, M. 1972. *Wirtschaft und Gesellschaft*. 5th ed. Tubingen: J. C. B. Mohr.

Wildavsky, A. 1979. *Speaking Truth to Power*. Boston: Little, Brown.

Wilson, V. S., and O. P. Dwivedi. 1982. *The Administrative State in Canada*. Toronto: McGraw-Hill Ryerson.

Wright, V. 1974. Politics and Administration under the Fifth Republic. *Political Studies* 22:44–65.

Yates, D. 1982. *Bureaucratic Democracy: The Search for Democracy and Efficiency in American Government*. Cambridge: Harvard University Press.

14

Ordaining Powers: Rediscovering the State Through Policy Studies

Douglas E. Ashford

IN MANY RESPECTS, the twentieth-century debate about states and societies is less clear than the well known constitutional debates of the nineteenth century. When states were confined to law and order functions, the boundary between the activities of states and the models of society was much clearer. Indeed, one can persuasively argue that the necessity for societal models was largely the result of the secularizing and equalizing forces unleashed by mass democracy in the late nineteenth century (Logue 1983; Hawthorne 1976). Whether justified by the eternal truths of the church or of the divine right of kings, so long as earthly existence was no more than a brief exposure to the evils of the flesh, the correct organization and conduct of society was not perplexing. In only a few countries, most notably England, did the proper organization of the daily affairs of government became a distinguishable problem before the decline of the church. This had profound effects on the development of British political thought and the emergence of an elusive, if not ephemeral, concept of an English state.[1]

What Pocock so brilliantly describes as the "apocalyptic republic," the seventeenth-century British concept of state and society, approximated the classical Greek model of mixed authority. By the end of Tudor rule, it was "easier to state how each may check the excesses of the others than to specify just what powers the lords and commons wield" (Pocock 1975, 364). As a result, Britain developed most of the instruments of modern government before many of the contemporary questions about demarcating states from societies were even asked. If social science still asks philosophical questions, an initial question might be whether the ancient concept of the British state makes it such a wild outlier among modern states as to defy comparison. But British stateness is so intellectually compelling that few modern states can be understood without first grasping the peculiar historical choices in which they are imbedded (Skinner 1974).

As Kumar (1987) describes so well, utopian models of society flourished throughout the nineteenth century as never before. Of all the modern states, the abrupt and violent achievement of mass democracy in France most urgently demanded the production of a rational model of society. The entire nineteenth-century history of French political thought might be viewed as a struggle to demonstrate the compatibility of individual and collective notions of the state. Comte's high priests of knowledge culminate with Durkheim, as the high priest of the Republic. Social theory was to provide what violence and revolution had denied France—an orderly base on which to test various definitions of the state. The French took the rationalization of state and society seriously but also erected a state structure that was given powers as though the social model existed, a kind of rash confidence in intellectuals that neither the British lords nor commoners ever displayed.

Despite the heavy-handed laborings of Spencer and Hobhouse (Collini 1979), British stateness remained curiously immune to philosophical musing. A young Churchill was no different than most turn-of-the-century British statesmen in disliking a mixture of "mathematics and politics" (Clarke 1978, 123). Well into the twentieth century, Oxford remained the citadel of the Greek classics, while a more modern Cambridge skillfully procrastinated making any commitment to anything that might be called social science (Collini, Winch, and Burrow 1973). Germany is of course an interesting variation, where the renewal of idealistic philosophy produced an uncritical concept of the state, thereby making Weber's work a heroic accomplishment in a state where the competing claims of state and society on individual loyalties had never undergone the democratic experiments of either France or Britain.

An appreciation of the close association between the development of social science during the nineteenth century and the superimposition of mass democracy on the liberal concept of democratic governance helps restore historical perspective to current reflections about state and society. Over much of the nineteenth century, the struggle between republicanism and various forms of liberalism was much more intense than the class struggles that inspire so many contemporary applications of Marxist social models to the analysis of states. The constitutional checks and balances built into early democracies were inspired more by Aristotelian apprehensions, which found the extremes of government to be tyranny and anarchy, rather than hypothetical tensions between presumably objective conditions of society and the malleability of states. Liberal precautions are most visible in the common use of property voting qualifications, indirect election methods, and especially in France, the long terms of elected office. The belief that property carries duties, which permitted a clear demarcation between state and society, steadily eroded even before Marx.

The era of classical liberal hegemony was, in fact, remarkably brief. In France, true political liberalism barely survived the Restoration, however much modern political sociologists may insist that the intransigent bourgeois habits of Frenchmen make the country a special case. In terms of intellectual history, this seems an enormous muddle, which assumes that political failings or strengths, depending on one's ideology, are necessarily the product of social forces. Put differently, the elaborate social models so enthusiastically undertaken by French philosophers may bias our perception of state-society relations in France. More to the point, in rethinking policy studies, social models attribute political salience to aggregate social characteristics and to episodic social tensions that might easily be less important were an independent assessment made of the policy process and actual political negotiations.

German liberals also suffered an ignominious fate by being abandoned by Bismarck in the late nineteenth century and crushed between Catholic and socialist parties in the twentieth century (Smith 1979, 12). Britain is an interesting case, because supreme confidence in the capabilities of the government, rarely thought of as a state in the continental sense, meant that mass democracy, radicalism, and secularism never depended on clear social models. By the end of the Victorian age, social theorists had produced little but impossible answers to the vaguely understood social ills of Britain (Wolfe 1975). The radicalism of Charles Bradlaugh and Sir Charles Dilke never penetrated the Liberal party. If a devout Gladstone was not suspicious of their secularism, he was most certainly totally discouraged by their marital infidelities. Joseph Chamberlain's Radical Programme of 1885 was a more viable formula to mobilize the middle class in an alliance of "usurers, stockjobbers and militant adventurers" (Royle 1980, 219). Nor should it escape our attention that, while radical republicans in Britain were being smothered by political stability, French radical republicans were mobilizing the Ligue d'Enseignement to convert the French educational system into a bulwark of republican sentiment. In early twentieth-century France, rabid republicanism bordered on tyranny, while the hypothetical excesses of Marxism were barely known (Auspitz 1982; Sorlin 1967).

Contrary to one book on boundaries between politics and society (Maier 1987), the ambiguities of states and societies may be no more than a curious product of Marxism and modern social science, often reinforced by behavioral social science and fervent academic liberals.

In the headlong dash to produce a discipline that left little room for moral judgment, narrative history, or legal distinctions, the concept of the state became a reservoir of intellectual confusion. Not too surprisingly, the extent to which social scientists talk only to themselves seems to correspond with the predominance of abstract social models, the trashing of philosophy and history, and the isolation of public and constitutional law from the study of politics. The immediate importance arises from the ease with which this simplification reduces the state, to use the austere language of variance, to a residual variable. Having spent nearly a century rejecting state theory under the deluge of rash claims in social models, social science now finds inspiration by setting out to eliminate the confusion that it has itself created. As the historical notes suggest, the first task is to see if the alleged ambiguity over the boundaries between state and society is an intellectual confusion rather than the product of predetermined social forces or bewildered, confused, and ultimately ineffective governance (Rose and Peters 1978; Taylor 1983). Neither Marxist glorifications of society nor liberal laments over the demise of law-and-order government will resolve the intellectual confusion that we have imposed on ourselves.

Governments Have Meanings

One of the similarities between Marxist and behavioral models of the state is the definition of states by their monopoly of coercion. To construct positivist explanations of states and societies, it is of course essential to have a clear empirical definition of states rather than definitions that might place more emphasis on the historical, developmental, or transcendental qualities of states. Not only is it virtually inevitable that societies emerge from such a biased competition of ideas as by far the most important object of social and political analysis, but it also means that the effects of society on states, the importance of social uprisings and violence, the socialization of the young, and the interactions of social classes take on preponderant importance in empirical research. In both research designs and in the imagination, states are derived from society.[2] Once any social demand becomes legitimate and any whim or fancy prima facie evidence of a failure of the state, radical republican and Marxist state models merge into an intellectual haze. Pluralism leaves nothing but the hidden hand of associational life to guide us toward the ephemeral goals of the state, while Marxism offers the grim inevitability of historical extermination. Either avenue of thought might lead to important societal or political truths, but neither provides the foundations for the study of the state conceived independently from society.

If one spends some time on the magnificent histories of how the liberal state gradually divorced itself from laissez-faire economics and its close association with property over the nineteenth century, the mystery of the state begins to unfold. The more nearly man is imagined as totally isolated in society and intellectually self-sufficient in politics, the more the issues of secularism, republicanism, and eventually socialism dominate political ideas and political life. To some extent, these trends were present in the creation of democratic governance—but certainly in varying degrees, as even the most rudimentary reading of constitutional history would tell us. But history readily shows how these struggles have centered on different political issues, on different facets of economic and social life, and most important, on radically different internal concerns about the renewal and viability of the state. In short, without endorsing any particular model of society, it is quite easy to grasp the critical phases and issues of rebuilding nineteenth-century liberal states into what today is most often called the advanced welfare state. Put differently, for those who wield authority, the conduct of government, the use of public authority, and the exercise of coercion (Thornton 1965; Critchley 1969) convey distinct meanings of what the state is. Whatever social virtues and vices are found, key actors make decisions, shape policies, implement programs, and in doing so, convey meaning. However misinformed, prejudiced, and even malevolent such persons may be in societal terms, they need ideas about governance and the state. At times these ideas have corresponded to economic and social principles, as was possibly the case in the early phase of democratic government. But property was the foundation of the franchise and of ownership for a surprisingly brief period.

My primary concern is not the methodologies by which the meaning of the state might be more clearly established, but it is important to note some of the possibilities that the overriding demands of positivist explanation have excluded. Not surprisingly, many of these possibilities arise because abstract society and state models cannot handle the complexity of policy making. First, the studies of organized complexity imply, if they do not always make explicit, that intricate behavior presupposes standards, values, and shared goals (Olson 1965). Second, there is the sizable literature on interactionist sociology, led by the work of Goffman (1971), urging more unorthodox methods to reveal hidden meanings and concealed relationships in dealing with the external, or "real," society. Third, there is a long tradition within cultural anthropology of probing for the "thick" descriptions used by people in order to make their time and situation comprehensible (Geertz 1973). Fourth, there is a highly respected, if controversial, body of thinking about history and the sociology of ideas illustrated by Pocock's work (1971). Last, there are the renewed efforts to review the study of institutions from which this chapter obviously takes inspiration (March and Olsen 1986; Douglas 1986; Thomas et al. 1987). But in linking policy studies to an independent concept of the state, the more pressing question concerns renewed awareness of how many institutionalized activities reveal internal meanings of the state. Put in more psychological terms, institutional reality testing may transcend the particular social realities or issues.

The real difficulty is not about methods as much as it is about devising a concept of the state that recognizes its independence from social and economic models. Tortured self-examinations over the nature of state autonomy rapidly lose significance once the state is given, so to speak, an equal intellectual chance to exist. This question would seem redundant to most eighteenth- and nineteenth-century philosophers, as well as to their political mentors. The institutions of statehood are manifested in numerous ways. For one thing, citizenship or full membership in a state never perfectly corresponded with being part of society. True to its neoclassical foundations, the British constitution did not define membership until faced with mounting racial problems in the 1960s and 1970s. Britain had subjects, and France had *citoyens*.

How one sacrifices the rights of membership are also important evidence about institutional powers. In Britain, these powers have always been more draconian than in any country, despite the fact that nationality was not defined until the British Nationality Act of 1982. Under the Riot Act of 1714, in force until 1967, unlawful assembly was a felony: the treason act of 1795 made incitement to treason a felony, with a loss of all civil rights. Nor were British policy makers reluctant to abolish citizenship in order to achieve social and economic ends; under the Poor Law Amendment Act of 1834, paupers were deprived of political rights. Though this arbitrary political punishment was compromised in Victorian Britain, exemptions required specific parliamentary approval, such as that given for those accepting school lunches in 1906.

A second area where statehood and social distinctions are clearly visible is in the oaths, procedures, and disciplines surrounding public office. Parliamentary immunities have similarities across nations, but the reasons for granting them and the legal recourse for violations of public trust by members of parliament, the civil service, and the police force are remarkably different. Having granted rational authority to certain persons on behalf of the state, states need procedures to deprive persons of office if their privileges display irrational tendencies. In the case of felonious crimes, criminal proceedings are identical to those used for private persons, although, as we have seen in the recent past, controversies remain over the right of privilege and secrecy in investigating and prosecuting officials. Reaganite indignance over public prosecutors is reproduced in disputes over the role of the solicitor general in Britain or the quasi-judicial activities of the *police judicaire* in France. Britain is again a limiting case, because the delay in secularizing government perpetuated the overlap of religious and political office well into the nineteenth century. Until 1855, members of Parliament were required to subscribe to the Thirty-nine Articles demanding allegiance to the monarchy and the Anglican church. Although a Judeo-Christian affirmation was permitted after 1870, until 1886 Jews and Protestants were barred from jury duty because of their inability to take the oath (Barker 1975, 212). Even more revealing of the prescriptive definition of office, roughly two-thirds of British localities were governed by royally appointed justices of the peace until the Local Government Act of 1888. In a political and legal system basically devised to protect land, it is hardly surprising that in 1850 ten men owned half of Scotland and a hundred, half of England (Thornton 1965, 220).

A third area where governments and constitutions acquire distinct meanings is the political imposition of social and economic constraints on private property. Before social models treated all forms of wealth as interchangeable, equality was primarily conceived as an individual contractual freedom. Today, the simple boundary of legal contract is hopelessly blurred, but this does not mean that either the political process or the social and economic limitations are alike across countries. Perhaps the most dramatic reconcilation of property and power was constructed in Sweden, where the sharp demarcation of private wealth and government was a precondition of Social Democratic success. Despite controversies within the Social Democratic party over the distinction between property and political power (Koblik 1975), it is hard to imagine how Social Democratic hegemony might have been achieved were private and public use of wealth and capital as diverse as is found in other democracies.

The controversy in Britain, a century before the Swedish compromise, was no less intense; there the introduction of limited liability was seen as an irreversible breach of private responsibility and the first step toward the moral degeneration of British life (Harding 1973, 372–82). For those interested in identifying the historical boundary between the classical (universal) liberal state and the partial liberal state of the late nineteenth century, there is probably no better dividing line than this transformation of property into an interlocking right and obligation. In no other state was the establishment of general rules about the convertibility of property into power more controversial. The intransigence of the Irish question in British politics arises in no small part due to fears of the Anglo-Irish landowning class. The first legal acknowledgment of social inequality as a limiting condition of contract was the Irish Land Act of 1881.

Despite Le Play's (1864) plea for primogeniture, the hopeless confusion of economic and political equality in France helps explain the strength of the bourgeoisie. Middle-class French society was reinforced by political equality, while large British landowners controlled Parliament until 1910. The Duke of Westminster and others even kept urban government in Tory hands well into the twentieth century. A political milestone in the revival of the Labour party was its victory in the London County Council elections of 1934. The resistance of the landed to elected county government was only overcome in 1888 by the derating (tax exemption) of half the value of agricultural land. The very tardy overall reform of urban government in 1929 was achieved by fully derating agricultural land. In social terms, Prime Minister Thatcher's abolition of domestic rates (local property tax) was good middle-class politics but, in political terms is no more than that claimed by urban liberals in other democracies a century or before. The self-destruction of the House of Lords in 1909 was also caused more by aristocratic outrage over a small land tax than by social objections to what was, in fact, a rather modest system of national insurance. Le Play is of course correct in thinking that primogeniture was the key to political and social stability, but his causal link is wrong. Like many French Anglophiles of the nineteenth century, he failed to see that the rigid link between property and politics was an enormous handicap to the modernization of British institutions.

The peculiar position of common law in British constitutional and political history helps explain why the state rarely needed conventional liberal and Marxist social models. Shorn of Marxist accretions, the law of torts and contracts (the main body of common law) established total individual freedom over the disposal and use of property. In Holmes's words, the "general purpose of the law of torts is to secure a man's immunity against certain forms of harm to person, reputation, or estate, at the hands of his neighbours, not because they are wrong, but because they are harms" (Friedmann 1951, 97). In other words, *property* is not objectively defined in common law, but the rights and procedures of freely acting individuals to transform, dispose of, and inherit property are spelled out in great detail. Natural rights and positive law, the two competing interpretations of basic rights under law, are not necessarily incompatible with common law, but unlike the definition of property rights in every other modern democratic government, social definitions of property were rejected in Britain for political reasons. British law provides no intrinsic right or general principle of property from which social justice might be inferred. To be sure, this highly individualistic concept of property has been severely amended over the past fifty years, but few major inroads were made until the 1930s. As late as 1933 in the Liesbosch case, the House of Lords held that a government contractor who, through no fault of his own, was unable to fulfill his obligation had no claim to exemption, because poverty is a misfortune that the law of damages cannot cover (ibid., 36). The language is the same used to condemn the undeserving poor to poorhouses a century earlier.

The elevation of common law to constitutional status was of course not an anticipated outcome of developments in the Middle Ages, but in English political history the institutionalization of common law depended on Parliament (Maitland 1963, 343–87). From the fourteenth century, the paramount political struggle was between the king and the lords. Asserting the primacy of common law meant limiting royal prerogatives to proclaim law, to impose taxes, and to deliver summary justice. Though probably outdated when written, Dicey's view that there is no law but "judge-made" law represents the prevailing legal opinion of his day and perfectly reflects supreme confidence in common law (Wade 1939, 475–642). To Maitland (1963), common law was enshrined in British constitutional history by Coke and elevated to sovereign importance by Blackstone (Sieghart 1950, 418). Dicey's view that parliament represented the "ordinary law of the land" really means that whatever social and economic complications arose, common law must not be qualified. As a result, the crown and other oddly omnipotent agencies became a "convenient cover for ignorance" (Maitland 1963, 416). Once secured in 1688, the unwritten constitution remained in a state of "perpetual emergency" for several centuries (Allen 1950, xiv). There were and are cumbersome ways to qualify this elevation of common law—writs, petitions, and tribunals—of which more later.

For the moment, the essential point is to know that, in constitutional terms and in the jargon of contemporary social science, the autonomy of the state is the ordaining power of the king now lodged in Parliament.[3] If definitions of states are to have causal importance, such political elements must be distinguished from social and economic forces. The most interesting political feature of the British state, and perhaps part of the explanation of why socioeconomic models are so easily confused with British politics, is that British political institutions have never defined the state, because to do so would mean establishing general principles that might be used against it. A precise definition of the British state would endanger the common law, which bestows power on Parliament. This of course helps explain why, in a strict sense, Parliament is not a law-making but a law-defending body. The social and economic characteristics of members of Parliament, of elections, and of legislation notwithsanding, Parliament is made up of lawyers who scrutinize proposed laws rather than draft them.

Many social and economic historians have ably demonstrated how British society, the British economy, and the British class structure have been remarkably unaffected by industrialization and modernization (Wiener 1981; Barnett 1986). To a greater degree than in any other democracy, the explanation is political, in the distinct sense of British stateness, rather than social. For centuries the most adaptive institution in British life has been the Parliament, not because it responds to every economic tremor or social whim, but because ordaining powers are well defined. The autonomy of British political institutions are demonstrated by its immunity to external social and economic realities. Whether the society, the economy, or the social classes might have, in some sense, improved the socioeconomic existence of the British people is a separable, if fascinating, question but readily demarcated from the history of the British state.

There are of course many possible ways that the ordaining power in British politics might have changed, but as Sieghart (1950, 1–88) so clearly shows, in British political and legal history, arbitrary power means discretionary power. In contrast, in France and in most continental countries, a vast judicial superstructure of state courts is seen as the barrier to the arbitrary exercise of royal power. A generation of French historical writing celebrates more than it explains the atomistic and anarchic tendencies of Frenchmen, so that we know more about Lyonnaise bakeries and Parisian beggars than about the transformation of state power. The political significance of French administrative law comes to life more readily in Maitland's (1963) attacks on Dicey and, later, in the writing of British constitutionalists such as Allen (1950) Wade (1939), and Jennings (1959). The full force of the political difference can only be grasped in a historical context, but as Sir Henry Maine realized in the nineteenth century from the study of primitive societies, the ascribed foundations of British political life are more clearly feudal than modern. The landed aristocracy had a perfectly rational strategy to preserve its privileges, but it is not a strategy that has benefited or suffered (depending on one's values) from the abstract social and economic reasoning needed in a republican era. There never was of course a radical political revolution or, apart from Henry VIII's marital problems, a true secularization of British government.

The failure of such efforts in the nineteenth century displays the extraordinary staying power of a government built on common law and landed property. The late nineteenth-century radicalism of Joseph Chamberlain, Sir Charles Dilke, and William Bradlough fell on deaf ears (Jenkins 1958). Even the surge of popularity for American populist Henry George (1881) rapidly dissipated once Disraeli's "one nation" philosophy launched modern social and economic reform for the oppressed—not surprisingly, still regarded as much an agricultural as an industrial problem. To the frustration of nascent British republicans and the socialists who followed them, the British could not be mobilized on behalf of radical institutional reform. As Beer (1965) makes clear, political ingenuity and foresight, rather than socioeconomic forces, saved the British constitution, because the two-party system provided the incentive and possibility for change within the existing institutional framework. But at the core of this amazing capacity for survival is the deep suspicion that Coke labeled the "crooked cord of discretion" and that can be traced through three centuries from Coke to Dicey. Only the immense complications of policy making in the twentieth century have produced timid modifications of Parliament's ordaining power.

Ordained Decisions

In societies with strong radical republican and secular histories, the presumption of political and societal equality cries out for theoretical reconciliation. Despite the scorn heaped upon the French bourgeoisie as a pernicious and greedy influence, both the middle class and working class of France needed a model of a rational society much more than the British did. The search for rational authority was most intense in the state that first proclaimed there is no higher authority than man. Durkheim provided the same service for the middle class that Marx provided the working class. The stormy history of French Marxism may indeed be the result of Durkheim having done his job so well. In any event, postwar intellectual preoccupation with the Jacobin qualities of the French state, however inaccurate, are a natural consequence of the explicit institutionalization of ordaining powers in French government (Rosanvallon 1985). British intellectuals, like British politicians, cannot protest what they cannot see. The opposition between French society and politics may be exaggerated for the glorification of social science, but political social realities interlock in ways that Britain lacks. On the one hand, there is what Annan (1959) so adroitly referred to as the curious strength of positivist political thought in British academe. On the other hand, there is the odd indifference to ideological politics best seen in the much lamented failure of the Labour party to become a truly Marxist instrument. Although Marxist historians have worked strenuously for a generation to show that British capitalism unleashed alarming social forces and social tensions (Himmelfarb 1987, 70–93), outside their charmed circle, history fails to explain the durability of the British state.

One of the paradoxical similarities of such unlikely bedfellows as pluralism and Marxism is that both see societal conditions as determining the vitality and endurance of the state. To the extent that these conditions are met, political failure is inevitably rooted in social forces, while any social failure is incontrovertible evidence of political ineptitude. Thus the renewed state-society debate always risks becoming a hopeless dichotomy. The intellectual effort to get "the state back in" is not so much about finding better social models as about finding characteristics of states that are not socially derived. If the state has no independent meaning, then it can never be studied as other than dependent on society. As suggested above, the importance of the British state is precisely that its political definition has never been socially subservient. If anything, British leaders have anticipated societal needs more often then they have reacted to them (Ashford 1986).

There are several areas of policy analysis for such inquiries, but one of special interest is administrative justice and administrative law, the ordaining powers of the state. The preceding excursion into common law and its critical role in giving virtually unlimited ordaining powers to British political institutions prepared the ground to analyze how other states exercise ordaining power. The incarnation of common law in British government means that there is no bordlerine between administrative discretion and public policies. (Friedmann 1951, 49). Whether one wishes to call this intentional insulation a constitutional fiction or a political hoax makes little difference. What is not ideological is the elaborate and delicate system of institutions that enables the British government to retain an ordaining authority probably unequaled in any other democratic political system. Dicey's judge-made law is only the most recent of numerous historical illustrations of the elaborate political measures taken to exclude discretionary decision making from British law. But as Jennings (1959) points out, there is no judge-made law without discretion, nor is there any administrative decision without discretion.

The external validity of the ordaining feature as a device to establish state autonomy for comparative purposes is best demonstrated in Britain by the peculiar problems of regulating social and economic questions in relation to the state. One major area, now causing immense embarrassment to British officials in the areas of civil rights, sexual and racial equality, and equal opportunity, is the absence of a bill of rights. Throughout the nineteenth century, the reluctance to abolish the property qualification for voting as well as the extraordinary delay in giving women equal voting rights were, in part, the function of a constitutional framework in which the rights of property, contract, and tort are closely associated with common law. There is still no right of association, one of the most basic of republican reforms in the Third Republic. Combining for economic or noncommercial reasons still remains cumbersome. The easily abused laws of trust for charitable organizations are only lightly supervised by the remnants of a Crown agency. Unlike the wild abandon allowing registered associations in France, British government is jealous of its power to grant public privileges (Harding 1973, 425). The potential abuse of discretionary powers bestowed by registration is important in the longstanding mutual suspicion between government and trade unions. All of these situations present British policy makers with dilemmas, contradictions, and ambiguities rooted in ordaining powers and the ancient refusal to generate a judicial body with discretionary power.

A second area of vast confusion emerging from the fictional preservation of parliamentary supremacy is intragovernmental and intergovernmental relations. Under the ultra vires rule, the political status of local government has barely changed from Elizabethan times. Two exhaustive inquiries during the 1960s produced a barely satisfactory local government reform, which many think remains "a chaos as regards to authorities, a chaos as regards to rates [taxes], and a worse chaos than all as regards to areas," and which Goschen described a century ago (Redlich and Hirst 1903). Lamentable as Thatcher's destruction of the remnants of local self-government in Britain may be, her attitude toward local government is no different than were her predecessors'.[4]

There is no consistent spatial or functional logic to regional agencies of central government (Hogwood and Keating 1982) and immense disparities exist between the political formulas establishing the Scottish and Welsh offices, not to mention the quasi-federal authority bestowed on Stormont. As the social role of British government grew in the 1930s, the first of many studies of the confusing and cumbersome procedures for delegating legislative power was made and was only recently (imperfectly) resolved by placing an enormously complex task on the shoulders of a parliamentary committee (Franks Committee 1957). The most arbitrary governments of the world have seldom enjoyed the powers of seizing, zoning, judging, and regulating given to British ministers.[5] Maintaining the fiction of discretionary control has resulted in a system in which questions of property, services, and delegated powers are most often arbitrarily resolved by a single person holding ministerial office with powers that would shock the French, the Germans and even the regulation-minded Americans.

A third area of immense importance arose with the development of the British welfare state. Discretionary powers could not be excluded from the provision, regulation, compensation, and provision of social and economic benefits. The proliferation of administrative tribunals is, in principle, no different from the overburdened administrative courts found on the Continent. The only difference is the absolute ordaining powers that such tribunals enjoy once the ordaining powers have become a constitutional fiction. Without consistency across the country or even in the same ministry, administrative tribunals hear complaints concerning rights of union members, bargaining agreements, working conditions, industrial training, national pensions, supplementary benefits (social welfare), public housing rents, land use and building permits, public health standards, agricultural marketing agreements, and medical malpractice disputes, to mention only a few. In most instances, such tribunals are appointed by ministers, and appeals terminate in their offices. The Franks Committee (1957) identified about seventy tribunals hearing about fifteen thousand cases a year.[6]

The national Council on Administrative Tribunals and Enquiries was created in 1958 to impose a measure of order and consistency on tribunals, but ministers resisted its meager inroads in the case of pensions until 1965 and national health until 1963 (Elcock 1969, 23). Not surprisingly, the first impulse of policy makers in the 1930s was to try to subsume the enormous discretionary powers of government to common law practicies and principles (Friedmann 1951, 87–93). But in an age of growing unemployment and poverty, the procedure soon meant that regular courts were unequal to the task. As might be expected, a strong-minded Beveridge wanted his welfare state plan totally insulated against the courts, because the more generous damages commonly awarded in civil cases would easily cripple the meagerly financed British welfare state. As a result, inconsistencies, variations, and contradictions abound in treating social and economic problems.

The Policy Connection

The burden of this chapter is to show that unique features of British constitutional and legal history materially affect the conduct of state affairs. The roots of the problem are not an unwillingness to deal with social grievances or economic problems but an insistence that the state retain a particular identity in British political life. The origin of the legal and constitutional conflict is found within the common law, which, as noted by Renner (1949), never defined property but dealt with how property is acquired, disposed of, and handled under bankruptcy, inheritance, and trust. To be accurate, the term *property* in Britain means total worth or economic value. Historical circumstance permitted the landed aristocracy to make common law their domain in order to control the unchecked appropriation and taxation powers of absolute monarchy. Despite the formidable efforts of British social historians to show that these ancient events are compatible with Marxism, their political significance for the definition of the state and the observation of modern problem-solving capabilities remains.

The peculiar nature of the ordaining powers of British government has been widely recognized since late Victorian Britain. Maitland (1953) was no doubt the most vigorous critic, writing "it seems to me impossible so to define constitutional law that it shall not include the constitution of every organ of government, whether it be central or local, whether it be sovereign or subordinate" (501). In contrast, the interlocking nature of private and public law preoccupied the French, not only in a legal and constitutional sense but in the continuous stream of rationalizations provided by positivist philosophers and sociologists, who quite literally set out to build a social model that would be congruent with French political and legal circumstances. Dicey's misunderstanding of French administrative law is most evident in his sanguine repetition of an inaccurate notion of the similarity of judge-made law in Britain and France.[7] To be sure, French decrees and British orders deal with similar questions, provide similar kinds of administrative and social justice, and struggle with the same political challenges of social and economic changes. The result is that, in solving policy problems, the English displayed "a genius for changing content without changing form" (Wiener 1981, 43), while the French sacrificed content to form.

For present purposes, the policy relevance rests more with how such powers reveal states at work. The English (later British) constitution emerged from a sequence of victories over absolute power rather than the unmistakable failures in France. As Sieghart (1950, 6) so aptly suggests, the English were constantly expounding upon the past to arrive at a manageable present, while the French struggled to perfect the present in order to be in harmony with an imagined future. As the ordaining illustration shows, understanding policy making in Britain is a radically different exercise than in France—and possibly in many other continental democracies. Being a state is not only distinguishable, but the historical and contextual knowledge captures true meanings rather than the arbitrary, hypothetical meanings common to social science. The aim is not simply to deepen our knowledge of the legal and constitutional origins of the state, though this is surely one of the most neglected aspects of the state-society discussion, but to uncover the empirical dimensions of being a state that help explain how policies are formulated, considered, and resolved. The aim of such structural analysis of public policy is not to explain policies in terms of external standards or conditions but to derive from policy-making behavior evidence of the underlying contextual elements of stateness itself.

Legally speaking, what the French call *puissance publique* does not exist in Britain, hence the overpowering necessity to retain some foundation for ordaining power. In France, the Constitution of 1791 forbade judges to rule on administrative matters and created the now formidable *droit administratif.* In almost precisely reverse reasoning of the British, the revolutionary republicans believed democracy required that civil law be sharply demarcated from administrative matters (Dupuis and Guédon 1986, 68–124). Following the injunction of the Declaration of the Rights of Man, the Council of State was to assure that the executive powers of state were scrupulously separated from judicial powers. In the turbulent political history of the early nineteenth century, how this was to be accomplished was not entirely clear, but the Council of State took on its present form under the Constitution of 1848, when it was given powers to review all rules (*réglements*) issued by the executive and special powers to supervise the police (*réglement de police*).[8] As a final guarantee to citizens, any case not open to appeal to the Council of State can be brought before the Cour de Cassation, the highest court of equity, on ultra vires grounds. The contrast should not be missed. In France, ultra vires protects citizens from the state; in Britain, ultra vires protects the state from citizens. In Britain, ultra vires is the cornerstone of ordaining power; in France ultra vires has been made a popular defense.

The elaborate development of *droit administratif* has of course had enormous effect on the conduct of French government, not to mention the organization of the higher civil service and state-run education.[9] There is no major legislation without a confusing set of legal footprints leading to the Council of State, nor is any lawmaker unaware of the sweeping power of annulation bestowed on the Council of State (Sieghart 1950, 210–48). Within policy-making circles, the early ministerial discussions with the Council of State over the *avant-projet* (draft law) of new bills are a trial by fire of new intentions and new purposes. Whatever the truth of Crozier's (1970) charges of social and economic stagnation leading to new enroachments of the state on French society, each major policy change is accompanied by an exchange of proposals, forecasts, and interpretations that makes French law making an uncertain and demanding process. Beer's (1965) interpretation of nineteenth-century British politics as primarily a case of party reform and realignment and Williams's (1954) superb study of the instability of the Fourth Republic both reflect national traditions concerning the foundations of democratic government. The careful effort to contain the arbitrary powers of the French state through administrative law are rarely seen as the equivalent to other complexities and uncertainties in the policy-making requirements of other democracies. Even less understood are the policy-making advantages of clearly stated formulas for public corporations, associations, and local government in France.[10]

The critical importance of the definitions and procedures for ordaining powers in the two states leads back to comparative policy studies as a way of understanding modern democratic states. The aim is not to restore the highly formalized examination of government so common at the close of the nineteenth century, nor to rationalize behavioral studies that isolate political studies from public law and public administration, but to return to an implicit assumption of the policy and politics series, namely, that policy making is not only a rich source of instrumental knowledge about government but of constituent knowledge. Governments were constituted by people, not social theorists, and these people worked within particular time frames and historical contexts. Societies are no less influenced by such pressures, but states are influenced by them in other ways, with different time lags and different objectives. If corporative policy studies are confined to comparing performance by whatever standards social scientists or others wish to impose, then shifting policy studies to the constituent questions becomes impossible.

The much debated question of the autonomy of the state is less mysterious if one begins with the constituent nature of all states and then limits the comparison to states holding common values about individual liberties—that is, democratic states. As ordaining power suggests, an enormous intellectual and political effort went into formulating the constituent elements of democracies. From this it follows that an explanation of constituent power is not necessarily an explanation of societal tensions and economic events. More important, to some degree all policy decisions incorporate constituent power as well as an instrumental effort to address social and economic needs. To confine comparative policy studies to identifiable, hypothetical, social and economic objectives is to exclude the state as a reality—that is, to ignore its intrinsic constitutional nature located in history. The choice often rests with what model of humankind most appeals to the investigator. For the past century, much of social science has concentrated on building the rational model of humankind that democracy required. Britain is the limiting case, because its model was heavily influenced by the ascriptive status of the landed aristocracy and best articulated in common law. Britain's constituent problems were very different from those of the French Revolution or the painful unification of imperial Germany.

From a comparative perspective, a final word should be said about the difficulties of using policy studies to understand historical institutional definitions. If policy-making behavior is always some mix of the enduring, then the constituent elements of states rooted in particular historical circumstances pose different constituent questions regarding the general social needs and preferences of a liberated people. The primary aim of comparative policy analysis, then, is to identify how the constituent aspects of stateness affect policy making. What sociologists, economists, planners, and others do with the residual knowledge (those abstract relations common to democracies) is a secondary question for the analyst of states. In the search for constituent truth, what we all do alike is marginal, if not trivial, in understanding states. What we do differently, given the diverse nature of democratic governance, is the prerequisite explanation.[11]

Such a change in social science methods and purposes should not be underestimated, and it goes well beyond the interdisciplinary quarrels that so easily distract us. First, states are probably best described in the classical sense of being limited by anarchy and tyranny, that is, by the destruction of their constituent elements by mob rule or by abuse of power. Allen (1950, xiv) is quite clear on this point. The abuse of *decret-loi* in France led to Vichy. The opposite condition, less frequently noted, may be in Britain, where government is virtually deprived of instruments to examine its own operation or, as Harden and Lewis (1986, 159) so aptly put it, a state governed by institutions "without rules." Isolation from the past can become an excuse to ignore serious threats to democratic governance. Second, democracies exist in a bewildering variety of forms. The vitality of democratic governance rests in its capacity to generate states under widely differing conditions rather than relying on a compelling ideology or an arbitrary definition of state objectives or, even more senseless, allowing hypothetical social disasters to define our analyses. Third, and perhaps most ominous, the crooked cord of discretion remains an oddly particularist, ascriptive necessity of modern government that binds us to our feudal and classical ancestors. The secular, universal values espoused by the democratic revolutions have not eliminated the need for discretion in performing the tasks of government (Freund 1928). Though we are surrounded by laws and institutions, discretion remains a timeless element of constituting a democratic state.

NOTES

1. Thus, it is not coincidental that Stubbs (1979) concerns political changes from the twelfth through the fourteenth centuries. The elusiveness of the British concept of the state is, in small degree, due to the political identification of an English state centuries before Scotland or Wales acquired modern political meaning.

2. In terms of the quest to revive interest in the state, the most damaging result is that the concepts of social harmony and political legitimacy are used synonymously. Regardless of the variety and causes of social disorder, any form of social breakdown is instinctively attributed to political deficiencies, while the inability of a state to conduct essential business for social or economic reasons is quite acceptable.

3. The common description of Parliament is as a deliberative rather than a law-making body. Parliament's function is to scrutinize legislation in much the same way a court scrutinizes evidence in cases. Of course, its historical roots are more closely linked to the development of British courts and their abuse through Star Chambers than with the design and implementation of laws. Maitland 1963, (343–87).

4. Until the Municipal Reform Act of 1835, local government was entirely subordinated to national ordaining powers exercised through the landed aristocracy. The great German jurist Gneist mistakenly saw similarities to the ancient origins of German law, and for this reason, he encouraged Hirst and the Englishman Redlich to write their history of English local government. In fact, royal ordaining powers were more or less transferred to justices of the peace in 1688, when these powers were subjected to parliamentary control through private bills. Until the Local Government Act of 1929, most local legislation took the form of individual private bills for each authority. See Keith-Lucas and Richards 1978.

5. Ordaining powers over land were transferred to the local government board in 1871, passed on to the Ministry of Health, and eventually lodged with the Ministry of Town and Country Planning at the close of the war. The historic case was Local Government Board vs. Hammersmith, wherein an appeal on natural law rights was rejected by the House of Lords as inapplicable to government departments.

6. The question first arose in 1932 when the Committee on Ministers' Powers investigated the powers being granted to unemployment and national insurance tribunals, as well as land-zoning appeals. On the continued confusion of ministerial powers, see Marshall 1984.

7. In the last of his editions of *Lectures on the Law and Public Opinion in England during the Nineteenth Century*, Dicey (1924) has a long appendix, arguing that there is no judge-made law in France, while British judges have wide latitude because of common law.

8. Though not explored here, the organization of police presented similar legal difficulties under the British constitution. See Marshall 1984, 128–49, on the confusions over the quasi-judicial nature of policing, unresolved until the 1964 Police Act made constables "servants" of chief constables following the recommendations of the Royal Commission on the Police (1962).

9. Sieghart (1950, 210–48) provides a succinct account of these powers. See also the account of Goodnow (1897), which provides similar comparative material on Germany and the United States.

10. Lest this statement be misunderstood, it does not mean that having such formulas necessarily produces better policies. For this reason, the terms *better*, *success*, and *efficiency* presume an external set of standards imposed on the policy process, not an identification of a thread of state power that runs through any decision in the same country.

11. Explanation is set apart, because the epistemological implications of my argument lead to a reconsideration of the nature of explanation and possibly to a revised concern with *Verstehen* in social science. See Dallmayr and McCarthy (1977) for a representative collection of alternative views, nearly all excluded from conventional social science. The meaning of constituent elements of states requires a better grasp of subjective meanings than is possible with present methods.

SOURCES

Allen, C. K. 1950. Introduction to M. A. Sieghart, *Government by Decree*. London: Stevens.

Annan, Noel. 1959. *The Curious Strength of Positivism in English Political Thought*. London: Oxford University Press.

Ashford, Douglas E. 1986. *The Emergence of the Welfare States*. Oxford: Basil Blackwell.

Auspitz, Katherine. 1982. *The Radical Bourgeoisie: The Ligue de l'Enseignement and the Origins of the Third Republic, 1866–1885*. Cambridge: Cambridge University Press.

Barker, Michael. 1975. *Gladstone and Radicalism, Liberalism: The Reconstruction of Liberal Policy in Britain, 1885–1894*. New York: Barnes and Noble.

Barnett, Corelli. 1986. *The Audit of War: The Illusion and Reality of Britain as a Great Nation*. London: Macmillan.

Beer, Samuel H. 1965. *British Politics in the Collectivist Age*. New York: Knopf.
Clarke, Peter. 1978. *Liberals and Social Democrats*. Cambridge: Cambridge University Press.
Collini, Stephan. 1979. *Liberalism and Socialism: L. T. Hobhouse and Political Argument in England, 1880–1914*. Cambrige: Cambridge University Press.
Collini, Stephan, Donald Winch, and John Burrow. 1973. *That Noble Science of Politics: A Study in Nineteenth-Century Intellectual History*. Cambridge. Cambridge University Press.
Committee on Ministers' Powers. 1932. *Report*. Cmd. 4060. London: HMSO.
Critchley, T. A. 1969. *The Conquest of Violence: Order and Liberty in Britain*. London: Constable.
Crozier, Michel. 1970. *La Société bloquée*. Paris: Grasset.
Dallmayr, Fred R., and Thomas A. McCarthy, eds. 1977. *Understanding and Social Inquiry*. Notre Dame: University of Notre Dame Press.
Dicey, A. V. 1924. Appendix to *Lectures on the Law and Public Opinion in England during the Nineteenth Century*. London: Macmillan.
Douglas, Mary. 1986. *How Institutions Think*. Syracuse: Syracuse University Press.
Dupuis, Georges, and Marie-José Guédon. 1986. *Institutions Administratives: Droit Administratif*. Paris: Colin (Collection U).
Elcock, H. J. 1969. *Administrative Justice*. London: Longmans.
Franks Committee. 1957. *Report of the Committee on Administrative Tribunals and Enquiries*. Cmnd. 218. London: HMSO.
Freund, Ernst. 1928. *Administrative Powers over Persons and Property: A Comparative Survey*. Chicago: University of Chicago Press.
Friedmann, W. 1951. *Law and Social Change in Contemporary Britain*. London: Stevens.
Geertz, Clifford. 1973. *The Interpretation of Cultures*. New York: Basic Books.
George, Henry. 1881. *The Land Question: Property and Land: The Condition of Labor*. New York: Doubleday.
Goffman, Erving. 1971. *Relations in Public*. New York: Harper.
Goodnow, Frank J. 1897. *Comparative Administrative Law*. New York: Putnam.
Harden, Ian, and Norman Lewis. 1986. *The Noble Lie: The British Constitution and the Rule of Law*. London: Hutchinson.
Harding, Alan. 1973. *A Social History of English Law*. Gloucester: Peter Smith.
Hawthorne, Geoffrey. 1976. *Enlightenment and Disparity: A History of Sociology*. Cambridge: Cambridge University Press.
Himmelfarb, Gertrude. 1987. *The New History and the Old: Critical Essays and Reappraisals*. Cambridge: Harvard University Press.
Hogwood, Brian W., and Michael Keating, eds. 1982. *Regional Government in England*. Oxford: Clarendon.
Jennings, W. I. 1959. *The Law and the Constitution*. 5th ed. London: University of London.
Jenkins, Roy. 1958. *Sir Charles Dilke: A Victorian Tragedy*. London: Collins.

Keith-Lucas, Brian, and Peter G. Richards. 1978. *A History of Local Government in the Twentieth Century.* London: Allen and Unwin.

Koblik, Steven, ed. 1975. *Sweden's Development from Poverty to Affluence, 1750–1970.* Minneapolis: University of Minnesota Press.

Kumar, Krishan. 1987. *Utopia and Anti-Utopia in Modern Times.* Oxford: Basil Blackwell.

Le Play, M. F. 1864. *La Réforme sociale en France.* Paris: Plon.

Logue, William. 1983. *From Philosophy to Sociology: The Evolution of French Liberalism, 1871–1914.* DeKalb: Northern Illinois University Press.

Maier, Charles S., ed. 1987. *Changing Boundaries of the Political.* Cambridge: Cambridge University Press.

Maitland, F. W. 1963 (1908). *The Constitutional History of England.* Cambridge: Cambridge University Press.

March, James G., and John P. Olsen. 1986. Popular Sovereignty and the Search for Appropriate Institutions. *Journal of Public Policy* 6:341–70.

Marshall, Geoffrey. 1984. *Constitutional Conventions: The Rules and Forms of Political Accountability.* Oxford: Clarendon.

Olson, Mancur. 1965. *The Logic of Collective Action.* Cambridge: Harvard University Press.

Pocock, J. G. A. 1971. *Politics, Language and Time: Essays on Political Thought and History.* New York: Atheneum.

———. 1975. *The Machiavellian Tradition: Florentine Political Thought and the Atlantic Republican Tradition.* Princeton: Princeton University Press.

Redlich, Josef, and Francis W. Hirst. 1903. *Local Government in England.* Vol. 1. London: Macmillan.

Renner, Karl. 1949 (1904). *The Institutions of Private Law and their Social Function.* London. Routledge and Kegan Paul.

Rosanvallon, Pierre. 1985. *Le moment Guizot.* Paris: Gallimard.

Rose, Richard, and Guy Peters. 1978. *Can Governments Go Bankrupt?* New York: Basic Books.

Royal Commission on the Police. 1962. *Report.* Cmnd. 1782. London: HMSO.

Royle, Edward. 1980. *Radicals, Secularists and Representatives: Popular Freethought in Britain, 1866–1915.* Manchester: Manchester University Press.

Sieghart, Marguerite A. 1950. *Government by Decree: A Comparative Study of the History of the Ordonnance in English and French Law.* London: Stevens.

———. 1974. Some Problems in the Analysis of Political Thought and Action. *Political Theory* 2:277–303.

Smith, Gordon. 1979. *Democracy in Germany: Parties and Politics in the German Republic.* New York: Holmes and Meier.

Sorlin, Pierre. 1967. *Waldeck Rousseau.* Paris: Colin.

Stubbs, William. 1979 (1874). *The Constitutional History of England.* Abridged ed. Chicago: University of Chicago Press.

Taylor, Charles Lewis. 1983. *Why Governments Grow: Measuring Public Sector Size.* Beverly Hills: Sage.

Thomas, George M., et al. 1987. *Institutional Structure: Constituting State, Society and the Individual*. Beverly Hills: Sage.

Thornton, A. P. 1965. *The Habit of Authority: Paternalism in British History*. London: Allen and Unwin.

Wade, E. C. S. 1939. Introduction and appendix to A. V. Dicey, *Introduction to the Study of the Law of the Constitution*. 9th ed. London: Macmillan.

Wiener, Martin J. 1981. *English Culture and the Decline of the Industrial Spirit, 1850–1980*. Cambridge: Cambridge University Press.

Williams, Philip. 1954. *Politics in Post-War France*. London: Longmans.

Wolfe, Wilard. 1975. *From Radicalism to Socialism: Men and Ideas in the Formation of Fabian Socialist Doctrines, 1881–1889*. New Haven: Yale University Press.

15

Conclusion: The Policy Connection: Subject or Object?

Douglas E. Ashford

THE POLICY CONNECTION does not mean simply that policy making is linked to institutions, states, and societies in diverse ways, but that policies may provide a method of analyzing these larger units of behavior in ways that political, economic, and social macrotheory does not permit. The argument implies that the various efforts to build new concepts of interest intermediation and policy process over the past decade or so are incomplete, while further efforts to subsume policy making under generalizations about larger units of political and social behavior can be misleading. Although the work of Beer, Lowi, and Schmitter alerted the political science community to the shortcomings of macrotheory, their ideas mainly concern structures whose behavior is explained by more general theories. Renewed interest in the state has achieved a certain notoriety (Evans 1985) but has yet to clarify many basic methodological issues about policy making (Ashford 1990a).

To argue, as this conclusion does, that none of these recent efforts adequately deals with the behavioral, philosophical, and epistemological complications of policy making may seem harsh. However one emerges from these ontological quandries, this volume and a good deal of additional new writing on policy analysis suggest that (1) few policy makers actually behave as macrolevel theories suggest; (2) policy makers are sensitive to the moral, ethical, and partisan limitations of problem solving; and (3) the formal rules of disaggregation from macro- to microgeneralizations deal only indirectly with the actual accumulation of policy-based experience. All this suggests that policy studies are no longer the prodigal son of political science but that policy studies might participate in its redefinition.

There are several interesting confrontations in policy studies that help explicate how a reversal of intellectual priorities might come about. Among the leading arguments, barely known outside the world of policy studies, is the intriguing suggestion by Dunn (1988, 727) that, within the universe of policy making—and by implication within the real world of political behavior in democratic governments—methodological questions of the second order are more important than those of the first order, that is, the selection of the appropriate technique to resolve a given public issue. As the policy book series from which this volume takes its inspiration suggests, policy makers are subject to unpredictable and diverse pressures in deciding how to respond to public problems. Put more simply, policy makers live in their particular worlds, worlds that macrotheory neither knows nor acknowledges. Weiss (1977) calls this the "enlightenment function" of policy analysis.

At the outset, it should be acknowledged that drawing generalizations from microlevel behavior is a much more ambitious enterprise than disaggregating from the macro- to the microlevel under hypothetical procedures. In some respects, this is what this book is about. Again, it is instructive to return to Dunn (1982), who takes issue with the individualist strategy of Kiser and Ostrom (1982) on the use of macrotheory. In what was then known as the structuralist controversy, Dunn argues that in the methodology of working from policy to process, the system or state is fundamentally different from simply expanding rational choice models to accommodate the institutional and procedural complexity that indeed characterizes the policy-making process. The presumption of positivist social science is that the hypothetical lawlike behavior at more general levels is consistent with lawlike behavior at lower levels of political, economic, and social decision making. For reasons outlined in chapter 1, the possibility that there may be two (or more) sets of aggregation rules at work is necessarily excluded. This is the essence of the challenge that policy studies presents to conventional political science. It is not only that the search for abstract regularities in political and social behavior may be too weak or too demanding a test, but that it may be no test at all.

Such an admission may not be as destructive as it appeared to the behaviorally inclined social sciences of the 1970s. As outlined in chapter 1, Eckstein, Verba, and Eulau are united in their view that lawlike behavior based on individual self-interest remains the foundation for a scientific social science. It is interesting that an even more flexible Lijphart (1975, 161) argues that there is "no unambiguous line" between comparative and statistical methods. For him, as for more hardline behavioralists, cases make "only one basic observation . . . in which the independent and dependent variables do not change." In other words, cases are easily subsumed within the rules of conventional social science.

The aim of this book, and many other new initatives in policy studies, is to show that cases are more than a crude form of statistical accumulation. Rather than reject cases as ways of dealing with background or uncontrollable situations (ibid., 163), we must make the richness and diversity of cases the subject rather than the object of analysis. There were signs in 1975 that this possibility was understood. Lijphart (ibid., 170) notes how France was too low on Dahl's polyarchy scale to be included in the range of countries he chose to study. Methodological exclusion was being practiced within a social science claiming methodological neutrality.

The conventional social science answer to these objections might well be that these objections are all manageable within the realm of an individualist social science. The contradictions raised by case studies could be no more than the failure to include a large enough universe or the failure to measure accurately. Leaving aside the way in which the claim to a statistically determined universe betrays the aims of social inquiry (anything not hypothetically universal is, by implication, more reliable), the problem remains that how policy makers (and possibly clients, citizens, etc.) perceive the policy process differs substantially within countries.

While there are reasons to question the major methodological study of Przeworski and Teune (1970), many of which the two authors now share, the levels argument was never clearly specified. Those committed to behavioral methods never wanted to see the question specified. Because they had no clear way to deal with the problem, they insisted that laws of human behavior transcend political action. A major misunderstanding followed. The critics of Easton, Almond, and Dahl never claimed that there might not be such lawlike principles but only that there remained enormous contradictions between highly generalized rules of political behavior and what policy makers do.

For this reason, as many of the essays in this volume suggest, policy studies are a kind of Pandora's box for the behavioralists. As suggested in chapter 1, so long as policy-related studies can be kept within the rules of normal social science, they are a welcome source of support and even a legitimation of the prevailing paradigm. There is a world of difference between Lindblom's "muddling through" (1959) and the unstructured situations that Cohen, March, and Olsen (1972) label the garbage can model. The first suggests that there may be no reason to look for microlevel generalizations—or as Lindblom says (1963, 118), there are virtues in "getting along without theory when necessary." All this is of course deeply rooted in the assumptions of pluralist political science, whose voting models assume rationality and in which governments exercise no discretion and have no strategic priorities. To give credit where credit is due, many of the same persons went on to discover that the implementation process was extremely intricate and unreliable (Pressman and Wildavsky 1973), but the remedies were essentially to restore free-market conditions. It is at about the same time that Caiden and Wildavsky (1974, 309) suggest the virtues of "thinking small."

Whether incrementialism is an accurate description of policy making, and there are good reasons to think that under conditions of great uncertainty it not only is but should be, the important point is that this formulation of policy making was imagined in hypothetical terms consistent with pluralist political models. It is worth recalling that, at roughly the same time the microeconomists were beginning to account for economic irrationalities in producing public goods and representing public interests (Olson 1964), the macrosociologists were mounting a formidable attack on social rationality by arguing that sudden, dramatic changes were indeed the important historical turning points (Tilly 1984). In the language of critical theory, conventional social science still portrayed policy making in a way that ceded "all conversations and symbolic rights to an allegedly technocratic minority," which in turn reinforced "passive acquiescence to a status quo" (Aggar 1985, 12, 14). The irony or, if one wishes, the contradiction of pluralist policy-making ideas is that they inadvertently defend an elitist process and minimal government. In a fundamental sense that would have been perfectly clear in the eighteenth and nineteenth centuries and that was recently revived by the state-society group (Evans 1985), the pluralists do not address the possible autonomy of the state, the meaning of sovereignty or national identity, or the nature of the discretionary and coercive powers of officials.

There were perhaps two important steps in rediscovering the subjectivity of policy making. Two vitally important discoveries were made: (1) the observational rules of macrolevel generalizations are not valid at the microlevel, and (2) the rules of statistical aggregation often used to organize such objective properties have little or no meaning to microlevel actors. In both an objective (hypothetical) and subjective (actor) sense, political science has failed to develop a persuasive ontology of policy making. The first shift is clearly visible in Lowi's early efforts to construct a policy-making matrix that would categorize policies as various forms of political conflict (1964). Over the years, this search has become more outspoken, until it finally emerges in Lowi's (1972) claim that "policy determines politics." If policies are, in some sense, independent rather than dependent variables, then the entire pluralist universe has been stood on its head. At the very least, the possibility arises that macrolevel behavior is superimposed on microlevel behavior within government and that many other activities linked to government are not objective according to the rules of the macrolevel explanation. This is not to say, as March and Olsen (1989) and Simon (1973) make clear, that organizational and group behavior is not, in some sense, rational, but only that there are many forms of rationality.

In many respects, Lowi's attack remains behavioral; that is, at the microlevel, rules of behavior are still potentially generalizable within categories that presumably operate across cultures, time, and settings. The implication is that policy-making behavior has some intrinsic features that approximate the abstract regularities of objective social science (Kjellberg 1977). Though never systematized, an important addition to this line of attack is the elaboration of the concept of policy community (Heclo 1974; Jordan and Richardson 1983). The term *community* itself, of course, suggests internal norms and values, frameworks of communication, and even shared notions of external realities among groups of policy makers. Heclo's and Wildavsky's (1979) village metaphor in their study of the British Treasury is noteworthy not only because it evokes anthropological concepts, which were later to virtually overtake all of Wildavsky's thinking, but because it also asserts, much as interpretative and critical theory does, that, within a large government process, there may be groups whose rules, understandings, and goals radically diverge from both professed and hypothetical rules and norms.

The second and more lethal attack arose with the revival of the policy style argument (Richardson 1982). The concept of policy style is of course consistent with much that Lowi, Heclo, and Wildavsky argue, but it further defines the application of policy style and eventually differentiates policy making from other forms of political behavior. Richardson and others are unmistakably making a cultural argument that implies that the external meanings or the aggregation of outcomes and policy objectives are of secondary importance to policy makers. In this sense, the cultural argument is a more radical attack on conventional social science than the Lowi case. It was perhaps first dramatized in an intense and, on the whole, unproductive argument between Wilensky and Castles over the place of ideology in explaining Scandinavian social policy (Castles 1978; Wilensky 1975). There is now of course a good deal of historical information suggesting that, within the intimate world of Swedish policy making, a small circle of policy makers often anticipated policy conflicts and fashioned policies to circumvent potential problems.

The cultural argument goes further in the sense that it suggests that behavior within agencies, networks, and communities of policy makers is distinguishably different from macrolevel, systemic behavior described by the pluralists or by mediating organizations and corporatism (Ott 1989). Once policy making is subjectively defined, the empirical link between macro- and microlevel analysis is broken. The disjunction means that the compositional rules (Ashford 1986), historical explanations, or contextual knowledge discussed in this volume become crucially important. Policy analysts compare the properties of policy outputs or outcomes not only in terms of macrolevel redistributive, resource, or popular meanings but also in terms of self-defined subgroups found throughout the system, the different capabilities these groups acquire in the policy process, and how these groups define their own behavior in relation to more general norms and values of the system. In other words, policy making is neither the elitist preoccupation implied by pluralists nor the threat to democratic governance suggested by corporatists but should be studied in terms of the professed framework of the action of policy makers themselves. The possibility then arises that policy studies might contradict received knowledge about political systems. The United States, for example, may not be simply an incrementalist backwash among more purposeful democracies, but a system within which subgroups, such as the Clean Air Coalition (Sabatier 1988), can have enormous impact. Like Derthick's (1975) "uncontrollable spending" for social assistance in the early 1970s, local spending for clean air multiplied twenty times over a decade. In brief, the array of policy communities, policy networks, and organizational interdependencies revealed in policy studies generate hypotheses about microlevel behavior rather than confirming or denying macrolevel hypotheses.

The Institutional Foundations of Policy Making

Tracing the intellectual saga of the shift from conventional to interpretive social sciences is, in many respects, the story of how the field of policy studies generated its own intellectual foundations, initially by criticizing the pluralist-liberal paradigm and later by overturning it. The attack is similar to, but much more significant than, the discovery that Marxist macrosocial laws do not work (Skocpol 1980). If policy making in the political arena has never been a pluralist paradise, then one needs a better theory of democratic governance. To be sure, there are important implications for research strategies and research methodologies, but the much larger challenge is the integration of the bewildering variety of microlevel behavior in alternative explanatory designs. If policy studies, in particular, comparative policy studies, have succeeded in demolishing the abstract macrotheories that were the core of the behaviorist ontology, what might take its place? The aim of this book, and of much related writing in policy analysis, is to show that there are no single solutions to this question. Hypothetical universality and firm distinctions between facts and values make the lawlike quest possible. To suggest that a new synthesis or integration of political knowledge based on policy making must adopt the same philosophical and epistemological rules is simply to fall back on received knowledge (Ashford 1990a).

Microtheory permits finer differentiation of political institutions and enriches policy comparisons. The problem of understanding institutionalized behavior has gained new popularity. Simon (1973, 186) notes that "ill-structured" problems are more common in social activities than in simple, goal-directed agencies. Indeed, it is probably a misreading of Weber to consider his concept of rational legal authority a macrotheory of institutional and bureaucratic behavior. He never claimed that ideal types or categorical concepts might resolve the problem of intersubjective meanings. At best, intersubjective reliability can be established within configurational or situational contexts, but the ideal types were never wholly objective variables, nor did behavior within a given context mean that subjective understandings (*Verstehen*) no longer qualified political meaning (Portis 1986, 76–82; Mommsen 1979; Dallmayr and McCarthy 1977). Unlike abstract theories of social and political action, institutionalized activity cannot be imagined without some prior understanding or trust concerning the nature of the activity itself. Within the framework of this book, and for policy making generally, institutions provide the contextual or situational foundations for collective action.

Like Weber, Dunn recognizes that first-order policy-making problems are relatively easy to solve by selecting the appropriate technique or instrument of public policy. But institutional contexts are composed by complex, possibly unique, events, many of which have been raised in this study. The historical formulation of trust and the accumulation of ideas, practices, and operating codes give internal coherence to institutions. An understanding of these experiences is likely to revive an interest in many traditional concerns of political science. Both the Kumar and Ashford essays in this volume consider legal structure and legal foundations in order to raise these issues in the Victorian setting. The prolonged Whig debate over the constitution, like the similar debate over Benthamite collectivism (Hart 1965), questioned the foundations of the British constitution in part because of profound political differences within British government in mid-Victorian England. McAuslan and McEldowney (1985, 1–38) provide a persuasive argument that the foundations of political legitimacy and the grounds for political trust were never entirely clear within the British constitutional tradition. One might look upon the elite civil service and the long adherence to governance by gifted amateurs as first-order solutions to problems of government that were defined and selected because of the intractable second-order problems. Thus, we find an internal, rather than an external, explanation for the British government being unable to provide solutions to pressing problems.

Well before the new institutionalism revived such questions, British policy makers and leaders were preoccupied with the rigidities and inefficiencies of British government (Ashford 1981; Williams 1988; Hall 1986). But the failure of British policy making, if such it was, was surely not the inability to acquire and to apply new instrumental forms of policy making. The scientific and technical aspects of British government changed with more sophisticated economic models, cost-benefit techniques, high-powered think tanks, and elaborate scientific and research advisory boards. Explanations of British failure that are limited to instrumental notions of policy making suggest a kind of willful, almost self-destructive, behavior (Barnett 1987) that conflicts with internal evidence. Nor, to return to the conventional wisdom concerning British society, do its deferential social habits seem to inhibit innovation and change. In specifying the difficulty of fundamental restructuring of British institutions, Nairn's (1988) metaphor of the enchanted glass is revealing. There are simply too many examples of unyielding and unimaginative governance over the past century or more to think that British decline is owed primarily to instrumental or policy-making deficiencies.

The historical invariability of British institutions make it a particularly instructive illustration of failure to develop new forms of trust and understanding within, rather than about, political institutions. The contextual argument is strengthened because, unlike most continental powers during the twentieth century, British government was never severely threatened by external forces or violent political movements. As argued in this book, a macrotheory of British failure is unlikely to discover the limitations of institutionalized power in Britain, because it cannot grasp the subjective meanings on which institutions rest. The empirical evidence of government failure can be accumulated only from microlevel studies of how officials, politicians, and leaders actually decide issues. It is not simply philosophical limitations that make behavioral methods less useful in such situations but the exclusion of the subjective knowledge that makes institutionalized behavior possible. The argument that government is largely about unstructured problems and that the essense of policy making is a problem of the second order (Dunn et al. 1986; Dryzek 1983; Linder and Peters 1985) points toward problems of reality testing, intersubjective learning, and collective problem solving that presuppose some form of contextual knowledge.

As described by Dunn (1988, 728–29), methods of a second type are no less empirical than hypothetical social science. In the hand of some, most notably Lasswell (Torgerson 1985), behavior of the second type may even acquire therapeutic meaning, but this is not necessarily the main goal of more explicit concern with subjective aspects of policy making. Dunn outlines four tasks: (1) identifying the elements of the decisions, (2) exploring preferred instruments related to the goal, (3) estimating the boundary or limiting conditions of expected change, and (4) evaluating the internal linkages of the decision. Linder presents the decision process as either a deliberative-procedural process that may involve ethical discourse (Macrae 1976), considerations of institutional design (Anderson 1979), or the discussion of individual meanings attached to the decision (Fischer 1980). In a sense, decision makers cannot avoid simultaneous reviews of the institutional context as they seek solutions to public problems. Institutional experimentation is thereby made a part of policy making rather than an instrument of policy making. A second, and possibly more demanding process, places a premium on prior consensus as a condition of finding the best solutions (Dryzek 1983; Dunn et al. 1986; Torgerson 1985, 1986).

Though not necessarily as radical as the solutions to intersubjective knowledge offered by critical theory, recognition of the inseparability of policy making and its institutional context is a radical departure from the rational choice, behavioral techniques for observing the policy process. First, the subjective dimensions of policy making no longer totally engage decision makers. There is less emphasis on the adequacy, efficiency, or popularity of outcomes as the main tests of effective policy making. Of course, it has always been the case that decision makers must satisfy themselves and their superiors that they are engaged in the best course of action. Both the deliberative and consensual processes of Linder, Dunn, and others stress the contextual and cognitive effects on the institutions themselves. There is, for example, an immense difference between an analysis of the effects of New Deal social policies based on hypothetical constructs rooted in conventional macrosociological theory, such as that done by Weir, Orloff, and Skocpol (1986), and the perception of the relation of social assistance to social security institutions as seen by New Deal policy makers (Balogh 1988; Coll 1988). American policy makers never lacked social convictions, but they saw the rapid growth of social assistance in the late 1930s as a threat to building more lasting and more elaborate social institutions. Outcomes of the second order take their meaning from the institutional context itself rather than from imputed goals, abstract values, or external conditions.

The second, and more formidable, implication of second-order policy-making questions concern institutional designs and institutional choices. Some of these implications are raised by Linder and Peters (1988) and Sabatier (1988). Unlike the more abstract, hypothetical evaluations of public policy, these options have institutional consequences, and in some cases, such consequences are of greater importance than the policy itself. Put differently, policy makers may have a choice of institutional contexts and are, to this extent, constantly involved in institutional experimentation and innovation. Again, the New Deal offers interesting illustrations from U.S. social policy. By most objective standards, the United States was unable to build a system of medical insurance until the 1960s. The objective truth may blind policy analysts to the importance that the Social Security Administration attaches to medical insurance, its efforts to lay the foundations for such insurance by developing the Public Health Service and enlarging the scope of disability insurance, the importance to the Social Security Administration of not becoming a social assistance agency in order to keep open the option of medical insurance (Stone 1984; Scotch 1984). The proliferation of federally provided health services for the handicapped, the disabled, the aged, and the mentally handicapped is an elaborate institutional alternative to the objective solution of simply nationalizing medicine. However persuasive more radical solutions might be in hypothetical terms, medical insurance threatens a partially institutionalized social security system. Even in welfare states, which by external standards have more advanced welfare benefits, medical insurance produces stalemate (Safran 1967; Heidenheimer and Erlander 1980).

Third, contextual analysis of public policy places a high priority on internal government networks, improved official communication, and teamwork. These concerns put the traditional interests of public administration in a new light and, of course, date from the major comparative administration studies of recent years (Armstrong 1977; Dyson 1980) as well as pioneering studies of national administrative systems (Suleiman

1974; Hanf and Scharpf 1978). All these studies show how administrative behavior interlocks with institutional and historical constraints on policy making. Much of this work departs from received knowledge—usually of Weberian origin, even if based on misinterpretations of Weber's thoughts on bureaucracy (Portis 1986; Mommsen 1979). Weber probably never believed that a thoroughly scientific bureaucracy was possible, though he saw controlling Germany's predemocratic bureaucracy as a critical element in building a democratic Germany. Deprived of its context, Weber's argument provides grounds for asserting an unrealistic bureaucratic political neutrality and operational objectivity. This simplified account of bureaucratic behavior reinforces the behavioral model of government but also helps divorce the study of administrative behavior from policy analysis. Explanations of a second type are, in part, an effort to underscore the interdependence of the organizational context and the substance of policy making.

Fourth, policy making of a second type enhances our ability to assess institutional change and institutional capabilities. The heavily instrumental perspective on policy making found in behavioral models excludes institutional variables of this kind, partly because they do not conform to the distinction conventional social science makes between facts and values. From being unable to make interesting statements about institutions, it was only a short step to the Eastonian conclusion of banishing the state from social science. Curiosity dimmed about why institutions are neither uniformly adaptable to similar policy goals nor automatically able to produce the desired policy outcome. The hypothetical model and its reliance on external measures of change effectively ignore these complications. Thus, while the state-society revival is a welcome return to institutional questions, it has not yet produced the institutionally grounded variables needed to weigh state explanations against the more common macrosocial explanations of social and political change. The risk is to relapse into macrotheoretical assertions based on very limited evidence or, worse perhaps, to assume that contextual problems can be analyzed in the same way that we measure government performance and outcomes (Ashford 1990a). Having no such evaluation at hand makes it easy, for example, to consider the United States a "belated welfare state" in comparison to a highly generalized concept of a "European welfare state" (Weir, Orloff, and Skocpol 1986). Contextual policy analysis does not necessarily defend institutional rigidities or traditions, but it does imply that the policy analyst, like the policy maker, needs to know the guidelines, assumptions, and past experience of institutions.

Policies as Institutional Variables

The general conclusion of this book is that an input-output model of politics, perhaps the most important analytical innovation of the behavioral revolution in political science, discounts policy making because it lacks the concepts and methodology needed to understand it. As we have seen, the other social science disciplines were, in their various ways, abandoning this form of thinking at roughly the same time it acquired general acceptance within political science. The criticisms came from many quarters. Referring to the risks of turning politics into a metaphoric marketplace, Macpherson called *equilibrium* "a nice tune for whistling in the dark" (1985). Arrow's (1984) paradox shows how, under majority rule, almost any ordering of preferences is possible. The ordering of demand often bears little resemblance to the ordering of public goods and services. One of the most striking of studies along these lines was, perhaps not too surprisingly, done in Germany, the democracy with strongly institutionalized policy making in nearly every area of public endeavor. Anticipating the new institutionalism, Scharpf and his collaborators found that partisan opinions were rarely associated in any clear pattern with policy options. The result was depoliticized decision making (Hanf and Scharpf 1978, 104–06). Much the same conclusion is reached by von Beyme and Schmidt (1985), who consider the political costs of dismantling institutional frameworks so high that, at least in the German case, no party can accept the immense political risks.

As many of the early studies of implementation and intergovernmental networks cited in this book indicate, the grounds for assessing outcome, outputs, and performance as useful institutional indicators were never strong. Indeed, if scholars of the 1960s had taken Schattschneider (Adamany 1972), Kaufman, and the Chicago policy analysts of the late 1930s seriously, they would have spared us a long and tiresome detour into barren territory. As Kristensen (1984) writes, an unexpected effect of the collapse of the demand model was to revive the idea that politics matter. Much the same evolution of ideas can be seen by tracing the study of government performance. Many of the statistical studies of variation in outcomes among sectors, through time, and in intergovernmental networks uncovered the problem but did little to explain how or why such variation occurs. The more difficult question, now posed in many comparative policy analyses, is why governments pursue apparently similar goals in so many different ways. Contextual analysis offers two possible answers, both of which are highlighted in comparative policy research.

The first is, of course, that pursuing a goal in objective terms may not be the same as pursuing the same goal in subjective terms (Ashford 1982; Dryzek and Leonard 1988; Loriaux 1989). A variety of evidence suggests that this is true. At one extreme, it is easy to produce policy makers who frankly admit that governments have institutionally imbedded agendas. As Abel-Smith said, while discussing British difficulties in coming to grips with the deficiencies of the Beveridge plan, public housing "always had center stage." His observation is not simply an implied criticism of the Conservative reversal of Labour party priorities but an acknowledgment that housing decisions took place in an institutional setting that enabled housing to more easily influence government. Much the same occurs in Germany, where the confluence of interests among *Autobahn* enthusiasts (touring clubs, local governments, safety experts), the steel and auto industries, and metalworkers easily overcomes ecological and environmental concerns. Successful policies legitimate institutions in ways that popularity and partisan advantage cannot.

At the other extreme are the numerous studies, some historical and some contemporary, of how governments develop institutional differentiations that gradually became policy-making realities. Though consistent with policy network and policy community studies, the aim is to extend behavioral results to institutional and organizational settings. For example, both contemporary and historical policy-making studies reveal how the British Ministry of Education erected formidable barriers to worker education, adult education, and continuing education (Ashford 1989). The reasons for this are many: the Ministry of Health, created in 1918, was seen as the major threat to the then Board of Education, as is clearly visible in Chamberlain's fight with the Ministry of Education over local government reform in the 1920s (Ashford 1982); the Ministry of Health reacted sharply to Butler's push for stronger educational laws at the end of the war and took steps in cabinet meetings to see that the new educational legislation would not affect health (Ashford 1986); quarrels erupted again in the Callaghan government of the 1970s between Shore and Williams, as Shore tried to reverse Tory local government reforms at some risk to education. There is both a historical persistence and an institutional consistency that make the institutional limits of British policy making remarkably clear. In sum, the educational outputs of British policy making make little sense without explaining why the Ministry of Education put such a high value on its own autonomy. The failures of British education are not understood by using external measures of social needs and interests, nor are they adequately explained by instrumental, rational shortcomings. There were, in the interpretive sense, multiple causes, among which institutional traditions of the ministry were most important.

From this digression, three conclusions may be made about the future of policy studies. First, policy-making results do not reliably differentiate institutions. There is an odd symmetry in the way that both pluralist indetermination and Marxist overdetermination of policy making diminish its importance. In their respective ways, each assumes the policy process to be totally flexible and perfectly adaptable. Second, the renewed interest in leadership, policy networks, and the socialization of decision makers (Rockman 1984; Campbell 1986) may restore the importance of leadership in decision-making processes, although how such individual interventions accumulate as institutions change is not entirely clear. Knowledge about individual decision makers does not easily reveal the operational codes of policy making nor the interlocking relationship within government that leaders rely upon. Third, it becomes increasingly clear that policy makers internalize the rules and procedures of their respective governments, but social science lacks concepts to link these behavioral findings to the content of public policies. This is of course a very large order, but it is also the crucial step between treating policies as an incoherent substrata of institutionalized behavior and treating them as manifestations of real differences among institutions.

To bring the concern of this book full circle, the inability of social science to come to grips with values and perception at high levels of decision making by prevailing standards of inquiry is hardly new. Anthropologists have had the same problem for years, and historians would not think of putting pen to paper without considering the ambiguities of intentions and motives. As Douglas (1986, 9) puts it, democratic theory has always acknowledged the common will, but the theory of "individual rational choice finds nothing but difficulties in the notion of collective behavior." In more specific terms, she argues that social science cannot assume with economics that equilibrium is natural (ibid., 48), meaning that it should have origins in physical, supernatural, or social arrangements. The full claim emerges later when she writes that "certainty about other persons' strategies " (55) is impossible without trust: in institutional if not social situations, actors need to know "that the institution's formal structure corresponds to formal structures in non-human realms." Douglas is not simply repeating Weberian formulas about rational legal authority, which Weber himself began to doubt after World War I, but asserting in anthropological language that institutions have proved points of leverage or elements of predictability, whose absence would make institutionalized behavior and, by implication, nearly all of modern civilization unworkable. Whether one prefers the utopian progress promised by Marxists or the sluggish progress anticipated by pluralists, they both make enormous institutional assumptions.

Like the institutionalists of the eighteenth and nineteenth centuries, Douglas is making a larger claim than can be provided by the individual reductionism of behavioral studies of implicit codes, learned behavior, and mutual understanding. In an interpretive sense, she is claiming that the existence of society cannot be easily differentiated from participation in society. The properties of the participants or the material evidence about the society do not fully explain trust, discretion, or authority. Using the same line of reasoning, this book elaborates three applications of policy studies to enable us to observe and compare the interlocking equality of governing institutions. In the first part, historical context is considered. Nearly all history is, in fact, faced with contextual issues. To be sure, the activity described in Kumar's essay on Victorian social reform, the emergent Social Democratic labor market hegemony policy in Rothstein's Sweden, or Blomkvist's stateless society can be reduced to behavioral terms. But in each of these cases, and in many other studies of the historical development of public policies, the contextual linkage among behaviors is readily visible.

The consequences of comparative policy studies are far-reaching. The longer the time span, the more momentous the implications. If we take, for example, MacFarlane's (1978) reconstruction of the origins of capitalism, an entire body of historical research and, by implication, common assumptions about the conditions and direction of modern capitalism are put in doubt. His study generates controversy because it relocates the conjunction of motive and action resulting in capitalist behavior in the seventeenth century. The sharp reactions against his interpretation of history are not so much about macroeconomic theories as about the reassessment of capitalist motives and attitudes that stress subjective meanings (MacFarlane 1987, 190–227). A very similar controversy arises over Clark's (1985) study of Britain's ancien regime. To the intense arguments over the meaning of Benthamite collectivism (Hart 1965) are added important questions about the meaning of partisan differences in Victorian England. By relocating British party history, the Victorian foundation of partisan differences and party growth are put in doubt. If, as Innes (1987, 169) states, "high political maneuvers" of the seventeenth century helped formulate recent political differences, then the interpretation of choices and preferences since then must be recalculated.

History provides a rich source of new interpretations of the present, which are only partially subsumed by macrosociological history (Skillen 1985; Atkinson and Coleman 1989). Many consequences of such major reinterpretations of history are raised in a study edited by Maier (1987)—but with one or two exceptions, how to proceed is not well specified. As Kousser (1982) points out, rewriting the present in terms of past policies is not a task that historians are likely to perform. As many of the historically rooted policy studies cited in this volume indicate, one way to test abstract conclusions is to see how actors in fact imagined their environment, modeled their choices, and organized their information. Major historical reinterpretations imply paradigmatic change in the study of policy making and policy processes. They raise fundamental questions about the origins and meaning of dominant ideologies, the foundations of partisan politics, and the origins of democratic government. It is no exaggeration to suggest that each major historical exercise implies a subsequent rewriting of the meaning of policy making. Though his recommendations were translated primarily into social history, Braudel's observation that "historical research must force open the gates of the present" (quoted in Paci 1987, 179) presses home the point. For this reason, policy analysts ignore historical interpretation at their peril.

The second part of the book moves on to alternative frameworks of contextual evaluation. In various guises, part 2 is basically what Anderson (1979) calls a critique of instrumental rationality. As he argues, to systematically introduce normative concerns into policy analysis is not necessarily to make policy making a totally normative activity. For Anderson, the "criteria of choice is the first element in any theory of policy evaluation" (ibid., 712). Similarly, the argument in this book is that the substitution of social science for normative analysis places severe limits on policy studies and necessarily confines policy comparisons to a particular form of reasoning. In structuralist terms, Boudon's (1971, 281) argument is that we need to know the "dialectic of interdependence." Once again there is an implicit attack on conventional social science. Aggregate effects may or may not constitute change in human relationships. This becomes a crucial question for policy studies, first, because highly generalized evidence may not capture momentous changes in societal, political, or economic relationships, and second, because aggregate change cannot identify unintended or unanticipated results.

There are numerous ways interpretive policy analysis might overcome these limits. Wittrock and Wagner draw on Gidden's notion of agency and the variety of institutional forms found in applying knowledge to public problems. Skillen gives an interpretation of welfare state norms. Furniss reflects on the function of the state, not in the teleological sense now widely rejected, but in reference to how institutions "systematically direct individual memory and channel our perceptions into forms compatible with the relations they authorize" (Douglas 1986, 92). Farr argues that situational concepts better capture action-oriented behavior in institutional settings. None of these contributions requires a paradigmatic reformulation of policy making, as frequently happens in the case of historical contextual studies, but each provides ways of breaking through the behavioral constraints on generalizations about collective behavior.

In organizing our knowledge and our behavior, contextual concepts of the second order concretely illustrate the various ideas that governments use to define, regulate, and monitor collective behavior. Institutional and organizational behavior is linked to norms in very different ways across countries and are critically important in defining, implementing, and evaluating policies. The idea of limited liability has a similar meaning across countries in an abstract legal and economic sense but not in relation to industrial structures, credit markets, tax policies, and government regulatory objectives. For example all the democracies guarantee freedom of association, but the groundings for this freedom in constitutional and judicial practices and its integration into policy making very widely. If one traces the organizational and political implications of major activities within specific policies, as Immergut (1986) does for redundancy benefits in three countries, it is clear that meaning permeates public policy.

The third part of the book assesses the place of contextual argument in relation to several traditional interests of political science. Rockman reviews the literature on political parties and concludes that the incidence between policy making and partisan behavior varies widely across countries and that much policy making takes place outside the sphere of partisan politics. This is certainly a major concession from Saint-Simon's claim (Portis 1986, 122) that the word *government* should be banished from the social science vocabulary. The interface between partisan politics and policy making is clearly a contextual problem. Since Weber, Ostrogorski, and Michels, bureaucracy has always figured among the major contextual issues of politics. It is no discredit to Peters's contribution to suggest that we have yet to successfully relate the many forms, practices, and principles of bureaucratic behavior in ways needed to make well-grounded, cross-national institutional comparisons. Constitutional theory may be promising ground, insofar as the question of the use and abuse of discretionary powers is defined within the constitutional framework of each country and seldom takes the same form in policy making and in the organization of governments (Ashford 1990b).

For reasons explored in chapter 1, contextual arguments may be particularly suitable to political science, and possibly of less pressing need in the other social sciences, because policy making is an action-based, empowering activity. Lacking the formal, abstract theories of economies and sociology, political science adapts other macrotheories to politics, even though political action is never totally distinguishable from policy making. The uniqueness of political science is not because it deals with issues of paradigmatic importance while reformulating ideas imbedded at the institutional level and trying to arrive at an instrumental understanding of human behavior in the conventional sense of social science. Its uniqueness lies in the fact that it has not developed constructs permitting an orderly transition between three questions of paradigm, concept, and instrumentation. As argued in chapter 1, this was partly due to the exclusion of those aspects of political action, in particular normative, legal, and administrative questions, that raise questions of contextual meanings and that require specification of settings, situations, and configurations.

For this reason, the conclusion of this book is that policy studies must revive concern with history, context, and meaning. This is not to say that formal and instrumental reasoning about policy choices is irrelevant or even misleading but only that such a rigid framework provides only a partial understanding of political action. Because of the subjective dimension of political action and because of the ambiguities of outcomes, performance, and achievements, politics has more acute need of interpretive and critical thinking than the other social sciences. Democracy was built on the ideas of authority, trust, and civic value. Only by reintroducing these values into alternative paradigms, the evaluation of concepts and the comparison of rational choices in the real world can a fully developed discipline emerge.

SOURCES

Adamany, David. 1972. The Political Science of E. E. Schattschneider. *American Policial Science Review* 56:1321–35.

Aggar, Charles. 1985. The Logic of De-Industrialization: An Essay in Advanced Capitalism. In J. Forester, ed., *Critical Theory and Public Life*. Cambridge: MIT Press.

Anderson, Charles W. 1979. The Place of Principles in Policy Analysis. *American Political Science Review* 73:711–23.

Armstrong, J. A. 1977. *The European Administrative Elite.* Princeton: Princeton University Press.

Arrow, Kenneth. 1984. *Individual Choice Under Uncertainty.* Cambridge: Harvard University Press.

Ashford, Douglas E. 1981. *Policy and Politics in Britain: The Limits of Consensus.* Philadelphia: Temple University Press.

———. 1982. Policymaking in France: Illusion and Reality Reconsidered. *Comparative Politics* 14:227–50.

———. 1986. Structural Analysis and Institutional Change: The Case of the Welfare State. *Polity* 19:97–122.

———. 1989. Death of a Great Survivor: The Manpower Services Commission in the United Kingdom. *Governance* 2:365–83.

———. 1990a. Bringing the Welfare State Back In. *Comparative Politics* 23: 351–75.

———. 1990b. *Discretionary Politics: Intergovernmental Social Transfers in Eight Countries.* Greenwich: JAI.

Atkinson, Michael M., and William D. Coleman. 1989. Strong States and Weak States: Sectoral Policy Networks in Advanced Capitalist Economies. *British Journal of Political Science* 19:47–67.

Balogh, Brian. 1988. Securing Support: The Emergence of the Social Security Broad as a Political Actor, 1935–1939. In D. T. Critchlow and E. W. Hawley, eds., *Federal Social Policy.* University Park: Pennsylvania State University Press.

Barnett, Corelli. 1987. *The Pride and the Fall: The Dream and Illusion of Britain as a Great Nation.* New York: Free Press.

Boudon, Raymond. 1971. *The Uses of Structuralism.* Trans. Michelina Vaughan. London: Heinemann.

Caiden, Naomi, and Aaron Wildavsky. 1974. *Planning and Budgeting in Poor Countries.* New York: Wiley.

Campbell, Colin. 1986. *Managing the Presidency: Carter, Reagan and the Search for Executive Harmony.* Pittsburgh: University of Pittsburgh Press.

Castles, Francis G. 1978. *The Social Democratic Image of Society.* London: Routledge and Kegan Paul.

Clark, J. C. D. 1985. *English Society 1688–1832: Ideology, Social Structure, and Political Practice during the Ancien Regime.* Cambridge: Cambridge University Press.

Cohen, M. D., J. G. March, and J. P. Olsen. 1972. A Garbage Can Model of Organizational Choice. *Administrative Science Quarterly* 17:1–25.

Coll, Blanche D. 1988. Public Assistance: Reviving the Original Comprehensive Concept of Social Security. In G. D. Nash, N. H. Pugach, and R. F. Tomasson, eds., *Social Security: The First Half-Century.* Albuquerque: University of New Mexico Press.

Dallmayr, Fred R., and Thomas A. McCarthy, eds. 1977. *Understanding and Social Inquiry.* Notre Dame: University of Notre Dame Press.

Derthick, Martha. 1975. *Uncontrollable Spending.* Washington, D.C.: Brookings.

Douglas, Mary. 1986. *Do Institutions Think?* Syracuse: Syracuse University Press.

Dryzek, J. 1983. Don't Toss Coins into Garbage Cans: A Prologue to Policy Design. *Journal of Public Policy* 3:345–67.

Dryzek, John S., and Stephen N. Leonard. 1988. History and Discipline in Political Science. *American Political Science Review* 82:1246–59.

Dunn, William N. 1982. The Theory of Exceptional Clinicians. Unpublished.

———. 1988. Methods of the Second Type: Coping with the Wilderness of Conventional Policy. *Policy Studies Review* 7:720–34.

Dunn, William N., A. G. Cahill, M. J. Dukes, and A. Ginsberg. 1986. The Policy Grid: A Cognitive Methodology for Assessing Change Dynamics. In W. N. Dunn, ed., *Policy Analysis: Perspectives, Concepts and Methods*. Greenwich: JAI.

Dyson, Kenneth. 1980. *The State Tradition in Western Europe*. Oxford: Oxford University Press.

Evans, Peter B., ed. 1985. *Bringing the State Back In*. Cambridge: Cambridge University Press.

Fischer, Frank. 1980. *Politics, Values and Public Policy: The Problem of Methodology*. Boulder: Westview.

Hall, Peter, 1986. *Governing the Economy*. New York: Oxford University Press.

Hanf, Kenneth, and Fritz Scharpf. 1978. *Interorganizational Decisionmaking*. London: Sage.

Hart, Jennifer. 1965. Nineteenth Century Social Reform: A Tory Interpretation of History. *Past and Present* 31:39–61.

Heclo, Hugh. 1974. *Modern Social Politics in Britain and Sweden*. New Haven: Yale University Press.

Heclo, Hugh, and Aaron Wildavsky. 1979. *The Private Government of Public Money*. New York: Macmillan.

Heidenheimer, Arnold, and Nils Erlander, eds. 1980. *The Shaping of the Swedish Health Care System*. New York: St. Martin's.

Immergut, Ellen. 1986. Between State and Market: Sickness Benefits and Social Control. In M. Rein and L. Rainwater, eds., *Public/Private Interplay in Social Protection: A Comparative Study*. Armonk: Sharpe.

Innes, Joanne. 1987. Jonathan Clark, Social History and England's "Ancien Regime." *Past and Present* 115:165–200.

Jordan, A. G., and J. J. Richardson. 1983. Policy Communities: The British and European Style. *Policy Studies Journal* 11:603–15.

Kiser, Larry, and Eleanor Ostrom. 1982. The Three Worlds of Action: A Metaphysical Synthesis of Institutional Approaches. In E. Ostrom, ed., *Strategies of Political Inquiry*. Beverly Hills: Sage.

Kjellberg, Francesco. 1977. Do Policies (Really) Determine Politics? And Eventually How?. In D. Ashford, ed., *Symposium on Public Policy, Policy Studies Journal*, special Issue, 554–69.

Kousser, J. Morgan. 1982. Restoring Politics to Political History. *Journal of Interdisciplinary History* 12:569–95.

Kristensen, Ole P. 1984. On the Futility of the "Demand Approach" to Public-Sector Growth. *European Journal of Political Research* 12:309–24.

Lijphart, Arend. 1975. The Comparable-Cases Strategy in Comparative Research. *Comparative Political Studies* 8:158–77.

Lindblom, C. E. 1959. The "Science" of Muddling Through. *Public Administration Review* 19:79–88.

———. 1963. *Politics, Economics and Welfare*. New York: Harper.

Linder, Stephen H., and B. Guy Peters. 1985. From Social Theory to Policy Design. *Journal of Public Policy* 4:237–59.

———. 1988. Integration of Policy Studies Through Policy Design. Unpublished paper.

Loriaux, Michael. 1989. Comparative Political Economy and Comparative History. *Comparative Politics* 21:355–77.

Lowi, Theodore H. 1964. American Business, Public Policy, Case-Studies and Political Theory. *World Politics* 16:677–715.

———. 1972. Four Systems of Policy, Politics and Choice. *Public Administration Review* 32:298–310.

McAuslan, Patrick, and John F. McEldowney. 1985. *Law, Legitimacy and the Constitution*. London: Sweet and Maxwell.

MacFarlane, Alan. 1978. *The Origins of English Individualism: The Family, Property, and Social Transition*. New York: Cambridge University Press.

———. 1987. *The Culture of Capitalism*. Oxford: Basil Blackwell.

Macpherson, C. B. 1985. *The Rise and Fall of Economic Justice*. New York: Oxford University Press.

Macrae, Duncan. 1976. *The Social Function of Social Science*. New Haven: Yale University Press.

Maier, Charles S., ed. 1987. *Changing Boundaries of the Political*. Cambridge: Cambridge University Press.

March, James G., and Johan Olsen. 1989. *Rediscovering Institutions: The Organizational Basis of Politics*. New York: Free Press.

Mommsen, Wolfgang. 1979 (1954). *Max Weber and German Politics, 1890–1920*. Trans. M. S. Steinberg. Chicago: University of Chicago Press.

Nairn, Tom. 1988. *The Enchanted Glass: Britain and Its Monarchy*. London: Radius.

Olson, Mancur. 1964. *The Logic of Collective Action*. Cambridge: Harvard University Press.

Ott, J. Steven. 1989. *The Organizational Culture Perspective*. Pacific Grove: Brooks Cole.

Paci, Massimo. 1987. Long Waves in the Development of Welfare Systems. In C. Maier, ed., *Changing Boundaries of the Political*. Cambridge: Cambridge University Press.

Portis, Edward B. 1986. *Max Weber and Political Commitment*. Philadelphia: Temple University Press.

Pressman, Jeffrey, and Aaron Wildavsky. 1973. *Implementation*. Berkeley and Los Angeles: University of California Press.

Przeworski, Adam, and Henry Teune. 1970. *Logic of Comparative Inquiry*. New York: Wiley.

Richardson, J. J., ed. 1982. *Policy Styles in Western Europe*. London: Allen and Unwin.

Rockman, Bert. 1984. *The Leadership Question: The Presidency and the American System*. New York: Praeger.

Sabatier, Paul A. 1988. An Advocacy Coalition Framework of Policy Change and the Role of Policy-Oriented Learning Therein. *Policy Sciences* 21:129–68.

Safran, William. 1967. *Veto-Group Politics: The Case of Health Insurance Reform in West Germany*. San Francisco: Chandler.

Scotch, Richard K. 1984. *From Good Will to Civil Rights: Transforming Federal Disability Policy*. Philadelphia: Temple University Press.

Simon, Herbert A. 1973. The Structure of Ill-Structured Problems. *Artificial Intelligence* 4:181–201.

Skillen, Anthony. 1985. Welfare State versus Welfare Society. *Journal of Applied Philosophy* 2:3–17.

Skocpol, Theda. 1980. Political Response to Capitalist Crisis: Neo-Marxist Theories of the State and the Case of the New Deal. *Politics and Society* 10:155–201.

Stone, Deborah A. 1984. *The Disabled State*. Philadelphia: Temple University Press.

Suleiman, Ezra. 1974. *Politics, Power and Bureaucracy in France*. Princeton: Princeton University Press.

Tilly, Charles. 1984. *Big Structures, Large Processes, Huge Comparisons*. New York: Russell Sage.

Torgerson, Douglas. 1985. Contextual Orientation in Policy Analysis: The Contribution of Harold D. Lasswell. *Policy Sciences* 18:241–61.

———. 1986. Between Knowledge and Politics: Three Faces of Policy Analysis. *Policy Sciences* 9:33–59.

von Beyme, Klaus, and Manfred G. Schmidt. 1985. *Policy and Politics in the Federal Republic of Germany*. New York: St. Martin's.

Weir, Margaret, Ann Sholoff Orloff, and Theda Skocpol, eds. 1986. *The Politics of Social Security*. Princeton: Princeton University Press.

Weiss, Carol. 1977. Research for Policy's Sake: The Enlightenment Function of Social Research. *Policy Analysis* 3:531–45.

Wilensky, Harold. 1975. *The Welfare State and Society*. Berkely and Los Angeles: University of California Press.

Williams, Walter. 1988. *Washington, Westminster and Whitehall*. Cambridge: Cambridge University Press.

Notes on Contributors

DOUGLAS E. ASHFORD is Andrew W. Mellon Professor of Comparative Politics at the University of Pittsburgh, with appointments in both political science and history. He has written and edited numerous books and articles on European policy and politics, most recently *Discretionary Politics* (1990) and *The Emergence of the Welfare States* (1986). His earlier interest in comparative local politics and participation now extends to the politics of social policy making and the institutions of the welfare state. Throughout his work, Ashford has had a lively interest in problems of theory formation and empirical methodology, especially as these questions relate to the democratic process of governance.

HANS BLOMKVIST is Associate Professor in the Department of Government, Uppsala University, in Sweden. His Ph.D. thesis, *The Soft State*, concerns the housing problem in a great Third World city, Madras, in south India. The empirical study is discussed in a general context of the "soft" state and clientelistic politics. Blomkvist is currently working on a project comparing the administrative development of northern Europe and south India in precolonial times. In this project he tries to view European history from an Indian viewpoint, as it were. Why did a universalistic state administration develop in Europe and not in India?

JAMES FARR is Professor in the Department of Political Science at the University of Minnesota and specializes in political theory. He is the coeditor of *Political Innovation and Conceptual Change* (1989), *After Marx* (1984), and *Discipline and History: Political Science in the United States* (1992). He is also the author of a number of recent essays in the history and philosophy of political inquiry published in the *American Political Science Review*, the *American Journal of Political Science*, and the *Journal of Politics*. He is currently writing a history of American political science understood as a series of discourses on the state.

NORMAN FURNISS's academic interests are in the areas of comparative politics and public policy. His research focuses on problems of modernization and political change in advanced industrial states, in particular the role of property rights, comparative public policy, and political futures for the "welfare state." In addition to publishing extensively in academic journals, he has edited and contributed to *Futures for the Welfare State* and *Turkish Workers in Europe;* he has contributed chapters to *The Democratic State,* ed. Roger Benjamin and Stanley Elkin; *Ethnic Autonomy—Comparative Dynamics,* ed. Raymond Hall; *Public Policy and Social Institutions,* ed. Harrell Rogers; and *Dilemmas of Change in British Politics,* ed. Jerold Waltman and Donley Studlar.

KRISHAN KUMAR is Professor of Social Thought at the University of Kent at Canterbury. He has bee a BBC Talks producer, a visiting fellow at Harvard University, and a visiting professor of sociology at the University of Colorado, Boulder. Among his publications are *Prophecy and Progress: The Sociology of Industrial and Post-Industrial Society* (1978), *Utopia and Anti-Utopia in Modern Times* (1987), *The Rise of Modern Society* (1988), and *Utopianism* (1991). He is also the editor of *Revolution* (1971) and, with A. Ellis, *Dilemmas of Liberal Democracies: Studies in Fred Hirsch's Social Limits to Growth* (1983).

B. GUY PETERS is Maurice Falk Professor of American Government and chair of the Department of Political Science at the University of Pittsburgh. He was cofounder of the International Political Science Association Research Committee on the Structure and Organization of Government and of its journal *Governance.* His publications include *Comparing Public Bureaucracies, The Politics of Taxation,* and *The Politics of Bureaucracy.*

BERT A. ROCKMAN is University Professor of Political Science and Research Professor at the University Center for International Studies at the University of Pittsburgh. He is also a nonresident Senior Fellow at the Brookings Institution where he was in residence from 1990 to 1992. Among his most recent works are *Do Institutions Matter? Government Capabilities in the United States and Abroad,* edited with R. Kent Weaver, and *The Bush Presidency: First Appraisals,* edited with Colin Campbell, S.J. He is currently working on a study of executive and political change in Washington, D.C., 1970–1991, with Joel D. Aberbach. Despite this, his tennis game continues to be mediocre.

BO ROTHSTEIN is Associate Professor in the Department of Government, Uppsala University, in Sweden. Among his publications in English are "State Structure and Variations in Corporatism," *Scandinavian Political Studies* 14 (1991); "The Success of the Swedish Labour Market Policy: The Organizational Connection," *European Journal of Political Research* 13 (1985); and "Social Justice and State Capacity," *Politics and Society* (1992). He has been a visiting scholar at Cornell University and at the Center for European Studies at Harvard University. He is currently working on English editions of his two books published in Swedish: *The Social Democratic State* and *The Corporatist State.*

ANTHONY SKILLEN is a Senior Lecturer in Philosophy at the University of Kent at Canterbury, and has held visiting posts at the Universities of Colorado and Michigan. He was an undergraduate at Sydney, Australia, and his postgraduate studies were at Oxford. He is the author of *Ruling Illusions* (1977) and has contributed several articles to the British journals *Radical Philosophy* and *The Journal of Applied Philosophy*. He has written articles recently on justice, citizenship, racism, and enterprise. He currently teaches courses in aesthetics, philosophy in literature, and cultural studies and is conducting research for two studies of conflicting strains in contemporary culture: one on sport and one on the British monarchy.

Peter Wagner, a political scientist, is Research Fellow at the Wissenschaftszentrum Berlin für Sozialforschung. His main research interest is in the long-term development of modern societies, focusing on the interrelations of societal discourses, technologies, economic organization, and political institutions. He is the author of *Sozialwissenschaften und Staat, Frankreich, Italien und Deutschland 1870–1980* (1990) and is coeditor of *Social Sciences and Modern States* (1991).

Björn Wittrock is Professor of Political Science at the University of Stockholm and director of the Swedish Collegium for Advanced Study in the Social Sciences in Uppsala. His main research interests are in social and political theory, the study of transformations of social knowledge, universities, and political institutions in historical and comparative perspective. His recent publications include *The University Research System* (1985) and *Social Sciences and Modern States* (1991), both of which he coedited; *Social Theory and Human Agency* (1991); and *Fact and Idea in the European and American University Since 1800* (in press).

PITT SERIES IN POLICY AND INSTITUTIONAL STUDIES

Bert A. Rockman, Editor

The Acid Rain Controversy
James L. Regens and Robert W. Rycroft

Affirmative Action at Work: Law, Politics, and Ethics
Bron Raymond Taylor

Agency Merger and Bureaucratic Redesign
Karen M. Hult

The Aging: A Guide to Public Policy
Bennett M. Rich and Martha Baum

Arms for the Horn: U.S. Security Policy in Ethiopia and Somalia, 1953-1991
Jeffrey A. Lefebvre

The Atlantic Alliance and the Middle East
Joseph I. Coffey and Gianni Bonvicini, Editors

The Budget-Maximizing Bureaucrat: Appraisals and Evidence
André Blais and Stéphane Dion, Editors

Clean Air: The Policies and Politics of Pollution Control
Charles O. Jones

The Competitive City: The Political Economy of Suburbia
Mark Schneider

Conflict and Rhetoric in French Policymaking
Frank R. Baumgartner

Congress and Economic Policymaking
Darrell M. West

Congress Oversees the Bureaucracy: Studies in Legislative Supervision
Morris S. Ogul

Democracy in Japan
Takeshi Ishida and Ellis S. Krauss, Editors

Demographic Change and the American Future
R. Scott Fosler, William Alonso, Jack A. Meyer, and Rosemary Kern

Economic Decline and Political Change: Canada, Great Britain, and the United States
Harold D. Clarke, Marianne C. Stewart, and Gary Zuk, Editors

Executive Leadership in Anglo-American Systems
Colin Campbell, S.J., and Margaret Jane Wyszomirski, Editors

Extraordinary Measures: The Exercise of Prerogative Powers in the United States
Daniel P. Franklin

Foreign Policy Motivation: A General Theory and a Case Study
Richard W. Cottam

"He Shall Not Pass This Way Again": The Legacy of Justice William O. Douglas
Stephen L. Wasby, Editor

History and Context in Comparative Public Policy
Douglas E. Ashford, Editor

Homeward Bound: Explaining Changes in Congressional Behavior
Glenn Parker

How Does Social Science Work? Reflections on Practice
Paul Diesing

Imagery and Ideology in U.S. Policy Toward Libya, 1969-1982
Mahmoud G. ElWarfally

The Impact of Policy Analysis
James M. Rogers

Iran and the United States: A Cold War Case Study
Richard W. Cottam

Japanese Prefectures and Policymaking
Steven R. Reed

Making Regulatory Policy
Keith Hawkins and John M. Thomas, Editors

Managing the Presidency: Carter, Reagan, and the Search for Executive Harmony
Colin Campbell, S.J.

The Moral Dimensions of Policy Choice: Beyond the Market Paradigm
John Martin Gillroy and Maurice Wade, Editors

Native Americans and Public Policy
Fremont J. Lyden and Lyman H. Legters, Editors

Organizing Governance, Governing Organizations
Colin Campbell, S.J., and B. Guy Peters, Editors

Party Organizations in American Politics
Cornelius P. Cotter et al.

Perceptions and Behavior in Soviet Foreign Policy
Richard K. Herrmann

Pesticides and Politics: The Life Cycle of a Public Issue
Christopher J. Bosso

Policy Analysis by Design
Davis B. Bobrow and John S. Dryzek

The Political Failure of Employment Policy, 1945-1982
Gary Mucciaroni

Political Leadership: A Source Book
Barbara Kellerman, Editor

The Politics of Public Utility Regulation
William T. Gormley, Jr.

The Politics of the U.S. Cabinet: Representation in the Executive Branch, 1789-1984
Jeffrey E. Cohen

Politics Within the State: Elite Bureaucrats and Industrial Policy in Authoritarian Brazil
Ben Ross Schneider

The Presidency and Public Policy Making
George C. Edwards III, Steven A. Shull, and Norman C. Thomas, Editors

Private Markets and Public Intervention: A Primer for Policy Designers
Harvey Averch

Public Policy in Latin America: A Comparative Survey
John W. Sloan

Reluctant Partners: Implementing Federal Policy
Robert P. Stoker

Roads to Reason: Transportation, Administration, and Rationality in Colombia
Richard E. Hartwig

Site Unseen: The Politics of Siting a Nuclear Waste Repository
Gerald Jacob

The Struggle for Social Security, 1900-1935
Roy Lubove

Tage Erlander: Serving the Welfare State, 1946-1969
Olof Ruin

Traffic Safety Reform in the United States and Great Britain
Jerome S. Legge, Jr.

Urban Alternatives: Public and Private Markets in the Provision of Local Services
Robert M. Stein

The U.S. Experiment in Social Medicine: The Community Health Center Program, 1965-1986
Alice Sardell